D0216368

Second Edition

GLOBAL INFORMATION WARFARE

The New Digital Battlefield

OTHER TITLES FROM AUERBACH PUBLICATIONS AND CRC PRESS

A Comprehensive Look at Fraud
Identification and Prevention
James R. Youngblood
ISBN 978-1-4987-0032-0

Analytical Evaluation of Nonlinear
Distortion Effects on Multicarrier Signals
Theresa Araújo and Rui Dinis
ISBN 978-1-4822-1594-6

Cognitive Radio Networks: Efficient
Resource Allocation in Cooperative
Sensing, Cellular Communications,
High-Speed Vehicles, and Smart Grid
Tao Jiang, Zhiqiang Wang, and Yang Cao
ISBN 978-1-4987-2113-4

Configuration Management: Theory,
Practice, and Application
Jon M. Quigley and Kim L. Robertson
ISBN 978-1-4822-2935-6

Corporate Security Intelligence and
Strategic Decision Making
Justin Crump
ISBN 978-1-4665-9270-4

Cybersecurity: Protecting Critical
Infrastructures from Cyber Attack and
Cyber Warfare
Edited by Thomas A. Johnson
ISBN 978-1-4822-3922-5

Design Science Research Methods and
Patterns: Innovating Information and
Communication Technology, 2nd Edition
Vijay K. Vaishnavi and William Kuechler
ISBN 978-1-4987-1525-6

Directing the ERP Implementation: A
Best Practice Guide to Avoiding Program
Failure Traps While Tuning System
Performance
Michael W. Pelphrey
ISBN 978-1-4822-4841-8

Emerging Technologies in Healthcare
Suzanne Moss Richins
ISBN 978-1-4822-6262-9

Human–Computer Interaction:
Fundamentals and Practice
Gerard Jounghyun Kim
ISBN 978-1-4822-3389-6

Knowledge Discovery Process and
Methods to Enhance Organizational
Performance
Kweku-Muata Osei-Bryson
and Corlane Barclay
ISBN 978-1-4822-1236-5

Lean for the Long Term: Sustainment
is a Myth, Transformation is Reality
William H. Baker, Jr. and Kenneth Rolfes
ISBN 978-1-4822-5716-8

Odyssey—The Business of Consulting:
How to Build, Grow, and Transform
Your Consulting Business
Imelda K. Butler and Shayne Tracy
ISBN 978-1-4987-2912-3

Securing Systems: Applied Security
Architecture and Threat Models
Brook S. E. Schoenfield
ISBN 978-1-4822-3397-1

Simple Statistical Methods for Software
Engineering: Data and Patterns
C. Ravindranath Pandian
and Murali Kumar
ISBN 978-1-4398-1661-5

The International Manager:
A Guide for Communicating,
Cooperating, and Negotiating with
Worldwide Colleagues
Frank Garten
ISBN 978-1-4987-0458-8

The "Success or Die" Ultimatum:
Saving Companies with Blended,
Long-Term Improvement Formulas
Steven Borris and Daniel Borris
ISBN 978-1-4822-9903-8

Transforming Business with Program
Management: Integrating Strategy,
People, Process, Technology, Structure,
and Measurement
Satish P. Subramanian
ISBN 978-1-4665-9099-1

Web Security: A WhiteHat Perspective
Hanqing Wu and Liz Zhao
ISBN 978-1-4665-9261-2

Second Edition

GLOBAL INFORMATION WARFARE

The New Digital Battlefield

Andrew Jones
Gerald L. Kovacich

CRC Press
Taylor & Francis Group
Boca Raton London New York

CRC Press is an imprint of the
Taylor & Francis Group, an **informa** business

CRC Press
Taylor & Francis Group
6000 Broken Sound Parkway NW, Suite 300
Boca Raton, FL 33487-2742

© 2016 by Taylor & Francis Group, LLC
CRC Press is an imprint of Taylor & Francis Group, an Informa business

No claim to original U.S. Government works

Printed on acid-free paper
Version Date: 20150504

International Standard Book Number-13: 978-1-4987-0325-3 (Hardback)

Library of Congress Cataloging-in-Publication Data

Jones, Andy, 1952-
    Global information warfare : the new digital battlefield / Andrew Jones and Gerald L. Kovacich. -- Second edition.
        pages cm
    Includes bibliographical references and index.
    ISBN 978-1-4987-0325-3
    1. Information warfare. 2. Business--Data processing. I. Kovacich, Gerald L. II. Title.

U163.J66 2015
303.48'33--dc23   2015016378

Visit the Taylor & Francis Web site at
http://www.taylorandfrancis.com

and the CRC Press Web site at
http://www.crcpress.com

This book is dedicated to all those info-warriors who do battle every day to protect our systems and information from those who seek to do us harm.

*Quotes on Warfare**

"The supreme art of war is to subdue the enemy without fighting."

"All warfare is based on deception. Hence, when able to attack, we must seem unable; when using our forces, we must seem inactive; when we are near, we must make the enemy believe we are far away; when far away, we must make him believe we are near."

"The greatest victory is that which requires no battle."

"So in war, the way is to avoid what is strong, and strike at what is weak."

"To win one hundred victories in one hundred battles is not the acme of skill. To subdue the enemy without fighting is the acme of skill."

"If you know the enemy and know yourself, your victory will not stand in doubt; if you know Heaven and know Earth, you may make your victory complete."

"Rouse him, and learn the principle of his activity or inactivity. Force him to reveal himself, so as to find out his vulnerable spots."

---

* *The Art of War* by Sun Tzu.

Contents

Forewords to the Second Edition

War is merely the continuation of policy by other means.

Carl von Clausewitz
*On War**

Dr. Jones' second edition of *Global Information Warfare* is timely as we witness new and more effective cyber attacks on governments, corporations, and individuals. I am writing this as I read the news that the White House takes the view that the Sony Pictures Entertainment hacking attack is a serious national security matter. It was probably a nation-state's professional computer network operations organization in action, achieving national goals.

Writing in the early years of the nineteenth century, Clausewitz remarked that "the political object is the goal, war is the means of reaching it, and means can never be considered in isolation from their purpose." Information warfare is applying this today as another means of achieving the political goal without the devastating consequences of a *hot* war.

We are bombarded daily in the media with stories of wars taking place, ruining people's lives and destroying states. Warfare is viewed by many as tanks, ships, fighter jets, and soldiers fighting each other or rag-tag bands of militias committing atrocities as acts of terror. Yet public consciousness of information warfare remains low, and therefore it is simpler and more effective for nations to fight in cyber space to achieve national goals. Global information warfare is not new, but it has taken on a new lease of life as our dependence on computers at all levels, whether personal gaming machines or sophisticated industrial control systems running nuclear power stations, makes states and their peoples vulnerable to exploitation and potentially domination by another power.

Global information warfare is taking place today, with many nation-states actively pursuing attacks on actual or perceived enemies. We have had the Stuxnet,

---

* Michael Howard and Peter Paret (ed), Carl von Clausewitz, *On War* (Princeton 1984) p. 87.

xx ■ *Foreworls to the Second Edition*

Aramco, RSA, and Dragonfly attacks, as well as an increasing awareness of twenty-first-century Chinese cyber warfare, all of which indicated professional, state-sponsored information warfare capabilities in action. Advanced persistent threat (APT) attacks are reported every day. APT attacks are being made against private and public organizations, often through their third-party suppliers. It is not just major states who are active in information warfare; other smaller nations are also in action. As an example, the Syrian Electronic Army has continued to wage information warfare in defense of the Assad Syrian state. Moreover, we have witnessed the rise of criminal groups who provide sophisticated hacking tools for sale or rent, enabling thieves to steal vast sums of money or allow nation-states to destabilize smaller states.

Dr. Jones' second edition of *Global Information Warfare* provides us with an expert and former soldier's insight into the nature of this warfare. He takes the reader through nation-state defensive and offensive capabilities while considering nonstate actors. I am pleased that this excellent book analyses the corporate world and its resilience as a part of national infrastructures. Many nations are wholly dependent on the corporate world for their national information technology systems, and the changing environment means that that these companies are part of the critical national infrastructure. Dr. Jones highlights both the reality and the awesomeness of global information warfare. Perhaps I could amend Carl von Clausewitz's famous line to "InfoWar is merely the continuation of policy by other means."

The reality that global information warfare is taking place today means that we need to understand it as citizens of our respective nations. This book will provide that insight. I hope you enjoy reading the second edition of Dr. Jones' *Global Information Warfare* and use it to challenge our own political leaders to defend critical national infrastructures properly as well protecting our citizens' online activities. Encourage your friends to read it.

William G. E. Millar
Global CISO Infrastructure Services Capgemini

I had a dream.

Perhaps, more accurately, it was a crystal clear, somnambulistic vision under the tumbling waters of a morning shower.

I saw first one, then two, then an infinite onslaught, along with a massive retaliative return fire of hostile software aimed at stealing, modifying, and destroying data and systems. I saw unrepentant electronic eavesdropping of wireless signals, satellite interruptions, network-cable interceptions, and invisible listening to Van-Eck radiations. I saw extreme electromagnetic interference and the disruption of finance, power, transportation, and communications infrastructures by high-energy radio signals, microwaves, and nonnuclear pulses.

When the hot water ran out, I came to. That was 1987.

Then I wrote about it; initially in *Terminal Compromise*, later updated to *Pearl Harbor Dot Com*, which became *Die Hard IV*. That was 1989–1990.

That changed my life.

I have been inaccurately cited as coining the term *cyber Pearl Harbor*. I did not. Let me clarify.

Somehow, I do not recall how or by whom I was asked, on June 27, 1991, I testified before the Congressional Subcommittee on Technology and Competitiveness's Committee on Science, Space and Technology about the state of security in the private sector and government. The following quotes (available from the official congressional record as well) sum it all up.

> Government and commercial computer systems are so poorly protected today they can essentially be considered defenseless—an Electronic Pearl Harbor waiting to happen. As a result of inadequate security planning on the part of both the government and the private sector, the privacy of most Americans has virtually disappeared.

To be accurate, the etymology of the current meme *cyber Pearl Harbor* is

"Electronic Pearl Harbor"
Winn Schwartau to Congress, June 27, 1991

"Electronic Pearl Harbor"
CIA director John Deutch to Congress, June 26, 1996

"Digital Pearl Harbor"
US cyber czar Richard Clark, December 8, 2000

Now "infowar experts" use the word *cyber* instead, but I stand by my original choice of word, *electronic*, as being ultimately more descriptive, accurate, and allowing greater integration of hardware and material science innovation into information systems.

Encouraged to write nonfiction, my vision remained constant.

> AT ONE POINT, if not already, you will be the victim of Information Warfare. If not you, then a member of your family or a close friend.
>
> Your company will become a designated target of Information Warfare. If not yesterday or today, then definitely tomorrow. You will be hit.
>
> Why? Because the United States is at war, a war that few of us have bothered to notice. The twentieth century information skirmishes, which are the prelude to global Information Warfare, have begun. Information Warfare is coming. For some, it has already arrived.

Imagine a conflict between adversaries in which information is the prize, the spoils of war. A conflict with a winner and a loser. A conflict which turns computers into highly effective offensive weapons. A conflict which defines computers and communications systems as primary targets forced to defend themselves against deadly, invisible bullets and bombs.

Imagine rival economies battling for a widening sphere of global influence over the electronic financial highways, sparing no expense to ensure victory.

Then imagine a world made up of companies that compete and settle disputes by regularly blitzkrieging each other's information infrastructure. A world where electronic and competitive espionage are the expected manner of conducting business.

Or imagine a world in which personal revenge, retribution! getting even is only a keystroke away.

What kind of world is this? This is the world of Information Warfare, and we, as individuals and as a country, are not prepared for the future we are creating.

At that time, 1991–1992, I employed a simple definition to describe what I came to call information warfare:

Information Warfare is the use of information and information systems as offensive tools against other information and information systems.

In my mind, this allowed the inclusion of present and future software, hardware, and the human mind (influence, psychological operations, etc.) as both offensive and defensive elements in the conflict.

Drs. Kovacich and Jones asked me for a perspective on information warfare today, and I fear that almost three decades of apathy, arrogance, and ignorance have allowed my initial visions to become reality, despite my incessant hopes that leadership would take hold. Sadly, no such realization has taken place.

In an attempt to granularize information warfare back in 1991 or so, I found it convenient to portray it in three classes:

Class I: Personal, where the average person is the victim of identity theft and a near absolute collapse of privacy. Where are we today?

Class II: Corporate, where private organizations wage legal, illegal, ethical, and unethical attacks on each other, utilizing the ancient mantra *business is war*; think advanced persistent threats (APTs) in today's terms.

Class III: Global, where nation-states, NGOs, terrorists, hactivists, and well-supported agenda-driven groups use the tools of the information warrior in the pursuit of their particular goals. The concept of hostile forces *chipping*, or making counterfeit hostile integrated circuits for commercial and military use, was finally accepted more than 20-some years after its introduction in 1992–1993. Why is that?

Sadly, these have all come true. The United States has spent untold gobs of money trying to define information warfare. I argue that since the nature of information warfare is asymmetric in nature, defining it as rigidly as kinetic warriors would like to has destroyed our ability to operate in that realm as efficiently as our adversaries (and some partners) can. (Oddly enough, the only license offered for the first edition of *Information Warfare* was to a Chinese "organization." From where I sit, they followed it, especially in terms of how to build and organize an information army, as I called it.)

Back in the mid-1990s, several of us encouraged the Pentagon to view information warfare as an additional domain of excellence, echoing the emergence of the Air Force from the Army Air Corps in 1947. How many years has it taken to realize USCYBERCOM? Again, I feel sadness.

Regrettably, the future of information warfare is even more dire, and as I reread portions of the first volume of *Information Warfare*, I feel little need to change many of my thoughts.

To put a point on our failures, in early 2015, US Army General Dempsey, the chairman of the Joint Chiefs of Staff, said in an interview with *Fox News* that we do not have an advantage in cyber warfare. After almost 30 years, this comment is an indictment of lack of our national will and leadership on so many levels; again, chagrin is a continuing emotion.

Politicians and lawyers have sought the equivalent of the Law of War, which has been formative for a couple of millennia, and to apply it to information warfare. The missed, and obvious point, is that the Law of War is a kinetic mindset, where symmetry existed and nation-states were the contenders. They have been trying and failing to shift their view from one of Clauswitzian, and indeed, Trojan through medieval siege mentality... and have remained comfortable doing do.

Fortress mentality is a failure, asymmetry is the rule, and the number and type of actors is so very different than ever in history. The weapons of the information warrior do not necessarily need to wait a generation to find themselves in the hands of our adversaries. They are often developed at the same time, and we have seen that criminal and NGO groups have, on their own, developed incredibly sophisticated information warfare weapons, to our collective detriment.

Imagine I were a terrorist or NGO hostile to, say the United States, the United Kingdom, the European Union, or another developed region; recent technological developments have given me such a suite of weapons available on Amazon, why should I bother developing my own?

Imagine: A handful of $200, 8-ounce drones, each fitted with a small quantity of highly explosive chemical, remotely flown into K-12 schools across middle

America. How many kids show up the next day, and how we do rebuild confidence in our ability to protect our progeny?

Imagine: The above weapons aimed at suburban malls. Or public mass transportation systems.

This scares the livin' I.T. out of me. Someone is going to do it, and outside of a few private conversations, fear overrides a public discussion.

Imagine: Huge progress in prosthetics, bioelectronic implants, and amazing technologies allow quadriplegics embedded with brain-control devices to reanimate their lives. They allow the blind to see and the deaf to hear, and they permit the reconstruction of nervous system circuits. What do directed energy pulses or streams do to these devices, and what happens to the victim human counterparts? I shudder at what will happen, especially to our veterans who greatly benefit from these technologies.

Imagine: Tens of millions of people connecting their home security, automation, entertainment, and endless Internet of things (IoT) devices to an already insecure internet. Autonomous vehicles, Wi-Fi, poor security, and unvetted technology represent a recipe for disaster, knee-jerk reactions by the technically illiterate (law makers) and for the compounding of one error with another more egregious one.

In my view, we are still attempting to build great castles on mesas, high walls, and wider moats—a siege mentality concept—as the primary defense method (defense in depth sound familiar), in the most integrated, bidirectional, high-speed environment you can conceive.

Our current cyber-defensive posture is still largely based on a simple singular model developed in the early 1970s: before the Internet, before networking, before information warfare. And it has not, in my opinion, been improved upon.

Our current operating theater was an experiment initially conducted in the late 1960s; it seemed useful, and today we run the world based on its flawed foundations.

Our current defensive view is one of stasis versus the continuously variable dynamics of the world we have created.

Worst of all, too many security experts preach that we have to accept the fact that the majority of our systems have already been penetrated by hostiles (of some flavor) and are probably "owned" on a continual basis.

I find these antique acceptances to be the basis for our ongoing failures, and, unless radically and rapidly changed, they will likely be the ingrained foundation of future catastrophe: Electronic Pearl Harbor, if you wish.

So what so we do?

Go back to go to the future.

I grew up as an analogue audio engineer. I think in analogue terms. I do not tend to believe that static condition analysis is realistic in information security or warfare; these are nonconflicting terms. I do not approve of universal binary decision-making. Digital is not necessarily binary. It is a matter of scale.

For the last decade or so, I have been preparing a comprehensive treatise on new ways to look at security. Perhaps, instead of repeating the mistakes over again… again… especially with IoT, a few thoughts will resonate.

- Global communications protocols, such as TCP/IP, need to be redesigned from scratch, with the fundamentals of security and privacy as core design goals.
- Engineers test things before deploying. If much of the current breed of software engineers worked on the space program, the results likely would have been very different. Commercial interests tend to allow the user base to beta new technologies versus greater internal stress testing.
- Almost every hardware-based technology uses real-time feedback as a governor to avoid runaway conditions. Haptics is essential to man–machine integration; limiters to acoustic control; negative feedback to control amplification circuits; thermometers to avert nuclear core meltdowns. But as an industry, we have ignored this simple analogue process in the vast majority of IT and security controls.
- I would like to see more looping, such as that formalized by Col. John Boyd's OODA loop. It works in the military, in marketing, and notably in education. Looping is resultant function of the math from time based security.
- How about a greater focus on engineering processes, the history of security, and "lessons learned" to help us stop repeating the same mistakes over and over again?
- Embrace failure. Society focuses on and rewards success. Would you rather hire a person who has succeeded on paper 100% of the time to protect your networks, or someone with a demonstrable degree of failed attempts, a learning curve, and greater operational experience? I cannot tell you how many failures have taught me so much.
- Hire the unhireable. The FBI acknowledged in 2014 that they cannot find qualified security people who do not smoke pot. Then change the fricking rules established in the early days of the Cold War. It seems we prefer to hire raging alcoholics.
- Find a way to hire those on the autism spectrum. Who can be better trained to find miniscule coding errors in mission-critical systems?
- Adapt a policy of graceful degradation. For ease's sake, we treat networks as a binary state—protect everything equally, connect everything, put in a firewall and you will be fine. All static mistakes we seem to repeat. When found under attack, an organization should be able to rapidly isolate system components and maintain the highest degree of availability versus a total shut down.
- Get rid of passwords. I have been breached at JP Morgan Chase three times in two years because of another static failure. In 1990, security dynamics developed a constantly changing (analogue) method of access control. Yet credit cards and the majority of the financial industry are still using antique identification techniques that invite costly breaches over and over. Repeat after me: Get rid of passwords.
- The Social Security Administration must quickly develop a process whereby people can easily be reissued a new social security number (SSN) when their identity has been stolen. SSNs were originally never meant for proof-positive ID but have morphed into that failed modality.

- Increase legal penalties for professional espionage and organized cyber crime to the point of pain, not mere hand slaps of a few million dollars to huge corporate entities. APTs should be punished severely—on the global scale.
- Out of band (OOB) communications is essential and largely unknown in the security community. Even in the 1970s audio world, we used OOB. This represents another software engineering design failure, in my opinion.
- Employ more side channel processing to replace the inherent inefficiencies of in-channel processing, especially as it relates to security.
- Root must be killed. My new mathematical models may help.
- The security industry has no common metric so security folks, risk people, and management have a means to quantitatively communicate.

A comprehensive security model that might work better than today's approaches, which clearly favor the attackers (the offense in information warfare), needs to look not only at today's technology but also the anticipated metatechnological developments for the next half century.

From my standpoint, information security and information warfare are virtually interchangeable (politics notwithstanding). But, after spending more than a decade as a human pin cushion for my original warnings to the likes of Al Gore, countless military brass around the world, politicos —the usual suspects—I quit in information warfare 2003. I had had it.

Today, I cannot claim to be an information warfare expert. But I can state that I am dedicated to finding solutions to the mess we have created in network security.

That being said, the silver bullet does not exist.

A new product from any big company will not fix things either.

We must encourage and fund unpopular approaches. We have to accept that today, no amount of technology will fix the human security problem. We have designed technology and asked humanity to adapt to it. Something is fundamentally askew here, and is it any wonder There Is No Patch For Poor Human Behavior?

In any model that will significantly enhance the strength of corporate network defenses or the Information Warrior, we must conceptually integrate software, hardware, wetware, and the emergence of artificial intelligence at a minimum. There are other emerging technologies I would want to add to the equation, if it were up to me.

Imagine: A simple Von Neumann automata machine, sufficiently imbued with swarming intelligence, suddenly disconnected from its command and control. Built by the good guys, I shudder at the possibilities. Built by the bad guys? Game over.

Our job, as I suggested almost 30 years ago, is to think like the bad guys, then get out of our own way, and, as with the Kobayashi Maru, learn how to change the rules when the going gets rough.

I feel honored to have been asked to preface this much-anticipated work of Drs. Kovacich and Jones. I hope my thoughts offer some food for future thought.

Winn Schwartau

Foreword to the First Edition

As we transition from the information age to the knowledge age, successful organizations are the ones that actively manage their information environment. Since knowledge and the data and information on which it is built are so important, having the capabilities to conduct offensive and defensive information warfare is absolutely essential. Many countries, cartels, and terrorist organizations possess sophisticated information warfare know-how and will do what they can—at times and in places of their choosing—to disrupt a nation's freedom, safety, economy, and social fabric. The information environment is a battleground of the future, affecting not just the military but governments, businesses, and citizens as well. The cascading effects of information warfare attacks could prevent a country from effectively projecting political, economic, military, and social power.

The concepts behind the coherent knowledge-based operations detailed in this book operate at the corporate level as well. Blending control of the information environment and knowledge management with an organization's network-centric business processes is absolutely essential in order for organizations to be competitive. The increasing reliance on the Internet indicates that not only will countermeasures and security measures become increasingly necessary and valuable, but so will concepts like coherent knowledge-based operations that embrace extended enterprises and infrastructure interdependencies.

At Northrop Grumman Corporation, we envision a future where information warfare powered by knowledge-based systems will be prevalent on the battlefield. One of our primary organizing strategies has been to create systems central to business and military transformation. We are developing technologies that help protect critical infrastructures by detecting, deflecting, and diverting cyber attacks. We are also working on the new concept of *information resiliency*. We want to recover critical data—automatically and in real time. Extensive cooperation is needed between businesses and governments to make the best use of ideas and resources in order to solve information warfare issues.

To operate effectively in this new era, governments must be as adaptive and agile as their private-sector counterparts. It is important that the global government, military, and business communities get it right and move forward together. The concepts and recommendations in *An Introduction to Global Information Warfare: How Businesses, Nation-States, and Others Use IW Tactics to Achieve Their Objectives* are a good place to start and ones that I heartily endorse.

Kent Kresa
Chairman and Chief Executive Officer (retired)
Northrop Grumman Corporation

Preface

The first edition of this book was published in 2002. Since then, much has happened in the world of politics, governments, spying, technology, global businesses, mobile communications, and global competition on nation and corporate levels; as well as the almost total annihilation of privacy worldwide, and so much more—all having an impact on how global information warfare is waged and what must be done to counter the attacks.

The authors believe it was time to write and have published a second edition of this popular and important book based on the increase in global information warfare incidents.

The second edition builds on the success of the first edition by revising it to discuss the changes and impacts of global information warfare, focusing primarily, but not entirely, on the time since the first printing in 2002.

It will focus on the threats, vulnerabilities, attacks, and defenses from perspectives of various players, for example, governments and corporations; moreover, to a limited extent, we will cover its impact on individuals and groups, from private citizens to terrorists.

In doing so, with referrals back to the first edition, it is hoped that the reader will be sufficiently interested in more details cited, in part, in the first edition that they will want to read the first edition, and thus they will have as a reference—as well as a good read—both editions of *Global Information Warfare*.

Acknowledgments

No writing project can be done in isolation only by the authors. It truly takes a team. We thank the following people for their help in making this project a success: Perry Luzwick, who was our coauthor on the first edition of our original *Global Information Warfare* book. We thank him for contributing to this edition of this book. We wish you well, ol' information warfare warrior.

To Kath, Andy's wife, we would like to give thanks for her support, encouragement, and tolerance for the disruption to normal life.

Thanks to Motomu Akashi, a true old-time information warfare veteran. Rest in peace, ol' buddy.

A special thanks to a dear friend of more than 15 years and freelance editor, Sandy Green, who is always kind enough to edit my (Kovacich's) manuscripts so that my books receive quality edits prior to submissions for publications.

Of course we must thank our friends and professional staff at Taylor & Francis Group/CRC Press, who of course made this book possible. Thanks to Richard O'Hanley Publisher—ICT, Business, and Security; Jennifer Abbott, associate editor for Homeland Security; Jessica Vega, editorial assistant; Stephanie Morkert, project coordinator; and the many others that make up the dedicated staff involved in the production of the book.

Authors

Andy Jones has more than 40 years of military, government, business, and academic experience in the areas of intelligence, security, and digital forensics, both in the United Kingdom and overseas. He has been a practitioner for the whole period and a researcher in these areas for more than 20 years. He is currently an academic, international consultant, lecturer, and writer and is involved in research with a number of universities in the United Kingdom and Australia.

Gerald L. Kovacich has over 45 years of experience in industrial, business, and government security, investigations, intelligence/counterintelligence, source handling, information systems security, and information warfare, both in the US government as a special agent and in international corporations and subsequently as an international consultant and lecturer. He retired from his position as the information warfare technologist at Northrop Grumman Corporation to pursue a career as an international consultant, lecturer, and writer.

Introduction

Chapter 1: Introduction to Global Information Warfare

This chapter provides an introduction to and discussion of global information warfare and sets the stage for the chapters that follow. It begins with a fictional scenario that soon can become all too real—some of it already has occurred. Some aspects of information warfare attacks have already been tested by government agencies, terrorists, hackers, organized crime members, and the general criminal out to get rich at our expense, either through theft or blackmail or by denying the adversary the ability to function.

Chapter 2: From Information Warfare to Information Operations and Cyber Warfare

In this chapter, the discussion centers on a "holistic" and historical view of where we started and where we are now, looking at what the different terms mean and why there has been the change.

Chapter 3: War Stories from the Digital Battlefield

When discussing the various aspects of global information warfare, it is important to also be aware of the actual, various types of information warfare attacks being conducted 24/7 around the world against individuals, groups, businesses, and governments. In this chapter, a number of reports of actual attacks are listed, together with related commentaries. The information warfare warriors should learn from these war stories to help build their offensive and defensive global information warfare capabilities.

Chapter 4: Pre 9/11

The first edition of this book was written through the period up to 2002 and was published in 2002. The terrible tragedy of 9/11 took place in the final stages of the completion of the book. At the time of the writing of the first edition, no one realized the profound effect on many aspects of life in the United States and around the world that the attacks of 9/11 would have, and it is understandable that in light of the attacks, the focus for security changed totally.

This chapter gives a condensed review of Information Warfare as it was understood before that hugely significant event and then goes on to look at the impact that the events of 9/11 had on the subject.

Chapter 5: Effect of 9/11 and US Homeland Security (DHS)

This chapter looks back at the ramifications of the terrorists' attack against the World Trade Center in New York City on September 11, 2001, focusing on the reorganization of the US federal government agencies to support combating terrorists in the future and the new, digital, global battlefield.

Some think that homeland security displaced information warfare and that the funding and attention to information warfare dropped as the Department of Homeland Security (DHS) became the "thing." A look at DHS is a good introduction to the United States' approach to combating terrorists and other sensitive, national security-related activities. It is also an excellent example of a typical government bureaucracy using the slower twentieth-century bureaucratic management structure and techniques to deal with the twenty-first century's need for nanosecond responses.

Chapter 6: Nation-State Defensive and Offensive Information Warfare Capabilities: North America

In this and the subsequent five chapters, we look at the current, known levels of information operations capability in a number of nations and organizations around the world. There has been significant change since the first edition of this book was published, and a number of countries have now developed or are considering developing capability. None of this should be a surprise, as we increasingly live in a world that is dependent on the high-tech, and the protection of the critical infrastructure is of increasing importance to everyone. The nations that have been reviewed were those that were considered by the authors to be either those with the most advanced capabilities or those that were of the most interest. This is not intended to be a comprehensive review, and there are certainly more countries that either already have capability or are developing it.

In this chapter we look at North America.

Chapter 7: Nation-State Defensive and Offensive Information Warfare Capabilities: Middle East Nation-States

In the Middle East, the two countries that were considered to have the greatest information warfare capabilities were Iran and Israel. While other countries, particularly Syria, have been active in the cyber arena since the Arab Spring events that started at the end of 2010, the ongoing war there and the rise of ISIS have resulted in the disruption of many of the state organizations in the region. As a result, there is little information as to the current state of information operations developments in most of the countries in the region.

Chapter 8: Nation-State Defensive and Offensive Information Warfare Capabilities: Asia Pacific Region

The Asia Pacific region includes a large number of countries and is, from an Information Warfare perspective, one of the most diverse. Within the region are very Western first-world countries such as Australia, as well as one of the most isolated and anti-Western countries, North Korea.

Chapter 9: Nation-State Defensive and Offensive Information Warfare Capabilities: Europe

In this chapter, the term Europe is used in the context of the European Union, which consists of 28 countries (Austria, Belgium, Bulgaria, Croatia, Republic of Cyprus, Czech Republic, Denmark, Estonia, Finland, France, Germany, Greece, Hungary, Ireland, Italy, Latvia, Lithuania, Luxembourg, Malta, the Netherlands, Poland, Portugal, Romania, Slovakia, Slovenia, Spain, Sweden and the United Kingdom), and Switzerland.

The three countries with the best defined information warfare capabilities and largest standing military establishments (France, Germany, and the United Kingdom) have been reviewed.

Chapter 10: Nation-State Defensive and Offensive Information Warfare Capabilities: The Russian Federation

The Russian Federation has a large standing military organization and is an old antagonist of the West. It has shown a willingness to take action in the countries that surround it, as evidenced in actions in Estonia, Georgia, and the Ukraine.

Chapter 11: International Organizations' Defensive and Offensive Information Warfare Capabilities

There are two international organizations that have to be included in this review—the European Union and NATO. While some of the countries that have been reviewed belong to one or both of these organizations, the organizations themselves both set policy and, in the case of NATO, have some capability.

Chapter 12: Nonstate Actors

In this chapter, the nonstate global information warfare actors will be discussed. Actually, not much has changed since we last discussed these people. More have joined the global information warfare arena, but they come under the same headings of individuals and groups.

Chapter 13: The History of Technology

In this chapter, the history of technology will be discussed, as one can argue that, without microprocessor technologies, there would not be any global information warfare.

Chapter 14: Corporate and National Resilience

In this chapter, the ability to defend and bounce back from global information warfare attacks will be discussed. The potential impact of global information warfare on both nation-states and corporations will be reviewed in the context of the changed environment.

Chapter 15: Awareness

In this chapter, there is a general discussion of aspects of "awareness" of global information warfare threats, vulnerabilities, risks, and related topics; these will be explored on a nation-state, business, group, and personal level. "Collateral damage," for example, private citizens, requires that awareness be at all levels.

Chapter 16: The Tallinn Manual

This chapter will look at the implications of the Tallinn Manual on both offensive and defensive global information warfare. "The Tallinn Manual on the

International Law Applicable to Cyber Warfare" was written by an independent "international group of experts" at the invitation of the NATO Cooperative Cyber Defence Centre of Excellence (CDCE). The manual was the product of a three-year project to examine how existing international law applies to this "new" form of warfare.

Chapter 17: A Look at the Future: The Crystal Ball

In this final chapter, we will look to the future and some of its possibilities as they relate to our global, more-interconnected-than-ever society; governments, businesses, groups, and individuals' actions and reactions; technology; and the impact all that these topics have on information warfare.

Chapter 1

Introduction to Global Information Warfare

War does not determine who is right—only who is left.

Bertrand Russell

This chapter provides an introduction to and discussion of global information warfare (GIW) and sets the stage for the chapters that follow. It begins with a fictional scenario that could soon become all too real—some of it already has occurred. Some aspects of information warfare (IW) attacks have already been tested by government agencies, terrorists, hackers, organized crime members, and the general criminal out to get rich at our expense either through theft or blackmail or by denying their adversary the ability to function.

This scenario is presented as part of an introduction to GIW so that the reader can see what devastation can be caused by GIW—global devastation, because it can happen from anywhere to anywhere. It is something that the GIW defender must consider when addressing GIW issues.

Let us look at the possibilities of a worst-case IW attack scenario on the United States.

Possibilities

At first, some thought it was a massive solar eruption worse than that of 1998, since communications, including microwave and cellphone towers, were made inoperable. Then it was theorized as being a software glitch similar to the scare of the

2000 millennium bug years earlier. Then, all too soon, the real reason for the power losses and its domino effect became clear—a GIW attack on a massive scale.

It first started on Christmas Eve in the United States, for the attackers knew only minimal staffing would be in place, with many on vacation and out of the communication loop—those being vital to getting systems up and running again. They unleashed the attack late at night in order to cause the most havoc; it started in the Northwest, in the Seattle area, moving south to Portland, San Francisco, and Los Angeles and at the same time moving east. The power went out, first on the western grids, shutting down power station after power station, blackening each neighborhood, each town, each city, moving slowly from the Pacific Ocean eastward like a swarm of locusts to the Atlantic Ocean, into parts of Canada and Mexico, who were unfortunate enough to share America's power grids. They called the attack program "Locust Swarm."

America's energy grid slowly went down; for those who had contingency plans that included generators, it brought them more time, but time was not on their side. Eventually, the gas-powered generators ran out of gas. Gas was not forthcoming as electrical power was out from gas stations to oil refineries, and the oil pipes leading to them had no power to move the oil. Gas pumps were closed, and panic ensued. The alarm systems in stores, banks, and everywhere else in the country ceased operation.

Local power companies found that some transformers had exploded, and it would take from days to months to find replacements as so many were dead; some estimated it would take as long as six months to replace many of them. Electricity is crucial to powering technology, and technology runs everything. It did not matter whether facilities used solar, windmill, coal, natural gas, or diesel fuel energy, as all were controlled and run by computers. Even the monitoring systems were run by technology, and when false readings were sent through them, they also helped cause chaos and the overloads that ensued. Systems monitoring everything from nuclear facilities to dams were affected.

Just before the rolling blackout hit an area, there were a number of Twitter broadcasts—"Power is out, bank alarms are out, store alarms are out, come take your share of the bounty." When the miscreants of each area where power failed got the message, they joined their friends, and soon police and fire fighters were occupied with emergencies. Mobs broke into any place that offered money, furniture, televisions, and other goods free for the taking, setting fire as they went. They acted with impunity as even CCTV cameras were out.

Fire departments were overwhelmed, and fire trucks eventually ran out of gas and could not respond. The same thing applied to police departments and even the National Guard and other military facilities.

Medical equipment in hospitals vital to keeping people alive ceased to operate as generators failed, and thousands of patients across the country died, many on the operating table.

Aircraft did not lose communications with control towers, however; the "locusts" that had infected the country did not shut down the control towers as rapidly. No one thought to ask why until it was too late. And it was too late when the locusts were uploaded to aircraft and wormed their way into the computer systems, changing the instrumentation settings on the aircraft without the knowledge of the flight crews on both commercial and military aircraft.

Aircraft pilots had learned to fly using computers and their instruments; long gone were the pilots who "flew by the seat of their pants." Programming errors caused planes to crash and thousands to die. Some that were running out of fuel tried landing but, relying on false instrument readings, burned up on runways, stopping other aircraft from trying to land. While some made it down safely, others crashed and burned in adjacent fields and taxiways. The skies glowed with the fires of crashed aircraft, and bodies were strewn everywhere. Some survived for a while, but the emergency teams were overwhelmed and many died.

The locusts program wormed its way into automated home systems. It was the middle of winter, and heaters were turned off and air conditioners turned on. Many vulnerable people in the northern region of the nation froze to death, and those in nursing homes and animals in shelters could not be cared for.

Water pumping stations ceased operation, sewerage systems failed. So when water was needed the most, bottled water started flying off store shelves until it ran out. People turning on their water faucets found nothing but stinking, brown water coming out; and then not even that.

All modern nations reliant on technology are vulnerable to such attacks. Of course there are those who say it cannot happen. Really?

Over 1000 US and European power plants and their equipment manufacturers have been penetrated by Dragonfly malware. Distributors of equipment updated software and data systems, spreading the malware further into systems. This malware may be of Russian descent.*

Introduction to Warfare

Wars have been fought ever since there were human beings around who did not agree with one another. These conflicts continue to this day, with no end in sight. The use of information in warfare is nothing new. Those who had the best information the fastest and were able to correctly act on it the soonest were usually the victors in battles.

Is it any wonder that since we are now in the information age that we should also have IW? Because we now look at almost everything on a global scale, it should also not be surprising then that IW is viewed on a global scale. IW is today's much-talked-about type of warfare. A search of the Internet on the topic using Google.com disclosed that in 2002 there were 472,000 hits for IW, but that in 2014 there were 27,700,000 hits. IW is becoming an integral, digital part of warfare of all types in the modern era.

---

* David Kennedy interview on Fox Business News, 8.37 am, July 1, 2014

Four Generations of Warfare

Military historians and professionals over the years have discussed the various generations of warfare. Some believe there are four generations of warfare to date[1]:

- First-generation warfare started with the rise of the nation-state and included a top-down military structure, limited weapons, and armies made up of serfs; this tended in the early 19th century, about the time of the Napoleonic Wars.
- Second-generation warfare began in about 1860 during the US Civil War. This generation of warfare included artillery, machine guns, mass weapons development, and logistics supported by trains. This generation of warfare ended some time after World War I.
- Third generation of warfare attributed its beginning to the Germans in World War II, when "shock-maneuver" tactics were used.
- In 1989, the US *Marine Corps Gazette*[2] contained an article by several military personnel. The article, entitled "Changing the Face of War: Into the Fourth Generation," discussed the fourth-generation battlefield, which is likely to include the

> whole of the enemy's society....The distinction between civilian and military may disappear....Television news may become a more powerful operational weapon than armored divisions.

If one were to have any doubts about the accuracy of that statement, one just has to remember the US television news showing a dead American military man's body being dragged through the streets of Mogadishu, Somalia. The loss of national will can be closely correlated with how quickly the United States departed that country. This, too, is part of the IW campaigns being waged on a worldwide scale.

One can argue that IW has existed in all generations of warfare and has included spying, observation balloons, breaking enemy codes, and many other functions and activities. True, IW is as old as man, but many aspects as to how it is being applied in our information-dependent, information-based world are new.

Introduction to Global Information Warfare

In the early 1990s, several people in the US Department of Defense (DoD) articulated a unique form of warfare termed *information warfare* (IW). The Chinese say they were developing IW concepts in the late 1980s. Who is correct? Does it matter? As the areas embraced by IW have been developed over the centuries and millennia, these have been a normal part of human activities from mankind's beginning. What is unique about IW is that it is the first instantiation of trying to tie together all the areas that make up the information environment (IE). The IE runs through every part of your country, organization, and personal life. At the present time, there is no cookbook recipe for doing the extremely complex task of bringing together all the areas.

What is IW? The general working definition of IW employed in this book is as follows: IW is a coherent and synchronized blending of physical and virtual actions to have countries, organizations, and individuals perform, or not perform, actions so that your goals and objectives are attained and maintained, while simultaneously preventing competitors from doing the same to you. Clearly, this embraces much more than attacking computers with malicious code. The litmus test is this: If information is used to perpetrate an act that was done to influence another to take or not take actions beneficial to the attacker, then it can be considered IW.

The definition is intentionally broad, embracing organizational levels, people, and capabilities. It allows room for governments, cartels, corporate, hacktivists, terrorists, other groups, and individuals to have a part. It is up to each enlightened enterprise to tailor the definition to fit its needs. This should not be a definition of convenience, to "check the box."

Exhibit 1.1 shows many information warfare areas.

You are asked, and many times forced by government and businesses, to depend on the Internet; the Internet that is home to hackers, crackers, phreakers, hacktivists, script kiddies, net espionage (network-enabled espionage), and information warriors; the Internet that is home to worms, Trojan horses, software bugs, hardware glitches, distributed denial-of-service (DDoS) attacks, viruses, and various forms of malware. All this, and the Internet is only a portion of the areas that IW addresses. Although the Internet touches many critical infrastructures and these in turn affect the many IEs with which you interface, most of the IW areas were around before the Internet.

As "competition" is analogous to "enemy" or "adversary," other business–military analogies can be made with profit, shareholder value, competitive edge, and industry rank to achieve brand recognition and customer loyalty, exerting power, influence, and market share. A business leader or military leader must train and equip forces; gather intelligence; assemble, deploy, and employ forces at decisive places and times; sustain them; form coalitions with other businesses and nation-states; and be successful. There are many physical and virtual world parallels, as can be seen in the following headline:

> Cisco to use SNA as weapon against competition…Cisco believes its experience in melding SNA and IP internet works can be used as a weapon in the company's battle with Lucent and Nortel for leadership in converging voice, video, and data over IP networks.[2]

Purists will focus on warfare as a state of affairs that must be declared by a government and can only be conducted by a government. Guerrilla warfare, economic

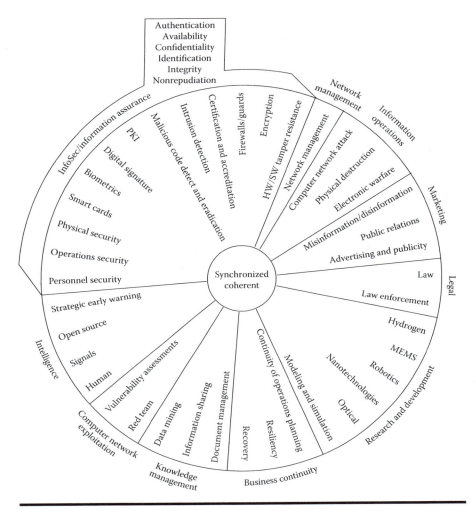

Exhibit 1.1 Information warfare areas.

warfare (either one country "forcing" another country to spend itself into bank-ruptcy, as allegedly the United States did to the Soviet Union), or a company adjust-ing prices to damage its competition (e.g., taking a long time horizon to use volume and time to adjust prices downward). "Conflict" or "that's business" does not carry the same sound of ultimate struggle as referring to business as "war." Clausewitz stated "War is an extension of politics." By analogy, because business is the imple-mentation of a country's laws, economic policy, and values, business is an extension of politics.

In a free market economy, competition is central to business strategy aimed at winning customers and market share. Competition, like war, is a struggle for a winning position. The marketplace can then be compared analogously to a battle-field with winners and losers. It follows that business is analogous to war. Therefore, using military phraseology in a business context is appropriate. In fact, one just has to remember September 11, 2001, and the destruction of New York's World Trade Center to see that in today's world, warfare is waged on many levels by vari-ous adversaries against various targets. These targets can be nation-states and their governments, groups, businesses, or individuals. The tools will be any that can be applied for attackers to successfully attain their goals.

The counterargument is that some insurance companies' contracts state that if a loss is due to an act of terrorism or war, they will not pay for damages. In the United States, attacks on computers are, by default, criminal acts and are thus in the purview of law enforcement. Often, only after an investigation determines that the criminal act is a national security issue will intelligence agencies and other gov-ernment organizations take the lead.

There are adversaries, winners, and losers. All the writing on IW focuses on weaknesses, defenses, and losses. Despite the gloomy forecasts by government offi-cials and the media, IW is also about strengths, offenses, and gains. These positive features are within the grasp of any government or business organization with a desire to seize and maintain a competitive advantage—to be a winner on the IW battlefield. Importantly, unlike in some of today's physical wars and those of the past, those without a great deal of resources—a small nation like North Korea, for example—have the power to successfully attack global and a nation's businesses as well as governments.

What possible application can IW have outside specialized military circles? From a practical viewpoint, how does IW shorten decision cycle times, raise rev-enue, lower or avoid costs, and improve performance? If IW cannot improve effec-tiveness or efficiency or bring about innovation, why do it? IW does do these things and ought to be the approach used rather than the top management fads that come and go, leaving businesses worse off for trying them. The purpose of IW is to gain power and influence over others. Power and influence are at the heart of all such relationships. Because IW requires effort, the effort needs to resolve into some aspect of power, such as profit or economic or military domination on the battle-field or in the marketplace.

Information Warfare Will Hit You in Your Pocketbook

There are some events that were not expected. Hannibal crossed the Alps. Clay defeated Liston for the heavyweight boxing title. CD Universe did not think crack-ers would break into its systems. Buy.com did not expect a DDoS attack, nor did Sony, Target, and other victims too numerous to mention. It seems new websites are discovered and hacked within minutes of being on the Internet. One honey-pot project was attacked within five minutes. It will happen: One day, your IE defenses are going to be beaten. When they go down, your revenues and profits will go down. The Internet age has again proven the adage that "time is money." Suppose a company has US$1 billion in electronic and mobile commerce revenue. That equates to $2,739,726 per day, $114,155 per hour, $1903 per minute, and $32 per second.[3] How long can your business afford to be adversely affected due to an attack? In other words, what are the risks and consequences you are willing to accept?

In a portent of crippling events to come, since early 2000 there have been thousands of automated computer-based distributed attacks, extortion attempts for tens and hundreds of millions of dollars, and posting on the Internet of millions of supposedly protected credit card details and other private information. Apparently, the laws and court sentences for computer crimes lack deterrent value. Of course, if hardware and software products, communications systems, e-commerce sites, and other information technology (IT) components were designed with security in mind, we would not have this predicament—something that even Bill Gates of Microsoft finally realized.

In many cases, the dollar loss is secondary to the loss of trust. Banks and insurance companies especially feel customers' wrath. When customers believe their trust has been compromised, they vote with their pocketbooks and take their business elsewhere. That is when revenues and profits decline, which leads to a decline in the stock price, which, in the not too distant future, will lead to shareholder lawsuits for negligence and other claims.

IW conjures up many images: computers, networks, and telecommunications-savvy experts in the military and intelligence communities, corporate espionage, and pale 14-year-olds looking like they could be the next-door neighbor's kids—or yours. Dire prognostications about how an "electronic Pearl Harbor" threatens national security and the daily media coverage of viruses and DoS attacks, interchangeably using phrases like IW, cyber warfare, and cyber terrorism, may make IW seem distant and surreal.

Some of the attacks, whether premeditated or unintentional, resulted in billions of dollars in damages. Computer emergency response teams (CERTs) and law-enforcement agencies stress protection and defense of information, information infrastructure, and information-based processes to ward off malicious attacks. What do these and many other aspects of operating in the IE have to do with managing a government organization or running a business? For businesses, this may mean new business generation, cost avoidance, profit, customer retention, market leadership, and positive public perception. For nation-states, this may be economic, political, or military power, influence, or defeat.

Once high-profile events such as the Morris worm and Citibank's $400,000 loss ($10 million was stolen, and all but $400,000 allegedly recovered) should have been sufficient warning shots across the bow that a different approach was needed. However, such attacks of "long ago," in technology terms, pale in comparison to the number, sophistication, and scale of losses of today's attacks.

NOTE: Many of us in the late 1980s and into the 1990s and beyond have been warning of the potential for IW attacks and what should be done to prepare for them. Of course, as usual when it comes to security, management in businesses and in government agencies ignored our warnings and are now reaping the results. We predict the worse is yet to come.

The much-needed security fixes are years away as defenses continue to lag behind the attackers in sophistication. However, there are pockets of government-sponsored sophisticated attacks; some may even be called "defensive attacks" or preemptive strikes against an adversary. Demand is low because the general public appears to be uninterested in cracker exploits and has become indifferent to the almost daily news stories. Said differently, the public has come to expect identity thefts, theft of their credit cards, and such. However, since corporations are held liable in most cases, and credit card corporations absorb the losses of their customers, the general public remains complacent in general and personally outraged only when it is their own identity or financial instruments that have been compromised.

Business Is War

An advertising campaign can be considered a subset of an IW campaign. Here is a perhaps not so hypothetical example. Taking grocery-store shelf space, due to product or packaging redesign, from a competitor is notionally no different than denying use of a radar or a seaport to the enemy. Instead of cereal boxes that stood and poured vertically, what if they stood horizontally and had spouts for pouring (besides, vertical boxes are prone to tipping)? This would result in more shelf space needed for the same amount of cereal boxes. The packaging will carry a message that conveys "new" and "improved." The boxes will be at eye level—easy for the consumer to spot. In-store advertising will attempt to vector shoppers to the cereal aisle. Newspaper and magazine advertising will attempt to convince customers to try the "new" and "improved" product, and coupons will be used as further enticement. There may even be an in-store demonstration. Because there is limited shelf space and if the cereal company has bargaining power, other cereals will have to lose space. Lost space then hopefully translates to lost product sales, which in turn leads to reduced revenue and profits as well as a lower stock price.

In business, the IW target can be the customer, the competition, or another entity. The purpose of the IW campaign is to have the competitor take action that will result in increased profits for your company. In the best of all outcomes, your revenues go up and the competitors' revenues decline. Even if your sales were constant, just having less space to sell should make competitors' sales decline, so your industry ranking will improve. What will the competition do? Redesign packaging? Alter ingredients? Lower the product's price? Counter with coupons? Have a television campaign employing a doctor to extol the health benefits of their cereal? Play hardball with the supermarket chain? Use combination of these tactics? Do nothing, taking a wait-and-see approach? This is physical and virtual IW at the corporate level. It embraces the media, perception management, physical operations, intelligence collection, and more.

This is no different than one country observing another and bringing to bear economic, diplomatic, and military means. These means may include very advanced open-source searches and analyses, and covert means involving manipulation of the radio-frequency (RF) spectrum. From a business perspective, operations, marketing, public relations, manufacturing, finance, transportation, and other parts of the company must operate in a synchronized and coherent fashion. The competition must be monitored and intelligence collected so the company can be in a position to agilely and effectively respond to any countermoves.

IW Broadly Encompasses Many Levels and Functions

IW is not the sole purview of a modern, technology-based and dependent government; otherwise, only wealthy countries could practice it. A narrow interpretation of IW flies in the face of reality. In addition to a unique set of capabilities that are based on unlimited deep pockets and specialized espionage capabilities, more brainpower, and perhaps more capabilities, reside external to a government. Any organization, and even individuals, can conduct offensive and defensive IW. IW is about seizing control of perceptions, physical structures, and virtual assets. Seizing control can be done from both offensive and defensive positions. That squarely puts any organization in control of its destiny. Those that are unenlightened will never perform at or near the top of the pack, and may well cease to exist. Those that embrace IW have a much better chance of surviving and reaping the rewards.

The military, the intelligence community, and law enforcement generally do not embrace this perspective. Why? They have capabilities that are highly classified. If used by industry, then "all hell would break loose." Certainly, there are unique offensive and defensive capabilities that only can be developed by the government due to their high risk of success and the funding they require. However, there has been an explosion of brainpower with regard to physical and virtual capabilities. The majority of brainpower in genetics, robotics, nanotechnology, microelectromagnetic systems (MEMS), and hydrogen technologies resides outside the military, the intelligence community, and law enforcement. What is to prevent these capabilities from falling into the hands of nation-states, individuals, businesses, and organizations that wish to perpetrate some form of hostile behavior? Absolutely nothing.

What IW Is…and Is Not

IW is not about a one-time silver bullet for a quick fix and looking good on a quarterly financial report. IW is not restricted to using computers to attack other computers. It is not confined to the cyber realm. *Virtual* means electronic, RF, and photonic manipulation. Organizations need to use the capabilities within the virtual and physical domains in a manner that optimizes what they wish to do. The best approach for IW, as it should be with a business or government organization, is to conduct physical and virtual operations in a synchronized and coherent fashion. This is easier said than done. Goddard's experiments contributed to manned space flight—four decades later. As virtual capabilities become more practical for the government, military, and business, the greater their importance becomes in operations. Fifteen years ago, laptops, mobile phones, and personal digital assistants (PDAs)—remember them?—were bulky, seldom more capable than their traditional counterparts, and much more expensive. For some people, the time-saving and cost-reducing capabilities of the gadgets borders on technological cocaine, and these people almost cannot function without their gadgets. Some business and government organizations have bought into technology to such an extent that their operations can truly be termed "network-centric business." What better way to counter this than with IW? Not many years from now, IW will be mainstream, and those who do not participate will fail.

Much hype surrounds hacker exploits and computer-based viruses. Most hacker, cracker, and phreaker exploits and viruses qualify as falling within IW, albeit at the low end of the spectrum, because there is an attempt to influence others, either directly or indirectly, to take an action. Approaches range from altruistic ("I found a hole in the software. Develop a patch for it") to anger ("I will make them miserable for firing me") to social awareness ("Stop drug research on animals") to criminal ("Here is how to defeat the fraud control and computer security systems of fill-in-the-blanks of the corporation as all are vulnerable more or less."). Almost all of the events and attacks fall into the realm of theft, extortion, fraud, and related criminal behavior. Measures must be employed to protect and defend corporate and government systems because individual losses have already been in the tens and hundreds of millions of dollars.

Even if you have taken all the appropriate measures to protect and secure your physical and virtual assets, much falls outside your span of control: protected and secured power, financial systems, communications, transportation, water, and continuity of government infrastructures; security-rich and bug-free commercial off-the-shelf (COTS) software; and the creativity of crackers and phreakers in finding new vulnerabilities in technology to exploit. Also, you probably cannot control your business partners', customers', financial stakeholders', and suppliers' IEs that are connected to yours. If you are an Internet-based company, then electronic and mobile commerce accounts for the majority of your revenue. Any disruption and your customers will go to your competitors. If you are a traditional bricks-and-mortar company expanding into the Internet to enhance your customers' ability to do business with you, business interruptions and disclosure of customer data will taint your reputation and credibility. Business interruption can be costly on many levels.[3]

When properly employed, IW is an agile capability that can be tailored to any situation. It can bring a multitude of functions to bear. It can be implemented in both the physical and virtual worlds. Central to IW is how it is used to influence decision makers. Magazines, radio, television, newspapers, leaflets, e-mail, web pages, social media, and other forms of media can all be used as a vehicle to deliver IW.

IW should not be restricted to a small cadre. Certainly only a few people should know about the sensitive details that will make or break the execution of the IW plan. All parts of an enterprise, not just an organization, need to be linked for the most effective implementation of IW. Any organization has a finite portion of resources. Partnerships, alliances, consortiums, and other relationships can serve to expand an organization's capabilities.

Proper use of information is central to profitable business and successful military operations. IW is used to provide your organization with a competitive advantage while at the same time limiting the competition's capability to reduce your advantage and increase their own. Effective IW is not possible without control of your IE.

An IE is the interrelated set of information, information infrastructure, and information-based processes. Data includes the measurements used as a basis for reasoning, discussion, or calculation. Data is a raw input. Information applies to facts told, read, or communicated, which may be unorganized and even unrelated. Information is the meaning assigned to data. Knowledge is an organized body of information. It is the comprehension and understanding consequent to having acquired and organized a body of facts. Information as used here means data, information, and knowledge. No doubt horrific to purists, there is no one good word in the English language that embraces all three concepts together. All three processes exist within any organization. At any given time, one of the processes will be of greater value than the others. Your competition wants your information, so do not believe that "gentlemen don't read other gentlemen's mail."

Information moves across information infrastructures in support of information-based processes. The information infrastructure is the media within which we display, store, process, and transmit information. Examples are people, computers, fiber-optic cables, lasers, telephones, and satellites. Examples of information-based processes are the established ways to obtain and exchange information. This includes people to people (e.g., telephone conversations and office meetings), electronic commerce/electronic data interchange (EC/EDI), data mining, batch processing, and surfing the web. Attacking (i.e., denying, altering, or destroying) one or more IE components can result in the loss of tens of millions of dollars in profit, can degrade national security, and can be more effective than physical destruction. Degrade or destroy any one of the components and, like a three-legged stool, the IE will eventually collapse.[4]

Exhibit 1.2 shows the major components of an IE.

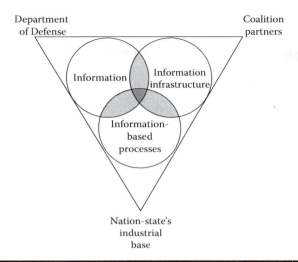

Exhibit 1.2   Major components of an information environment (IE).

Bad things happen, such as floods, hurricanes, and earthquakes; power surges and sags; and fires. Disgruntled employees can steal, manipulate, or destroy information. Crackers work their way through the electronic sieve of protection mechanisms (e.g., firewalls and intrusion detection devices) into information assets.

Sound disaster recovery, business continuity, and contingency operating plans are essential. For every minute information systems are not up and fully running, revenues, profits, and shareholder value are being lost. The last thing a general counsel needs is a lawsuit from unhappy shareholders who are suing for millions because the corporation did not follow best practices to protect information. One problem is that COTS hardware and software are very difficult to protect. Another concern is that firewalls, intrusion detection devices, and passwords are not enough. The state-of-the-art in information assurance (IA) works against script kiddies and moderately skilled hackers. What about the competition, drug cartels, and hostile nation-states that are significantly better funded? There is no firewall or intrusion detection device on the market that cannot be penetrated or bypassed. Password dictionaries can cover almost any entire language, and there are very specific dictionaries (e.g., sports, Star Trek, or historic dates and events).

Exhibit 1.3 shows the possible breakdowns in an IE. IEs exist internal and external to an organization. An IE is tailorable so it can support many actors. The example that follows involves a corporation, its customers, and the government. Another IE can be a military, its allies and coalition partners, and the government. Whatever comprises a specific IE, the important fact remains: If its elements are not protected and secured, the consequences can range from irritants to catastrophes.

Exhibit 1.4 depicts an enterprise IE.

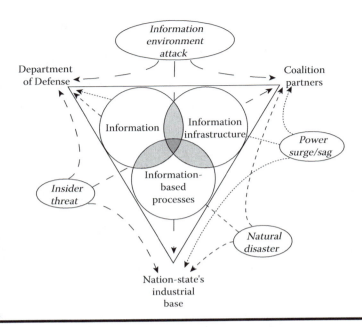

Exhibit 1.3   Possible breakdowns in an IE.

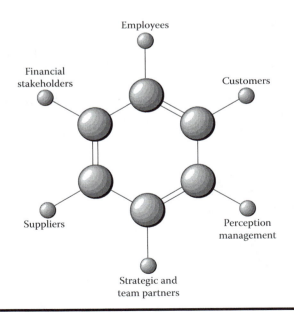

Exhibit 1.4   Enterprise IE.

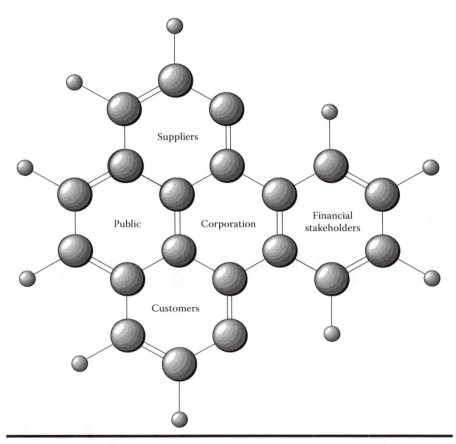

Exhibit 1.5 Extended IE.

An organization has employees. These employees deliver products, services, and processes to the organization and its customers. To keep the organization running, suppliers deliver products, services, and processes. Financial stakeholders—venture capitalists, banks, stockholders, and others—provide capital. The public has a positive, neutral, or negative view of the organization. Strategic teaming partners provide physical, financial, cerebral, and other capabilities. Every entity with which the organization is linked has its own IE. IEs are connected to, and are interdependent on, other IEs.

Exhibit 1.5 depicts an extended IE.

Going beyond Three Blind Men Describing an Elephant: IW Terms of Reference

IW cuts across national borders, educational backgrounds, and cultural views. To ensure a consistent understanding during this discussion, working definitions of

IW and many supporting terms are offered. This does not preclude national interpretations and certainly does not attempt to rationalize, harmonize, and normalize definitions. Common terms of reference (TOR) permit a shared understanding, as well as a point of departure for applying TOR within specific organizations.

George Santayana said "Those who ignore the lessons of history are condemned to repeat them."

Here is an example of how parochialism caused a disaster.

In August and October 1943, the Allies launched air raids against Schweinfurt with disastrous consequences—for the Allies. In the August raid, of 600 planes, 60 were lost, along with 600 crewmen. Why? There was no long-range fighter escort. Why? In the 1920s and 1930s, resources were allocated for strategic bombardment over pursuit. Why? General Emilio Douhet and others postulated that air power alone could win wars by striking the enemy's strategic centers. Lesson learned: The decisions made in the 1920s and 1930s led to the wrong tactical employment a decade later. We must not make the same mistake with IW. If we do, national security, economic viability, and corporate capabilities will be lost.

It seems that there are as many definitions of IW and related topics as there are people. It is reminiscent of three blind men describing an elephant by touching the animal's various parts. One blind man said, "An elephant is a reptile and is thin and long," as he was touching the tail. Touching the tusks, another blind man said, "An elephant is like a big fish with its smooth and pointed body." The third blind man said, "An elephant resembles a large leaf with a hole in the middle," because he was touching the ears. None of them could extrapolate their interpretations to a real elephant. Similarly, what one sees is not necessarily what one gets. "Qu'est-ce que c'est?" will be mispronounced if one does not have a basic understanding of French diction. So, too, is it with terms used to describe various practices in the information realm.

Although the names are initially obtuse to those who do not work in those areas, these information practices have been a normal evolution in communications and computers and also in the dark side move/countermove/counter-countermove "cool war." There are many other variations. Little wonder the terms are understood by few people and erroneously used interchangeably. Few understand the difference between a hacker, cracker, and phreaker, much less a white-hat hacker.

In some cases, more terminology only detracts from meaning. *Cyber* is too limiting. It is as if, rather than pushing through difficult points to achieve philosophical insights and technical understanding, people create terms to differentiate themselves without knowing what they are doing.

Information and knowledge are now in vogue. We are in the information age, rapidly transitioning into the knowledge age. Acquiring the right data, deriving good information, and applying it to make sound decisions to positively affect the bottom line are essential. Search engines have made finding information on the Internet very simple. Witness during the past at least 40 years the explosion of terminology related to the protection of information and use of information for national security purposes. The most important point is to understand the meaning of these terms and what the different functions can—and cannot—do to make an informed decision whether or not to commit resources (i.e., people, money, and time).

Many countries have developed definitions. IW, information assurance, information operations, information superiority, information dominance, and other constructs popular in the US military are part of the revolution in military affairs (RMA) and revolution in security affairs (RSA). Government organizations and businesses have developed additional terms, and some do not agree with the national version. So there can be a point of departure for this discussion; definitions accepted by many are put forth. In some cases, working definitions will be used. The following definitions are taken from the US *Department of Defense Dictionary of Military and Associated Terms*[5].

Command and Control Warfare (C2W)

This refers to the integrated use of operations security, military deception, psychological operations, electronic warfare, and physical destruction, mutually supported by intelligence, to deny information to, influence, degrade, or destroy adversary command and control capabilities, while protecting friendly command and control capabilities against such actions. Command and control warfare (C2W) is an application of IW in military operations and is a subset of IW. Command and control warfare applies across the range of military operations and all levels of conflict. C2W is both offensive and defensive.

Defense in Depth

This means the siting of mutually supporting defense positions designed to absorb and progressively weaken attack, prevent initial observations of the whole position by the enemy, and to allow the commander to maneuver the reserve.

Information

This is defined as facts, data, or instructions in any medium or form: the meaning that a human assigns to data by means of the known conventions used in their representation. Here are some terms—"oldies but goodies"—that are still valid today as they describe IW-related environment:

■ *Information assurance (IA)*: Information operations that protect and defend information and information systems by ensuring their availability, integrity, authentication, confidentiality, and nonrepudiation. This includes providing for restoration of information systems by incorporating protection, detection, and reaction capabilities.

- *Information-based processes*: Processes that collect, analyze, and disseminate information using any medium or form. These processes may be stand-alone processes or subprocesses that, taken together, comprise a larger system or systems of processes.
- *Information environment*: The aggregate of individuals, organizations, or systems that collect, process, or disseminate information; also included is the information itself.
- *Information security*: The protection of information and information systems against unauthorized access or modification of information, whether in storage, processing, or transit, and against DoS to authorized users. Information security includes those measures necessary to detect, document, and counter such threats. Information security is composed of computer security and communications security. Also called INFOSEC.

An older definition focused on only physical protections: locks, alarms, safes, marking of the documents, and similar physical-world capabilities.

Information System

This means the entire infrastructure, organization, personnel, and components that collect, process, store, transmit, process, display, disseminate, and act on information.

Information Warfare (IW)

These are information operations conducted during a time of crisis or conflict to achieve or promote specific objectives over a specific adversary or adversaries.

We can expand on this because of the definition of IW. What is IW? It is more than computer network attack (CNA) and defense (CND). That almost everyone agrees on. But what else is encompassed by IW? Heated debates go on today about what IW should embrace and accomplish. IW is an umbrella concept embracing many disciplines. IW is most effective when performed in a synchronized and coherent fashion. That is why knowledge management (KM) complements it so well. All components of an organization, as well as across the enterprise, need to be included in an IW action plan.

The good news is that IW embraces marketing, public relations, counterintelligence, and other functions you now perform. IW is not these functions renamed. They continue to be run by the subject-matter experts. IW is the coherent application and synchronized approach of these functions. What is needed are experts who, by analogy, are conductors of the orchestra. They know where the expertise resides within the organization, understand what the functions can and cannot do, and bring them to bear for optimum performance. At present, only the military in a few countries come close to understanding the relationships and functions of linking the physical domain with the virtual realm and have begun policy development and allocation of resources. For the most part the equivalent does not exist in industry—yet.

The purpose of IW is to control or influence a decision maker's actions. An area of control can be directly manipulated, whereas an area of influence can only be indirectly manipulated. Control and influence are the essence of power. From a business perspective, sector and industry-leading market share and profit are the results of proper IW execution.

What would make a decision maker act or not act? Perhaps false or misleading information, an analysis of open-source information, documents mysteriously acquired, or intelligence from an employee hired away from the competition. IW at the corporate level manifests itself in marketing, public relations, legal issues, research and development, manufacturing, and other functions. With the introduction of commercial high-resolution satellite photography, some companies have altered their delivery and shipment schedules to include using empty rail cars and semi-tractor trailers to mask inventory, production capability, and customer quantities. IW is a full spectrum of capabilities. Ingredients are carefully selected and tailored to each case.

IW can be conducted without using physical destruction. Both military psychological operations (PsyOps) and commercial advertising heavily depend on psychology and sociology, the study of individual and group behavior. The implications of this insight are enormous. Businesses engage in IW all the time, or is it that only the effective ones do?

IW enables direct and indirect attacks to be made from anywhere in the world in a matter of seconds. Physical proximity to a target is not necessary. How is this possible? Because we have made conscious and unconscious decisions to have speed and connectivity without complementary security. In Sun Tzu's and Genghis Khan's eras, physical, personnel, and operational security were all that was needed for protection. Today we have fiber optics, satellites, smart phones and tablet computers, infrared and laser communications, interactive cable television, and a host of other technology marvels that allow us to reach anywhere in a few seconds. Now, in seconds, our information can be intercepted, modified, manipulated, and stolen.

No simple sentence or paragraph effectively describes IW. There are broad and narrow interpretations within national and international government, business, and academic communities, and some even totally reject the notion of IW. The overall view of IW must be expansive. Information is everywhere. We find information, for example, in mass media such as radio, television, and newspapers, on World Wide Web (WWW, or web) sites, in communications systems, and in computer networks and systems. Any and all of these may be subjected to attack via offensive IW (OIW). It follows that all these areas must be defended with defensive IW (DIW).

OIW can make a government, society, nation, or business bend to the will of the attacker. Attacks can be very large, devastating, and noticeable, such as economic or social disruption or breakdown and the denial of critical infrastructure capabilities (e.g., power, transportation, communications, and finance). They can also be small, low key, and unassuming, such as a request for publications and telephone calls (as the basis for social engineering). Businesses do not have the deep pockets of a government, but that does not restrict them from engaging in IW.

A business wants to deny the competition orders, customers, and information about its research and development (R&D). Industrial espionage has its share of illegal activities: theft, monitoring communications, and denying use of servers to conduct electronic commerce. Governments engage in psychological operations (with the subsets of mis-/dis-information, propaganda using leaflets, and television and radio broadcasts). Businesses must identify when disinformation is being used to lure customers away and have the means to counter it. Of course, that is starting from a position of weakness. What is a proactive, DIW approach to counter the attack? Inoculate the customers, suppliers, business partners, and others in the IE.

DIW is the ability to protect and defend the IE. Defense does not imply being reactive.

Measures can be taken to forewarn of attacks and to preposition physical and virtual forces. Examples of virtual forces are software and brainpower. The acme of skill is to present a posture to prevent a competitor from attacking and to achieve victory without having to attack. Perception management is as important as demonstrable physical and virtual capabilities.

Information Operations (IO)

As stated above, for the purposes of this book, IW is not restricted to war, so information operations (IO) as described below is included in IW. IO refers to actions taken to affect adversary information and information systems while defending one's own information and information systems.

■ *Defensive IO*: The integration and coordination of policies and procedures, operations, personnel, and technology to protect and defend information and information systems. Defensive information operations are conducted through IA, physical security, operations security, counterdeception, counterpsychological operations, counterintelligence, electronic warfare, and special information operations. Defensive information operations ensure timely, accurate, and relevant information access while denying adversaries the opportunity to exploit friendly information and information systems for their own purposes.

■ *Offensive IO*: The integrated use of assigned and supporting capabilities and activities, mutually supported by intelligence, to affect adversary decision makers to achieve or promote specific objectives. These capabilities and activities include, but are not limited to, operations security, military deception, psychological operations, electronic warfare, physical attack or destruction, and special information operations, and they could also include computer network attack.

- *Information superiority*: The degree of dominance in the information domain that permits the conduct of operations without effective opposition. Information superiority is the relative state of influence and control of the IE between two or more actors. Some argue that the opposite of "superiority" is "inferiority." This is not the case. All actors have equal access to open-source information. Restricted, sensitive, and classified information can be acquired through overt or covert operations. Having data, information, and knowledge is not the key to attaining and maintaining information superiority. What is done with the information and the speed at which it is done is the gold nugget. Information sharing, automation, cross platform information sharing, automating processes (like air-traffic control; sales-manufacturing/production-inventory-transportation; and military intelligence-platform maneuver-weapons selection and release-battle damage assessment) are essential to have execution cycles faster than those of the competition.

- *Operations security*: A process of identifying critical information and subsequently analyzing friendly actions attendant to military operations and other activities to (1) identify those actions that can be observed by adversary intelligence systems; (2) determine indicators that hostile intelligence systems might obtain what could be interpreted or pieced together to derive critical information in time to be useful to adversaries; and (3) select and execute measures that eliminate or reduce to an acceptable level the vulnerabilities of friendly actions to adversary exploitation. Also called OPSEC.

- *Vulnerability*: In information operations, a weakness in information system security design, procedures, implementation, or internal controls that could be exploited to gain unauthorized access to information or information system.

In addition to the above definitions, the US National Security Telecommunications and Information Systems Security Committee (NSTISSC) 4009 National Information Systems Security (INFOSEC) Glossary14 offers the following:

- *Attack*: Type of incident involving the intentional act of attempting to bypass one or more security controls

- *Confidentiality*: Assurance that information is not disclosed to unauthorized persons, processes, or devices

- *Critical infrastructure*: Those physical and cyber-based systems essential to the minimum operations of the economy and government

- *Integrity*: Quality of an IS, reflecting the logical correctness and reliability of the operating system; the logical completeness of the hardware and software implementing the protection mechanisms; and the consistency of data structures and occurrence of the stored data. Note that, in a formal security mode, integrity is interpreted more narrowly to mean the protection of unauthorized modification or the destruction of information.

- *Nonrepudiation*: Assurance that the sender of the data is provided with proof of delivery and the recipient is provided with proof of the sender's identity so that neither can later deny having processed the data
- *OPSEC*: Process denying information to potential adversaries about capabilities or intentions by identifying, controlling, and protecting unclassified generic activities
- *Probe*: Type of incident involving an attempt to gather information about an IS for the apparent purpose of circumventing its security controls
- *Risk*: Possibility that a particular threat will adversely impact an IS by exploiting a particular vulnerability
- *Risk management*: Process of identifying and applying countermeasures commensurate with the value of the assets protected based on a risk assessment

Neither NSTISSC 4009 nor the US DoD *Dictionary of Military and Associated Terms* define consequence and consequence management. Risks are the intersection of threats and vulnerabilities. Residual risks are those that remain after mitigating actions. To plan effectively, decision *makers* need to know the consequences of various courses of actions. The residual risks influence the outcomes. The outcomes are best represented via consequence management cascading effects. Third- and fourth-order effects, or further, need to be well estimated for the best course of action to be chosen.

Information Warfare Is a Powerful Approach for Attaining and Maintaining a Competitive Advantage

The purpose of a business is to create value for its shareholders, and the purpose of a government is to provide for the common good. From a business viewpoint, being effective and efficient in current markets and opening new lines of business are key to sustained revenue generation and profits. From a national security perspective, we should expect the military, intelligence community, and law enforcement to develop and use capabilities to maintain sovereignty, create and sustain peace and economic prosperity, and ensure public safety from criminals and monopolies. These entities cannot survive by insulating themselves. They must embrace, within their value system, whatever it takes to go beyond surviving to thrive.

Exhibit 1.6 shows how to use IW to achieve goals and objectives.

Complexity interwoven across government, industry, and society presents a daunting challenge for IW. It is in the best interests of any government, business, and other organization to take prudent action to defend against IW attacks and to be able to launch them.

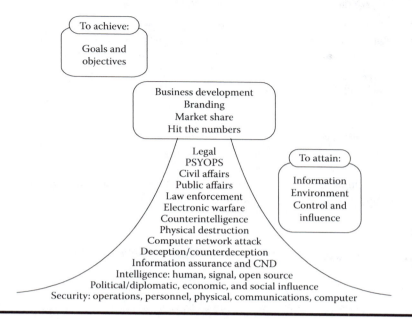

Exhibit 1.6   How to use IW to achieve goals and objectives.

The advanced hacker breaks into online shopping exchanges, manipulates orders, steals merchandise, plunders credit card numbers—the modern-day pirate, highway robber, and Wild West outlaw. Those who would be part of the online shopping population come to expect this malicious behavior but are not dissuaded from shopping online.

Espionage, disinformation, physical destruction (normally permitted by law only for the military and law enforcement), and other actions are a means to an end. IW is a higher level, cerebral activity. The target can be a population (the national will or a specific political, religious, or ethnic group), a despot, a general, or anyone in an organization. How, then, should IW be applied to industry? After all, is war not a declaration of Congress, parliament, or other government entity? If a business is destroyed by an act of war or terrorism, it will not be remunerated by insurance. Is this a misnomer? By no means!

Because business is war, the principles of war normally associated with the military ought to be applied. These are not rigid, and their application is tailored to each use. Objective, offensive, mass, economy of force, unity of leadership, maneuver, security, surprise, and simplicity are generally recognized principles that will benefit any organization. Applying those principles to coherent and synchronized IW will produce a positive return on investment (ROI).

In the IT world, determining ROI is considered the holy grail. The problem for quantitative metrics for IW is that orders of magnitude are more difficult because of the many disciplines, organizational levels, and the sheer scope involved. Some prefer it that way, because it allows them to hide behind classified information and black magic. If IW is to be successful, metrics are necessary. Existing traditional measures are a good start (e.g., how many probes did our intrusion detection system pick up?), but they are not sufficiently expansive and precise. What is the value of a database? What it the value of that database after it has been successfully data mined? Because quantitative metrics need to be developed, qualitative ones will need to be used.

IW is an embracing approach, customizable to produce positive results in any organization and tailorable to meet the demands of the marketplace. By balancing tried and true capabilities with leading-edge technologies and concepts, IW remains a fresh and useful approach for achieving goals and objectives on the way to attaining and maintaining a competitive advantage.

Coherent Knowledge-Based Operations (CKO)

IW for its own sake is senseless. IW must help countries achieve their national security objectives and help businesses attain their goals. When IW is combined with KM and how business is done, the combination provides a powerful capability. Applying IW in conjunction with KM results in information superiority. When KM is applied to how business is done, situational awareness will result. Combining IW with how business is done delivers tactics, techniques, and procedures to attain a competitive advantage. The intersection of IW with KM and how business is done is called coherent knowledge-based operations (CKO). CKO enables a country or a business to attain and maintain a competitive advantage through the synchronization and coherent application of all of its capabilities in the extended IE.

Organizations dabble in many pop management fads. Well-intentioned or not, these often are stovepipe solutions that divert finite resources—people, money, and time—from the organization's central interests and objectives. CKO brings together what appear to be several disparate components. *Coherent* means an orderly or logical relation of parts that affords comprehension or recognition. The parts are network-centric business (NCB) (how business is done), KM, and IW. When used in concert, their sum is far more powerful than the individual components, creating a powerful means of attaining and maintaining a competitive advantage. CKO can be used to execute and to survive IW attacks.

Network-Centric Business (NCB)

We are told that we are in the information age, ride the information highway, and are part of the knowledge-based economy. We conduct electronic commerce (EC), have electronic data interchange (EDI) between computers, allow employees to telecommute and have remote access, and spend millions of dollars on websites to attract customers to sell products and services. Computers and robots are in the manufacturing plants, personnel and medical records are automated, and many of us participate in automated deposits and bill payments. If the computers stopped, not enough trained and skilled people could take over the functions in a manual system, and many businesses and government functions would quickly come to a halt. Computers, databases, and networks are as vital to a business as the circulatory and nervous systems are to your body. Computers and networks have become as ubiquitous as toasters, and network-centric appliances are in the works. The current generation of smartphones are the forerunners of tools with tremendous capability, limited only by human creativity. If you do not quickly gain control of your IE, doing so in the future will be exponentially more difficult—and expensive. The main advantage of controlling your IE is that your bottom line will improve.

There is no faster, more effective, or more efficient means to beat the competition than to use network-centric business (NCB). NCB allows an organization to take maximum advantage of its business processes: taking and placing orders, using the supply chain, conducting just-in-time production, and using distribution channels to field products and services. NCB leverages not only all the resources within an organization but also its customers and business partners. They are all part of the solution set that drives the bottom line. The resources within the organization—people, money, and time—are finite, but they can be effectively and efficiently allocated to provide optimal support to customers and to maximize the bottom line.[4]

Knowledge Management (KM)

KM integrates technologies, processes, and cultural changes to provide a means for well-informed, rapid decision-making via collaborative information and knowledge sharing by varied and dispersed organizations and individuals. KM tenets include support for organizational processes, tailored content delivery, information sharing and reuse, the capture of tacit knowledge as part of the work process, situational awareness of information and knowledge assets, and valuation. KM enables an organization to be more agile, flexible, and proactive. The approach is ideal for integrating, for example, intelligence (e.g., economic and open source) and security (e.g., physical, personnel, and operations); sales and production; and research and development with business development.[4]

Summary

IW is an embracing concept that brings to bear all the resources of a nation-state or business organization in a coherent and synchronized manner to control the IE and to attain and maintain a competitive advantage and to gain power and influence. Judicious use of IW, when coupled with KM and NCB, leads to reduced or avoided costs, increased revenues, more satisfied customers, larger profits, and increased national security. Governments and businesses can use IW offensively and defensively in the physical and virtual domains. Counters to IW do not have to be in kind; they can be no, low, or high technology and they can be asymmetric. Not conducting IW will result in a reduced market presence and lower national security. Although the name may change over the years, IW will evolve from its nascent stage and become mainstream within 20 years. We projected that in 2002. We are in fact there already.

IW occurs when, in the physical and virtual domains, you attack your competition or they attack you. IW is about synchronized and coherent relationships and capabilities. As previously discussed, central to IW are those physical and virtual capabilities to control the IE.

CKO couples IW in a useful approach with KM and how the organization does business. Not only is the corporation's IE engaged; the resources of its enterprise are also brought to bear to use all its capabilities in a coherent and synchronized manner to seize as great a competitive advantage as possible. In this fashion, a country can call on its allies and coalition partners, and a business can call on its suppliers and business partners, so as much knowledge and as many capabilities as possible can be brought to bear.

References

1. Omicinski, J. (Gannett News Service) (2001). Analysis: Terror attack sends American into "fourth generation of warfare," *Greenville News*, September 26.
2. Lind, W.S., Schmitt, J.F., and Wilson, G.I. (1989). The changing face of war: Into the fourth generation, *Marine Corps Gazette*, October, pp. 22–26.
3. Luzwick, P. (2001). Most of your revenue is from e-commerce, then cyber insurance makes sense. "Surviving Information Warfare" column, *Computer Fraud and Security*, March. Reed-Elsevier.
4. Luzwick, P. (1999). What's a pound of your information worth? Constructs for collaboration and consistency. American Bar Association, Standing Committee on Law and National Security, National Security Law Report, August.
5. DoD. 2001. *Department of Defense Dictionary of Military and Associated Terms*, April 12.

Chapter 2

From Information Warfare to Information Operations and Cyber Warfare

In this chapter, the discussion is centered on the "holistic" and historical view of where we started and where we are now. It looks at what the different terms mean and why there has been a change.

When the first edition of this book was published in 2002, the concept of information warfare was not new. It had been discussed by government, the military, and in research laboratories. What was not clear then (and still is not now, some 12 years later) is what the term actually means. Different governments, agencies, and organizations have defined it in a range of ways to meet their own needs and the fashion of the moment, whether this is to adopt the latest thinking, policy, technology, capability, or hype.

The terms *information warfare* and *cyber warfare* (CW) are now used fairly interchangeably, although the reality is that information warfare covers a much wider scope than CW. In this book, the term CW will be used rather than the alternatives *cyberwarfare* or *cyberwar*. The term *information operations* is also used in more recent publications and has largely replaced the term information warfare. In the 2006 revision of *Joint Publication 3–13, Joint Doctrine for Information Operations*, the term information warfare was removed as a term from the joint information operations doctrine.

There is a significant history to the adoption of the word *operations* in place of *warfare*, which is largely based on the political acceptability of the use of the emotive term warfare, and this can be seen in the past in the move from the use of terms such as *psychological warfare* to *psychological operations* (PSYOP).

Description of Information Warfare

In a 2002 paper[1], Dan Kuehl gives a history of the term information warfare, in which he attributes the earliest reference to the term in the United States to Dr Tom Rona in 1970. In an investigation into the relationship between control systems, Dr Rona used the term information warfare to describe the competition between competing control systems, with the explanation that it was

> in the sense that control systems can be described as the means for gathering, processing, and disseminating information, processes which can be diagrammed and described with flow and feedback charts.

In 1993, the Department of Defense (DoD) published an official definition of the term in the highly classified *DoD Directive TS3600.1*. At that time, there were actually several definitions of the term at differing classification levels. The *Joint Publication 3–13, Joint Doctrine for Information Operations*, published in October 1998, was the document that was current at the time of writing of the first edition of this book and offered a description of information warfare (IW):

> Information Operations (IO) conducted during time of crisis or conflict (including war) to achieve or promote specific objectives over a specific adversary or adversaries. Within the context of the joint force's mission, the joint force commander (JFC) should apply the term "adversary" broadly to include organizations, groups, or decision makers that may adversely affect the joint force accomplishing its mission.

Current DoD Definition of Information Operations

The 2012 *Joint Publication 3-13, Joint Doctrine for Information Operations* defines information operations as

> The integrated employment, during military operations, of information-related capabilities in concert with other lines of operation to influence, disrupt, corrupt, or usurp the decision-making of adversaries and potential adversaries while protecting our own. Also called IO. Approved for incorporation into JP 1-02 with JP 3-13 as the source JP.

One other term that has been added to the IW catalogue is that of strategic communication (SC). This is defined in the *Commander's Handbook for SC and Communication Strategy*[2]:

> Focused United States Government efforts to understand and engage key audiences to create, strengthen, or preserve conditions favorable for the advancement of United States Government interests, policies, and objectives through the use of coordinated programs, plans, themes, messages, and products synchronized with the actions of all instruments of national power. (JP 5-0).

The aim of SC is to exert influence on the strategic and political levels over a longer period of time and is not necessarily limited to a specific conflict. SC is not viewed as an integrated component of information operations. It is also clear that military deception (MILDEC) and SC are not necessarily parts of each other.

SC is seen as a whole-of-government approach. The concept appears to have been adopted early in the twenty-first century and was described in the February 2006 *Quadrennial Defense Review* (QDR). In this review, SC was identified as one of five specific "areas of particular emphasis" that was an ability critical to the DoD to enable it to address a strategic environment "characterized by uncertainty and surprise." The QDR went on to state that DoD

> must instill communication assessments and processes into its culture; developing programs, plans, policy, information and themes to support Combatant Commanders (CCDRs) that reflect the US Government's overall strategic objectives.

The primary military capabilities that contribute to SC include public affairs (PA), information operations (IO), and defense support to public diplomacy (DSPD).

In 2011, however, Rosa Brooks[3], a professor of law at Georgetown University Law Center, when giving testimony before the House Armed Services Sub-Committee on Evolving Threats and Capabilities, commented "that the term has caused far more confusion that clarity." She went on to add: "Specifically, in the government context strategic communication' is often confused with related terms such as 'information operations,' 'public diplomacy' and 'communications.'" The paper goes on to explain that

> It's important to draw some distinctions between these concepts, however, since otherwise we can start getting very muddled up, and conflate capabilities with processes, aspirations with tools for achieving those aspirations.

It is clear from a 2012 Government Accountability Office (GAO) report[4] that there was still a need for the DoD to change its approach to SC, and the report commented that the

DOD has taken some initial actions toward integrating the strategic communication process into its policy making, plans, and operations at every level, such as ensuring that top leadership is driving the effort. DOD officials acknowledge that DOD staff across the department do not currently integrate the process into their efforts in a consistent manner.

This is more than 10 years since the concept was introduced.

A 2012 Rand report[5] stated that Douglas Friedly, a senior analyst with the Office of the Under Secretary of Defense for Policy, Information Operations Directorate, contributed the following summation of the problem from the perspective of his Pentagon office:

> There has been confusion within DoD, and especially in the field, because the terms Strategic Communication, Information Operations, and Psychological Operations (PSYOP) (now Military Information Support Operations [MISO]) are frequently used interchangeably.

He goes on to say that

> Although the term "IO" is often used in a way that implies [that] it is synonymous with individual capabilities such as PSYOP, the term is only appropriately applied when information-related capabilities are coordinated to achieve a military objective. [PSYOP are] the dissemination of information to influence foreign audiences to take action favorable to the U.S. Information Operations describes the integrated employment of a wide range of capabilities to influence adversary decision-making. Although [PSYOP] can be used to inform, persuade, and influence friendly foreign audiences as well as adversaries, PSYOP as part of military activities [are] always integrated into IO.

While there are DoD definitions for the terms SC, information operations, and psychological operations, all three overlap and are, to some degree, ambiguous. The distinction between SC and information operations is blurred even further because SC involves the integration of issues of audience and stakeholder perception and response into policymaking, planning, and operations at all levels.

Perhaps the easiest way to think of this is that information operations should be consistent with the goals and objectives of the government strategy, but that the military will be either the lead or a major contributor to achieving government strategic goals.

SC is not only about the spoken or written word, but is also affected by the actions that are taken. For example, the projection of force through the presence of troops, aircraft, or ships in a region may communicate the government's intentions far more clearly than any other form of communication.

A research paper by Col. Michael J. Dominique[6] gives a good description of the relationship between SC and information operations:

> Strategic communication is one of the primary weapons to battle mis-information and disinformation at the strategic level. IO, the military arm of the national information effort, supports strategic communication and public diplomacy through its actions and supporting information efforts.

He goes on to say that "If the strategic communication and the military themes are contradictory then credibility is lost."

Developing World View

We are all, to some level, guilty of introversion, inasmuch as we understand the perspective of the United States and other Western nations. What we have consistently failed to do is to understand how our traditional enemies see information operations and the developing world view on the subject. The next part of the chapter looks at the approaches and perspectives of a number of other nations.

Russian View of Information Operations

There is no publically available Russian definition for IW; however, the background to this area of operations in the former USSR, now Russia, is extensive. In Russia, a much broader view of the concept of information weapons is taken, wherein the cyber element is one component among a number of others, including the human, social, and spiritual. The Russians take the view that information can take either an artificial or natural form. Cyber is seen as being artificial and is the technical representation of information. Natural information includes thoughts in a person's head and information contained in books and documents. The Russians believe that information in the cyber domain cannot be addressed separately, and that the subject of information operations encompasses all information, not just a subset (i.e., cyber). It is probably for this reason that they do not have a separate concept of CW.

By 1995, the information warfare theorist Vitaliy Tsygichko,[7] among others, stated that "the development of a [US] national, and then an international, information superhighway" would "create new conditions for the effective employment of information weapons" and furthermore that "the prototype of this superhighway already exists. That is the Internet, a worldwide association of computer networks."

Tsygichko went on to warn that "although we live in an era of global information systems and we understand that economic vegetation awaits the country if it is not connected to the world information space." He goes on to say that Russia's participation in international telecommunications and information exchange systems would not be possible "without the comprehensive resolution of the problems of information security."

This publication shows that the requirement for information security, or network defense, was understood from a very early stage in the development of the Internet.

Since 1998, Russia has regularly introduced a resolution at the United Nations (UN) calling for an international agreement to combat "information terrorism." The Russian leadership are concerned that the Internet potentially makes it very easy for people to communicate and that a foreign government could use the Internet to challenge another country's political system.

The Information Security Doctrine of the Russian Federation,[8] which was approved by Vladimir Putin on September 9, 2000, characterizes information security as the "protection of its national interests in the information sphere, as determined by the overall balanced interests at the level of the individual, society and the state." The document goes on to cover a wide range of issues, including data protection, personal privacy, the hacking of state secrets, and access to information.

In 2007, a paper published by Sergei Korotkov et al.[9] representing the Russian Ministry of Defense at a UN disarmament forum stated that

> the use of computer networks crossing the territory of a neutral state
> to conduct information operations could be considered as a violation
> of its territory. These forms of aggression can therefore be considered
> illegitimate acts of warfare against a neutral state

In 2001, a number of countries, including China, Russia, Kazakhstan, Kyrgyzstan, Tajikistan, and Uzbekistan formed an organization called the Shanghai Cooperation Organisation (SCO). The stated main goals of the SCO are strengthening mutual confidence and good-neighborly relations among the member countries; promoting effective cooperation in politics, trade and economy, science and technology, and culture as well as education, energy, transportation, tourism, environmental protection, and other fields; making joint efforts to maintain and ensure peace, security, and stability in the region, moving toward the establishment of a new, democratic, just, and rational political and economic international order.

In a report[10] on the June 2009 meeting of the SCO, it was noted that there had been significant progress in the development and implementation of the latest information and communication technologies and the means for creating global information space. Concern was expressed about the threats connected with the possibilities of the use of such technologies. The members proposed a collaboration with the stated aim of limiting threats to international information security and providing information security to the member states. It was agreed that the three main threats that were being faced were

1. The development and use of the information weapon and the preparation and conducting of information war
2. Information terrorism
3. Information crime

Using the term "mass psychologic brainwashing," the agreement stated that the dissemination of information "harmful to the spiritual, moral and cultural spheres of other states" should be considered a "security threat."

In the Military Doctrine of the Russian Federation,[11] approved by Russian Federation Presidential Edict on February 5, 2010, there is a characterization of the features of contemporary military conflicts, among which is "the intensification of the role of information warfare." Later in the document, in the section on the tasks of equipping the armed forces and other troops with armaments and military and specialized equipment, is a requirement "to develop forces and resources for information warfare."

In September 2011, Russia, China, Tajikistan, and Uzbekistan, all members of the SCO, jointly presented an "International Code of Conduct for Information Security" at the UN.[12] Among other requirements, the code of conduct included the statement that each state voluntarily subscribing to the code pledges

Not to use information and communications technologies, including networks, to carry out hostile activities or acts of aggression, pose threats to international peace and security or proliferate information weapons or related technologies;

To cooperate in combating criminal and terrorist activities that use information and communications technologies, including networks, and in curbing the dissemination of information that incites terrorism, secessionism or extremism or that undermines other countries' political, economic and social stability, as well as their spiritual and cultural environment;

To endeavour to ensure the supply chain security of information and communications technology products and services, in order to prevent other States from using their resources, critical infrastructures, core technologies and other advantages to undermine the right of the countries that have accepted the code of conduct, to gain independent control of information and communications technologies or to threaten the political, economic and social security of other countries;

To reaffirm all the rights and responsibilities of States to protect, in accordance with relevant laws and regulations, their information space and critical information infrastructure from threats, disturbance, attack and sabotage;

To lead all elements of society, including its information and communication partnerships with the private sector, to understand their roles and responsibilities with regard to information security, in order to facilitate the creation of a culture of information security and the protection of critical information infrastructures;

To settle any dispute resulting from the application of the code through peaceful means and to refrain from the threat or use of force.

One of the major differences between what is referred to as the "Western consensus" and the view held by Russia and the other members of the SCO is the Russian perception of the threat that results from information content. This is identified as the "threat of the use of content for influence on the social-humanitarian sphere."

The Western view recognizes the potential threat from hostile code but generally discounts the issue of hostile content. For example, an Organisation for Economic Co-operation and Development (OECD) "Communiqué on Principles for Internet Policy-Making"[13] includes the free flow of information and knowledge; the freedom of expression, association, and assembly; and the protection of individual liberties as critical components of a democratic society and cultural diversity. The Russian view, meanwhile, as expressed by the Russian communications and media minister Igor Shchegolev at the London Conference on Cyberspace in 2011, is that "this should be subject both to national legislation, and to counter-terrorism considerations," which is consistent with another principle on the list, "restrictions of rights and freedoms only in the interests of security."

In May 2014, Chinese President Xi Jinping and Russian President Vladimir Putin said in a joint statement[14] that the two countries would seek to defend the "information space" together. "The sides are concerned over use of IT technologies running counter to tasks of maintaining international stability and security in detriment to state sovereignty and inviolability of private life," the statement said.

These developments give a clear indication that the Russian view of the topic is significantly different to that of the West, and the 2012 document "Conceptual views on the activities of the Armed Forces of the Russian Federation in the information space[15]" defines some of the terms as

Information Warfare

This is defined as "a confrontation between two or more states in the information space with the aim of causing harm to information systems, processes and resources, and other critical structure." The Russian view of the term varies from that held in the West as it goes on to include the undermining of political, economic, and social systems; massive psychological effects on the population to destabilize society and the state; and the forcing of a state to take decisions in the interests of the opposing side.

Information Weapons

This is defined as information technologies, tools, and methods used in order to carry out information warfare.

Information Space

This is defined as a sphere of activity that is related to the formation, creation, transformation, transmission, use, and storage of information that will have an impact, including on individual and social consciousnesses, the information infrastructure, and the information itself.

Definitions of the kinds and types of information weapons used from as early as 2001 can be found in *Information Challenges to National and International Security*, a book edited by Fedorov and Tsygichko of the PIR Center.[16]

The authors state that information weapons are divided into either defensive or offensive weapons and describe defensive information weapons as those that perform missions of defensive IW. The things they describe as defensive weapons include multilevel computer security systems and systems of active countermeasures to enemy information weapons. They describe offensive information weapons as those that are intended to create an effect on the enemy by destroying the critical structures of the system supporting the decision-making cycle.

In their book, Fedorov and Tsygichko highlight a number of information weapons that can, from a theoretical standpoint, be singled out:

- The means of accurately locating equipment that is emitting in the electromagnetic spectrum and of destroying it through the prompt detection and recognition of the target and guidance of weapons against individual elements of the command and control information system
- The means of creating an effect on the components and the power supplies of electronic equipment for the temporary or permanent disabling of the these components of electronic systems
- The means of affecting the software used in electronic control modules that disables them or changes their functioning through the use of special software
- The means of affecting the data transfer process to prevent or disrupt the functioning of information exchange subsystems by affecting the signal propagation medium and on their operation
- The means of propaganda and disinformation to affect the information of command and control systems, to create an image of the situation that differs from reality, to affect a person's system of values, and to create a negative effect on the religious and moral values of the enemy population
- Psychotronic weapons (psychological warfare), intended to create an effect on a person's mind and subconscious to degrade and suppress their will or temporarily disable them

The book goes on to state that

> It cannot be asserted that this classification takes in all kinds of information weapons that possibly may appear in the future. It completely

encompasses, however, all known practical developments being carried on at the present time.

The book then goes on to provide a classification of information weapons as

- Single purpose and multipurpose or general purpose
- Close range and long range
- Individual, multiple, or mass destruction
- Type of platform
- Destructive effect

The book categorizes information weapons by their type of effect and gives three categories:

- Weapons based on information technologies
- Weapons having an energy
- Weapons having a chemical effect

Russia has adopted a three-pronged approach to information-related developments. The three prongs are the international front, the domestic front, and the military front. This approach, which has been in development since the late 1990s, has shown the greatest progress on the international and domestic fronts, but progress on the military front appears to have accelerated as a result of the Russian–Georgian crisis, which escalated in 2008.

In the first prong (on the international front), Russia has continued its efforts to shape the international information environment by influencing international opinion at the UN and through the SCO and other forums. Russia has also focused efforts on shaping international opinion at a range of conferences on the development of an information society.

The second prong (the domestic front) has been advanced through the development of doctrines and policies to enhance domestic information security, particularly regarding the impact of news media on the Russian population. These internal policies are aimed at issues such as cyber crime and the information-psychological stability of society. Concepts such as information-psychological stability are not well understood by military policy and decision makers in the West.

The third prong (the military front) is continuing with efforts to modernize the military force and develop a relevant and effective military strategy for the twenty-first century.

The 2008 Russian–Georgian conflict helped Russia to identify the need for significant improvement in command and control and for the development of information-based equipments. In addition to making improvements in tactics and equipment, the Russian military believes that it needs to enhance the psychological stability of its servicemen. In an effort to address this, the *Red Star* (*Krasnaya Zvezda*), the newspaper of the Ministry of Defense, now periodically prints articles dedicated to IW's impact on soldiers' psychological stability.

In 2007, Professor Selivanov[17] wrote that Russia is now obligated to speak about the need for information subunits in the armed forces to shape patriotism and a fighting spirit, to counteract enemy information-ideological operations, and to conduct information-ideological operations against an actual or potential enemy. These reforms were designed to make improvements in both the technical and psychological components of IW.

To date, no publically available documents have been seen that indicate the existence of either the command structure or units specifically tasked with IW.

Col. P. Koayesov[18] defined IW in the following way in January 2009, some five months after the conflict between Russia and Georgia ended:

> Information warfare consists in making an integrated impact on the opposing side's system of state and military command and control and its military-political leadership.

He goes on to describe the desired effect as being an impact that, in peacetime, would cause the adoption of decisions favorable to the party initiating the action and, during a period of conflict, would paralyze the functioning of the enemy's command and control infrastructure.

This statement clearly shows the differences between the Western and Russian views regarding the scope and purpose of IW.

Chinese View of Information Warfare

One of the earliest documents to give the Chinese view of IW is a paper by Major General Wang Pufeng, a former director of the Strategy Department, Academy of Military Science, Beijing, in the *China Military Science Journal*[19] (spring 1995).

In the same timeframe, PLA senior colonels Wang Baocun and Li Fei of the Beijing Academy of Military Science published papers[20,21] on the US military view of IW, including references to papers on the digitized battlefield and the informatization of the military.

One of the recurring themes that has been apparent throughout the development of the Chinese IW policy is that they have devoted a great deal of intellectual capital and effort to studying and understanding the development of policy and tactics in the United States and other Western nations.

The Chinese view is based on four parameters:

- Preemptive strike capability
- Asymmetric warfare (inferior versus superior)
- High-tech local war
- People's war

One of the more significant elements in the Chinese concept of IW, that of deception, originates from Sun Tzu's 36 stratagems described in the famous *Art of War*, which was written around 2500 years ago. The Chinese concept of IW can be applied over a long period of time and is not limited to a specific period or conflict.

The Chinese view is that the US doctrine is far too technology driven and does not consider, to any extent, the strategic dimension. They feel that it is too strongly focused on the information and information systems of the opponent and does not adequately address the human, psychological factors.

In the Chinese view, IW must also consider issues such as the opponent's will and ability to fight. The following quote from the writings of Sun Tzu gives an insight into the Chinese thinking

> To win the war without the fight is the greatest victory.

The Russian view is similar to that of the Chinese in that there is an emphasis on the psychological impact of IW as well as the idea that IW is conducted over longer time periods, in peacetime, and in the period prior to a conflict, as well as in wartime. Both Russian and Chinese approaches seem to view IW as something that is conducted on a more or less continuous basis at a strategic level as well as on the operational and tactical levels.

Deception is widely seen as an essential element of IW, both in the West and by the Chinese and Russians. In the United States, MILDEC is considered a core capability of information operations. The Russians use the term *Maskirovka* (Маскировка), and while the Chinese do not seem to have a specific term to encapsulate the meaning, the concept is well embedded in Chinese military doctrine. The Chinese view is perhaps best described in another quote from Sun Tzu's *Art of War*:

> I make the enemy see my strengths as weaknesses and my weaknesses as strengths while I cause his strengths to become weaknesses and discover where he is not strong … I conceal my tracks so that none can discern them; I keep silence so that none can hear me.

The Russian military treat Maskirovka as a separate and specific type of combat support to influence an adversary. While the Western view of deception is more apparent at the operational and tactical levels, the Russians take a longer term view, and for the Chinese, it may cover decades.

For more than two decades, the People's Liberation Army (PLA) has carefully studied the range of American and other Western nations' military publications on network-centric warfare and the evolution of their doctrine on IW. They also keenly observed the victory of the coalition forces in the Persian Gulf War and the Balkan conflicts, which were the first "information"-driven conflicts; in these, the PLA saw the effect of modern information operations, both on the battlefield and in the international arena, and started to examine how such practices could be applied by its own military.

As a result of this, the Chinese military has now developed IW concepts compatible with its own organization and doctrine. These have evolved from its own organization, traditional Chinese tactics, and Soviet and American doctrine. In parallel, China has significantly modernized and improved its own psychological warfare operations.

The Chinese call their development of IW and other hi-tech means to counter what they perceive to be the overwhelmingly superior conventional military capabilities of the West as *acupuncture warfare*, a term that was first used in 1997.[22] Acupuncture warfare (also called *paralysis warfare*) is described as

> Paralysing the enemy by attacking the weak link of his command, control, communications and information as if hitting his acupuncture point in kung fu combat.[23]

Strategic deception, the denial of information, and the achievement of psychological surprise are an integral part of Chinese military doctrine. The Chinese view IW as an asymmetric tool that will help them to overcome their relative lack of modern military hardware. They have invested heavily in perfecting their IW techniques to target the rapidly modernizing Western armed forces, which they have seen to be increasingly dependent on software to run their communications and computer networks. The Chinese view IW as a tool that will help to project power and level the playing field in future wars.

It is still not clear from the available literature whether IW is fully integrated with the doctrine of "people's war under modern conditions" or whether it is treated as a separate but complementary pattern of war. There is also some confusion as a result of the use of the term *informationized warfare* (xinxihua zhanzheng) instead of IW (xinxi zhanzheng). The Chinese definition of IW comprises

■ Intelligence operations, which include intelligence reconnaissance and protection
■ Command and control (C2) operations to disrupt enemy information flow and weaken the enemy's C2 capability while protecting one's own
■ Electronic warfare, involving seizing the electromagnetic initiative through electronic attack, electronic protection, and electronic warfare support
■ Targeting enemy computer systems and networks to damage and destroy critical machines, networks, and the data stored on them
■ Physical destruction of enemy sources like information infrastructure (such as C4ISR) through the application of firepower

In late 2003, the Central Military Commission (CMC) made the decision that China needed to build computerized armed forces in order to win the new strategic goal of IW. The term the *Three Warfares* was endorsed and used to describe the PLA's IW concept, aimed at preconditioning key areas of competition in its favor.[24]

Chinese military papers have highlighted the importance that they place on the influencing of global public opinion in order to gain support or compliance without having to go to war and to gain international support and to influence the enemy's leadership, military, and domestic population in the event of conflict.

The Three Warfares are codified for the PLA in the "People's Liberation Army Political Work Regulations." They utilize the whole range of national resources, including military and civilian, driven by the overall military strategy: to secure the political initiative and psychological advantage over an opponent. The PLA's operational hierarchy of combat is separated into three levels: war, campaigns, and battles. Each level is driven by its own strategy, campaign methods, and tactics, respectively. The Three Warfares are normally considered to be a campaign method but also have potential application at the strategic and tactical levels.

The Three Warfares are defined[25] as

- Psychological warfare, which seeks to undermine an enemy's ability to conduct combat operations through operations aimed at deterring, shocking, and demoralizing enemy military personnel and supporting civilian populations.
- Media warfare, which is aimed at influencing domestic and international public opinion to build support for China's military actions and dissuade an adversary from pursuing actions contrary to China's interests.
- Legal warfare, which uses international and domestic law to claim the legal high ground or assert Chinese interests. It can be employed to hamstring an adversary's operational freedom and shape the operational space. Legal warfare is also intended to build international support and manage possible political repercussions of China's military actions. China has attempted to employ legal warfare in the maritime domain and in international airspace in pursuit of a security buffer zone.

At a press release held on May 25, 2011, in the PLA Daily,[26] Senior Colonel Geng Yansheng, spokesperson for the Ministry of National Defense and director general of the Information Office of the Ministry of National Defense, stated that the PLA had established an "Online Blue Army" in order to enhance Chinese troops' network protection level. He went on to say that

> network security had become an international issue that influences not only the social arena but also the military domain as well and that China was also the victim of network attack.

He added that

> Currently, China's network protection is comparatively weak. Enhancing the informationization level and strengthening network security protection are important components of military training for an army.

In 2013, China conducted its first "digital" technology military exercise in north China's remote Inner Mongolia region to "test new types of combat forces including units using digital technology amid efforts to adjust to informationalized war."[27]

Another development that highlights the Chinese Military IW capability development in line with the Chinese philosophy can be seen in the PLA Units 61398 and 61486. A 2013 report[28] by Mandiant gave a description and examined the activities of PLA Unit 61398 (otherwise known as the 2nd Bureau of the PLA's General Staff Department's Third Department). The Mandiant report stated that "the nature of 'Unit 61398's' work is considered by China to be a state secret; however, we believe it engages in harmful 'Computer Network Operations.'" The report went on to say that "We estimate that Unit 61398 is staffed by hundreds, and perhaps thousands of people based on the size of Unit 61398's physical infrastructure" and that "APT1 (Unit 61398) has systematically stolen hundreds of terabytes of data from at least 141 organizations, and has demonstrated the capability and intent to steal from dozens of organizations simultaneously." The Mandiant report speculates that the unit may have been in operation from as early as 2006.

A 2014 report from the threat intelligence firm Crowdstrike[29] reported that a second PLA unit (61486), based in Shanghai and subordinate to the 12th Bureau of the PLA's Third General Staff Department (GSD) had carried out a "Targeted economic espionage campaigns compromise technological advantage, diminish global competition, and ultimately have no geographic borders." The report went on to state that this unit had been in operation since at least 2007 and has been observed targeting the US defense and European satellite and aerospace industries. The group, which is nicknamed Putter Panda, is also known by the name MSUpdater and is reported to deploy custom malware focused on exploiting popular productivity apps including Adobe Reader and the Microsoft Office family.

According to a 2014 report in the *China Daily*,[30] China has not yet fully developed its IW strategy, as it quoted President Xi as stating that the army must "strive to establish a new military doctrine, institutions, equipment systems, strategies and tactics and management modes" for IW and that

> We should cast off the paradigm of mechanized warfare and embrace
> an approach to war featuring information technology. The principle of
> protecting traditional security interests should also be shifted to one for
> the country's comprehensive security and strategic interests.

Cyber Warfare

While the terms IW and CW are often treated as being interchangeable by many practitioners in Western nations, the main problem with the terms occurs when the perspective of some of the other major players such as Russia and China is considered. However, even in the West, there are significant differences in the actual meanings of the terms.

In most countries, CW is seen as a subsection of IW, with IW spanning a much broader field of action than CW.

Today, most armed forces view information operations (IW) as a core military competency. They see information as both a weapon and a target in warfare, and they believe that information and knowledge dominance can win conflicts. There are a range of factors that make the concept of CW attractive:

- It is cheaper to deploy than conventional weapons as it utilizes "off the shelf" technologies and freely available tools.
- It has a low entry cost.
- It does not require large numbers of troops and weapons.
- It can be used to achieve "instant" effects and can remove the delay inherent in the deployment of conventional weapons.
- The size of the Internet and the complexity of the global network give the potential for stealth and anonymity as a result of the difficulty in tracing the origin of an attack.
- The low cost of entry, the ability to remain anonymous, and the free availability of CW tools enable a disproportionate effect to be achieved by actors that would not be significant in a conventional force conflict.
- It may allow for the reduction, or avoidance, of the need to engage in kinetic operations.
- The systems of the adversary can be disrupted rather than destroyed, which leads to lower post conflict restoration costs and timescales.

In 2010, CW was defined by the vice chairman of the US Joint Chiefs of Staff[31] as

> An armed conflict conducted in whole or part by cyber means. Military operations conducted to deny an opposing force the effective use of cyber space systems and weapons in a conflict. It includes cyber attack, cyber defense, and cyber enabling actions.

The UN Interregional Crime and Justice Research Institute (UNICRI)[32] defines the term cyber warfare: "While some claim that cyber warfare is the fifth domain of warfare (after land, sea, air and space) others simply claim the term is an attempt at sensationalism." The definition goes on to state that "from a more specific perspective, cyber warfare refers to any action by a nation-state to penetrate another nation's computer networks for the purpose of causing some sort of damage," and also that broader definitions of the term claim that cyber warfare also includes acts of "cyber hooliganism," cyber vandalism or cyber terrorism.

Cyber warfare can consist of many threats, namely:

- Online acts of espionage and security breaches, which are acts done to obtain national material and information of a sensitive or classified nature through the exploitation of the Internet (e.g., exploitation of network flaws through malicious software)
- Sabotage—the use of the Internet by one nation state to disrupt online communications systems of another nation state (e.g., military communication networks) with the intent to cause damage and disadvantage
- Attacks on supervisory control and data acquisition (SCADA) networks and nuclear control institutes (NCIs)

CW is viewed as both a military and intelligence function and refers to the conduct of military operations according to information-related principles. It is typically referred to in two aspects—computer network defense (CND) and computer network attack (CNA). Some experts identify a third area—computer network exploitation (CNE), although this is often classed as being a part of CNA. The respective terms from the publication[33] are here given in more detail:

- CND consists of all measures necessary to protect own ICT means and infrastructures against hostile CNA and CNE.
- CNA describes operations designed to disrupt, deny, degrade, or destroy information resident in computers and computer networks or the computers or networks themselves.
- CNE describes the retrieving of intelligence-grade data and information from enemy computers by ICT means.

CW is also sometimes also referred to as computer network operations (CNO).

CNA, or the deliberate Denial of Service or destruction of enemy network capabilities, is only one of the available tools in the framework of military operations. While the importance of CNA is acknowledged as being of increasing significance, it is still immature and its integration into the wider field of military operations is largely untested. One of the major issues is how to measure the impact of CNA. The conventional indicators used for battle damage assessment are not suitable as, for the most part, there will be no physical destruction associated with CNA and the time needed to recover will involve too many variables to be able to be consistently and accurately predicted. Another issue is that of *unintended consequences* or *collateral damage*. Most of the potential targets for CNA that can be accessed will be connected to the Internet. The result of this is that any tools deployed to attack the target may also affect systems that are connected to it, the ultimate effects of which will not be known. This is still an issue of most significance to the United States and other Western nations, as they have the highest dependency on network infrastructures.

CND—more commonly known as information security or information systems security—is the activity that is more widely understood and undertaken. It is the activity that is, or should be, carried out at some level on every computer system and network, particularly those that are connected to the Internet.

Systems that are stand alone or communicate over private networks can be given a degree of additional protection through physical and procedural security measures, as access to the system is required to carry out an attack. However, following the introduction of the Stuxnet malware that was programmed to target Iran's uranium-enrichment performance in the Natanz nuclear facility and was intended to cause actual physical damage, it has since been reported to have affected systems in a Russian nuclear plant and systems in Indonesia, India, Azerbaijan, Pakistan, and the United States. The systems that were affected at the Natanz facility were "air gapped" and not connected to the Internet but, as often happens, the weakest link in the security screen failed and a person carried the malware into the facility allegedly on a USB device.

As with much of modern technology, the drivers for many of the recent developments are in the commercial arena—or as one Chinese general put it, involve economic warfare—rather than in the military, and because commercial systems are connected to the Internet, they are as exposed as any military system to an attack. As a result of this, considerable experience in computer network defense has developed in the private sector, and much of the knowledge and experience in developing, deploying, and managing security now exist there.

The military has an important role in the protection of its own systems, and the government has a major role in the protection of systems that come together to form the *critical infrastructure* (CI),* also known as the *critical national infrastructure*. Increasingly, however, the protection of these systems can only be achieved with the active collaboration and input from the private sector, which "owns" the individual elements of the CI and possesses the resources and the breadth of skills required to maintain and protect it.

CNE is the up-to-date version of espionage, and while the objectives have not changed, the method of achieving it has adapted to the opportunities that have been presented by the ubiquity of computer networks and our increasing reliance on them. The gathering of intelligence through spying activities is undertaken by all governments, both in peacetime and during conflicts, and continues to take place both in the physical and cyber realms. Some of the advantages of CNE are

---

* Critical infrastructure is defined by the Department of Homeland Security as:

> Critical infrastructure is the backbone of our nation's economy, security and health. We know it as the power we use in our homes, the water we drink, the transportation that moves us, and the communication systems we rely on to stay in touch with friends and family.

> Critical infrastructure are the assets, systems, and networks, whether physical or virtual, so vital to the United States that their incapacitation or destruction would have a debilitating effect on security, national economic security, national public health or safety, or any combination thereof.[34]

that it can be conducted from a remote location, and the source of the activity can be hidden in the complexity of the modern networks. Massive resources can be applied to a single target, and the target can be attacked over a considerable period of time with very little risk. The term advanced persistent threat (APT)* has come into common usage to describe this type of activity.

There has been considerable and ongoing debate with regard to the role and potential impact of CW. One argument is that it acts as a *force multiplier* and enhances the capabilities and effect of conventional kinetic operations. Another is that it is the next generation of warfare and will eventually replace some conventional operations. What is clear is that it is a low-cost option that also has a low entry cost. The general consensus is that it is unlikely that there will ever be a war fought exclusively with cyber weapons, as the normal basis for war is the control of territory and this can still, currently, only be achieved by the use of conventional forces.

Cyber forces, as with any other military capability, need to be integrated into the overall battle strategy as part of a planning process. The most likely use of cyber weapons will be as part of a combined operation together with conventional kinetic weapons. The major concern is that the United States and other Western nations have economies and infrastructures that are critically dependent on interlinked networks to support their communication systems and the processing and exchange of information. The complexity of these networks, while perceived to offer some degree of resilience is, in itself, proving to be a vulnerability that can be exploited.

The disruption or denial of both critical national and civilian infrastructures is a potential target for both nations and nonstate actors† that want to engage in *asymmetric warfare* and lack the capacity to compete on the traditional battlefield.

Cyber Warfare Approaches of Some Other Nations

Earlier in this chapter, the approaches that are being taken to IW by Russia and China were reviewed, but there is clear evidence that a number of other countries are also developing CW capabilities. The CW capabilities of China and other countries that have been identified and the approaches being taken are given in the remainder of this chapter. There is little information on the cyber capabilities of Russia, although there is evidence of cyber attacks that have originated in Russia, which will now be discussed.

---

* An advanced persistent threat (APT) is a network attack in which an unauthorized person gains access to a network and stays there undetected for a long period of time. The intention of an APT attack is to steal data rather than to cause damage to the network or organization. APT attacks target organizations in sectors with high-value information, such as national defense, manufacturing, and the financial industry.[35]
† Nonstate actors are nonsovereign entities that exercise significant economic, political, or social power and influence at a national, and in some cases international, level. National Intelligence Council.[36]

Russia

In the Russia 2010 military doctrine,[37] there is an acknowledgment of the requirement for the "intensification of the role of information warfare," and a task to "develop forces and resources for information warfare" was outlined. As a result of the very different philosophy in Russia, the approach that has been taken appears very different from that which we understand in the West.

A statement made in August 2013 by Andrei Grigoryev,[38] chief of the newly-created Foundation of Advanced Military Research (the Russian equivalent of the US Defense Advanced Research Projects Agency [DARPA]), which came into being in October 2012, said: "The decision to create a cyber-security command and a new branch of the armed forces has already been made." He went on to say that the agency had singled out three main areas of military research and development (R&D)—"futuristic weaponry," "future soldier" gear, and "cyber warfare." However, there are some indications that there has been some capability to date embedded in the radio technical troops.

It is reported that there are at least 12 institutes in Russia that provide education in dual-use information security and electronic warfare technologies, and the students are then employed by the Ministry of Defense and the security services for both offensive and defensive operations. However, there is evidence that Russia is currently outsourcing its CW efforts and there have been a number of reports highlighting an extensive reliance on youth groups such as the Kremlin-controlled Nashi (the Youth Democratic Anti-Fascist Movement) and cyber-crime groups such as the Russian Business Network (RBN), although this has not been seen to be active for some time.

What is clear is that, whether the activity is considered to be IW or CW, Russia has actively been sponsoring computer-based attacks since at least 2007 when we saw the Estonian conflict.

This involved a series of cyber attacks that began on April 27, 2007, which used distributed denial-of-service (DDoS) attacks; these overwhelmed the websites of a number of Estonian organizations, including the Estonian parliament, a number of government ministries, banks, newspapers, and broadcasters. The background to the conflict concerned the relocation of the Bronze Soldier of Tallinn, a Soviet-era grave marker. At the peak of the crisis, bank cards and mobile-phone networks were unable to operate. In a panel discussion on IW in the twenty-first century, Sergei Markov, a state duma deputy from the pro-Kremlin Unified Russia party, stated "About the cyberattack on Estonia... don't worry, that attack was carried out by my assistant." This was the first time that Russia had actually claimed responsibility for the activity. The *Financial Times* reported that on March 10, 2009, Konstantin Goloskokov, a "commissar" of the Kremlin-backed youth group Nashi, claimed responsibility for the attack.

In Russia's war with Georgia in 2008, there was the first clear evidence of a combined cyber and kinetic attack by Russia on Georgia. Although not completely successful, it was a clear demonstration and first use of the approach. During the period, DDoS attacks were made on the Georgian president's website and other government websites. These started more than two weeks before the conventional kinetic Russian forces invaded. On the same day that the invasion started, a number of websites such as stopgeorgia.ru sprang up. These sites were clearly in support of the invasion and contained lists of sites to attack and instructions on how to go about it. A number of reports have implicated the RBN (a criminal group) in this activity.

In 2014, during the invasion of Crimea, a number of news agencies reported that Russian troops had disrupted the telecommunication networks in Ukraine. In a report by the BBC, the Ukrainian security chief stated that Russian forces had "installed equipment" at Ukrtelecom, a Ukrainian telecom firm in Crimea, which "blocks [the security chief's] phone, as well as the phones of other deputies, regardless of their political affiliation." Members of the Ukrainian parliamentary also reported that the mobile phone service had been disrupted. In a Reuters report, Ukrtelecom officials said that armed men had trespassed onto their Crimean facilities and damaged fiber-optic cables. The cyber attack was attributed to Russian military intelligence (GRU). Other activity included attacks on government websites and news and social networks.

China

According to a 2004 report[39] from the Institute for Security Technology Studies at Dartmouth College, training for future cyber-attack operations is of primary importance to the PLA. The report goes on to state that

> other formal training for PLA officers includes the usage of information weapons, simulated cyber warfare, protection of information systems, computer virus attacks and counterattacks, and jamming and counter-jamming of communications networks.

In 2010, in what was seen as a response to the creation of the cyber command in the United States, China's then-President Hu Jintao issued a presidential decree that China was to build a Chinese equivalent. He ordered the creation of an information assurance base to maintain China's version of a pure Chinese Internet, with the intention of creating a Chinese command to handle cyber threats and to strengthen the nation's cyber infrastructure. As he was leaving office, he proclaimed that the PLA would "strive to basically complete military mechanization and make major progress in full military IT application by 2020" and that they "should attach great importance to maritime, space and cyberspace security." Since then, his successor, President Xi, is believed to have maintained and accelerated the cyber policies.

According to a report in BrinkNews,[40] the fundamental Chinese cyber principles are

- To train large numbers of a new type of high-caliber military personnel, to carry out intensive military training under computerized conditions, and to enhance the integrated combat capability based on the extensive use of IT
- To implement a military strategy of active defense for the new period and to enhance military strategic guidance
- To strengthen national defense to safeguard China's sovereignty, security, and territorial integrity and ensure its peaceful development
- To enhance China's ability to accomplish a wide range of military tasks, the most important of which is to win a local war in an information age

The first recorded PLA CW exercise took place in October 1997 in the Shenyang Military Region, with cyber detachments conducting both defense and attacks against each other.

China has adopted the approach of integrating the country's civilian computer experts into military reserve units within the PLA, and military reserve units specializing in CW are in development in several cities.

Israel

In 2009, Gabi Ashkenazi, chief of staff of the Israeli army, stated that he considered cyber space as an area of both strategic and operational warfare. The Israeli military have set up a cyber unit within Unit 8200 of the Israeli Military Intelligence (AMAN) with the purpose of guiding and coordinating the activities of the Israeli Army in cyber space. In December 2009, Amos Yadlin, then head of Israeli military intelligence, explained that the role of the unit was to provide good defense for the Internet networks operating in Israel and to carry out attacks against external targets in cyber space.

On May 18, 2011, Israeli prime minister Benjamin Netanyahu announced the establishment of the "national cyber committee" in Israel. He stated that the main objective of the national cyber committee would be to enhance Israel's CI systems' defense capabilities against "terrorist attacks" that may be carried out either by "foreign states or terrorist organizations."

Iran

According to a report from the Israeli Institute for National Security Studies (INSS),[41] in 2013 Iran had developed its CW capability to become "one of the most active players in the international cyber arena." The report states that the changes are a result of two factors—"an easing of the restraints on offensive activity in cyberspace by Iranian decision makers, and a qualitative leap by the Iranian cyber warfare system."

According to the authors, Iran has applied lessons learned from the Stuxnet attacks, which set its nuclear program back by several years, and they have seen evidence that Iran has made significant advances in three key areas:

- Creating a defense envelope against cyber attacks on critical infrastructures
- Neutralizing cyber operations by opposition elements and regime opponents
- Keeping Western ideas and content out of Iranian cyber space

With regard to offensive capabilities, it has seen the potential for cyber space to level the playing field with regards to its perceived adversaries in the West who maintain a "clear military superiority," while the difficulties with the attribution of attacks allows them "a margin of denial."

The INSS report goes on to state that "during 2013, CW became a key tool used by Iran to attack Western targets in response to the sanctions and as a means of deterring escalation by Western countries against Iran." The report continued, "The scope, targets, and relative success of those cyber attacks of the past year ascribed to Iran show its improved capabilities."

The Iranian Islamic Revolution Guards Corps (IRGC) set up its first CW division in 2010 and since then has continued to grow its CW capabilities. The IRGC budget for its cyber capabilities is reported to be in the region of US$76 million.

The range of the IRGC's CW arsenal is believed to include

- Wireless communications jammers
- Computer viruses and worms
- Embedded Trojan time bombs
- Computer and network reconnaissance
- Cyber data collection exploitation

In 2013, Mojtaba Ahmadi, the man reportedly in charge of Iran's cyber-warfare headquarters, was reportedly assassinated near the town of Karaj, northwest of the capital, Tehran.

Iran has been accused of being responsible for the Shamoon virus, which wiped more than 30,000 computers at the Saudi Aramco oil company in 2012. Reports from US officials interpreted this attack as Iranian retaliation for the Stuxnet worm and other acts of sabotage. From September 2012 onward, a number of attacks on more than a dozen Western banks and on unclassified US Navy computers have been blamed on Iran.

India

In August 2010, the Indian government informed its agencies that there was a need to enhance their CW capabilities and directed them to develop capabilities to break into networks of unfriendly countries, set up hacker laboratories, set up a testing facility, develop countermeasures, and set up computer emergency response teams (CERTs) for several sectors. The lead agencies for this strategy were identified as the National Technical Research Organization (NTRO), the Defence Intelligence Agency (DIA), and the Defence Research and Development Organization (DRDO).

In December 2010, after an attack by hackers from the Pakistan Cyber Army had defaced the Central Bureau of Investigation, one of India's most secure websites, the government called for increased capabilities in cyber security.

An Indian Institute for Defence Studies and Analyses (IDSA) task force report was published in March 2012.[42] The document laid out the structures and organizations that would be required for both cyber defense and cyber attack. The document stated that efforts "must be coordinated by the National Security Council Secretariat (NSCS)" and that there was a need to create a directorate or special wing in the NSCS to oversee and coordinate both defensive and offensive cyber operations. The document identified the agencies that could be tasked to take on the CW challenge, which include the NTRO, Headquarter Integrated Defence Services (HQ IDS), DRDO, the Research and Analysis Wing (RAW), and Intelligence Bureau (IB) and representatives of India's CERT and National Association of Software and Services Companies (NASSCOM). Each would operate under guidelines and through proxies.

The list of proxies includes:

- Cyber command
- Territorial army (TA) battalions for CW
- Perception management and social networks

The Indian view is that CW is an ongoing activity during both peacetime and war and will form an essential part of the preparation of the battlefield in any future conflict. It also believes that it could also form part of the strategic deception process. The cyber command, which has yet to be developed, will probably be modelled on the USCYBERCOM (US cyber command), which plans, coordinates, integrates, synchronizes, and conducts activities to:

> direct the operations and defense of specified Department of Defense information NWs and; prepare to, and when directed, conduct full spectrum military cyberspace operations in order to enable actions in all domains, ensure US/Allied freedom of action in cyberspace and deny the same to our adversaries.[43]

The role of the organizations would include monitoring traffic, disseminating information, and ensuring remedial measures to ensure ongoing security to networks and systems. It may also be given responsibility for the protection of the CI of each service; that is, communication backbone, power systems, high-priority networks, and a defense CERT would work in concert with each service CERT.

A Defense Intelligence Agency already exists under HQ IDS. It has cyber and information operations elements, and the Indian view is that intelligence gathering is an accepted reality and cyber space may provide the best scope for this in addition to information operations, which are required for preparation of the battlefield.

The role of the TA battalions for CW would be to create and maintain a "surge capacity" for crisis or warlike situations. In addition to purely defense requirements, these could also provide for the protection of CI.

One element of the Indian view of CW is that, with the growth of social networks, there is scope for perception management and the manipulation of information. This media is seen as a potential tool for psychological warfare and should form part of any offensive or defensive action.

It is interesting to note that India has observer status at the SCO.

North Korea

North Korea has been developing a CW capability for a number of years. In 2009, according to an unverified report, the country's then-leader Kim Jong-il ordered Pyongyang's cyber command to be expanded to 3000 hackers. Other estimates speculate that North Korea has been investing resources into CW since the 1980s.

Gen. James Thurman, commander of US forces in South Korea, told Congress in 2012 that "the newest addition to the North Korean asymmetric arsenal is a growing cyber warfare capability,"[44] in which North Korea "employs sophisticated computer hackers trained to launch cyber infiltration and cyber attacks" against South Korea and the United States.

The South Korean National Intelligence Service (NIS) quoted North Korean leader Kim Jong-un as saying[45] that, alongside nuclear weapons and missiles, CW capabilities are "a magic weapon" that empowers the North Korean army to launch "ruthless strikes" on the South. The report also stated that the North has established a cyber-strike command under the General Reconnaissance Bureau, and that it operates seven hacking organizations consisting of some 1700 hackers under the National Defense Commission and the Workers Party, and that "now that it has finished manning cyber strike organizations that it can mobilize in a war."

The North Korean State Security Department and an agency known as *Bureau 225* under the Workers Party are also producing anti–South Korean propaganda through spy networks in China and Japan, and it is also active on some 400 social media sites to carry out psychological warfare abroad, using South Korean resident registration numbers to sign up.

The NIS revealed a document that suggests the North has worked out ways to manipulate online opinion here by posting articles on blogs or sending e-mails to South Korean journalists. It has developed a Trojan program to take over computer networks and power supply systems, including power stations and substations, throughout the South, the NIS claims.

Other plans include disturbing the GPS systems for aircraft and ships in and near the Seoul metropolitan area and Chungcheong provinces, according to the NIS. Then, of course, there is the alleged most serious attack against Sony Corporation.

Pakistan

Pakistan is reported to have had a CW capability since at least 1998, when it was engaged in defacing websites in India. This activity appears to have escalated in 2003 when it was reported to have attacked Indian government servers. In 2010, Indian cyber hackers are reported to have attacked Pakistan's infrastructure, and Pakistan responded by attacking similar Indian infrastructure. Pakistan still does not appear to have a formal CW coordination center or any specifically designated agency or department responsible for CW, and to date, any cyber attacks appear to have been carried out by individual cyber sections that are attached to government departments.

Summary

When the first edition of this book was published in 2002, there was considerable confusion as to the scope of IW and the meaning of the term. In the intervening years, considerable progress has been made in refining the concepts of IW, and it has matured into what we now call information operations.

References

1. Kuehl, D.T.(2002). Information operations, information warfare, and computer network attack: Their relationship to national security in the information age. In *Computer Network Attack and International Law*. International Law Studies, Vol. 76. Newport, RI: Naval War College.
2. US Joint Forces Command Joint Warfighting Center. 2010. *Commander's Handbook for Strategic Communication and Communication Strategy*, Version 3.0. June 24.
3. Brooks, R. (2011). Ten years on: The evolution of strategic communication and information operations since 9/11. Testimony before the House Armed Services Sub-Committee on Evolving Threats and Capabilities, July 12.
4. Government Accountability Office. (2012). GAO-12-612R Strategic Communication. Michael Courts, Acting Director, International Affairs and Trade, John Pendleton, Director, Defense Capabilities and Management, DOD Strategic Communication: Integrating Foreign Audience Perceptions into Policy Making, Plans, and Operations, May 24, 2012, http://gao.gov/assets/600/591123.pdf.
5. Rand. (2001–2010). U.S. military information operations in Afghanistan: Effectiveness of psychological operations. http://www.rand.org/content/dam/rand/pubs/monographs/2012/RAND_MG1060.pdf.
6. Dominique, M. J. (2009). Information operations: The military's role in gaining information superiority. http://usacac.army.mil/cac2/IPO/repository/COLDominiquethesis.pdf.
7. Smolyan, G., Tsygichko, V., and Chereshkin, D. A. (1995). Weapon that may be more dangerous than a nuclear weapon: The realities of information warfare. *Nezavisimoye voyennoye obozreniye*, November 18.

8. Ministry of Foreign Affairs, Russian Federation. (2008). Information Security Doctrine of the Russian Federation. Approved by President of the Russian Federation Vladimir Putin on September 9, 2000. http://www.mid.ru/ns-osndoc. nsf/1e5f0de28fe77fdcc32575d900298676/2deaa9ee15ddd24bc32575d9002c442b? OpenDocument.
9. Komov, S., Korotkov, S., and Dylevski, I. (2007). Military aspects of ensuring international information security in the context of elaborating universally acknowledged principles of international law. Disarmament Forum. UNIDIR/DF/2007/3.
10. CIS legislation. (2009). The agreement between the governments of state members of the Shanghai organization of cooperation about cooperation in the field of ensuring the international information security. http://cis-legislation.com/document.fwx?rgn=28340.
11. The Military Doctrine of the Russian Federation. (2010). Approved by Russian Federation presidential edict. February 5, 2010. http://www.sras.org/ military_doctrine_russian_federation_2010.
12. International Code of Conduct for Information Security. 2011. Annex to the letter dated 12 September 2011 from the Permanent Representatives of China, the Russian Federation. Tajikistan and Uzbekistan to the United Nations addressed to the Secretary-General (A/66/359). 2011.
13. OECD. (2011). Communiqué on principles for internet policy making. The Internet economy: Generating innovation and growth. http://www.oecd.org/internet/innovation/48289796.pdf.
14. *South China Morning Post.* (2014). China and Russia say they will seek to defend "information space." http://www.scmp.com/news/china/article/1516748/china-and-russia-say-they-will-seek-defend-information-space. May 21, 2014.
15. PIR Center (2011). Conceptual views on the activity of the armed forces of the Russian Federation in information space. http://pircenter.org/en/articles/532-conceptual-views-on-the-activity-of-the-armed-forces-of-the-russian-federation-in-information-space.
16. Polikanov, D. (2001). *Information Challenges to National and International Security.* Moscow: PIR Center Library.
17. Selivanov, A. (2007). How our land can become foreign land: On the architecture of the "information war" against Russia. *Voyenno-Promyshlennyy Kuryer*, March 21.
18. Koayesov, P. (2009). Theater of warfare on distorting airwaves. Georgia versus South Ossetia and Abkhazia in the field of media abuse. Fighting by their own rules. *Voyennyy Vestnik Yuga Rossii.* January 18, 2009.
19. Pufeng, W. (1995). *Xinxi zhanzheng yu junshi geming [Information Warfare and the Revolution in Military Affairs].* Beijing: Junshi kexueyuan.
20. Wang, B. and Li, F. (1995). An informal discussion of information warfare. *Liberation Army Daily*, June 13.
21. Wang, B. and Li, F. (1995). *Liberation Army Daily*, June 20.
22. Panchsheel. (2009). *South Asia Defence and Strategic Year Book.* 1997. PLA National Defence University publication entitled *On Commanding Warfighting under High-Tech Conditions.*
23. Kanwal, G. (2009). China's emerging cyber war doctrine. *Journal of Defence Studies.* July 2009. http://idsa.in/system/files/jds_3_3_gkanwal_0.pdf.
24. Halper, S. China: The three warfares. http://cryptome.org/2014/06/prc-three-wars.pdf.
25. Office of the Secretary of Defense. Annual report to congress on military and security developments involving the People's Republic of China 2011. http://www.defense.gov/pubs/pdfs/2011_cmpr_final.pdf.

26. Ye Xin. (2011). PLA establishes "Online Blue Army" to protect network security. *People's Daily Online.* http://english.people.com.cn/90001/90776/90786/7392182.html.
27. Reuters. (2013). China war games: Army to conduct its first digital technology military exercise. May 29.
28. Mandiant, APT1: Exposing one of China's cyber espionage units. http://intelreport.mandiant.com/Mandiant_APT1_Report.pdf.
29. Crowdstrike. http://www.crowdstrike.com/.
30. *China Daily.* (2014). Army needs "information warfare" plan, declares Xi. September 2014. http://www.chinadaily.com.cn/china/2014-09/01/content_18520930.htm.
31. Vice Chairman of the Joint Chiefs of Staff. 2011. Memo from the Vice Chairman of the Joint Chiefs of Staff to the Chiefs of Military Service, Commanders of the Combatant Commands and Directors of the Joint Staff Directorates entitled: Joint Terminology for Cyberspace Operations. http://www.nsci-va.org/CyberReferenceLib/2010-11-joint%20Terminology%20for%20Cyberspace%20Operations.pdf.
32. Cyber threats: Issues and explanations. UN Interregional Crime and Justice Research Institute. http://www.unicri.it/special_topics/securing_cyberspace/cyber_threats/explanations/.
33. Schreier, F. 2012. On-cyberwarfare. http://www.dcaf.ch/Publications/On-Cyberwarfare.
34. What is critical infrastructure?, http://www.dhs.gov/what-critical-infrastructure. Last Published Date: October 24, 2013.
35. Rouse, M., Advanced persistent threat (APT), http://searchsecurity.techtarget.com/definition/advanced-persistent-threat-APT.
36. Nonstate actors: Impact on international relations and implications for the United States. A report prepared under the auspices of the National Intelligence Officer for Economics and Global Issues. DR-2007-16D, 23 August 2007.
37. The Kremlin, The military doctrine of the Russian Federation, February 5, 2010, http://kremlin.ru/supplement/461.
38. RIA Novosti, Russian military creating cyber warfare branch. http://en.ria.ru/military_news/20130820/182856856/Russian-Military-Creating-Cyber-Warfare-Branch.html.
39. Billo, C., Chang, W. (2004). Cyber warfare: An analysis of the means and motivations of selected nation states. Institute for Security Technology Studies at Dartmouth College. http://www.ists.dartmouth.edu/docs/execsum.pdf.
40. Hagestad II, W. (2014). Past is prologue to China's cyber strategy. *Brinknews*, November 10. http://www.brinknews.com/past-is-prologue-to-chinas-cyber-strategy/.
41. Report on Iranian cyber warfare capabilities, Institute for National Security Studies (INSS). (2014). http://www.tripwire.com/state-of-security/top-security-stories/inss-issues-report-iran.ian-cyber-warfare-capabilities/.
42. IDSA Task Force Report, India's cyber security challenge. http://idsa.in/system/files/book_indiacybersecurity.pdf.
43. U.S. Cyber Command fact sheet. May 25, 2010. http://www.defense.gov/home/features/2010/0410_cybersec/docs/CYberFactSheet%20UPDATED%20replaces%20May%2021%20Fact%20Sheet.pdf.
44. Vlahos, K.B. (2014). Special report: The cyberwar threat from North Korea. FoxNews.com, February 14, 2014. http://www.foxnews.com/tech/2014/02/14/cyberwar-experts-question-north-korea-cyber-capabilities/.
45. Kim Jong-un boasts of "magic weapon" hacker unit. 2008. http://www.wantchinatimes.com/news-subclass-cnt.aspx?id=20131108000031&cid=1101.

Chapter 3

War Stories from the Digital Battlefield

When discussing the various aspects of global information warfare (GIW), it is important to also be aware of the actual and various types of IW attacks that are currently being conducted 24/7 around the world against individuals, groups, businesses, and governments.

Being aware of such attacks, one can get a better appreciation of the massive challenges ahead for those info-warriors trying, often in vain, to protect the information and information systems being used today.

It is also important to know of the latest technologies being developed and by whom, as well as to understand the politics of the time, because as tensions rise among people, businesses, groups, and nations, they are more apt to become aggressively involved in GIW.

As you read through these actual attacks and their related commentaries,* think of how to defend against them and also how to use them—how to piggy-back off them when conducting offensive operations against adversaries. Knowing the who, how, where, when, why, and what will help defend against GIW attacks as well as provide a basis that can be used for offensive GIW weapons.

To get some idea as to who are perpetrating such attacks, go to the United States' FBI website and read through the list of the FBI's most wanted cyber criminals,[1] as these are some of the people you must defend against.

The following reported digital battlefield attacks and related stories have been grouped into a number of categories, starting with those related to governments,

---

* All stories are edited, generally direct quotes from the cited websites, except where otherwise noted.

which includes both actions taken by governments and attacks on government systems.

Let us start with one of the most sophisticated attacks, allegedly made in July 2010 against Iran's nuclear program using a program called Stuxnet.

Stuxnet is a computer worm that was discovered in June 2010. It was designed to attack industrial programmable logic controllers (PLCs). PLCs allow the automation of electromechanical processes such as those used to control machinery on factory assembly lines, amusement rides, or centrifuges for separating nuclear material.[2]

Allegedly, this program was the work of the US and Israeli governments, although this is just speculation. The worm entered the Iranian network and destabilized over 1000 of their centrifuges.

Now, one can only speculate how it entered a "closed" network. Some allege it was entered via a CD/DVD or a flash drive by an insider. Others speculate that a disk or flash drive was left in a place where someone working in the Iranian facility found it and entered it into the closed Iranian nuclear network just to see what was on the media and thus unleashed the worm.

Regin malware[3] is allegedly the most powerful to date, even more powerful than Stuxnet, and it targets mostly Russian and Saudi Telecom Companies. It has been out there since 2008, and even when it is detected, it is impossible to tell what it is doing. It is supposedly in ten countries, with half the attacks being in Russia, as well as others in India and Iran. Some say that it is so good that it is believed it could only have been developed by a nation-state—a Western nation-state; interestingly, attacks have now been reported in the United States.

Every year, the US military academies of the army, navy, coast guard, and air force put together teams of cadet info-warriors to compete in an IW game using a points system to determine the winner. It begins with each academy selecting a team and building a secure network; all are then attacked over a three-day period by a "Red Team." This sophisticated IW game is used to help train the US military info-warriors of the future.[4]

According to a May 2014 DefenseTech report,[5]

> Defense Advanced Research Project Agency leaders told lawmakers the agency is making progress with an ongoing cyber security project known as Plan X to increase cyber visibility and provide a new foundation for the fast-developing world of cyber warfare moving into the future.

In May 2014, Fox News reported[6] that

> Gen. Zhu's comments were echoed during a spirited question-and-answer session following Hagel's speech. In the session, PLA Maj. Gen. Yao Yunzhu questioned America's repeated claim that it doesn't take sides in territorial disputes, asking how that can be true when the U.S.

also claims the disputed islands in the East China Sea are covered by a U.S. treaty with Japan.

In another May 2014 Fox News report,[7] it was stated that

> The U.S. plans to "keep up the pressure" on China as it gauges that nation's response to this week's indictment of five Chinese military officials for allegedly hacking into American corporate computers…If China doesn't begin to acknowledge and curb its corporate cyberespionage, the U.S. plans to start selecting from a range of retaliatory options.

In another Fox News report in the same month,[8] it was stated that

> between traffic-light cameras, blue-light cameras that scan neighborhoods for violent crime, cameras on board city trains and buses—not to mention private security cameras—there are few places you can go in Chicago without being monitored.

Yet another May 2014 Fox News report[9] stated that

> The Pentagon's research arm unveiled a new drone built with secure software that prevents the control and navigation of the aircraft from being hacked. The program, called High Assurance Cyber Military Systems, or HACMS, uses software designed to thwart cyber attacks. Citing the success of mock-enemy or "red-team" exercises wherein cyber experts tried to hack into the quadcopter and failed, Fisher indicated that DARPA experts have referred to the prototype quadcopter as the most secure UAS in the world.

Another May 2014 Fox News report[10] stated that

> China has warned the U.S. that it is jeopardizing its military ties with Beijing and demanded that Washington withdraw an indictment brought by the Justice Department against five Chinese military officials accused of hacking into U.S. companies to steal trade secrets.

Also in May 2014, another Fox News report[11] stated that

> Virtual Battlespace 3 (VBS3)…Using the system, the Army can build battlefield scenarios and tailor the game to reflect specific requirements. Soldiers, for example, can simulate driving a Stryker, conduct patrols, engage in close combat and drive down to the firing position to practice gunnery in realistic terrain.

In June 2014, Fox News reported that[12]

The mission data packages, now being developed by the Air Force's 53rd Wing are designed to accommodate new information as new threat data becomes available. The data base is loaded with a wide range of information to include commercial airliner information and specifics on Russian and Chinese fighter jets.

Another June 2014 Fox News report[13] stated that

The spy agency has relied more on facial-recognition technology in the past four years as a result of new software that can process the flood of digital communications such as emails, text messages and even video conferences...

Also in June 2014, another Fox News report[14] stated that

Concerned over network security following news last year suggesting German leader Angela Merkel had her phone tapped by the NSA, the government said it will transfer all its telecom and Internet-related services to German firm Deutsche Telekom...

In July 2014 Fox News reported[15] that

The Secret Service has confirmed what you've probably suspected for a long time: Public computers at hotels are ridiculously insecure, and you're taking a gamble with your personal data each time you use one.

Another July 2014 Fox News report[16] states,

The director of the CIA, in a rare apology, has acknowledged an internal probe's findings that CIA employees in the Executive Branch improperly spied on the Legislative Branch by searching Senate computers earlier this year.

Yet another July 2014 Fox News report[17] stated that

Hot on the heels of the NSA snooping firestorm, a leaked document appears to detail the cyber espionage tricks employed by its U.K. counterpart, GCHQ.

In another July 2014 report, Fox News stated that

U.S. authorities have charged a Chinese businessman with hacking into the computer systems of U.S. companies with large defense contracts, including Boeing, to steal data on military projects, including some of the latest fighter jets,…targeted fighter jets such as the F-22 and the F-35 as well as Boeing's C-17 military cargo aircraft program, according to court papers.

Another July 2014 Fox News report[19] stated that

An ironclad drone programming protocol, is about to go open-source, allowing both governments and enthusiasts to keep their autonomous flying machines secure.…seL4 is an operating system kernel that acts as a go-between for hardware and software in an electronic device.

Also in July 2014, Fox News reported[20] that

China took its investigation of "alleged monopoly actions" by Microsoft to a new level this week, raiding four of the company's offices and carrying away internal documents and computers.

Another July 2014 *Fox Business News* report[21] gave a quote from John Carlin of the US Department of Justice, which stated that

It's clear that the terrorists want to use cyber-enabled means to cause the maximum amount of destruction to our infrastructure.

In August 2014, Fox News reported[22] that

The National Security Agency's surveillance machinery is again in the spotlight after a media report claimed that it is secretly providing data to almost two dozen U.S. government agencies via a powerful "Google-like" search engine.

Again in August 2014, Fox News reported[23] that

The federal government is spending nearly $1 million to create an online database that will track "misinformation" and hate speech on Twitter…monitor "suspicious memes" and what it considers "false and misleading ideas," with a major focus on political activity online.

Also in August 2014, Fox News reported[24] that

Israeli's secret service intercepted Secretary of State John Kerry's phone calls during 2013 Middle East peace negotiations, according to the German publication *Spiegel*.

In August 2014, Fox News also reported[25] that

> More than 1,000 U.S. retailers could be infected with malicious software lurking in their cash register computers, allowing hackers to steal customer financial data, the Homeland Security Department…

Later in August 2014, Fox News reported[26] that

> Sony was the target of a double-barreled attack by hackers…with an executive's flight diverted due to a bomb scare at roughly the same time as its network was under attack.

In an October 2014 Fox News report,[27]

> One security expert noted healthcare.gov is a still a huge ripe target… and that unlike the private sector, no law requires the federal government to even inform you if your information has been hacked.

Also in an October 2014 Fox News report,[28] it was stated that

> The U.S. Department of Homeland Security is investigating about two dozen cases of suspected cybersecurity flaws in medical devices and hospital equipment that officials fear could be exploited by hackers.

Another Fox News report[29] in October 2014 stated that

> the source warned her about the threat of government spying. She was "shocked" and "flabbergasted"…scrutiny of her personal desktop proves that "the interlopers were able to co-opt my iMac and operate it remotely, as if they were sitting in front of it." And an inspection revealed that an extra fiber-optics line had been installed in Attkisson's home without her knowledge.

Yet another October 2014 Fox News report[30] stated that,

> Voting machines that switch Republican votes to Democrats are being reported in Maryland.

In November 2014, Fox News reported[31] that

> Australian defense officials are preparing for what could be a barrage of possible cyber attacks during the G20 leaders' summit this Saturday and Sunday in Brisbane. "Targeting of high profile events such as the

G20 by state-sponsored or other foreign adversaries, cyber criminals and issue-motivated groups is a real and persistent threat"

In November 2014 Fox News also reported[32] that

Recently a series of high-profile attacks hit U.S. infrastructure—computer networks at the White House, the State Department and U.S. Postal Service systems were compromised by hackers. Security experts speculated that the attacks were coordinated by groups of hackers backed by a foreign government, probably one of the state-sponsored crews that is targeting U.S. critical infrastructure.

According to another November 2014 Fox News report,[33]

Governments all around the world use malware and spyware to keep tabs on people, from visitors to residents...The Detekt tool was developed and supported by several human-rights groups. Detekt checks for malware that is often used against journalists, activists and others.

In another November 2014 Fox News report,[34] it was stated that

After decades of steady improvements in air travel, a new report from the Federal Aviation Administration shows a surge in near-collisions between commercial airliners and drones.

A November 2014 Fox News television program reported[35] that

Security attacks/breaches in U.S. Government from July 2014-Nov 2014: Health and Human Services; Energy Department; Postal Service; White House; State Department—and those just reported and may be more that are not reported or worse yet, not even know they were attacked.

In November 2014, Fox News also reported[36] that

Weeks before the State Department's Nov. 16 shutdown of its unclassified email system in the face of unprecedented hacking attacks, auditors took the department's management to task for ignoring warnings about their lax security habits and chronic failure to enact protections against high-tech intruders. The situation was so bad, the auditors say in a highly censored report, that they "identified control deficiencies across a total of 102 different systems reviewed over five years, yet many of the same deficiencies have persisted."

Again in November 2014, Fox News reported that[37]

> Throughout the flood of hacks and data breaches at retailers, restaurants, health care providers and online companies this year—Home Depot, Target, Subway, Adobe and eBay were just a handful...

Also in November 2014, Fox News reported[38] that

> Russia, China, Iran, and Islamists are waging unconventional warfare around the world, and the United States currently lacks a clear strategy to counter the threat, according to a recent report by the Army Special Operations Command. "This challenge is hybrid warfare combining conventional, irregular, and asymmetric means, to include the persistent manipulation of political and ideological conflict," states the Army white paper, "Countering Unconventional Warfare".

Later in November 2014, Fox News reported[39] that

> Malicious hackers have completely brought down Sony Pictures Entertainment's global internal network, forcing executives and employees to temporarily log off corporate PCs and potentially heisting internal documents. Every single computer pertaining to the company's network displayed an ominous message from the authors of the attack...the hacking organization responsible calls itself Guardians of Peace (or GOP).

In December 2014, Fox News reported[40] that

> With the finger of suspicion now pointing at North Korea in the Sony Pictures hack, a security expert warns that the rogue state has the tools at its disposal to wreak havoc on other western corporate networks.

A February 2015 report[41] from Threatpost stated that

> Iranian state-sponsored hackers have been singled out for attacks on critical infrastructure worldwide, including 10 targets in the United States.

A February 2015 BBC News report[42] stated that

> US and British intelligence agencies hacked into a major manufacturer of Sim cards in order to steal codes that facilitate eavesdropping on mobiles, a US news website says.

In a paper, L. Scott Johnson[43] of Tera Research, Inc., a contractor performing analysis on behalf of the Directorate of Intelligence, stated that

> IW is one of the hottest topics in current discussions of battlefield and geopolitical conflict. It has been addressed in writings, conferences, doctrine and plans, and military reorganizations, and it has been proposed as a fundamental element of 21st-century conflict. In a way, the IW situation is reminiscent of the concept of logistics as a military discipline, circa 1940:
>
> - Elements of the concept had been known and used for millennia.
> - The value of integrating those elements into a coherent discipline was just beginning to be recognized.
> - The discipline was to become a central element of modern warfare–it is now said that "amateur generals (that is, Saddam Hussein) talk strategy, professional generals talk logistics."

According to a CBS News report,[44]

> Many of America's military secrets can be stolen by exploiting the networks over which unclassified information is shared by military contractors and subcontractors…Chinese hackers are believed to have stolen the designs for "more than two dozen major weapons systems."

According to another CBS News report,[45]

> Pentagon was pushing to expand its cybersecurity forces. The U.S. military's so-called Cyber Command will grow five-fold over the next few years, from 900 employees at present, to about 5,000 civilian and military personnel, Orr reported.

In another CBS News report,[46]

> U.S. officials are blaming Chinese hackers for another serious data breach. Someone broke into secure government networks that hold personal information for all federal employees. The target appears to be workers applying for high-level security clearances.

A report[47] in *The Wire* stated that

> Ballistic-missile defenses, joint-strike fighters, Black Hawks, and more—Chinese hackers have their hands on plans for these and more of the Pentagon's most sophisticated weapons systems, just the latest sign that the culture of hacking in China continues to put America on the defensive.

What did you expect, an exploding pen?

Selected government malware

Year discovered	Malware	Possible source
2006	Greek Vodafone hack	?
2010	Stuxnet	US and Israel
2010	Aurora	China
2012	Flame	US and Israel
2013	Red October	Russia or China
2014	DarkHotel	South Korea
2014	Uroburos	Russia
2014	The Mask	?
2014	Regin	Britain and US

Sources: Anti-virus firms; press reports

Exhibit 3.1   Selected government malware.

In November 2014, the *Economist* published an article on "The spy who hacked me" and gave a table of the most notable attacks that were suspected to have been state sponsored (Exhibit 3.1).[48]

The next group of reports looks at issues that have affected corporations. According to a September 2014 Fox News report,[49]

Home Depot said Thursday a recent cyber attack on its computer network affected a colossal 56 million customer payment cards…is believed to be the biggest ever hack of a retail firm's computer systems…used malware to collect customer information.

According to an October 2014 *New York Times* report,[50]

Hackers had broken into the phone network…and routed $166,000 worth of calls from the firm to premium-rate telephone numbers in Gambia, Somalia and the Maldives.

In another Fox Business report,[51]

a company, along with 1.2 billion other websites, was targeted by Russian hackers utilizing a massive "bot" attack. These bots aggressively attempted access to websites with username and password options.

In a February 2015 CNN Money report,[52] it was stated that

> Hackers have stolen information on tens of millions of Anthem Inc. customers, in a massive data breach that ranks among the largest in corporate history.

The next group of reports looks at what terrorists and hackers are doing. In October 2014, Fox News reported[53]

> Hackers would love to weasel their way on to your smartphone or tablet…mobile gadgets are a bit harder to crack…hackers have to be even sneakier and use malicious apps, hidden Wi-Fi attacks or simply walk off with your gadget.

According to a Gizmodo report,[54]

> On average, the hackers would spend nearly a year perusing a targeted company's systems looking for sensitive information to steal: Product development plans, manufacturing techniques, business plans and the email messages of senior executives. The point is to help Chinese companies be more competitive.

In a 2014 *Washington Post* report,[55]

> Hackers may have breached the Office of Personnel Management's network…intrusion has been traced to China, although it is not clear that the Chinese government is involved.

Yahoo News reported[56] that

> Syrian Twitter user appeared to break the news of U.S.-led airstrikes in Syria overnight before the Pentagon announced it had launched them.

In May 2014, the *Herald* of Everett, Washington, reported[57] that

> Four Monroe High School students are in hot water after a teacher's online grade book was hacked into earlier this month.…One of the students inserted a keylogging device into the teacher's computer. It allowed them to covertly record the sequence of key strokes the teacher used as the password to the electronic grade book.

In May 2014, Fox News reported[58] that

> Hackers apparently based in Iran have mounted a three-year campaign of cyber-espionage against high-ranking U.S. and international

officials, including a four-star admiral, to gather intelligence on economic sanctions, antinuclear proliferation efforts and other issues… according to cybersecurity investigators.

In May 2014 Fox News also reported[59] that

The infamous hacker known as Sabu who cooperated with the FBI for three years to take down his former associates and help authorities disrupt or mitigate cyber attacks including those targeting U.S. military, Congress and law enforcement websites was sentenced on Tuesday to time served.

Again in July 2014, Fox News reported[60] that

Chinese computer hackers were able to access the computer network of the federal agency that houses the personal information of all government employees in an apparent attempt to target workers who have applied for security clearances, according to a published report.

In July 2014, Fox Business News reported[61] that

Hackers and scammers know that travelers are in a hurry and might not be paying much attention to the security of Wi-Fi. And unbeknownst to travelers, they may have unwittingly connected to an unverified rogue network.

In July 2014, the *Guardian* reported that[62]

A Chinese hacking group has been accused of stealing data from Israel's billion-dollar Iron Dome missile system. The state-sponsored Comment Crew hacking group, thought to operate out of China, was responsible for attacks from 2011 onwards on three Israeli defence technology companies Elisra Group, Israel Aerospace Industries (IAI) and Rafael Advanced Defense Systems all involved with the Iron Dome project.

In August 2014, Fox News reported[63] that

Malicious software used to steal millions from bank accounts has re-emerged a month after US authorities broke up a major hacker network using the scheme, security researchers say…a Russian crime ring has amassed some 1.2 billion username and password combinations makes now a good time to review ways to protect yourself online.

In September 2014, Fox News reported[64] that

Jihadists in the Middle East are ramping up efforts to mount a massive cyber attack on the U.S., with leaders from both Islamic State and Al Qaeda—including a hacker who once broke into former British Prime Minister Tony Blair's Gmail account—recruiting web savvy radicals, FoxNews.com has learned.

In November 2014, Fox News reported[65] that

Islamic jihadists worldwide have launched a barrage of recruitment messages amid the latest unrest in Ferguson, Mo., using Twitter accounts to call on African-Americans and others in the United States to join their cause.

In November 2014, the Radware Blog posted[66] that

Cybercrime and hacktivism are on the rise and commercial and governmental organizations are common attack targets. But, based on recent evidence, an increasing number of cyber-attack targets are other attackers. That's right—attackers attacking other attackers. Recently, Radware security researchers have analyzed samples of a potentially new attack tool called "ddos.exe." This tool challenges the concept of honor among thieves. The alleged Denial of Service (DoS) attack tool, "ddos.exe" as implied by its name, is actually a new variant of NJRAT agent installer.

In January 2015, Fox News reported[67] that

The Twitter account for U.S. Central Command was hacked on Monday and for several minutes carried incendiary messages promoting the Islamic State—including one that said, "AMERICAN SOLDIERS, WE ARE COMING, WATCH YOUR BACK. ISIS."

Also in January 2015, Fox News reported[68] that

Hacking group Anonymous declared war on Islamist extremists after the deadly terror attack on Paris satirical publication Charlie Hebdo...also warned that those who stand in the way of freedom of expression can expect "a massive frontal assault...because the struggle for the defense of these freedoms is the foundation of our movement."

The next group of reports looks at attacks that affect the individual.

First, let us talk about a simple attack. A journalist tells the story[69] of how his devices were allegedly hacked, and his photos and e-mails—basically his entire cyber life—was deleted. He was able to contact the hackers, who were teenagers, and they said they just did it for "fun." He agreed not to press charges and not to identify them, but he wanted to know how they did it.

They allegedly told him that they did not hack his passwords but basically did the following: They began by "social engineering" their way into his accounts, taking advantage of loopholes in the system.

- They first called Amazon.com as him and gave them a false credit card number.
- Then they received a temporary password from Amazon.
- They now owned his Amazon account.
- They then got the last four numbers of his actual credit card.
- Apple was also using it as an identity verification method.
- Apple gave "him" (the hackers) a password reset.
- They now owned his Apple account.
- They then moved on to take over his Google and then his Twitter accounts.

As you can see, today's GIW attacks can range from being as nontechnical as using social engineering techniques to the more sophisticated covert malware types of attacks, a combination of both, and everything in between.

Do you ever get the feeling you are being watched? According to a Fox News report,[70] if you have got a webcam, you might be right; it is stunningly easy since most companies, in an effort to be helpful, put installation manuals online, manuals that make public the default passwords for their products.

In November of 2014, Fox News reported[71] that

> The story of a 12-year-old girl's kidnapping fuels concerns about the dangers of the Internet—even as it demonstrates how today's devices can come to the rescue.

The last group of reports are about technology companies and the technologies themselves.

According to a Yahoo News Canada report,[72]

> Taiwanese government is investigating whether Xiaomi Inc, China's leading smartphone company...is a cyber security threat...as governments become increasingly wary of potential cyber security threats from the world's second-biggest economy....The smartphone maker recently came under fire for unauthorized data access.

A June 2014 Fox News report[73] stated that

> Samsung Electronics said five of its Galaxy-branded smartphones and tablets that come with its enterprise security software recently received approval from the U.S. Defense Information Systems Agency, allowing them to be listed as an option for officials.

In another June 2014 Fox Business News report,[74] it was stated that

> EyeVerify working on innovative biometric security for smartphones and tablets. The software scans the eyes of the user in place of a password, and if it's not the right person, the software won't open.

A Fox News report[75] in July 2014 stated that

> BlackBerry has announced a deal to acquire German anti-eavesdropping specialist Secusmart…provides its technology to German Chancellor Angela Merkel, who is at the center of a controversy over an alleged National Security Agency phone tap.

An August 2014 Fox News report[76] stated that

> As more devices and appliances with Internet capabilities enter the market, protecting those devices from hackers becomes critical. Unfortunately, many of these non-computer, non-smartphone devices from toilets to refrigerators to alarm systems—weren't built with security in mind.

According to a September 2014 Yahoo News report,[77] there are at least 19 bogus cellphone towers operating across the United States that could be used to spy on, and even hijack, passing mobile phones.

A Yahoo Tech report[78] stated that

> In the field of Artificial Intelligence there is no more iconic and controversial milestone than the Turing Test, when a computer convinces a sufficient number of interrogators into believing that it is not a machine but rather is a human. Having a computer that can trick a human into thinking that someone, or even something, is a person we trust is a wake-up call to cybercrime.

Summary

The articles shown in this chapter are given as just a very small example of the range and level of activity that we are seeing on a daily basis. They were collected over a 9-month period and represent just a few of the reports that were made. It may seem from the selected reports that Fox News is the only show in town—this is not true, it just happens to be the favorite news source of one of the authors! There are interesting lessons that can be learned.

References

1. FBI. (n.d.). Cyber's most wanted. http://www.fbi.gov/wanted/cyber.
2. Razvan, B. (2014). Stuxnet. Wikipedia. Retrieved March 28. http://en.wikipedia. org/wiki/Stuxnet.
3. Varney & Company, Business News Program. (2014). Fox Business TV Channel, November 24.
4. –. (2014). *Cyber Wargame.* Fox Business Channel TV. August 25.
5. Osborn, K. (2014). DARPA sets cyber foundations with "Plan X." Defensetech. May 14. http://defensetech.org/2014/05/14/darpa-sets-cyber-foundations-with-plan-x/#ixzz32V4YPy00.
6. –. (2014). Chinese general warns that US is making "important" mistakes in region. *Wall Street Journal*, May 31. http://www.foxnews.com/world/2014/05/31/chinese-general-warns-that-us-is-making-imporant-mistakes-in-region/?intcmp=HPBucket.
7. –. (2014). US to rev up hacking fight against China. *Wall Street Journal*, May 24. http://www.foxnews.com/politics/2014/05/24/us-to-rev-up-hacking-fight-against-china/.
8. Tobin, M. (2014). Security camera surge in Chicago sparks concerns of "massive surveillance system." Fox News, May 12. http://www.foxnews.com/politics/2014/05/12/security-camera-surge-in-chicago-sparks-concerns-massive-surveillance-system/.
9. Osborn, K. (2014). DARPA unveils hack-proof drone. Fox News, May 22. http://www.foxnews.com/tech/2014/05/22/darpa-unveils-hack-proof-drone/?intcmp=obnetwork.
10. Fox News. (2014). China summons US envoy, warns that cyberspying charges could harm ties. May 20. http://www.foxnews.com/politics/2014/05/20/china-summons-us-envoy-as-justice-dept-brings-cyberspying-case/.
11. Barrie, A. (2014). Army battles with brawn and beer bellies. Fox News, May 22. http://www.foxnews.com/tech/2014/05/22/army-battles-with-brawn-and-beer-bellies/?intcmp=features.
12. Osborn, K. (2014). Air Force develops threat data base for F-35. Fox News, June 19. http://www.foxnews.com/tech/2014/06/19/air-force-develops-threat-data-base-for-f-35/?intcmp=obnetwork.
13. Fox News. (2014). NSA steps up digital image harvesting to feed its facial recognition program, June 1. http://www.foxnews.com/politics/2014/06/01/nsa-steps-up-digital-image-harvesting-to-feed-its-advancing-facial-recognition/.
14. Mogg, T. (2014). German government ends contract with Verizon following NSA revelations. Fox News, June 27. http://www.foxnews.com/tech/2014/06/27/german-government-ends-contract-with-verizon-following-nsa-revelations/?intcmp=obnetwork.
15. Honorof, M. (2014). Secret Service warns hotels of data theft. Fox News, July 14. http://www.foxnews.com/tech/2014/07/14/secret-service-warns-hotels-of-data-theft/?intcmp=obnetwork.
16. Fox News. (2014). CIA director apologizes to lawmakers as probe finds officers read Senate emails. Fox News, August 1. http://www.foxnews.com/politics/2014/07/31/cia-director-apologizes-to-senate-leaders/?intcmp=latestnews.

17. Rogers, J. (2014). UK intelligence agency in cyber spying controversy. Fox News, July 15. http://www.foxnews.com/tech/2014/07/15/uk-intelligence-agency-in-cyber-spying-controversy/.

18. Associated Press. (2014). Chinese man charged with hacking into US computers. Fox News, July 12. http://www.foxnews.com/us/2014/07/12/chinese-man-charged-with-hacking-into-us-computers/?intcmp=latestnews.

19. Honorof, M. (2014). Hack-proof drones? This could make it happen. Fox News, July 29. http://www.foxnews.com/tech/2014/07/29/hack-proof-drones-this-could-make-it-happen/?intcmp=obnetwork.

20. Piper, D. (2014). Microsoft's China woes increase. Fox News, July 30. http://www.foxnews.com/tech/2014/07/30/microsofts-china-woes-increase/?intcmp=obnetwork.

21. Fox Business News. (2014). Varney & Company Program. July 28.

22. Rogers. J. (2014). "Google-like" search engine puts NSA snooping back in the spotlight. Fox News, August 26. http://www.foxnews.com/tech/2014/08/26/google-like-search-engine-puts-nsa-snooping-back-in-spotlight/.

23. Harrington, E. (2014). Feds creating database to track hate speech on Twitter. Fox News, August 26. http://www.foxnews.com/politics/2014/08/26/feds-creating-database-to-track-hate-speech-on-twitter/.

24. Fox News, (2014). Israel spied on Kerry's calls during 2013 peace talks, magazine reports. August 3. http://www.foxnews.com/politics/2014/08/03/israel-spied-on-kerrys-calls-during-2013-peace-talks-magazine-reports/.

25. Associated Press. (2014). Malicious software in cash registers could affect more than 1,000 US retailers, Gov't warns. August 22. http://www.foxnews.com/tech/2014/08/22/malicious-software-in-cash-registers-could-affect-more-than-1000-us-retailers/?intcmp=obnetwork.

26. Rogers, J. (2014). Hackers get personal in new Sony attack. Fox News, August 25. http://www.foxnews.com/tech/2014/08/25/hackers-get-personal-in-latest-sony-attack/?intcmp=obnetwork.

27. Angle, J. (2014). Is your ObamaCare information safe? Fox News, October 27. http://www.foxnews.com/politics/2014/10/27/is-your-obamacare-information-safe/.

28. Finkle, J. (2014). US government probes medical devices for possible cyber flaws. Fox News, October 22. http://www.foxnews.com/tech/2014/10/22/us-government-probes-medical-devices-for-possible-cyber-flaws/?intcmp=features.

29. Kurtz, H. (2014). The highly sophisticated hacking of Sharyl Attkisson's computers. Fox News, October 28. http://www.foxnews.com/politics/2014/10/27/highly-sophisticated-hacking-sharyl-attkisson-computers/?intcmp=HPBucket.

30. Ward, K. (2014). "Calibration issue" pops up on Maryland voting machines. Fox News, October 27. http://www.foxnews.com/politics/2014/10/27/calibration-issue-pops-up-on-maryland-voting-machines/.

31. Dorsey, S. (2014). Australia braces for G20 cyber attacks. Fox News, November 13. http://www.foxnews.com/tech/2014/11/13/australia-braces-for-g20-cyber-attacks/?intcmp=features.

32. Paganini, P. (2014). The looming cyberthreat to America's backbone. Fox News, November 25. http://www.foxnews.com/tech/2014/11/25/looming-cyberthreat-to-americas-backbone/?intcmp=ob_homepage_tech&intcmp=obnetwork.

33. Scharr, J. (2014). Free tool detects government spyware. Fox News, November 21. http://www.foxnews.com/tech/2014/11/21/free-tool-detects-government-spyware/?intcmp=ob_homepage_tech&intcmp=obnetwork.

34. Fox News. (2014). FAA: Near-collisions between drones and airliners spike. November 27. http://www.foxnews.com/politics/2014/11/27/faa-collisions-between-drones-and-airliners-spike/?intcmp=HPBucket.

35. Cavuto, N. (2014). Fox News TV Program, November 21.

36. Russell, G. (2014). Amid hacking attack, State Department info-security still in shambles. Fox News, November 25. http://www.foxnews.com/politics/2014/11/25/amid-hacking-attack-state-department-info-security-still-in-shambles/?intcmp=latestnews.

37. Komando, K. (2014). 5 steps to keep your accounts safe from hackers and scammers. Fox News, November 1. http://www.foxnews.com/tech/2014/11/01/5-steps-to-keep-your-accounts-safe-from-hackers-and-scammers/?intcmp=ob_homepage_tech&intcmp=obnetwork.

38. Gertz, B. (2014). US lacks strategy to counter unconventional warfare threats from states and terrorists. Fox News, November 26. http://www.foxnews.com/politics/2014/11/26/us-lacks-strategy-to-counter-unconventional-information-warfare-threats-from/.

39. Diaconescu, A. (2014). Sony Pictures Entertainment employees greeted by ominous message as network is hacked. Fox News, November 25. http://www.foxnews.com/tech/2014/11/25/sony-pictures-entertainment-employees-greeted-by-ominous-message-as-network-is/?intcmp=ob_homepage_tech&intcmp=obnetwork.

40. Rogers, J. (2014). Expert: Why the North Korean cyber threat is real. Fox News, December 1. http://www.foxnews.com/tech/2014/12/01/expert-why-north-korean-cyber-threat-is-real/?intcmp=ob_homepage_tech&intcmp=obnetwork.

41. Mimoso, M. (2014). Report connects Iran to critical infrastructure hacks worldwide. Threatpost, December 2. http://threatpost.com/report-connects-iran-to-critical-infrastructure-hacks-worldwide/109666.

42. BBC News Technology. (2015). US and UK accused of hacking sim card firm to steal codes. BBC News, February 20. http://www.bbc.co.uk/news/technology-31545050.

43. Scott Johnson, L. Toward a functional model of information warfare: A major intelligence challenge. https://www.cia.gov/library/center-for-the-study-of-intelligence/kent-csi/vol40no5/pdf/v40i5a07p.pdf.

44. Montopoli, B. (2013). How Chinese hackers steal U.S. secrets. CBS News, August 7. http://www.cbsnews.com/news/how-chinese-hackers-steal-us-secrets/2/.

45. CBS News. (2013). China military unit behind many hacking attacks on U.S., cybersecurity firm says. February 19. http://www.cbsnews.com/news/china-military-unit-behind-many-hacking-attacks-on-us-cybersecurity-firm-says/.

46. CBS News. (2014). U.S.: Chinese hackers got to federal workers' records. July 10. http://www.cbsnews.com/news/report-chinese-hackers-got-to-federal-workers-records/.

47. Abad-Santos, A. (2014). China is winning the cyber war because they hacked U.S. plans for real war. The Wire, May 28. http://www.thewire.com/global/2013/05/china-hackers-pentagon/65628/.

48. *The Economist*. (2014). The spy who hacked me: Malicious computer code is making the spook's job easier than ever. November 29. http://www.economist.com/news/international/21635044-malicious-computer-code-making-spooks-job-easier-ever-spy-who-hacked-me.

49. Mogg, T. (2014). Home Depot malware attack even bigger than Target's, 56m payment cards affected. Fox News, September 19. http://www.foxnews.com/tech/2014/09/19/home-depot-malware-attack-even-bigger-than-targets-56m-payment-cards-affected/?intcmp=obnetwork.

50. Perlroth, N. (2014). Phone hackers dial and redial to steal billions. *New York Times,* October 19. http://www.nytimes.com/2014/10/20/technology/dial-and-redial-phone-hackers-stealing-billions-.html?_r=0.
51. Emerson, C. (2014). Why your passwords should be at least 24 characters long. Fox Business, August 19. http://www.foxbusiness.com/personal-finance/2014/08/29/why-your-passwords-should-be-at-least-24-charcters-long/?intcmp=obnetwork.
52. Riley, C. (2015). Insurance giant Anthem hit by massive data breach. CNN Money, February 6. http://money.cnn.com/2015/02/04/technology/anthem-insurance-hack-data-security/.
53. Komando, K. (2014). Essential security apps for your smartphone and tablet. Fox News, October 19. http://www.foxnews.com/tech/2014/10/19/essential-security-apps-for-your-smartphone-and-tablet/?intcmp=obnetwork.
54. Estes. A. C. (2014). Why Chinese hackers stole 4.5 million US hospital records. Gizmodo, August 18. http://gizmodo.com/why-chinese-hackers-stole-4-5-million-us-hospital-recor-1623284602.
55. Barbash, F. and Nakashima, E. (2014). Chinese hackers may have breached the federal government's personnel office, U.S. officials say. *Washington Post*, July 10. http://www.washingtonpost.com/news/morning-mix/wp/2014/07/09/report-chinese-hacked-into-the-federal-governments-personnel-office/.
56. Stableford, D. (2014). Syrian Twitter user reports U.S. airstrikes 30 minutes before Pentagon. *Yahoo News*, September 23. http://news.yahoo.com/us-syria-air-strikes-live tweets-130215331.html.
57. Stevick, E. and Writer, H. (2014). Monroe High School students hack into computer, raise grades. *Daily Herald*, May 29. http://www.heraldnet.com/article/20140529/NEWS01/140529125/1057/Monroe-High-School-students-hack-into-computer-raise-grades.
58. *Wall Street Journal*. (2014). Iran-based hackers reportedly target US officials for sanctions, anti-nuclear intelligence. May 29. http://www.foxnews.com/politics/2014/05/29/iran-based-hackers-reportedly-target-us-officials-for-sanctions-anti-nuclear/.
59. Winter, J. (2014). Hacker who helped feds gets no more time in prison. Fox News, May 27. http://www.foxnews.com/tech/2014/05/27/prosecutors-say-hacker-helped-thwart-hundreds-cyberattacks/.
60. Fox News. (2014). Chinese hackers reportedly sought data on US workers with security clearance. July 10. http://www.foxnews.com/politics/2014/07/10/chinese-hackers-reportedly-sought-data-on-us-workers-with-security-clearance/?intcmp=latestnews.
61. Emerson, C. (2014). The truth about free wi-fi. Fox Business, July 25. http://www.foxbusiness.com/2014/07/25/truth-about-free-wi-fi/?intcmp=fbfeatures.
62. Gibbs, S. (2014). Chinese hackers steal Israel's iron dome missile data. *Guardian*, July 29. http://www.theguardian.com/technology/2014/jul/29/chinese-hackers-steal-israel-iron-dome-missile-data.
63. Fox News. (2014). How to strengthen and secure your passwords in 7 simple steps. August 6. http://www.foxnews.com/tech/2014/08/06/how-to-strengthen-and-secure-your-passwords-in-7-simple-steps/?intcmp=obnetwork.
64. Dettmer, J. (2014). Digital jihad: ISIS, Al Qaeda seek a cyber caliphate to launch attacks on US. Fox News, September 14. http://www.foxnews.com/world/2014/09/11/digital-jihad-isis-al-qaeda-seek-cyber-caliphate-to-launch-attacks-on-us/.

65. Edwards, S. (2014). Global jihadists tweet in bid to recruit Ferguson protesters. Fox News, November 27. http://www.foxnews.com/us/2014/11/27/global-jihadists-tweet-in-bid-to-recruit-ferguson-protesters.

66. Ofer, O. (2014). DDoS 2.0: Hackers getting a taste of their own medicine. Radware Blog, November 17. http://blog.radware.com/security/2014/11/ddos-2-hackers-getting-a-taste/?utm_source=outbrain&utm_medium=link&utm_campaign=outbrain.

67. Fox News. (2015). US central command Twitter account back online after pro-ISIS hack. January 12. http://www.foxnews.com/politics/2015/01/12/twitter-account-for-us-central-command-hacked-filled-with-pro-isis-messages/.

68. Fox News. (2015). Anonymous declares war on Islamist extremists after terror attack in Paris. January 11. http://www.foxnews.com/tech/2015/01/11/anonymous-declares-war-on-islamist-extremists-after-terror-attack-in-paris/.

69. Ambrosino, M. (2014). *NOVA* (television program), October 8.

70. Quain, J. R. (2014). Hacked webcams: Is your home next? Fox News, November 21. http://www.foxnews.com/tech/2014/11/21/hacked-webcams-is-your-home-next/?intcmp=ob_homepage_tech&intcmp=obnetwork.

71. Cantor, M. (2014). How technology led to 12-year-old's abduction…and rescue. Newser, November 28. http://www.foxnews.com/tech/2014/11/28/how-technology-led-to-12-year-old-abduction-and-rescue/?intcmp=ob_homepage_tech&intcmp=obnetwork.

72. Gold, M. (2014). Taiwan probes Xiaomi on cyber security. Yahoo! News Canada, September 24. https://ca.news.yahoo.com/taiwan-government-investigates-xiaomi-potential-cyber-security-concerns-044430946--finance.html.

73. Lee, M.-J. (2014). Samsung devices get nod from US Defense Agency. *Wall Street Journal*, June 9. http://www.foxnews.com/tech/2014/06/09/samsung-devices-get-nod-from-us-defense-agency/?intcmp=obnetwork.

74. Blanchard, L. (2014). Take a peek: Biometric security offers relief from passwords. Fox News, June 9. http://www.foxbusiness.com/industries/2014/06/09/take-peek-biometric-security-offers-relief-from-passwords/?intcmp=obnetwork.

75. Rogers, J. (2014). BlackBerry launches cybersnooping counterattack. Fox News, July 29. http://www.foxnews.com/tech/2014/07/29/blackberry-launches-cyber-snooping-counter-attack/?intcmp=obnetwork.

76. Rashid, F. Y. (2014). How to secure your (easily hackable) smart home. Fox News, August 26. http://www.foxnews.com/tech/2014/08/26/how-to-secure-your-easily-hackable-smart-home/?intcmp=obnetwork.

77. Wagenseil, P. (2014). Spying cell towers may be spread across U.S. Yahoo.com, September 4. http://news.yahoo.com/spying-cell-towers-may-spread-123451560.html.

78. IB Times. 2014. Turing test bested, robot overlords creep closer to assuming control. June 9. https://www.yahoo.com/tech/turing-test-bested-robot-overlords-creep-closer-to-88270310244.html.

Chapter 4

Pre 9/11

The first edition of this book was written through the period up to 2002 and was published in 2002. The terrible tragedy of 9/11 took place in the final stages of the completion of the book. At the time of writing of the first edition, no one realized the profound effect on many aspects of life in the United States and around the world that the attacks of 9/11 would have, and it is understandable that in light of the attacks, the focus for security changed totally.

This chapter gives a condensed review of information warfare as it was understood before that hugely significant event and then goes on to look at the impact that the events of 9/11 had on the subject.

> I know not with what weapons World War III will be fought, but World War IV will be fought with sticks and stones.
>
> **Albert Einstein**

> It is obvious that the media war in this century is one of the strongest methods; in fact, its ratio may reach 90% of the total preparation for the battles.
>
> **Osama Bin Laden**

> You ask, what is our aim? I can answer in one word. It is victory, victory at all costs, victory in spite of all terror, victory, however long and hard the road may be; for without victory, there is no survival.
>
> **Winston Churchill**

Two unrelated but significant technologies made their appearance in the early 1970s. These were computers and precision-guided weapons. It can be argued that precision-guided weapons had been deployed from a much earlier time, but they developed significantly from the 1970s onward.

These developments helped to create an environment on the modern battlefield that is characterized by an increased lethality, range, and precision of fire and units that are smaller, more mobile, and more effective due to the better integration of technology.

To give some idea of the effect of precision-guided weapons, according to Hallion,[1] in 1944, during the Second World War, only 7% of all bombs dropped by the Eighth Air Force hit within 1000 ft. of their aim point; even a "precision" weapon such as a fighter-bomber in a 40° dive releasing a bomb at 7000 ft. could have a circular error probability (CEP) of as much as 1000 ft. It took 108 B-17 bombers, crewed by 1080 airmen, dropping 648 bombs to guarantee a 96% chance of getting just two hits inside a 400×500 ft. German power-generation plant; in contrast, in the Gulf War, a single strike aircraft with one or two crewmen, dropping two laser-guided bombs, could achieve the same results with essentially a 100% expectation of hitting the target, short of a material failure of the bombs themselves.

The advent of the computer provided the commander with a facility that he had not enjoyed for a considerable time—a real-time view of the battlefield. Historically, the commander found a vantage point on the top of a hill and directed the battle from there, but with increasingly sophisticated weapons with greater range, this had become unrealistic. The development of the computer and communications networks has again given the commander this facility. With the information age that computers and communication systems facilitated came sensors that could be deployed to provide an electronic view of the battlefield.

Writings around the year 2000 included terms such as information security and information dominance, and they showed an understanding that future wars would be predicated on knowledge; they also reflected that the fighting of battles in the future would be similar to the activities already taking place in the business world.

The range of operations that the modern armed forces may be engaged in covers a wide spectrum, including conventional war fighting, peace enforcement, peacekeeping, counterterrorism, humanitarian assistance, and support to civil authorities.

In January 1994, the then deputy secretary of defense, William Perry, established a group to coordinate a Department of Defense (DoD)–wide project on the revolution in military affairs. The aim of the group was to define the most plausible defense environment for the years 2010–2015 and to identify the most promising technologies and operational concepts. It was then to conduct war games to examine the impact of the findings on military operations.

The Revolution in Military Affairs (RMA) was defined in an Air University paper[2] as

A Revolution in Military Affairs (RMA) is a major change in the nature
of warfare brought about by the innovative application of new technologies which, combined with dramatic changes in military doctrine
and operational and organisational concepts, fundamentally alters the
character and conduct of military operations.

RMAs are undertaken for a variety of reasons, with the most obvious being a
change in technologies. Historic examples of this include the invention of gunpowder, the internal combustion engine, the submarine, the airplane, and the atom
bomb. The introduction of these technologies led to fundamental changes in the
way in which wars were fought.

RMAs are not just undertaken as a result of technology change, and an appropriate operational concept is just as important as technological development in
bringing about a revolution in military affairs. The Gulf War in early 1991 highlighted some of the key components of the revolution in military affairs that took
place later in the decade. The deployment of a range of new technologies was seen to
significantly enhance the coalition forces' ability to collect, exchange, and use information and demonstrated the benefit gained by denying the adversary the ability to
communicate with his forces. Also seen was the effect of the use of precision-guided
weapons, wherein new guidance systems resulted in the deployment of munitions
that could be delivered with a significantly improved level of precision and which
could be delivered by artillery, aircraft, or cruise missiles.

The greatly improved accuracy of guided munitions meant that a target could be
destroyed with one or two munitions rather than, as previously, a large-scale bombing
raid. This had a significant impact of the number of high-value assets (such as aircraft)
that needed to be deployed to achieve the destruction of the target and also reduced
the level of collateral damage caused. The use of stealth aircraft and cruise missiles
also had the additional advantage that it enabled some attacks against highly protected targets to take place with virtually no warning and at a greatly reduced risk to
one's own forces. One interesting aspect of the new technologies was that, for the first
time, journalists observing the conflict from both sides had instant access to global
communications and, on a number of occasions, those based in a hotel in Baghdad
reported live on TV that they were observing cruise missiles passing their location.

According to Bolkcom and Tatman,[3] during the Gulf War, 6,250 tons of
precision-guided munitions (PGMs) were used compared with 81,980 tons of
"dumb" bombs. Between 80% and 90% of the PGMs hit their targets compared
with about 25% of dumb bombs.

The significance of the value of information in the Gulf War was less obvious but of equal importance. A range of systems, including surveillance, reconnaissance, and intelligence gathering systems, including human, were deployed,
including both proven land, air, and space systems and a number of prototypes.
In addition, significant use was made of satellites, both military and commercial,
belonging to the United States, the United Kingdom, France, and Russia. In some

cases, the military were competing for bandwidth on commercial satellites with the news channels that were reporting their activities.

The satellites provided the coalition forces with communications, navigation, surveillance, intelligence, and early warning. Global positioning systems (GPS) enabled the coalition forces to navigate and locate targets with greater accuracy than the enemy.

The overall effect of the use of this range of new technologies for the first time was to create the need for an RMA to ensure that they were used to the best effect in the future. Throughout the conflict, both the Russians and the Chinese had observed the effect of the use of these new technologies, and this also caused them to undertake their own RMAs.

In a 1993 paper, General Gordon Sullivan, former chief of staff of the United States Army, and coauthor Lt. Col. James M. Dubik[4] categorized the current trends in military technology as

■ Greater lethality
■ Increased volume and precision of fire
■ Better integrative technology leading to increased efficiency and effectiveness
■ Increasing ability of smaller units to create decisive results
■ Greater invisibility and increased detectability

This highlighted a trend toward smaller, more lethal forces that were able to deliver a high volume of accurate fire through the integration of delivery systems with effective sensor and information distribution systems. The same integrated systems provided an improved capability for the detection of hostile forces.

As in the past, the RMA identified the emergence of new warfare areas. A warfare area is a form of warfare that has unique military objectives and is characterized by an association with particular forces or systems. In 1998, an Air University publication[2] identified four potential new warfare areas: long-range precision strike, information warfare, dominating maneuver, and space warfare.

The development of precision strike systems has been ongoing since the 1970s. The current generation of systems include cruise missiles that can be launched from land, sea, and air, and PGMs delivered by aircraft and artillery.

According to the Air University study,

> Precision strike, in the context of the ongoing RMA, is the ability to locate high-value, time-sensitive fixed and mobile targets; to destroy them with a high degree of confidence; and to accomplish this within operationally and strategically significant time lines while minimizing collateral damage, friendly fire casualties, and enemy counterstrikes.

The second new area that was identified was information warfare. The value of information (intelligence) in warfare has long been understood. However, as we moved into the "information age", characterized by an increasing reliance on information systems and ever increasing volumes of information available, the importance of information has never been greater. The range of systems that were becoming available included sensors, information-gathering systems such as reconnaissance and early-warning satellites, a wide variety of manned and unmanned air-based systems such as Airborne Warning and Control Systems (AWACS), and advanced information distribution and communications systems.

The potential value of information systems and the information that they contained were considered to be a "force multiplier" for conventional forces, but at the same time the use of, and reliance on, these systems was also a potential vulnerability. Imagine the situation of the US-led coalition fighting the Iraqi War if suddenly their computer systems were attacked by malware and ceased to function.

In 1996, the United States Defense Science Board produced a comprehensive assessment of the information warfare threat,[5] which identified a number of possible sources of information warfare threats:

- Incompetent, inquisitive, or unintentional blunderers, mischief-makers, and pranksters
- Hackers driven by technical challenge
- A disgruntled employee or unhappy customer intent on seeking revenge for some perceived wrong
- A crook interested in personal financial gain or stealing services
- A major organized crime operation interested in financial gain or in covering their crimes
- An individual political dissident attempting to draw attention to a cause
- An organized terrorist group or nation-state trying to influence US policy by isolated attacks
- Foreign espionage agents seeking to exploit information for economic, political, or military intelligence purposes
- A tactical countermeasure intended to disrupt a specific US military weapon or command system
- A multifaceted tactical information warfare capability applied in a broad orchestrated manner to disrupt a major US military mission
- A large organized group or major nation-state intent on overthrowing the United States by crippling the national information infrastructure

A 1997 report[6] also examined the potential for using just the information systems as a way of disrupting both civil and military information infrastructure. In open warfare, however, information warfare is taken to include the potential use of physically destructive means—such as missile attacks and bombing—to knock out key information assets.

Some analysts have added information warfare as a fourth dimension of warfare, joining the traditional three of air, land, and sea.

As first wave wars were fought over land, and second wave wars were fought over physical resources and productive capacity, the emerging third wave wars will be for the access to and control of knowledge.[7]

The third new area was that of dominating maneuver. While maneuver has always been a fundamental element of military operations, the RMA examined the potential for it to be conducted faster, with smaller, more agile forces and on a global scale.

According to the Air War College study, dominating maneuver was defined as the positioning of forces—integrated with precision strike, space warfare, and information war operations—to attack decisive points, defeat the enemy's "centers of gravity," and accomplish campaign or war objectives. These centers of gravity are key points in command, organization, resources, transport, and so on, whose loss would severely erode an opponent's ability to wage war.

Dominating maneuver differs from the traditional concepts of maneuver in a number of ways. In 1989, the DoD defined maneuver as the "employment of forces on the battlefield through movement in combination with fires, to achieve a position of advantage in order to accomplish the mission." Dominating maneuver encompasses the positioning of all the forces that could be brought to bear in a theater of operations and the integration of the three other new areas of warfare.

The fourth new area was that of space warfare. The potential for the use of space systems for communications had been understood for some time, but it was the development of real-time surveillance, reconnaissance, and targeting systems, along with precision navigation and meteorological data systems that could be integrated into military operations, that changed its importance.

One of the issues that has to be taken into account is that not all nations and their armed forces will have the resources to be able to take advantage of this revolution, and today's information-age army must be prepared to deal with a broad spectrum of threats, not only from nations with these capabilities but also from agrarian and industrial-age adversaries and from the new threat of terrorism.

The US Joint Vision 2020 (JV2020) provides a useful background for the consideration of electronic warfare on the digitized battlefield. JV2020 builds upon the findings of Joint Vision 2010 and had the goal of transforming US forces to create a force that was dominant across the full spectrum of military operations.

At this time, it was becoming increasingly clear that the range of actions in which the modern armed forces had to be able to defeat adversaries now included conventional warfighting, peace enforcement, peacekeeping, counterterrorism, humanitarian assistance, and civil support.

Information Warfare

While the information age and other new technologies produced a revolution in military operations that offered the commander who could gather and exploit information most effectively the potential of a decisive advantage on the modern battlefield, it was also becoming apparent that there were significant risks from this information revolution. As communications and information systems became increasingly vital to both the military and to civilian society, they have also become significant targets in war. The military adoption of information technology has created new vulnerabilities. The same information technologies that have enabled the networks that support the commander also provide a vector through which they can be attacked.

The automated command systems that are used to increase a commander's situational awareness may also be used by an adversary who can attack them by either denying information or creating uncertainty and doubt by manipulating the information.

A paper by Bryan Lewis[8] estimated that during 1995 alone, the DoD computers, estimated at the time to number around 2.1 million computers, had been the victim of as many as 250,000 electronic attacks. The paper went on to report that the Defense Information Systems Agency (DISA) had estimated that 65% of these attacks on the DoD computers and networks had been successful. These figures lead to the frightening conclusion that DoD networks and computers had been penetrated at least 162,500 times during 1995 alone. This works out at approximately 445 successful intrusions into DoD computers and networks every day. Lewis goes on to qualify these figures, as many of the 250,000 electronic attacks may have been harmless incorrect login attempts by legitimate users, but he concludes that the number is still alarming.

The modern battlefield depends heavily on the use of a wide range of the electromagnetic spectrum for surveillance and target acquisition, the exchange of and processing of information, or the destruction of an adversary's forces capability.

At the time of writing the first edition of this book, the terminology and techniques of IW were still relatively ill defined and, even now, still do not have universal agreement. The view in the United States was that the objective of IW was to attain a significant information advantage that enables the rapid domination and control of an adversary. The US Army also recognized that the definition of IW at the time was more narrowly focused on the impact of information during actual conflict, and it chose a broader approach to the impact of information on ground operations and adopted the term *information operations* (IO). The definition of IO that was adopted was that it integrated all aspects of information to support and enhance the elements of fighting power, with the goal of dominating the battlespace at the right time, at the right place, and with the right weapons or resources. IO was defined by FM100-6[9] as

> Continuous military operations within the military information environment that enable, enhance, and protect the friendly force's ability to collect, process, and act on information to achieve an advantage across the full range of military operations; IO include interacting with the global information environment and exploiting or denying an adversary's information and decision capabilities.

The JV2020 document also added that IO also includes actions taken in a non-combat or ambiguous situation to protect one's own information and information systems as well as those taken to influence target information and information systems.

The warfighting application of IW in military operations is called *command and control warfare (C2W)*. FM100-6 (1996) defines the aim of C2W as being to influence, deny information to, degrade, or destroy adversary C2 capabilities while protecting C2 capabilities.[9]

The concepts of C2W are well established and have been in use for a considerable time. The 1996 version of JP 3–13.1: Joint Doctrine for Command and Control Warfare (C2W) defines both information warfare (IW) and C2W:

> Information warfare (IW) capitalizes on the growing sophistication, connectivity, and reliance on information technology. The ultimate target of IW is the information dependent process, whether human or automated. Intelligence and communications support are critical to conducting offensive and defensive IW. IW supports the national military strategy but requires support, coordination, and participation by other United States Government departments and agencies as well as commercial industry.
>
> Command and control warfare (C2W) is an application of IW in military operations and employs various techniques and technologies to attack or protect a specific target set—command and control (C2). C2W is the integrated use of psychological operations (PSYOP), military deception, operations security (OPSEC), electronic warfare (EW), and physical destruction, mutually supported by intelligence, to deny information to, influence, degrade, or destroy adversary C2 capabilities while protecting friendly C2 capabilities against such actions. C2W is applicable throughout the range of military operations. Effective C2W provides the joint force commander (JFC) an ability to shape the adversary commander's estimate of the situation in the theater of operations and allows the JFC to process information through the C2 decision cycle faster than an adversary commander, which is crucial to gaining and maintaining the initiative in military operations. Applicability to combatant commander's staffs or subordinate joint forces may vary due to staff resources and responsibilities. Most staffs already have C2W planning and coordinating cells. Integration of C2W resources into the larger IW cell can facilitate deconfliction of compartmented and noncompartmented IW activities and provide planners more resources to support operational planning.

The document goes on to describe the elements of C2W:

> OPSEC denies critical information necessary for the adversary commander to estimate the military situation accurately;

psychological operations are vital to the broad range of US political, military, economic, and informational activities, including support of C2 during C2-attack and C2-protect operations;

military deception focuses on causing the adversary commander to estimate incorrectly the situation in the operational area with respect to friendly force dispositions, capabilities, vulnerabilities, and intentions; electronic warfare includes electronic warfare support, electronic attack, and electronic protection; and

physical destruction in support of C2W refers to the use of "hard kill" weapons or other means such as sabotage or covert actions against designated targets as an element of an integrated C2W effort.

Much of the confusion both then and now stems from the fact that at no point are the words "computer" or "network" used. The concepts of C2W predate these innovations and it is only the medium that has changed.

By the second half of the 1990s, the concepts of IW had been developed and were incorporated into the training of the military in exercises and education. In 1997, the US Joint Chiefs of Staff ordered the first ever no-notice interoperability exercise (NIEX) based on an IO scenario as part of the ELIGIBLE RECEIVER exercise series. ELIGIBLE RECEIVER 97–1showed the power of "social engineering" when the Red Team players managed to persuade DoD personnel to reveal information in addition to the large amount of valuable information that they were able to collect from the Internet on a daily basis. The exercise revealed significant vulnerabilities in DoD information systems and flaws in the actions taken in response to attacks on their information systems.

A major wake-up call came in February 1998, when analysts with the Air Force Computer Emergency Response Team (CERT) in San Antonio, Texas, noticed a number of intrusions into their computer networks from several academic institutions, including Harvard. The hackers, who turned out to be three teenagers, had exploited a weakness in the network's operating system. The attack was called "the most organized and systematic attack to date" on US military systems by then US Deputy Defense Secretary, John Hamre. Subsequent investigations revealed that the "attack" had been carried out by two youths from California, who became known as the "Cloverdale kids," and another youth in Israel (Ehud Tenebaum, known as "Analyzer"). The incident took place at a time of increased tension between the United States and Iraq, from which country the UN weapons inspectors had been expelled. The initial concern was that this attack had been initiated by Iraq. The investigation into the attack involved resources from the army, navy, air force, FBI, NASA, CIA, NSA, and others and took more than two weeks to identify the attackers. This attack highlighted the difficulty in attributing the source of a cyber attack and also the level of resources required to initiate one.

In December 1998, the DoD established a Joint Task Force on Computer Network Defense to defend the department's networks and systems "from intruders and other attacks."

At the end of the twentieth century, new terms such as network-centric warfare and cyber warfare started to become commonly used. The term network-centric warfare first seems to have appeared in late 1998 in a paper by VADM Cebrowski and John H. Garstka,[10] in which they recognized that, as a result of the "fundamental changes in American society and business, military operations increasingly will capitalize on the advances and advantages of information technology. Here at the end of a millennium we are driven to a new era in warfare. Society has changed. "The underlying economics and technologies have changed. American business has changed. We should be surprised and shocked if America's military did not." The paper goes on to identify that

> For nearly 200 years, the tools and tactics of how we fight have evolved with military technologies. Now, fundamental changes are affecting the very character of war. Who can make war is changing as a result of weapons proliferation and the fact that the tools of war increasingly are marketplace commodities. By extension, these affect the where, the when, and the how of war.

The paper also addresses the ongoing RMA and quotes the then chief of naval operations, Admiral Jay Johnson, who called it "a fundamental shift from what we call platform-centric warfare to something we call network-centric warfare."

Network-centric warfare and the associated revolutions in military affairs were a result of the new and developing technologies and changes in American society that, in part, they had enabled. These changes have been enabled and driven by the developing economics, information technology, and business processes and organizations and had resulted in a shift in focus from the platform to the network and a recognition of the importance of making strategic choices to adapt and survive in the changing environment.

Cyber Warfare

By 2000, in the United States, the structures and organizations that would be required for cyber warfare were being put in place. By the end of 1998, the Joint Task Force-Computer Network Defense (JTF-CND) had reached its initial operational capability. Then, in 1999, under the Unified Command Plan, the president assigned the CND mission to the US Space Command, with the JTF-CND as the subordinate command responsible for executing CND operations. In 2000, the US Space Command was also given responsibility for computer network attack (CNA) missions. This was to enable the coordinating of all military space operations, including missile warning, communications, navigation, weather, and surveillance from DoD, civil, and commercial satellite systems. This allocation of joint responsibility for both CNA and CND was explained as being due to the growing understanding that during armed conflicts, military forces need to use information technologies to accomplish their military objectives in the context of the law of armed conflict, denying our adversary the ability to use their computer networks to conduct military operations.

In a news report from Space Command,[11] it was stated that CNA operations may also be used in other situations. An example was given of combating terrorist threats when appropriate authority was in place. The article went on to say that the integration of CNA into a broader military operation would help US military forces to prevail on future battlefields. In some instances, CNA might allow an operation to succeed with less loss of life and physical destruction.

The Chinese View

Around this time, the Chinese were also undergoing an RMA and were starting to identify cyber warfare in their military doctrine, organization, and training. The Chinese view of warfare is significantly different to that in the West and is based on both the *people's warfare* concept and the old 36 stratagems. The Chinese view is also heavily influenced by Marxist-Leninist concepts and has a strong emphasis on deception, knowledge-based warfare, and gaining an asymmetric advantage. The Chinese approach is that of developing battalion-size *net force* units supported by a large reserve force of experts (thought to be from the universities). The Chinese had been carrying out cyber-warfare exercises since the late 1990s.

The Russian View

The Russian view at this time was that the threat of cyber warfare ranked second only to nuclear warfare, and, as early as 1995, V. I. Tsymbal[12] was quoted as saying:

> from a military point of view, the use of information warfare against Russia or its armed forces will categorically not be considered a non-military phase of a conflict whether there were casualties or not

Tsymbal goes on to say that

> Russia retains the right to use nuclear weapons first against the means and forces of information warfare, and then against the aggressor state itself

On September 12, 2000, Russian President Vladimir Putin announced the Russian Information Security Doctrine. The new doctrine gives the government an enhanced legal framework for dealing with computer crime and the assurance of security in cyber space. The new doctrine was also, in part, an attempt by the Russian government to deal with cyber threats from both foreign and domestic sources.

Impact of the Attacks on September 11, 2001

The attacks on the World Trade Center and the Pentagon that took place on 9/11 led the way for a change from the old Cold War concepts of symmetric warfare to the new environment of asymmetric warfare. The US DoD Joint Vision 2020 document[13] that was published in the summer of 2000 discussed asymmetric conflict and recognized, prophetically, that it would have increased significance in the future. A relevant extract from the document says

> We have superior conventional warfighting capabilities and effective nuclear deterrence today, but this favorable military balance is not static. In the face of such strong capabilities, the appeal of asymmetric approaches and the focus on the development of niche capabilities will increase. By developing and using approaches that avoid US strengths and exploit potential vulnerabilities using significantly different methods of operation, adversaries will attempt to create conditions that effectively delay, deter, or counter the application of US military capabilities.
>
> The potential of such asymmetric approaches is perhaps the most serious danger the United States faces in the immediate future—and this danger includes long-range ballistic missiles and other direct threats to US citizens and territory. The asymmetric methods and objectives of an adversary are often far more important than the relative technological imbalance, and the psychological impact of an attack might far outweigh the actual physical damage inflicted. An adversary may pursue an asymmetric advantage on the tactical, operational, or strategic level by identifying key vulnerabilities and devising asymmetric concepts and capabilities to strike or exploit them. To complicate matters, our adversaries may pursue a combination of asymmetries, or the United States may face a number of adversaries who, in combination, create an asymmetric threat. These asymmetric threats are dynamic and subject to change, and the US Armed Forces must maintain the capabilities necessary to deter, defend against, and defeat any adversary who chooses such an approach. To meet the challenges of the strategic environment in 2020, the joint force must be able to achieve full spectrum dominance.

What the joint vision document did not envisage was a totally new type of threat, that of the Muslim extremist, which became apparent in the form of

Al Qaeda. All of the thinking and planning that had been carried out was based on an enemy that had a tangible base and a nation-state affiliation. Al Qaeda was to be a new type of threat that had no specific home base.

Summary

In the period up to the start of the twenty-first century, the concepts of IW had been developing for a number of years, and the military forces of a number of countries had started to include it in military doctrine and training and had recognized that the use of IW could have a potentially devastating effect on both a conflict and also on the infrastructure of a nation-state. The vulnerabilities of the military and national infrastructure had been repeatedly exposed through high-profile hacking attacks and through coordinated tests and exercises, and efforts had been made to improve the detection of attacks and the restoration of affected systems.

A range of new terms also came into common use, including IO, CNA, CND, cyber warfare (cyberwar, cyberwarfare), information assurance, and many more. As with IW itself, many of these terms were not well defined, nor was the responsibility for their application.

References

1. Hallion, R. P. (1995). Precision guided munitions and the new era of warfare, Australian Power Studies Centre Paper Number 53. Fairbairn, Australia: Air Power Studies Centre.
2. McKitrick, J., et al. (1998). *The Battlefield of the Future—21st Century Warfare Issues*, Chapter 3, The revolution in military affairs, p. 1. Air University, http://aupress.maxwell.af.mil/digital/pdf/book/b_0064_schneider_grinter_battlefield_future.pdf.
3. Bolkcom, C. and Tatman, J. A. (1997). *US Military R&D (Jane's Special report)*, Jane's Information Group, p. 175.
4. Sullivan, G. R. and Dubik, J. M. (1993). *Land Warfare in the 21st Century*. Carlisle, PA: Strategic Studies Institute.
5. Andrews, D. P. (1996). Report of the Defense Science Board Task Force on Information Warfare–Defense, Office of the Under Secretary of Defense for Acquisition and Techology, November 1996. Washington, DC. http://cryptome.org/iwdmain.htm.
6. NAA Science and Technology Committee. (1997). Information warfare and the millenium bomb [AP 237 STC (97) 7]. Lord Lyell, General Rapporteur, September 1.
7. Toffler, A. and T. Heidi. (1993). *War and Anti-War: Survival at the Dawn of the 21st Century*. Boston: Little, Brown.
8. Lewis B.C. (n.d.). Information warfare, Federation of American Scientists, http://fas.org/irp/eprint/snyder/infowarfare.htm.
9. Department of the Army. (1996). *Information Operations. US Army Field Manual FM100-6*. Washington, DC: HQ, Department of the Army.

10. VADM Cebrowski, A. K. and Garstka, J. J. (1998). USN. Director, Space, Information Warfare, Command and Control (CNO-N6). In *Proceedings on Network Centric Warfare—Its Origins and Future*, January 1998, p. 29.
11. *Space Daily*. 2000. US Space Command takes charge of computer network attack. Peterson AFB, October 2, 2000. http://www.spacedaily.com/news/milspace-00n.html.
12. Tsymbal, V.I. (1996). Kontseptsiya 'Informatsionnoy voyny', (Concept of information warfare). Speech given at the Russian–U.S. Conference on Evolving Post Cold War National Security Issues, Moscow, September 12–14, 1995 (cited in Col. Thomas, T., Russian views on information-based warfare, *Airpower Journal* special issue, July 1996).
13. United States Department of Defense. 2011. Joint Vision 2020, http://www.docstoc.com/docs/98469559/Joint-Vision-2020.

Chapter 5

Effect of 9/11 and US Homeland Security (DHS)

In this chapter, the US governmental changes caused by 9/11 and the new digital battlefield will be addressed.

> Let your plans be dark and impenetrable as night, and when you move, fall like a thunderbolt.

> **Sun Tzu**
> *The Art of War¹*

This chapter looks back at the ramifications of the terrorist attack on the World Trade Center in New York City on September 11, 2001, focusing on the reorganization of the US federal government agencies to support combating terrorists in the future and on the new digital battlefield.

Some think that *homeland security* displaced information warfare (IW) and the funding and attention to IW dropped as the Department of Homeland Security (DHS) became the "thing." A look at DHS (liberally quoted from their websites) is a good introduction to the way in which the United States is attempting to combat terrorists and other sensitive, national security–related activities.

Since the United States is the "world leader" and has led the world economically, militarily, and politically (at least until the current administration took, some may argue, less of a leadership role in the world), we will focus on the US government's changes relating to their focus on global information warfare (GIW), specifically as it relates to what was once the number one enemy after 9/11 (although that priority seems to have been somewhat clouded with time and the new administration treating some acts of terrorism as a function of law enforcement and an example of "workplace violence"): terrorists, which changed how the United States saw the world after 9/11.

This focus has been chosen because generally the nation-states of the world either follow the US lead or change their approach to that of an adversary or rival of the United States. Furthermore, it is believed that the world is still basically US-centric—countries around the world also responded in a similar manner and in reality, the United States was at the forefront, so we will discuss what happened from a US and DHS perspective.

The 9/11 Attack

On September 11, 2001, 19 Islamic terrorists linked to the group called Al Qaeda hijacked four airliners in order to carry out suicide attacks against the United States. One plane crashed into the US Department of Defense headquarters, known as the Pentagon; two others flew into the twin towers of the World Trade Center in New York City; and one plane crashed in a field in Pennsylvania after being taken over by some of its passengers. It is thought that this plane was to crash into the White House or the Congress building. Known forevermore as "9/11," the attacks resulted in the deaths of more than 3000 people.[2]

The attacks caused an immediate change of US focus and started initiatives and the restructuring of the US federal government to fight terrorism, including all the IW resources needed to support such efforts.

The United States attacked terrorists and their supporters in Afghanistan and Iraq; this is well documented and there is no need to go through that here. Suffice to say that of course all means available, including IW, were used to attack the Al-Qaeda terrorist group at that time. Some may think it still is the global terrorist leader, while others argue that ISIS has taken its place.

> The Islamic State of Iraq and the Levant (ISIL/'aısəll'), also translated as the Islamic State of Iraq and Syria (ISIS/'aısıs/; ad-Dawlah al-Islāmīyah fīl-'Iraq wa ash-Shlām), also known by the Arabic acronym Daʿish and self-proclaimed as the Islamic State (IS), [a] is a Sunni, extremist, jihadist rebel group controlling territory in Iraq and Syria. It has been designated as a terrorist organization by the United Nations, the European Union, the United Kingdom, the United States, Australia, Canada, Turkey, Saudi Arabia, Indonesia, the UAE and Israel.[3]

Effect of 9/11 on US Government and Homeland Security

Using a typical old twentieth-century management approach to meet twenty-first-century challenges, the bureaucrats of the US government decided to reorganize the departments using the same old twentieth-century organizational structure as in the past: a top-down hierarchy.

The theory was apparently that the threat could have been stopped if the agencies responsible for intelligence collection and counterintelligence actives within the US government would have broken down the political and legal barriers and shared information.* A commendable objective, but placing entire agencies under other agencies does not make it so.

Reaction to the World Trade Center and Pentagon Attacks

The following case shows the dangers of "vigilantes" and people who, with the best of intentions, take actions for which they have not researched the background information. The action in question was reported on September 27, 2001, by Brian McWilliam of Newsbytes,[4] who revealed that members of a coalition of vigilante hackers had mistakenly defaced the website of an organization that had had offices in the World Trade Center. The hacker group, called the Dispatchers, attacked the website of the Special Risks Terrorism Team.

The other sites that were attacked by this group were both in Iran, which, for the geographically challenged, is not in Afghanistan and is in fact hostile to the Taliban regime and Osama bin Laden. In fact, today, the US government is allegedly trying to work with Iran to help mitigate some of the threats in the regions; for example, ISIS.

One can understand the anger and frustration and the desire to strike out in the aftermath of the attacks, but this type of action by uninformed and nonrepresentative individuals does much to damage relationships with countries and organizations that have not (at least in recent years) caused any offense and are in fact may even be sympathetic to the cause.

US Homeland Security (DHS) Overview†

Let us look at the DHS and by doing so gain some insight as to the logic the United States is using; for example, its GIW battle plan in its war against "all enemies foreign and domestic."

Homeland Security Act of 2002[5]

> Title I: Department of Homeland Security
> Section 101. Executive Department; Mission
> (a) Establishment. "There is established a Department of Homeland Security, as an executive department of the United States within the meaning of title 5, US Code.

---

* At least the authors' opinion and voiced by others in and out of US government.
† The following information is quoted for the most part directly from the DHS website.

    (b)   Mission:
        (1) In General. The primary mission of the Department is to:
            (a)   Prevent terrorist attacks within the United States;
            (b)   Reduce the vulnerability of the United States to terrorism; and
            (c)   Minimize the damage, and assist in the recovery, from terrorist attacks that do occur within the United States." (From the Homeland Security Act of 2002)[6]

The focus of DHS is to be on terrorism; however, it can be asked whether that is still true today and, if it is, whether the terms *terrorism* and *terrorist* have been expanded. For example, is it an act of terrorism for a high-school student to shoot his fellow students?

Another excerpt from the USHS website states

> On May 23, 2012 President Obama issued Presidential Memorandum,- Building a Twenty-first Century Digital Government. The CIO released the strategy entitled "Digital Government Building a 21st Century Platform to Better Serve the American People", which provides agencies with a 12-month roadmap that focuses on priority areas enabling a more efficient and coordinated digital service delivery. The Department of Homeland Security will use this initiative in order to:
>
> ■ Enable the citizens of America to better leverage government data to spur innovation across our Nation and improve the quality of services for the American people,
> ■ Ensure we seize the opportunity to procure and manage smart devices, applications, and data safely, securely, and efficiently,
> ■ Unlock the power of data and be ready to deliver and receive digital information and services anytime, anywhere and on any device.
>
> The technology landscape is changing very rapidly. The introduction of Cloud Computing, Agile Development and Mobility has provided new and innovative ways to deliver value in Information Technology within the Federal Government. The DHS is working diligently to align with the White House's Digital Government Strategy. DHS is committed to enabling better utilization of departmental data to improve the quality of services to the American people. DHS will develop services that leverage the unique capabilities of mobile computing and promote innovation while maintaining enhanced security.

Do you see the word "terrorism" anywhere in the above "DHS Digital Strategy"? As government agencies tend to do, they expand the bureaucracy, are given more tasks, and may lose sight of why they were formed in the first place. One can see this coming when so many agencies with various missions, all of which maybe have some part in the war on terrorism mission, go about their business trying to fulfill all their mission statements.

Our Mission: Overview

The vision of homeland security is to ensure a homeland that is safe, secure, and resilient against terrorism and other hazards.

Three key concepts form the foundation of our national homeland security strategy, which is designed to achieve this vision:

■ Security
■ Resilience
■ Customs and exchange

In turn, these key concepts drive broad areas of activity that the Quadrennial Homeland Security Review (QHSR) process defines as homeland security missions. These missions are enterprise-wide, and not limited to the DHS. These missions and their associated goals and objectives tell us in detail what it means to prevent, to protect, to respond, and to recover, as well as to build in security, to ensure resilience, and to facilitate customs and exchange.

Hundreds of thousands of people from across the federal government; state, local, tribal, and territorial governments; the private sector; and other nongovernmental organizations are responsible for executing these missions. These are the people who regularly interact with the public, who are responsible for public safety and security, who own and operate our nation's critical infrastructures and services, who perform research and develop technology, and who keep watch, prepare for, and respond to emerging threats and disasters. These homeland security professionals must have a clear sense of what it takes to achieve the overarching vision articulated above.

The Core Missions*

There are five homeland security missions:

1. Prevent terrorism and enhancing security
   Protecting the American people from terrorist threats is our founding principle and our highest priority. The DHS's counterterrorism responsibilities focus on three goals:
   – Prevent terrorist attacks

---

* Quoted from DHS[7]; More on the DHS mission can be found in the Quadrennial Homeland Security Review (QHSR).

- Prevent the unauthorized acquisition, importation, movement, or use of chemical, biological, radiological, and nuclear materials and capabilities within the United States
- Reduce the vulnerability of critical infrastructure and key resources, essential leadership, and major events to terrorist attacks and other hazards

2. Secure and manage our borders

The DHS secures the nation's air, land, and sea borders to prevent illegal activity while facilitating lawful travel and trade. The department's border security and management efforts focus on three interrelated goals:

- Effectively secure US air, land, and sea points of entry
- Safeguard and streamline lawful trade and travel
- Disrupt and dismantle transnational criminal and terrorist organizations

3. Enforce and administer our immigration laws

The department is focused on the smart and effective enforcement of US immigration laws while streamlining and facilitating the legal immigration process.

The department has fundamentally reformed immigration enforcement, prioritizing the identification and removal of criminal aliens who pose a threat to public safety and targeting employers who knowingly and repeatedly break the law.

4. Safeguard and secure cyber space

The department has the lead for the federal government for securing civilian government computer systems, and it works with industry and state, local, tribal, and territorial governments to secure critical infrastructure and information systems. The department works to

- Analyze and reduce cyber threats and vulnerabilities
- Distribute threat warnings
- Coordinate the response to cyber incidents to ensure that our computers, networks, and cyber systems remain safe

5. Ensure resilience to disasters

The DHS provides a coordinated, comprehensive federal response in the event of a terrorist attack, natural disaster, or other large-scale emergency while working with federal, state, local, and private-sector partners to ensure a swift and effective recovery effort. The department builds a ready and resilient nation through efforts to

- Bolster information sharing and collaboration
- Provide grants, plans, and training to our homeland security and law-enforcement partners
- Facilitate rebuilding and recovery along the Gulf Coast

In addition, they department says it must "specifically focus on maturing and strengthening the homeland security enterprise itself".

Its tasks include

- Global aviation security
- Cargo screening

- Enhancing national preparedness and supporting state and local law enforcement
- Strengthening international partnerships
- Critical infrastructure protection
- Trade
- Trusted traveler programs
- Border security results
- Combating cyber crime
- Securing cyber networks
- Cyber-security results
- Planning and preparing for disasters
- Disaster response and recovery
- Department grants
- Disasters results (learning from disasters and improving the preparedness and response)

Of course one can make a case for all such tasks being associated with terrorism; for example, a plane flying into a building requires disaster response and recovery. US borders need to be controlled so terrorists do not sneak into the country. How is that working for them as "illegals" cross the porous US borders by the thousands?

> oversight report on the Department of Homeland Security…found major problems…not successfully executing any of its five main missions… spends more than $700 million annually to lead the federal government's efforts on cybersecurity, but struggles to protect itself, federal and civilian networks from the most serious cyberattacks.[8]

You can even go to their website and get a portrait of the secretaries of the DHS (past and present). If terrorists wanted to target the secretary, they can get a color photo of that person to hand out to all members of that assassination team. No need for covert stakeouts to get a photo.

Yes, one can argue that these are public figures and have bodyguards, and so on. However, do they have to make it easy for terrorists?

Department Components

The following list contains the components, directorates, and offices with websites or web pages on DHS.gov that currently make up the DHS (Exhibit 5.1).

US Citizenship and Immigration Services

US Citizenship and Immigration Services (USCIS) secures America's promise as a nation of immigrants by providing accurate and useful information to our customers, granting immigration and citizenship benefits, promoting an awareness and understanding of citizenship, and ensuring the integrity of our immigration system (Exhibit 5.2).

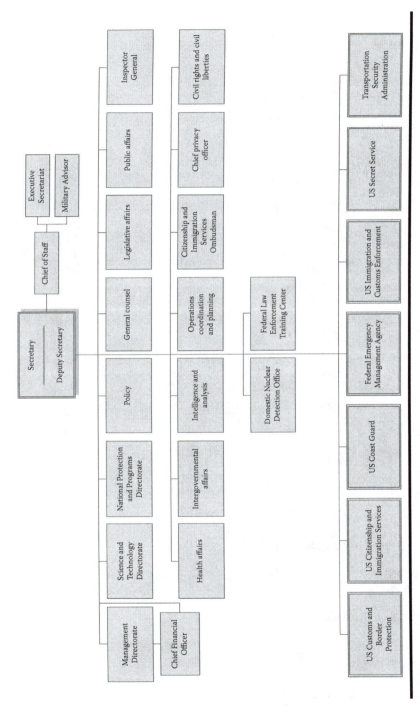

Exhibit 5.1   US Department of Homeland Security.

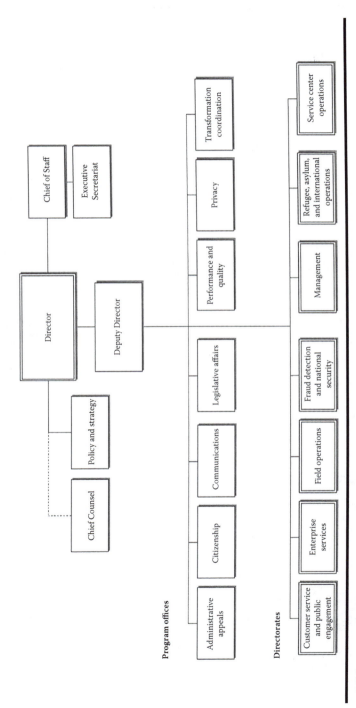

Exhibit 5.2 US Citizenship and Immigration Services.

US Customs and Border Protection

US Customs and Border Protection (CBP) is one of the DHS's largest and most complex components, with a priority mission of keeping terrorists and their weapons out of the United States. It also has responsibility for securing and facilitating trade and travel while enforcing hundreds of US regulations, including immigration and drug laws (Exhibit 5.3).

US Coast Guard

The US Coast Guard (USCG) is one of the five armed forces of the United States and the only military organization within the DHS. The USCG protects the maritime economy and the environment, defends our maritime borders, and saves those in peril (Exhibit 5.4)

Federal Emergency Management Agency

The Federal Emergency Management Agency (FEMA) supports our citizens and first responders to ensure that as a nation we work together to build, sustain, and improve our capability to prepare for, protect against, respond to, recover from, and mitigate all hazards (Exhibit 5.5).

Federal Law Enforcement Training Center

The Federal Law Enforcement Training Center (FLETC) provides career-long training to law-enforcement professionals to help them fulfill their responsibilities safely and proficiently (Exhibit 5.6).

US Immigration and Customs Enforcement

US Immigration and Customs Enforcement (ICE) promotes homeland security and public safety through the criminal and civil enforcement of federal laws governing border control, customs, trade, and immigration (Exhibit 5.7).

Transportation Security Administration

The Transportation Security Administration (TSA) protects the nation's transportation systems to ensure freedom of movement for people and commerce (Exhibit 5.8).

US Secret Service

The US Secret Service (USSS) safeguards the nation's financial infrastructure and payment systems to preserve the integrity of the economy, and it protects national

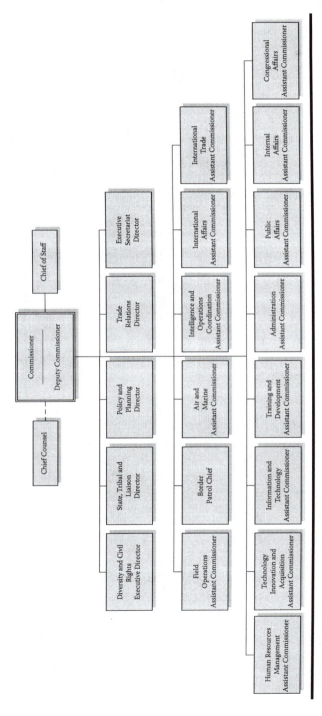

Exhibit 5.3 US Customs and Border Protection.

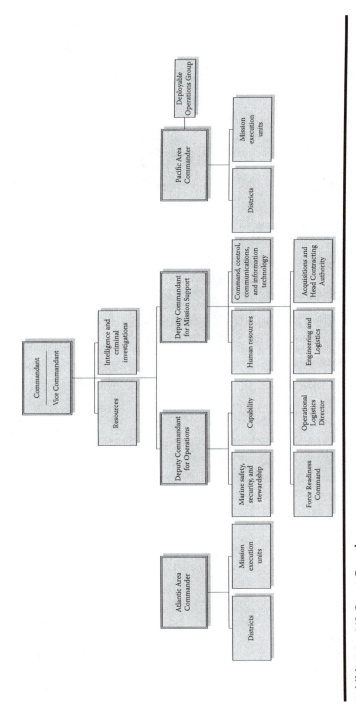

Exhibit 5.4 US Coast Guard.

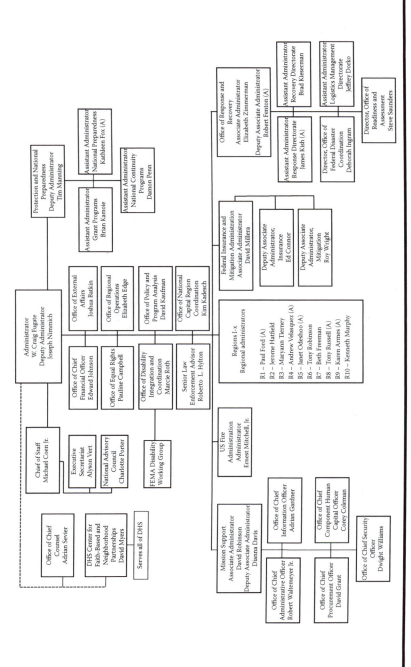

Exhibit 5.5   US Department of Homeland Security/Federal Emergency Management Agency.

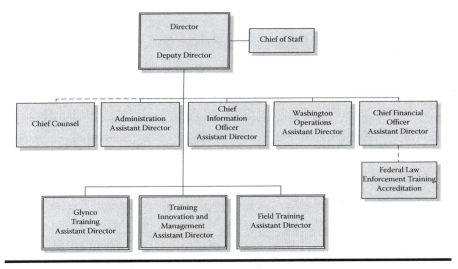

Exhibit 5.6   Federal Law Enforcement Training Center.

leaders, visiting heads of state and government, designated sites, and national special security events (Exhibit 5.9).

Management Directorate

The Management Directorate is responsible for department budgets and appropriations, expenditure of funds, accounting and finance, procurement, human resources, information technology systems, facilities and equipment, and the identification and tracking of performance measurements (Exhibit 5.10).

National Protection and Programs Directorate

The National Protection and Programs Directorate (NPPD) works to advance the department's risk-reduction mission. Reducing risk requires an integrated approach that encompasses both physical and virtual threats and their associated human elements (Exhibit 5.11).

Science and Technology Directorate

The Science and Technology Directorate (S&T) is the primary research and development arm of the Department. It provides federal, state, and local officials with the technology and capabilities to protect the homeland (Exhibit 5.12).

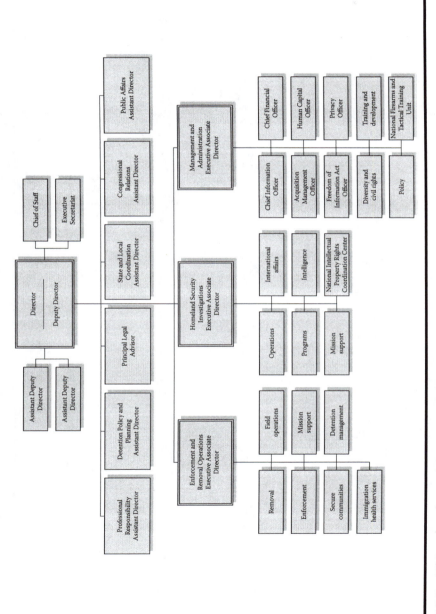

Exhibit 5.7   US Immigration and Customs Enforcement.

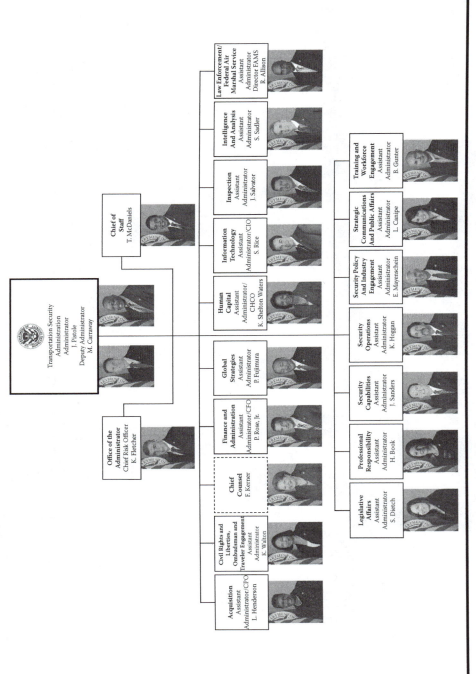

Exhibit 5.8 Senior Leadership Organization Chart.

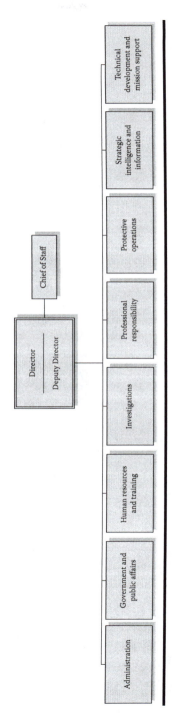

Exhibit 5.9   US Secret Service.

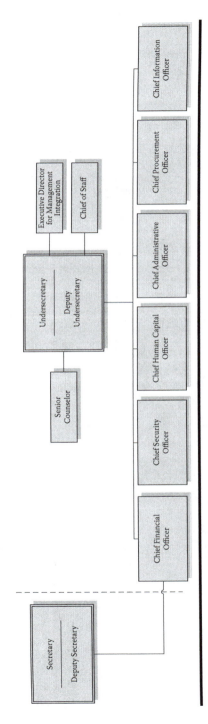

Exhibit 5.10 Management Directorate.

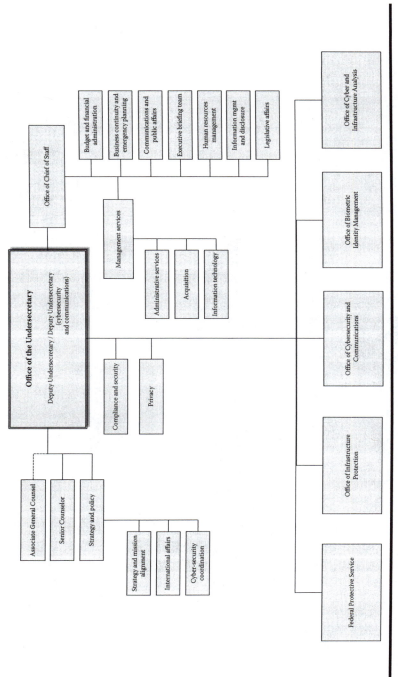

Exhibit 5.11 National Protection and Programs Directorate.

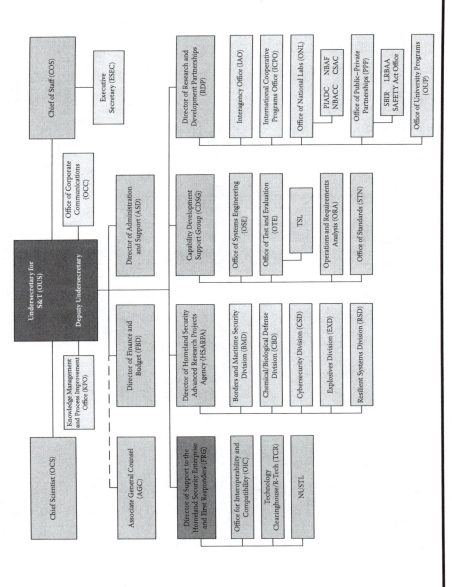

Exhibit 5.12 Science and Technology Directorate.

Domestic Nuclear Detection Office

The Domestic Nuclear Detection Office (DNDO) works to enhance the nuclear detection efforts of federal, state, territorial, tribal, and local governments, as well as the private sector, and to ensure a coordinated response to such threats (Exhibit 5.13).

Office of Health Affairs

The Office of Health Affairs (OHA) coordinates all the medical activities of the DHS to ensure appropriate preparation for and response to incidents having medical significance (Exhibit 5.14).

Office of Intelligence and Analysis

The Office of Intelligence and Analysis (I&A) is responsible for using information and intelligence from multiple sources to identify and assess current and future threats to the United States (Exhibit 5.15).

Office of Operations Coordination and Planning

The Office of Operations Coordination and Planning is responsible for monitoring the security of the United States on a daily basis and coordinating activities within the department and with governors, homeland security advisors, law-enforcement partners, and critical infrastructure operators in all 50 states and more than 50 major urban areas nationwide (Exhibit 5.16).

Office of Policy

The Office of Policy is the primary policy formulation and coordination component for the DHS. It provides a centralized, coordinated focus to the development of department-wide, long-range planning to protect the United States (Exhibit 5.17).

As you delve further into the DHS organizational charts, you will find more layers of this massive bureaucracy. Furthermore, it apparently has lost its focus as *the* terrorist fighting organization and has become deluded as to its primary mission and has basically become the federal government almost in its entirety (at least in the author's opinion).

The US Department of Defense also has its GIW organizations. In fact, each military service has its own:

> The *Joint Information Operations Warfare Center (JIOWC)* supports the Joint Staff in improving DOD ability to meet combatant command information-related requirements, improve development of information-related capabilities, and ensure operational integration and coherence across combatant commands and other DOD activities.

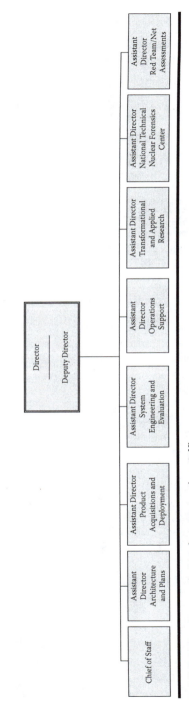

Exhibit 5.13 Domestic Nuclear Detection Office.

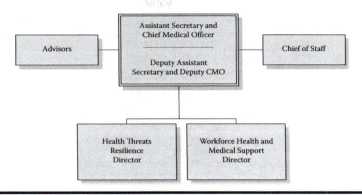

Exhibit 5.14   Office of Health Affairs.

IO involves the integrated employment, during military operations, of information-related capabilities in concert with other lines of operation to influence, disrupt, corrupt, or usurp the decision-making of adversaries and potential adversaries while protecting our own. They apply across all phases of an operation, the range of military operations, and at every level of war. They are a critical factor in the joint force commander's capability to achieve and sustain the level of information superiority required for decisive *joint operations.*

Located at Lackland AFB, Texas, the JIOWC's mission is to assist in planning, coordinating and executing information operations. The center deploys information operations planning teams worldwide at a moment's notice to deliver tailored, highly skilled support and sophisticated models and simulations to joint commanders, joint task forces and the *Joint Staff.*

Direct support is provided to unified commands, joint task forces, functional and service components, and subordinate combat commanders. Support is also provided to the Office of the *Secretary of Defense*, the Joint Staff, the services and other government agencies. The JIOWC has a balanced mixture of personnel from all four military services, the civil service and three allied nations.[9]

Mission

The US Army John F. Kennedy Special Warfare Center and School, the US Army's Special Operations Center of Excellence, trains, educates, develops and manages world-class Civil Affairs, Psychological Operations and Special Forces warriors and leaders in order to provide the Army special operations forces regiments with professionally trained, highly educated, innovative and adaptive operators.

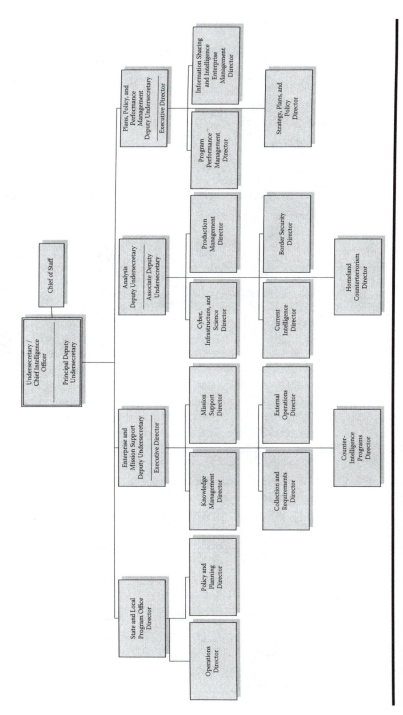

Exhibit 5.15 Office of Intelligence and Analysis.

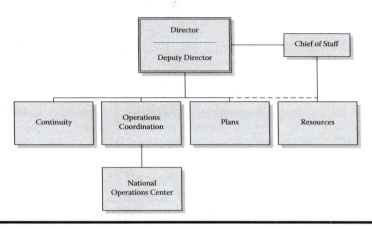

Exhibit 5.16   Office of Operations Coordination and Panning.

Vision

Professionalism starts here. We are an adaptive institution character-ized by agility, collaboration, accountability and integrity. We promote life-long learning and transformation. We are THE Special Operations Center of Learning whose credibility in producing the world's finest special operators is recognized and sustained by every single member of our three regiments.[10]

Air Force Information Warfare Center

The Air Force Information Warfare Center (AFIWC), collocated with the Air Intelligence Agency, was created to be an information superiority center of excellence, dedicated to offensive and defensive counterinformation and information operations.

AFIWC was originally activated as the 6901st Special Communication Center in July 1953. The following month, the 6901st was redesignated as the Air Force Special Communications Center. It was then redesignated as the Air Force Electronic Warfare Center in 1975.

Air-force successes in exploiting the enemy information systems during Desert Storm led to the realization that the strategies and tactics of command and con-trol warfare could be expanded to the entire information spectrum and could be implemented as information warfare. In response, the AFIWC was activated on September 10, 1993, combining technical skills from the former AFEWC, the Air Force Cryptologic Support Center's Securities Directorate; and intelligence skills from the former Air Force Intelligence Command. AFIWC's team of 1000 military and civilian personnel are skilled in the areas of operations, engineering,

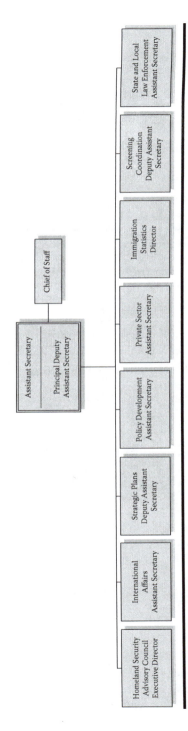

Exhibit 5.17   Office of Policy.

operations research, intelligence, radar technology, communications, and computer applications.

The members are dedicated to providing improved C2W/IW capabilities to the warfighting US Air Force major commands.

Mission

The mission of AFIWC is to explore, apply and migrate offensive and defensive IW capabilities for operations, acquisition and testing; and provide advanced IW training for the Air Force.

The AFIWC provides IW services to the warfighter in contingencies and exercises through quantitative analysis, modeling and simulation, data-base and technical expertise in communication and computer security. The AFIWC is divided into eight directorates:

Advanced Programs
Communications-Computer Systems
C2W Information
Engineering Analysis
Mission Support
Systems Analysis
Operations Support
Information Warfare Battlelab

The newest directorate, the *Information Warfare Battlelab*, supports the full spectrum of Air Force operations by rapidly identifying innovative and superior ways to plan and employ IW capabilities; organize, train, and equip Air Force IW forces; and influence development of IW doc-trine and tactics. *Advanced Programs* foster the development and employment of advanced IW capabilities using a multi-disciplined approach. They explore and advance technologies, techniques, talents and tactics for IW applications. Developing multi-disciplined (scientific, technical, intelligence and operation) solutions, they provide support for emerging warfare techniques.

Communications-Computer Systems provides the command, control, communication, computer and information systems infrastructure to support all AFIWC mission areas. SC develops C4I systems architecture and initiates programs for their implementation or acquisition.

Using all-source data, **C2W Information** develops, builds, extracts and integrates standardized C2W data into the Air Force Extended Integrated Data Base architecture. DB addresses the issues of control, quality assurance planning, training, development, deployment, technical support and implementation of new databases.

Engineering Analysis provides technical guidance in the areas of computer security during the development of information, sensor and weapon systems including in- depth analysis and electromagnetic measurements of aircraft.

The Air Force **Computer Emergency Response Team** is the Air Force's global command center for handling worldwide networked computer system security issues. The AFCERT is the single point in the Air Force for reporting networked computer intrusions and problems. AFCERT responded to 47 computer security incidents in 1996 and expanded its internal security database connectivity and capabilities. They educated worldwide Air Force and Department of Defense customers on computer security topics and provided assistance to other computer security organizations.

Mission Support maintains the research library that provides analysts, engineers and scientists with vital information for projects and studies. They also promote aware-ness of AFIWC capabilities through marketing and business development and provide a centralized education and training activity for the center. Additionally, they manage AFIWC safety, security, facilities and contracting functions.

The scientists and engineers of **Systems Analysis** provide quantitative analysis through modeling and simulation of offensive and defensive IW systems capabilities and vulnerabilities. SA develops and operates engineering, platform, mission, and campaign models for analysis of information, sensor and weapon systems. Evaluating vulnerabilities of US Air Force radar, communications, navigation, and IW systems; SA helps the warfighter to understand the potential vulnerabilities of friendly weapon systems, C2W systems and space systems. This understanding allows the warfighter to develop tactics and procedures to counter current, future and reactive threats.

Operations Support trains, equips and deploys personnel to provide IW and intelligence to the warfighter during contingencies, special operations and exercises. Deployable information warfare support teams provide planning support for operations security, military deception, command and other operations to Air Operations Centers and Joint Force Air Component Commanders.

In addition to these directorates are the staff support. Intelligence Requirements, Management Support and Technology Management Support complete the infrastructure, allowing AFIWC to strive for information dominance and supply the warfighter with the services needed in contingencies and exercises.[11]

Naval Network Warfare Command (NETWARCOM) is the US Navy's information operations, *intelligence*, networks and space unit. Its mission is to execute, under the Commander TENTH Fleet

Operational Control, is to operate and defend the Navy's portion of the Global Information Grid and to deliver reliable, secure Net-centric and Space warfighting capabilities in support of strategic, operational and tactical missions across the Navy.[12]

Summary

These digital battlefield centers and GIW organizations also fight terrorism and other adversaries of the United States. They also have intelligence and counterintelligence organizations, which are also used to fight terrorism and collect information as part of a GIW mission. One wonders if DHS and other US government agencies are putting political and power fights aside in an effort to more effectively and deficiently fight terrorism and other adversaries on the global digital battlefield. We doubt it.

The military GIW units are given in more detail in Chapter 6.

References

1. Tzu, S. *The Art of War* quotes. http://www.goodreads.com/work/quotes/3200649---s-nz-b-ngf.
2. History.com. 2010. 9-11 attacks. http://www.history.com/topics/9-11-attacks.
3. *Wikipedia*. Islamic State of Iraq and the Levant. http://en.wikipedia.org/wiki/Islamic_State_of_Iraq_and_the_Levant.
4. McWilliams, B. (2001). Hacking vigilantes deface WTC victim's site, Newsbytes. September 17. http://www.securityfocus.com/news/252.
5. DHS (Department of Homeland Security). (2012). Homeland Security Act of 2002. http://www.dhs.gov/homeland-security-act-2002.
6. DHS (Department of Homeland Security). (2002). Public Law 107–296.
7. DHS (Department of Homeland Security). (2012). Our mission. http://www.dhs.gov/our-mission.
8. Fox News (2015). Oversight report finds major problems with DHS. January 3. http://www.foxnews.com/politics/2015/01/03/oversight-report-finds-major-problems-with-dhs/.
9. *Wikipedia*. Joint Information Operations Warfare Center. http://en.wikipedia.org/wiki/Joint_Information_Operations_Warfare_Center.
10. US Army. US Army John F. Kennedy Special Warfare Center and School. http://www.soc.mil/swcs/.
11. Air Force Information Warfare Centre. http://fas.org/irp/agency/aia/cyberspokesman/97aug/afiwc.htm.
12. NETWARCOM (Naval Network Warfare Command). http://www.netwarcom.navy.mil/.

Chapter 6

Nation-State Defensive and Offensive Information Warfare Capabilities: North America

In this and the next five chapters, we look at the current, known levels of information operations (IO) capability in a number of nations and organizations around the world. There has been significant change since the first edition of this book was published, and a number of countries have now developed or are considering developing capability. None of this should be a surprise, as we live in a world that is increasingly dependent on high-tech, and the protection of the critical infrastructure is of increasing importance to everyone. The nations that have been reviewed were those that were considered by the authors to be either those with the most advanced capabilities or those that were of the most interest. This is not intended to be a comprehensive review, and there are certainly more countries that either already have capability or are developing it.

In this chapter, we look at North America.

Canada

Doctrine and Strategy

Canada has a National Cyber Security Strategy that was published in 2010, which states that "The Government is continuing its efforts to help secure Canada's cyber systems and protect Canadians online." The Canadian Government has established the Canadian Cyber Incident Response Centre (CCIRC) in order to monitor the Internet, provide advice on how cyber threats can be mitigated, and to "coordinate the national response to any cyber security incident." This strategy is built on three pillars:

- Securing government systems
- Partnering to secure vital cyber systems outside the federal government
- Helping Canadians to be secure online

Canada also has a defense strategy, and the Canada First Defence Strategy of June 2008 outlines one of the roles of the Canadian Forces:

> In such a complex and unpredictable security environment, Canada needs a modern, well-trained and well-equipped military with the core capabilities and flexibility required to successfully address both conventional and asymmetric threats, including terrorism, insurgencies and cyber attacks.

The Canadian defense strategy calls on the Department of National Defence and Canadian Forces (DND/CF) to strengthen its capacity to defend its own networks, work with other government departments to identify threats and possible responses, and work with allies to exchange best practices and develop policy and frameworks for the military aspects of cyber security.

In April 2011, the chief of the Canadian Defence Staff established a permanent Director General cyber space organization. This directorate is tasked with identifying and developing future cyber capabilities, including designing and building cyber capabilities. It incorporates the Canadian Forces Cyber Task Force with ongoing support from Level 1 organizations across the DND/CF. The DND/CF works in collaboration with the Communications Security Establishment (CSE) Canada and Shared Services Canada.

The Canadian National Defence Land Operations Manual, published in 2008,[1] contains a section on IO, which is defined in the manual as

> coordinated actions to create desired effects on the will, understanding and capability of adversaries, potential adversaries and other approved parties in support of overall objectives by affecting their information, information based processes and systems while exploiting and protecting one's own.

This definition is consistent with the one used in NATO doctrine.

The manual states that IO is conducted in three core activity areas: influence activity, which is the primary means of influencing will; countercommand activity, which counters information and command-related capability; and information protection activity, which safeguards friendly information, thereby inhibiting an adversary's understanding. The manual goes on to state that there are several capabilities, tools, and techniques that form the basis of most IO activity. They include psychological operations (PsyOps); presence, posture, and profile (PPP); operations security (OPSEC), information security (INFOSEC), deception, electronic warfare (EW), physical destruction, and computer network operations (CNO). The manual goes on to say that

> It is important to note that only when tools and techniques are used directly to influence will, affect understanding, or affect a decision-maker's command, control, communications, computer, intelligence, surveillance and reconnaissance (C4ISR) capability, they can be deemed part of Info Ops activity.

Defensive

Communications Security Establishment Canada

CSE is the Canadian equivalent of the National Security Agency (NSA) in the United States. Its mission and vision statements are

- ■ Mission: To provide and protect information of national interest through leading-edge technology, in synergy with our partners.
- ■ Vision: Safeguarding Canada's security through information superiority.

The role of CSE is given as:

> CSE is one of Canada's key security and intelligence organizations and focused on collecting foreign signals intelligence in support of the Government of Canada's priorities, and on helping protect the computer networks and information of greatest importance to Canada.

The CSE also provides assistance to federal law-enforcement and security organizations when they require its technical capabilities.

Canadian Cyber Incident Response Centre

The mandate for the CCIRC is that, in support of Public Safety Canada's mission to build a safe and resilient Canada, it contributes to the security and resilience of the vital cyber systems that underpin Canada's national security, public safety, and economic prosperity. CCIRC is Canada's national coordination center for the prevention and mitigation of, preparedness for, response to, and recovery from cyber events. It does this by providing authoritative advice and support and by coordinating information sharing and event response.

Canadian Armed Forces

Canadian Forces Information Operations Group

The Canadian Forces have an Information Operations Group that is part of the joint staff at the national headquarters and is located within the Canadian Forces Network Operations Centre (CFNOC). The Canadian army has an electronic warfare center and a network operation center to support military cyber capabilities.

Canadian Forces Network Operations Centre

The role of the CFNOC is to maintain IT services under all conditions and to operate, defend, and manage national systems and networks at all classifications. Its role is split into six areas:

- National systems operations
- Incident management
- Computer network defense
- Security operations
- ITI situational awareness
- Problem management

Canadian Forces Electronic Warfare Centre

The Canadian Forces Electronic Warfare Centre provides EW support to the Canadian forces through the use of a national database, electronic orders of battle to front-line troops, and deployable coordination and liaison.

21 Electronic Warfare Regiment (21 EW Regt) trains army EW operators and support personnel for the Canadian forces. This is a reserve EW squadron within the Canadian forces that is a part of the Regular Forces Regiment.

Offensive

Canada does not claim to have any offensive capability.

Research and Development

Defence Research and Development Canada

Defence Research and Development Canada (DRDC) is an agency of Canada's Department of National Defence (DND). DRDC states its mission thus:

DRDC provides DND, the Canadian Armed Forces and other government departments as well as the public safety and national security communities, with the knowledge and technological advantage needed to defend and protect Canada's interests at home and abroad.

The DRDC focus areas for cyber-related military activities fall into three areas:

- Capabilities for operating in the cyber environment
- Trust and confidence for conducting operations in the cyber environment
- Resilient networks and systems in a contested environment

Exercises

Cyber Storm Biannual Exercise Series

Cyber Storm I took place in 2006. Participants included the United States, the United Kingdom, Canada, Australia, and New Zealand. The scenario was an exercise overseen by the US Department of Homeland Security (DHS) to test the nation's defenses against digital espionage.

Participants of Cyber Storm II, which took place in 2008, were from the United States, the United Kingdom, Canada, Australia, and New Zealand, and they also included about 40 private-sector companies. The scenario for the exercise was a the launch by "persistent, fictitious adversaries" of an extended attack using websites, e-mail, phones, faxes, and other communications systems.

Cyber Storm III took place in 2010. Participants were from Australia, Canada, France, Germany, Hungary, Japan, Italy, the Netherlands, New Zealand, Sweden, Switzerland, and the United Kingdom and included more than 60 private-sector companies. The scenario for the exercise was to look at what happens when the infrastructure is unavailable and to see how organizations could respond.

United States

Doctrine and Strategy

In 2009, a subunified command of the US Strategic Command, the United States Cyber Command (USCYBERCOM), was established, and it became fully operational in October 2010. In 2010, the Pentagon formally recognized cyber space as the fifth domain of warfare, indicating that the US military considered cyber space to be equal in importance to military operations to the land, sea, air, and space domains.

New Strategy

A paper by William J. Lynn III,[2] the then US Deputy Secretary of Defense, gave the new Pentagon cyber strategy and explained that for Cyber Security, Cyber Command has three missions. First, it leads the day-to-day protection of all defense networks and supports military and counterterrorism missions with operations in cyberspace. Second, it provides clear and accountable way to marshal cyberwarfare resources from across the military. A single chain of command runs from the US president to the secretary of defense to the commander of Strategic Command to the commander of Cyber Command and on to individual military units around the world. To ensure that considerations of cybersecurity are a regular part of training and equipping soldiers, Cyber Command oversees commands within each branch of the military, including the Army Forces Cyber Command, the U.S. Navy's Tenth Fleet, the 24th Air Force, and the Marine Corps Forces Cyberspace Command. Because military networks are not impervious to attack, a critical part of the training mission is to ensure that all operational forces are able to function in a degraded information environment.

Cyber Command's third mission is to work with a variety of partners inside and outside the U.S. government. Representatives from the FBI, the Department of Homeland Security, the Justice Department, and the Defense Information Systems Agency work on-site at Cyber Command's Fort Meade headquarters, as do liaison officers from the intelligence community and from allied governments. In partnership with the Department of Homeland Security, Cyber Command also works closely with private industry to share information about threats and to address shared vulnerabilities. Information networks connect a variety of institutions, so the effort to defend the United States will only succeed if it is coordinated across the government, with allies, and with partners in the commercial sector.

Given the dominance of offense in cyberspace, U.S. defenses need to be dynamic. Milliseconds can make a difference, so the U.S. military must respond to attacks as they happen or even before they arrive. To grapple with this, the Pentagon has deployed a system that includes three overlapping lines of defense. Two are based on commercial best practices—ordinary computer hygiene, which keeps security software and firewalls up to date, and sensors, which detect and map intrusions. The third line of protection leverages government intelligence capabilities to provide highly specialized active defenses. And the government is deploying all these defenses in a way that meets its obligation to protect the civil liberties of U.S. citizens.

In July 2011, Deputy Lynn articulated a "five pillar" strategy for USCYBERCOM. The first pillar is to recognize that the new domain of cyber space is of equal importance to the other domains in the battlespace (land, sea, air, and space). The second pillar is the use of proactive (active) defenses as opposed to just passive defense. The third pillar is critical infrastructure protection (CIP) to ensure the protection of critical infrastructure. The fourth pillar is the use of collective defense, which would enable the early detection of threats and their incorporation into the cyber-warfare defense operations. The fifth pillar is to maintain and enhance and leverage US technological dominance and improve the acquisitions process.

In 2012, the United States made significant changes in its cyber-security policies with the introduction of Presidential Decision Directive 20 on US Cyber Operations Policy. The directive is classified, but the fact sheet for it states that

> "This policy is part of the Administration's focus on cybersecurity as a top Priority" and that "The policy establishes principles and processes for the use of cyber operations so that cyber tools are integrated with the full array of national security tools we have at our disposal."

The policy also states that it takes into account the evolution of the threat and the experience that has been gained. The policy makes it clear that it is a whole-of-government approach consistent with US values that have been promoted both domestically and internationally, and which have previously been articulated in the International Strategy for Cyberspace.

As a result of the presidential directive, USCYBERCOM, which was originally only responsible for dealing with threats to the military cyber infrastructure, may now have a wider national cyber-defense responsibility.

USCYBERCOM's mission is to plan, coordinate, integrate, synchronize, and conduct activities to direct the operations and defense of specified Department of Defense (DoD) information networks; to prepare to, when directed, conduct full-spectrum military cyber space operations (CSO) in order to enable actions in all domains; and to ensure US/allied freedom of action in cyber space and deny the same to our adversaries. According to a report in Defesetech,[3] USCYBERCOM has stated that it is developing a wide range of cyber weapons. These weapons will give cyber commanders a wide range of options when it comes to offensive and defensive retaliation. The capabilities that are being developed will include tools that would allow US cyber forces to deceive, deny, disrupt, degrade, and destroy information and information systems.

In a statement made before the Senate Committee on Armed forces on 27 February, 2014, by General Keith B. Alexander, the commander of USCYBERCOM, stated that

> USCYBERCOM is a subunified command of U.S. Strategic Command in Omaha, Nebraska though based at Fort Meade, Maryland. It has approximately 1,100 people (military, civilians, and contractors) assigned with a Congressionally-appropriated budget for Fiscal Year 2014 of approximately $562 million in Operations and Maintenance

(O&M), Research, Development, Test and Evaluation (RDT&E), and military construction (MILCON). USCYBERCOM also has key Service cyber components: Army Cyber Command/Second Army, Marine Forces Cyberspace Command, Fleet Cyber Command/Tenth Fleet, and Air Forces Cyber/24th Air Force. Together they are responsible for directing the defense ensuring the operation of the Department of Defense's information networks, and helping to ensure freedom of action for the United States military and its allies—and, when directed, for defending the nation against attacks in cyberspace. On a daily basis, they are keeping U.S. military networks secure, supporting the protection of our nation's critical infrastructure from cyber attacks, assisting our combatant commanders, and working with other U.S. Government agencies tasked with defending our nation's interests in cyberspace.

According to a US Air Force presentation,[4] the air force contribution to USCYBERCOM resources, as of 2013, was to provide 1,715 billets/39 teams. At that time there were 451 existing cyber billets tasked for FY13 and a shortfall of 166. A total of 1,264 billets were to be sourced, assigned, filled, and trained in FY14-16.

Defensive

Defensive cyber-command units include:

Army Forces Cyber Command
24th Air Force
Fleet Cyber Command
Marine Corps Forces Cyberspace Command

In addition, in 2010, in order to facilitate cooperation, the DoD and the DHS, which is responsible for government networks and working with the private sector, signed a memorandum of agreement on cyber security to increase interdepartmental collaboration.

At around the same time as the creation of USCYBERCOM, the US Air Force reported that it had transferred at least 30,000 troops from communications and electronics assignments to "the front lines of cyber warfare," and the Pentagon announced that "The US Army will consolidate 21,000 soldiers in its cyber warfare units under a new unified command led by a three-star general." Army Forces Cyber Command (ARFORCYBER) "will be fully operational by October at Fort Belvoir," with the aim of achieving "unprecedented unity of effort and synchronization of Army forces operating within the cyber domain."

Offensive

On the creation of the USCYBERCOM in 2010, the Joint Functional Component Command for Network Warfare (JFCC-NW), which had been in existence since 2005, was merged into USCYBERCOM. It is responsible for coordinating offensive CNO for the US DoD.

Subordinate to the JFCC-NW are the Joint Task Force-Global Network Operations (JTF-GNO) and the Joint Information Operations Warfare Center (JIOWC), both of which have direct responsibility for defense against cyber attack. The JTF-GNO defends the DoD Global Information Grid, while the JIOWC supports combatant commands with an integrated approach to IO. These include OPSEC, PsyOps, military deception, and EW. The JIOWC also coordinates network operations and network warfare with the JTF-GNO and with JFCC-NW.

Known Units

Detailed below is a list of US military units that are involved in IO. The details below were all taken from a single, open-source document from the Army War College.[5] We wish that other nations were as helpful!

Army Cyber Command

1st Information Operations Command (1st IO Cmd)

The 1st IO Cmd is a major subordinate command to the US Army Intelligence and Security Command (INSCOM) but is under the operational control and tasking of Army Cyber Command/2d US Army.

Mission: The mission of the 1st IO Cmd is to provide IO support to the army and other military forces through deployable IO support teams, IO reachback planning and analysis, and the synchronization and conduct of army CNO in coordination with other CNO and network operations stakeholders. In addition, it is responsible for operationally integrating IO, reinforcing forward IO capabilities, and defending cyber space in order to enable IO throughout the information environment.

Army Reserve Information Operations Command

The Army Reserve Information Operations Command (ARIOC) is subordinate to the US Army Reserve Joint & Special Troops Support Command (USARJSTSC) and is operationally tasked through the Army G-3 (Director of Operations, Readiness and Mobilization) and Forces Command (FORSCOM).

Mission: The mission of ARIOC is to undertake CNO in support of Army and Joint Commands to achieve information superiority of cyber space.

US Army Information Proponent Office

The US Army Information Proponent Office (USAIPO) is responsible for the development of capabilities and capacity across Army Doctrine, Organizations, Training and Education, Materials, Leadership, Personnel, and Facilities (DOTMLPF), which leverage the power of information to achieve mission success across the unified land operations.

Combined Arms Center (CAC) Capability Development Integration Directorate (CDID)—Information Proponent Office (IPO)

Mission: The mission of this body is to integrate capabilities and capacity across DOTMLPF to meet the Army's requirement for the successful planning, integration, and execution of Information Operations in full-spectrum operations.

US Marine Corps Forces Cyberspace (MARFORCYBER)

The Marine Corps established MARFORCYBER in October 2009.

Mission: MARFORCYBER's mission, in addition to its standard service component responsibilities, is to plan, coordinate, integrate, synchronize, and direct the Marine Corps' full spectrum of CSO. This includes DoD information network (DoDIN) operations, Defensive Cyber Operations (DCO), and the planning and execution of Offensive Cyberspace Operations (OCO). These operations support the Marine Air-Ground Task Force (MAGTF) and joint and combined cyber space requirements that enable freedom of action across all warfighting domains and deny the same to adversarial forces.

MARFORCYBER Subordinate Units

Marine Corps Network Operations and Security Center The Marine Corps Network Operations and Security Center (MCNOSC) provides the engineering functions for the effective integration and use of hardware, software, and computer network practices of the Marine Corps Enterprise Network (MCEN) and is responsible for the Marine Corps' network defense infrastructure.

Mission: The mission of MCNOSC is to direct global network operations and the computer network defense of the MCEN and to provide technical leadership in support of marine and joint forces operating worldwide. The MCNOSC is also responsible for intelligence gathering and analysis to develop future capabilities planning in accordance with DCO. The MCNOSC is the Computer Network Defense Service Provider (CNDSP) and is also the Marine Corps' Global Network Operations and Security Center (GNOSC). Under the Operational Control (OPCON) of MARFORCYBER, the MCNOSC conducts information network operations (NETOPS) and DCO in support of Marine Corps operational requirements in order to enhance freedom of action across all warfighting domains, while denying the efforts of adversaries to degrade or disrupt this advantage through cyber space.

Company L, Marine Cryptologic Support Battalion (MCSB) Company L is under the OPCON of MARFORCYBER **Mission**: Its mission is to plan and

conduct OCO in support of Service, Joint and combined cyberspace requirements. Company L may also provide support to defensive CSO.

Marine Corps Information Operations Center The Marine Corps IO Center is subordinate to Deputy Commandant for Plans, Policies and Operations (DC, PP&O) IO Planning Teams and Expeditionary PSYOP

resources will, in most cases, be attached to supported MAGTFs during operational deployments, including predeployment exercises via the Request for Forces (RFF) process.

The Marine Corps Information Operations Center (MCIOC) provides operational support to the MAGTF and provides IO subject-matter expertise in support of USMC IO to enable the effective integration of IO into Marine Corps operations.

Navy Information Operations Organizations

Fleet Cyber Command

The Fleet Cyber Command is an Echelon II Command reporting to the Chief of Naval Operations (CNO). The Fleet Cyber Command serves as the navy component command to the Strategic Command and Cyber Command, and the Navy's Service Cryptologic Component commander under the National Security Agency (NSA)/Central Security Service.

The US 10th Fleet is the operational arm of Fleet Cyber Command and executes its mission through a task force structure similar to other warfare commanders. It provides operational direction through its Maritime Operations Center, which has command and control (C2) over assigned forces in support of navy or joint missions in cyber/networks, information operations, EW, cryptologic/signals intelligence, and space.

Mission: The mission of Fleet Cyber Command is to direct Navy CSO globally to deter and defeat aggression and to ensure freedom of action to achieve military objectives in and through cyber space. Its mission also includes the organization and direction of navy cryptologic operations worldwide and support for information operations and space planning and operations and to manage the navy's portion of the Global Information Grid; to deliver integrated cyber IO, cryptologic, and space capabilities; and to deliver global navy cyber common operational picture.

Navy Cyber Forces Command

In October 2014, the Navy Cyber Forces Command (CYBERFOR) transitioned into a new organization known as Navy Information Dominance Forces. Navy Cyber Forces is the Type Commander for the navy's global cyber resources of around 14,000 sailors and civilians. CYBERFOR has a headquarters staff of approximately 600 and provides forces and equipment in cryptology/signals intelligence, cyber, EW, IO, intelligence, networks, and space.

Mission: The mission of CYBERFOR is to carry out all aspects of the organization and management of capabilities for command and control architecture/ networks, cryptologic and space-related systems and intelligence and IO activities, and to coordinate with type commanders to deliver interoperable, relevant, and ready forces.

Air Force Intelligence, Surveillance and Reconnaissance Agency

Mission: The mission of the Air Force Intelligence, Surveillance and Reconnaissance Agency is to deliver decisive advantage by providing and operating integrated cross-domain Intelligence, Surveillance and Reconnaissance (ISR) capabilities in coordination with service, joint, national, and international partners. Its vision is to be the preeminent ISR enterprise, providing the right ISR to the right person at the right time.

480th Intelligence, Surveillance, and Reconnaissance Wing

The 480th ISR Wing is the Air Force team responsible for leading the development of timely and relevant ISR from a variety of platforms in direct support of combat operations, air force leaders, key coalition partners, and combatant commanders worldwide. Its capabilities include global C2 for the collection, processing, exploitation, and dissemination of ISR data from the U-2 "Dragon Lady," RQ-4 "Global Hawk," MQ-1 "Predator" and MQ-9 "Reaper," in addition to numerous other ISR platforms, using the Air Force Distributed Common Ground System weapon system. The wing also conducts real-time cryptologic and SIGINT in direct support of combat operations and combatant commanders worldwide. The wing was activated on December 1, 2003.

70th Intelligence, Surveillance, and Reconnaissance Wing

The 70th ISR Wing is responsible for the integration of air force capabilities into global cryptologic operations, directly supporting national-level decision makers, combatant commanders, and tactical warfighters. The wing works closely with the NSA/Central Security Service, leveraging the Internet-centric capabilities of a worldwide cryptologic enterprise to conduct national missions and enable national-tactical integration for joint and combined air force combat operations around the world. The wing includes six intelligence groups in the United States, Pacific, and European theaters.

National Air and Space Intelligence Center

The National Air and Space Intelligence Center (NASIC) is the primary DoD producer of foreign air and space intelligence. NASIC supports warfighters, force modernizers and national policy makers with predictive intelligence products that integrate all available sources of intelligence data. The center analyzes the characteristics and performance of foreign weapons systems, assesses the capabilities and intent of potential adversaries, and serves as a national node for the processing, exploitation and dissemination of intelligence data from around the world. NASIC has four intelligence analysis groups and 18 squadrons, all located in its main complex at Wright-Patterson AFB.

361st Intelligence, Surveillance and Reconnaissance Group

The 361st ISR Group provides specialized ISR capabilities to the Air Force Special Operations Force community. They train, equip, and present more than 250 airmen to provide specialized SOF ISR forces for worldwide employment.

Air Force Technical Applications Center

The Air Force Technical Applications Center (AFTAC) carries out nuclear treaty monitoring and nuclear event detection. AFTAC provides national authorities with quality technical measurements to monitor nuclear treaty compliance and performs research and development of new proliferation detection technologies to enhance or assist treaty verification, thus limiting the proliferation of weapons of mass destruction and preserving the nation's security. AFTAC became operational in 1973.

Headquarters 24th Air Force

The 24th Air Force (24 AF) is the air force's operational warfighting organization responsible for conducting the full range of cyber operations. 24 AF establishes, operates, maintains, and defends the air force–provisioned portion of the DoD network to ensure the joint war fighter can maintain the information advantage while prosecuting military operations. The 24 AF is subordinate to Air Force Space Command (AFSPC). AFSPC was assigned the cyber mission when 24 AF was established in August 2009. AFSPC is 24 AF's "Organize, Train and Equip" entity, which has the role of enabling 24 AF to meet its operational mission requirements. AFSPC also provides a range of support services, including operational analysis, research and development, and training and education support to 24 AF.

Mission: The 24 AF mission is to extend, operate, and defend the air force portion of the DoD network and to provide full-spectrum capabilities for the joint war fighter in, through, and from cyber space.

Units subordinate to the 24th Air Force include

- 624th Operations Center. The 24 AF executes C2 over the AFNet and AF Cyber forces through the 624 Operations Center. The 624 OC is the single inject point for operational cyber taskings for the AF. The 624 OC's organizational structure is aligned with its operational counterparts (AOCs) to facilitate integration of 24 AF capabilities into the supported CCDR's existing structure.
- 67th Network Warfare Wing. The 67th Network Warfare Wing (67 NWW) executes the integrated planning and employment of military capabilities to achieve the desired effects across the interconnected analog and digital portion of the Battlespace—Air Force Network Ops. The wing's Cyber Warriors conduct network operations through the dynamic combination of hardware, software, data, and human interaction, which involves time-critical, operational-level decisions that direct configuration changes and information routing.
- 688th Information Operations Wing. The 688th Cyberspace Wing (688th CW) delivers proven information operations and engineering infrastructure capabilities integrated across air, space, and cyberspace. This wing is made up of two groups, the 38th Cyberspace Engineering Installation Group and the 318th Cyberspace Operations Group, creating a multidisciplined organization. Its mission is stated as being to deliver proven information operations, engineering and infrastructure capabilities integrated across air, space, and cyberspace domains.
- 689th Combat Communications Wing. The 689th Combat Communications Wing (689 CCW) is located at Robins Air Force Base, Warner Robins, Georgia. The 689 CCW's mission statement is to deliver combat communications for the joint/coalition war fighter supporting combat operations and humanitarian relief operations.

Research and Development

Within the United States, there have been a large number of military, defense, and academic organizations that have answered the call for research and development (R and D) in the area of IO.

As in most countries, the majority of the effort in research and development in the area of IO is for defense. As a result, funding is from a range of sources. One of the major sources of funding in the United States is the National Science Foundation. In 2013, more than 110 new cyber-security research projects were funded in 33 states, with award amounts ranging from about $100,000 to $10 million.

The Defense Advanced Research Projects Agency (DARPA) runs a Cyber Grand Challenge (CGC), which will utilize a series of competitions to test the abilities of a new generation of fully automated cyber-defense systems. The 2014 CGC has been set up to create a new generation of autonomous cyber-defense capabilities. This program aims to identify effective, integrated automation of cyber-reasoning tasks for the protection of compiled test software operated on a closed, monitored network.

The Cyber Systems and Technology Group (formerly the DARPA Intrusion Detection Evaluation Group), under DARPA and Air Force Research Laboratory (AFRL/SNHS) sponsorship, has collected and distributed the first standardized dataset for the evaluation of computer network intrusion detection systems.

In May 2012, DARPA announced the Plan X program, in which experts conduct novel research in the cyber domain and seek to create revolutionary technologies that will help the cyber workforce understand, plan, and manage DoD cyber missions in large-scale, dynamic network environments. According to DARPA's Plan X website, the program does not create cyber weapons or fund research and development efforts in vulnerability analysis.

DARPA has also contributed to the interagency Comprehensive National Cybersecurity Initiative, which aims to safeguard federal government information systems from cyber threats and attacks with the National Cyber Range (NCR). In January 2010, DARPA announced that it has moved to the second phase of its NCR program. This program aims to assess the readiness of the nation's cybersecurity systems and networks. The announcement stated that two contracts for Phase II had been awarded to Johns Hopkins University for $24,777,235 and to Lockheed for $30,803,319 in order to continue the program.

While by no means a complete list, the organizations listed below are all known to be carrying out education, training, research, and/or development in this area.

The US Army 1st Information Operations Command

This provides IO support to the army and other military forces. Its functional areas include IO intelligence, reachback teams, deployable IO support teams, and IO training. The OPSEC Support Element (OSE) is the primary coordinator for the army OPSEC programs, planning, training, assessments, policy, incident response team, and mission integration throughout the army.

Joint Special Operations University (JSOU)

JSOU is the educational component of US Special Operations Command (USSOCOM). The JSOU mission is to educate SOF executive, senior, and intermediate leaders and selected other national and international security decision makers, both military and civilian, through teaching, outreach, and research in the science and art of joint special operations. JSOU conducts research through its Strategic Studies Department. The stated mission of JSOU is to provide fully capable special operations forces to defend the United States and its interests and to plan and synchronize operations against terrorist networks.

United States Army Communications-Electronics Research, Development and Engineering Center (CERDEC)

The stated aim of the United States Army Communications-Electronics Research, Development and Engineering Center (CERDEC) Intelligence and Information Warfare Directorate (I2WD) is to provide effective intelligence and information warfare tools that equip US soldiers with the integrated systems needed to ensure information dominance, and it focuses on quick-reaction capabilities. This is achieved by transitioning new technologies into systems for rapid deployment in the field. The technologies that are identified include radar/combat identification, EW air/ground survivability equipment, information and network operations, SIGINT, modelling and simulation, information fusion, measurement and signatures intelligence (MASINT), EW countermeasures, and intelligence dissemination.

Air Force Institute of Technology Center for Cyberspace Research (CCR)

The Center for Cyberspace Research (CCR) was established in March 2002 and carries out defense-focused research at the postgraduate level. The CCR is responsive to the educational and research needs of the air force, DoD, and the federal government. Faculty members undertake research that focuses on understanding and developing advanced cyber-related theories and technologies.

A number of the military education organizations educate and train the military at all levels and also carry out research into information operations. The main establishments will now be detailed.

National Defense University Information Resources Management College (NDU iCollege)

The National Defense University Information Resources Management College (NDU iCollege) offers a multidisciplinary approach to cyber issues and approximately 50 courses focused on cyber, IT leadership, and related topics. The Cyberspace Integration and Integrated Operation (CI&IO) Department focuses on information assurance (IA), cyber security, and the supporting role of information integration in the planning and execution of national and military strategy.

Joint Force Staff College

The mission of the Joint C4I (Command, Control, Communications, Computers, and Intelligence) Staff and Operations Course (JC4ISOC) is to educate and train joint C4I decision makers in C4I concepts in the joint/coalition/interagency environments, the DoD's organization and how it supports the C4I process, and the management and operation of current joint C4I systems and joint operational procedures associated with both strategic and theater/tactical systems.

US Army War College

The US Army War College educates military, civilian, and international leaders in the global application of land power. The Center for Strategic Leadership and Development (CSLD) is the Army War College education center and high-technology lab, addressing strategic issues affecting the national security community, including cyber threats. The CSLD offers two courses in "Cyber Warfare" and "Cyber Warfare Planning," along with courses on technology applications and emerging threats to national security. Faculty members at the US Army War College have published journal articles and papers on cyber as a new operational domain, cyber infrastructure protection, and cyberspace theory.

Information Assurance Training Center, US Army Signal Center

The IA Division, US Army School of Information Technology, provides IA/Computer Network Defense training and certification for DoD personnel worldwide.

Department of Defense Cyber Crime Center (DC3)

Defense Cyber Crime Center (DC3) provides computer investigation training for forensic examiners, investigators, system administrators, and any other DoD members who must ensure that defense information systems are secure from unauthorized use, criminal and fraudulent activities, and foreign intelligence service exploitation.

US Army Reserve Readiness Training Center (ARRTC)

The Army Reserve Readiness Training Center (ARRTC) runs a number of computer security courses that are open to all federal government system and network administrators. The ARRTC Computer Network Defense Course is an advanced course designed to provide systems administrators and network managers with the knowledge to defend their systems, networks, and applications against the latest computer threats.

US Naval War College

The US Naval War College (NWC) promotes itself as a leader in developing concepts for operationalizing cyber warfare, CSO, and cyber conflict in joint military operations and planning. Aspects of cyber education are integrated across the full range of NWC academic programs as part of both the Joint Professional Military Education (JPME) and the M.A. in National Security and Strategic Studies curricula. Courses offered include:

Cybersecurity, which covers the topics of Cybered Conflict, Response to Surprise, and
Emerging Indicators of Global System Change
IO and Cyber Warfare, which looks at current issues in the information environment
Net-Centric and Cyber Operations

Naval Post Graduate School (NPS)

The Naval Post Graduate School (NPS) has established a Cyber Academic Group (CAG). CAG's objective is to enable NPS students to understand both how to defend networks from penetration and to employ cyber capabilities to ensure an advantage in future operations. A set of cyber-related courses and research lead to a master's of science degree in cyber systems and operations or a master's of science in applied cyber operations. The group also runs a Cyber Battle Lab, which hosts the NPS semiannual Cyber Wargames, designed to develop interdisciplinary cyber education and research ranging from high-level strategy to machine-level reverse engineering. The NPS has been certified as one of the National Centers of Academic Excellence in information assurance (IA)/cyber defense (CD) under the joint NSA and DHS program.

Navy Center for Information Dominance (CID)

The mission of the Center for Information Dominance (CID) is to deliver full-spectrum cyber-information warfare and intelligence training to achieve decision superiority. CID is the navy's learning center, providing the navy and joint forces with training in IO, IW, IT, cryptology, and intelligence. The CID has a staff of approximately 1300 military, civilian, and contracted staff.

Marine Corps Intelligence Schools (MCIS)

The MCIS provides training and education for all intelligence fields and serves as a proponent for intelligence language training and remote sensor operators in order to provide technically-proficient marines to both operational forces and supporting units. MCIS runs a Joint Network Attack Course (JNAC) to provide senior enlisted cryptologic ratings and officers with core knowledge and skills in planning to support computer network attack operations.

US Air Force Air War College (AWC), Air University

The role of the Air War College (AWC) Department of Leadership and Warfighting is the development of senior leaders with the skills to plan, deploy, employ, and control US and multinational forces throughout the range of military operations, including in cyber space. The AWC run a number of courses, including CSO, Cyberspace Requirements for the Warfighter, and Intelligence and Surveillance and Reconnaissance (ISR) Requirements for Cyberspace. Subordinate to the AWC is the Cyberspace and Information Operations Study Center (Air University), which states its purpose as being to contribute to the USAF and Joint Cyberspace and IO communities' strategic and operational understanding and application of twenty-first century information-age operations.

The NSA and the DHS jointly run a program of certification of National Centers of Academic Excellence in IA/CD. To date, 44 institutions have been designated as NSA/DHS National Centers of Academic Excellence (CAE) in IA/CD. The designation is based on academic criteria for cyber-security education and allows each CAE institution to distinguish its strengths in specific IA/CD focus areas. Certificates are awarded for both education and research.

The universities that have been certified under this program are as follows:

Boston University has a Center for Reliable Information Systems & Cyber Security (RISCS) and lists its current research to include cryptology, network and software security, software safety, economic and game-theoretic approaches to Internet computing, database security, robust monitoring, and fair and secure file sharing. The university runs a military postgraduate program in Computer Information Systems. It is an NSA Center of Academic Excellence in IA for research.

Prince George's Community College runs a number of information security courses. It is an NSA Center of Academic Excellence in IA for education.

California State Polytechnic University has a Center for Information Assurance (CfIA) and provides a number of information security courses. It is an NSA Center of Academic Excellence in IA for education.

California State University runs a National Security Studies (NSS) program. The program houses the CSU Intelligence Community Center of Academic Excellence (CSU-ACE).

CSU-ACE has received a multimillion dollar grant from the Office of the Director of National Intelligence (ODNI) and received a grant from the Defense Intelligence Agency in 2012. It is an NSA Center of Academic Excellence in IA for education and has a focus on cyber investigations and network security administration.

Carnegie Mellon University carries out research and education in IA and computer security. It is an NSA Center of Academic Excellence in IA for education and research.

Dartmouth University has an Institute for Security Technology and Society (ISTS). The university has received grants through the DoD Information Assurance Scholarship Program and the Federal Cyber Service: Scholarship for Service, which is funded through grants awarded by the National Science Foundation. It is a member of the Institute for Information Infrastructure Protection (I3P), which is a consortium of leading universities, national laboratories, and nonprofit institutions dedicated to strengthening the cyber infrastructure of the United States. Recent research has included work on Trustworthy Health and Wellness (THaW) and Trustworthy Cyber Infrastructure for the Power Grid (TCIPG). It is an NSA Center of Academic Excellence in IA research.

Florida Atlantic University has a Center for Cryptology and Information Security (CCIS), which carries out research into cryptology and information security. It is an NSA Center of Academic Excellence in IA research.

Florida Institute of Technology runs an IA and cyber-security program. It is an NSA Center of Academic Excellence in IA research.

George Mason University has a Center for Secure Information Systems (CSIS), which researches both the theoretical and applied aspects of information systems security. It is an NSA Center of Academic Excellence in IA education and research.

George Washington University provides a range of programs on highly technical topics, such as network and computer security and higher level systems engineering courses, including information security management. It is an NSA Center of Academic Excellence in IA education and research.

Georgia Institute of Technology (Georgia Tech) has the Georgia Tech Research Institute (GTRI), which is carrying out research to improve the safety and security of military personnel abroad and citizens at home by developing new technologies to defeat enemy threats and provide a strategic advantage against adversaries. It is an NSA Center of Academic Excellence in IA research.

Iowa State University has an IA Center and carries out education, research, and outreach in IA. Areas researched include problems of securing information in application areas ranging from software to networks to electronic democracy. It is an NSA Center of Academic Excellence in IA education and research.

Kansas State University has a Center for Information and Systems Assurance, which carries out research into a wide range of areas in cyber security and information assurance, including high-assurance software, network security, cloud security, mobile-system security, cyber-physical system security, usable security, privacy, and anonymity. It is an NSA Center of Academic Excellence in IA education and research.

Mississippi State University has a Computer Security Research (CCSR) program, which provides computer security education and carries out research into computer vulnerabilities to improve prevention and detection techniques. It is an NSA Center of Academic Excellence in IA education and research.

New York University has a National Science Foundation–funded Information Systems and Internet Security (ISIS) laboratory and runs a postgraduate program in cyber security. It is an NSA Center of Academic Excellence in IA research.

North Carolina State University has a Laboratory for Analytic Sciences (LAS), which was developed in partnership with the NSA to address big-data problems; and a defense laboratory to undertake security-related research. It is an NSA Center of Academic Excellence in IA research.

Northeastern University in Massachusetts has an Information Assurance Center, which provides organizations with education, information, and training in responding to cyber threats from terrorists or criminals and safeguards the nation's information assets. It is an NSA Center of Academic Excellence in IA research.

Norwich University is a private military college. It runs a postgraduate program in Information Security and Assurance. It is an NSA Center of Academic Excellence in IA education.

Princeton University has carried out research on the use of fiber optics as a secure means to communicate information and prevent wireless communications systems used by the military, police, and other first responders from interfering with one another; and other topics related to information security. It is an NSA Center of Academic Excellence in IA research.

Purdue University has the Center for Education and Research in Information Assurance and Security (CERIAS) for research and education in areas of information security that are crucial to the protection of critical computing and communication infrastructure. It is an NSA Center of Academic Excellence in IA research.

Rochester Institute of Technology has a Department of Computing Security that runs both undergraduate and postgraduate courses in the topic. Faculty and students have published a number of papers on information security and digital forensics. It is an NSA Center of Academic Excellence in IA education.

Southern Methodist University has a Darwin Deason Institute for Cyber Security, which has the stated aim to "advance the science, policy, application and education of cyber security through basic and problem-driven, interdisciplinary research." It is an NSA Center of Academic Excellence in IA education.

Stevens Institute of Technology has a Center for the Advancement of Secure Systems & Information Assurance. Some of the roles of the center are the exploration of the implications to information assurance and cyber security of ubiquitous computing and other visionary scenarios; the anticipation of cultural evolution resulting from the inception of innovative technologies such as social networking; and public-private partnerships for threat assessment, response, technology development, and deployment. The institute runs undergraduate and postgraduate courses in cyber security. It is an NSA Center of Academic Excellence in IA research.

Syracuse University has the Center for Systems Assurance, which has three main areas: research, education, and technology. Efforts to improve system assurance will comprise three major areas: research, education, and technology transfer. It is an NSA Center of Academic Excellence in IA education.

Pennsylvania State University has a Systems and Internet Infrastructure Security Laboratory and also runs a Security and Risk Analysis undergraduate program. They are part of a Collaborative Research Alliance, which is made up of Penn State, Carnegie Mellon University, Indiana University, University of California Davis, University of California Riverside, and the Army Research Laboratory. This research is carried out into models for enabling continuous reconfigurability of secure missions. This research has a five-year, $23.2 million funding for the core and enhanced program, with an additional $25 million for the optional five-year program. The project will fund research by 17 faculty and more than 30 graduate students among the partnering universities. It is an NSA Center of Academic Excellence in IA education.

The University of Alabama at Birmingham has a CfIA and Joint Forensics Research program, which carries out research on a broad spectrum of IA topics. The university offers a number of undergraduate information-security courses and a postgraduate program in Computer Forensics and Security Management (MSCFSM). It is an NSA Center of Academic Excellence in IA research.

The University of Arizona has an Information Assurance and Security Education Center (IASEC), which provides a range of information-security courses. The center carries out research into a wide range of related topics, including biometric identification and deception detection, network-centric warfare, detecting deception in the military infosphere, improving and integrating human detection capabilities with automated tools, explosives and IEDs in the dark web, and the capture of multimedia, multilingual open-source web-based terrorist content. It is an NSA Center of Academic Excellence in IA education.

The University of Texas at San Antonio's Advanced Laboratories for Infrastructure Assurance and Security (ALIAS) provides training in biometrics, data mining, intrusion detection, and cyber forensics at both the undergraduate and postgraduate levels. The faculty and students have produced a number of publications in the area of information security. It is an NSA Center of Academic Excellence in IA education.

Towson University offers a number of undergraduate and postgraduate courses on information security. It is an NSA Center of Academic Excellence in IA education.

The University of Arkansas has a Center for Excellence for Assurance, Security, and Software Usability, Research, and Education (ASSURE), which runs courses at both the undergraduate and postgraduate level on information-security topics and carries out research focused on the integration of fundamental security and forensics research with the latest technical advances in mobile computing, cloud computing, and social networks. It is an NSA Center of Academic Excellence in IA research.

The State University of New York, Buffalo, has a Center of Academic Excellence in Information Systems Assurance, Research and Education, which has the aims of providing graduate education and carrying out coordinated research in computer security and information assurance. It is an NSA Center of Academic Excellence in IA education and research.

The University of California at Davis caries out education and research to improve computer security. It is an NSA Center of Academic Excellence in IA research.

The University of Connecticut has a CfIA and Computer Systems Security (CIACSS), which carries out research into authorization and access control, cryptography and cryptanalysis, data security and privacy, information fusion and data mining for homeland security, and trustable computing systems. It is an NSA Center of Academic Excellence in IA research.

The University of Illinois at Urbana has a CfIA, which runs a cyber-security program through the Illinois Cyber Security Scholars Program. Research by the university includes:

Cryptographic Scalability in the Smart Grid,
Functional Security Enhancements for Existing SCADA Systems,
GridStat Middleware Communication Framework - Management Security and
    Trust,
Trustworthy Time-Synchronous Measurement Systems,
Analyzing the Cyber-Physical Impact of Cyber Events on the Power Grid,
a Game-Theoretic Intrusion Response and Recovery Engine,
Assessment and Forensics for Large-Scale Smart Grid Networks,
Detection/Interdiction of Malware Carried by Application-Layer AMI Protocols,
Intrusion Detection for Smart Grid Components by Leveraging of Real-Time
    Properties, and a
Specification-based Intrusion Detection System for Smart Meters.

It is an NSA Center of Academic Excellence in IA education and research.

The University of North Carolina's Laboratory of Information Integration, Security, and Privacy (LIISP) collaborates with other universities, government agencies, and industrial organizations to advance the state of information integration, security, and privacy and provides education and training programs in information integration, security, and privacy. It is an NSA Center of Academic Excellence in IA research.

The University of Maryland, Baltimore County, has the UMBC Center for Information Security and Assurance (CISA), which carries out research and education in information security and assurance. It is an NSA Center of Academic Excellence in IA education and research.

The University of Maryland University College's Center for Security Studies runs a number of undergraduate and postgraduate courses in cyber security and carries out applied research into the IA and homeland security fields. It is an NSA Center of Academic Excellence in IA education and research.

The University of Memphis has a CfIA, which runs a number of undergraduate and postgraduate courses in information security and also carries out research into negative authentication systems; intelligent security consoles; cougar-based intrusion detection systems; immunity-based intrusion detection systems; and security agents for network traffic analysis. It is an NSA Center of Academic Excellence in IA education.

The University of Pittsburgh has a Laboratory for Education and Research on Security Assured Information Systems (LERSAIS), which offers a number of undergraduate and postgraduate courses on information security and carries out research into a range of information security topics. It is an NSA Center of Academic Excellence in IA research.

The University of Texas at Dallas has a Cyber Security Research Institute and runs a cyber-security scholarship program. It delivers both undergraduate and postgraduate courses in cyber security. It has carried out research into a range of topics, including information operations via infospheres, stream and text mining for NASA, secure cloud, and adaptive malware detection. It is an NSA Center of Academic Excellence in IA education and research.

The University of Tulsa has a Center for Information Security (CIS), which carries out education and research in cyber-security education and research. It is an NSA Center of Academic Excellence in IA education.

Utica College runs undergraduate courses in cyber security and IA, specializing in digital forensics and investigation currently available to address the growing demand for expertise in defending critical infrastructure, both public and private, from the threat of cyber attack. It also runs an online M.S. in Cybersecurity to address ever-changing attack and infiltration techniques, which combines state-of-the-art practices in intelligence, forensics, and cyber operations. It is an NSA Center of Academic Excellence in IA education.

Virginia Polytechnic and State University has the Hume Center for National Security and Technology, which carries out research into defense and intelligence applications of cyber attack and defense. It also has a number of subject-specific security laboratories and provides undergraduate and postgraduate programs in cyber security. It is an NSA Center of Academic Excellence in IA research.

West Virginia University runs a number of undergraduate and postgraduate courses in specific topics in computer security, computer networking, communications, and management of information systems. The university also runs a computer forensics teaching and research laboratory in cooperation with the West Virginia State Police and conducts research in software engineering under the sponsorship of NASA. It is an NSA Center of Academic Excellence in IA education and research.

Worcester Polytechnic Institute's Cybersecurity Program runs a number of undergraduate and postgraduate courses on specific topics in computer security. The faculty and students also carry out research into a range of information-security topics, including hardware, embedded systems, wireless protocols, secure system architectures, software systems, and end-user security. It is an NSA Center of Academic Excellence in IA research.

Civilian Universities

Other civilian universities that run related information-security programs include

- Auburn University in Alabama. The university's Information Assurance Laboratory (IAL) studies and develops new techniques of assuring secure and accurate data transmission and reception.
- East Stroudsburg University provides undergraduate courses in Computer Security.

- Florida State University's Department of Computer Science has an initiative in Information Technology Assurance and Security, covering software reliability, information assurance, and computer and communications security.
- James Madison University provides an online distance education Information Security (InfoSec) program.
- Idaho State University has a National Information Assurance Training and Education Center.
- Johns Hopkins University has an Information Security Institute (ISI), which carries out research and education in information security, assurance, and privacy.
- Portland State University provides education in computer security, including introduction to security, network security, cryptography, forensics, and internetworking protocols.
- Stanford University's Security Laboratory is a part of the university's Computer Science Department and carries out research into various aspects of network and computer security.
- Texas A&M University has a Center for Information Assurance and Security (CIAS), which addresses the broad spectrum of issues involved in the expansion and protection of information and communications infrastructure systems.
- The University of Idaho has the Center for Secure and Dependable Systems (CSDS), which was established in response to the overwhelming need for computer-related security education and research.
- The University of Massachusetts has a Computer Science Research Center, which carries out wide-ranging research that includes information retrieval and data mining and distributed systems and security.
- The University of Nebraska at Omaha has the Nebraska University Center for Information Assurance (NUCIA), which, in addition to the traditional technical areas of information assurance, works in a wide variety of areas, including computer science, management information systems, criminal justice, public policy, law, national and international security, cyber terrorism, health informatics, and privacy.
- Walsh College, Michigan, has an Information Assurance Center, which provides organizations with education, information, and training in responding to cyber threats from terrorists or criminals and safeguards the nation's information assets.

Another project within DARPA is Cyberspace Operations Research and Development, which is described as

Cyberspace operations (CSO) are the employment of cyberspace capabilities where the primary purpose is to achieve objectives in or through cyberspace. Cyberspace superiority is the degree of dominance in cyberspace by one force that permits the secure, reliable conduct of operations by that force, and its related land, air, maritime, and space forces at a given time and place without prohibitive interference by an adversary.

Research and development (R&D) projects in CSO to achieve cyberspace superiority require specialized knowledge, skills, and experience. Often, these projects are classified and can only be solicited from a limited number of sources. The Defense Advanced Research Projects Agency (DARPA) must maintain up-to-date knowledge about potential performers to maximize the number of sources that can be solicited for classified, highly specialized, CSO R&D initiatives.

The mission of the AFRL Information Directorate is "to lead the discovery, development, & integration of affordable warfighting information technologies for our air, space, & cyberspace forces." The Air Force Research Laboratory Information Directorate (AFRL/RI) sponsors research to design, develop, test, evaluate, and experiment with innovative technologies and techniques for cyber awareness and resilience research. The main areas of interest are

- Cyber resilience
- Cyber-situation awareness
- Identity, authentication, and access management
- Cyber footprint reduction
- Counter-insider modelling

The Information Analysis and Research (IWAR) laboratory, referred to as the IWAR range, at the US Military Academy (USMA) is a unique resource at West Point. The IWAR range is an isolated laboratory for use by undergraduate students and faculty researchers and is part of the IA curriculum at West Point.

The Defense Research and Engineering Network (DREN) and Secret Defense Research and Engineering Network (SDREN). DREN is a system that provides secure data transfer with Non-Secure Internet Protocol Router Network (NIPRNet) and other federal and academic research networks. The Secret DREN (SDREN) is a virtual private network overlay of the DREN using SDREN Service Delivery Routers (SDR) and NSA Type 1 encryptors with a common key.

Exercises

Exercise Combined Endeavor Series

This series of exercises has been taking place for 20 years. In the 2010 exercise, which took place in Germany, there were approximately 1400 participants from more than 40 countries and organizations. The exercise included a cyber-defense component for the first time.

Cyber Guard Exercise Series

In August 2012, USCYBERCOM carried out the Cyber Guard excercise.

This was the first exercise to be carried out in collaboration with subject-matter experts from the NSA, National Guard, DHS, and FBI. The tactical-level exercise focused on national defensive cyber-space operations and C2, with mission integration between USCYBERCOM/NSA and the National Guard. The primary aim of the exercise was to establish long-lasting DoD/NSA relationships with the National Guard in order to increase cyber-space capability and situational awareness to better support the DHS and FBI in the defense of the nation. The exercise lasted for one week and included about 500 participants, of which approximately 100 came from National Guard units.

In 2013, the 2nd annual Cyber Guard Exercise was hosted by USCYBERCOM and involved the Army and Air National Guard, Army and Navy Reserves, NSA, DHS, Federal Bureau of Investigation, state and local officials, and simulated industry partners. The outcome of the 2013 Cyber Guard Exercise remains classified.

In June/July 2014, exercise Cyber Guard ran for two weeks and was manned by elements from the 175th Network Warfare Squadron, the army's 110th Information Operations Battalion, and the Maryland Defense Force. The exercise involved tactical-level cyber-space operations utilizing a simulated network wherein the participants tested their tools and internal tactics, techniques, and procedures against a world-class opposing force.

Exercise Cyber Guard 14-1 focused on the joint and interagency response to a cyber attack on the homeland and exercised relationships between the National Guard, the active component, and several other agencies and organizations, such as DHS and the FBI. There were over 550 participants, including the newly formed "Title 10" status cyber-protection teams, a team from the Army Reserve, and an international reserve team from the United Kingdom.

Cyber Flag Exercise Series

The Cyber Flag exercise started in 2011 and combines operational C2 and tactically focused training in a virtual environment. According to the Defence Industry Security Agency (DISA), the Cyber Flag exercises set the conditions for force-on-force maneuvers against a realistic enemy, fusing attack and defense across the full spectrum of operations.

In November 2013, more than 800 participants, including representatives from DISA, 40 states, and one ally nation, took part in Cyber Flag 14, and activities included conventional maneuvers and kinetic fires in conjunction with cyber operations.

Cyber Shield Exercise Series

Exercise Cyber Shield is a defensively focused cyber exercise that is run from the National Guard Professional Education Center in North Little Rock, Arkansas.

In September 2013, personnel from more than 40 states took part in exercise Cyber Shield 2013 to improve their ability to provide response capabilities to cyber attacks.

In April/May 2014, more than 300 soldiers, airmen, and civilians from 35 states as well as Puerto Rico, Guam, and the District of Columbia took part in the 2014 Cyber Shield Exercise.

Cyber Storm Exercise Series

This series of exercises, which began in 2006 and appears to have finished in 2012, was part of the DHS's effort to assess and strengthen the state of cyber preparedness, examine incident response processes in response to ever-evolving threats, and enhance information sharing among federal, state, international, and private-sector partners.

References

1. Director of Army Doctrine. (2008). National defense land operations manual. https://info.publicintelligence.net/CanadaLandOps.pdf.
2. Lynn III, W. J. (2010). Defending a new domain: The Pentagon's cyberstrategy. http://www.defense.gov/home/features/2010/0410_cybersec/lynn-article1.aspx.
3. Coleman, K. (2010). The challenge of attribution in cyber war: Bring on the lawyers. *Defensetech*, September 7. http://defensetech.org/2010/09/07/the-challenge-of-attribution-in-cyber-war/.
4. US Air Force (2013). Headquarters US Air Force, USCYBERCOMMAND Cyber Mission Force, February 5. http://www.safcioa6.af.mil/shared/media/document/AFD-140512-039.pdf.
5. US Army War College (2011). Information operations primer: Fundamentals of information operations. November. http://www.au.af.mil/au/awc/awcgate/army-usawc/info_ops_primer.pdf.

Chapter 7

Nation-State Defensive and Offensive Information Warfare Capabilities: Middle East Nation-States

In the Middle East, the two countries that were considered to have the greatest information warfare (IW) capabilities were Iran and Israel. While other countries, particularly Syria, have been active in the cyber arena since the Arab Spring events that started at the end of 2010, the ongoing war there and the rise of the Islamic State of Iraq and Syria (ISIS) have resulted in the disruption of many of the state organizations in the region. As a result, there is little information as to the current state of information operations (IO) developments in most of the countries in the region.

Iran

Policy and Strategy

In June 2011, Iran announced its plans to establish a cyber command for the armed forces to defend against cyber attacks and to centralize operations. A High Council of Cyberspace (*Shora-ye Ali-ye Faza-ye Majazi*) was created in 2012 by order of supreme leader Ayatollah Khamenei, and it includes high-level Iranian authorities such as

- Parliament
- The president
- Ministers of intelligence, telecommunication, culture, and science
- Heads of the judicial power
- Police
- Head of the state-run radio and television networks

The council has the mission of instituting high-level policies on cyber space, and all organizations carrying out cyber operations are under its jurisdiction.

A number of reports put the initial Iranian cyber-force budget at around $76 million annually; however, it is thought that by late 2011 it had committed at least $1 billion to the development of cyber technology, infrastructure, and expertise. According to a 2012 article in the *Wall Street Journal*,[1] the Islamic Revolutionary Guard Corps (IRGC) claimed that it had recruited and trained around 120,000 cultural soldiers over the past three years to combat "a soft cyber war against Iran."

In October 2011, a former IRGC commander of the Tehran province claimed that there were "two cyber war centers" in Tehran under the command of the IRGC and that some 2,000 bloggers had been recruited and trained as cyber army staff.

Defense

Passive Civil Defense Committee

The Passive Civil Defense Committee is responsible for coordinating a number of government organizations and agencies in the nonmilitary response to a military attack in order to minimize damage to the national infrastructure and facilities. This organization is subordinate to the Joint Staff of the Armed Forces.

Cyber Defense Command

This was created at the end of 2010. The Cyber Defense Command (Qarargah-e Defa-e Saiberi) operates in Iran under the authority of the Passive Civil Defense Organization (*Sazeman-e Padafand-e Gheyr-e Amel*), which is itself a subdivision of the Joint Staff of the Armed Forces (*Setad-e Kol-e Niruhay-e Mosalah*).

Police

In September 2009, the creation of the cyber police was announced. This special unit was named FETA Police in January 2011 (which in Persian stands for "the Police of the Space of Creating and Exchanging Information"). The main task of

FETA is to tackle Internet crimes, but it has the additional role of combating "political and security crimes." In November 2011, an official announced that FETA was going to use a group of hackers to assist the police in better understanding the technical weaknesses of government sites and ways to remove them.

Offensive

The Islamic Revolutionary Guard Corps is reported to have a cyber-warfare unit. This unit is estimated to have 2400 staff and potentially an additional 1200 in reserves. In June 2011, the commander of the Khatam al-Anbiya Air Defense Base stated that "the Iranian military base is equipped with necessary capabilities and knowledge to counter any possible cyber assault." This was followed in December 2011 by a statement by the head of the Passive Defense Organization, who said that "Iranian computer experts are adequately prepared to defend the country against any possible cyber attack," and that "Iran has set up a cyber defense base to track down and counter any form of attack against the country's cyberspace."

Iran's Cyber Army

Iran's cyber army is a group of highly skilled information technology specialists and professional hackers whose identities are unknown. The group is not officially acknowledged, and no agency or government organization has assumed responsibility for it. There is, however, strong evidence that it is affiliated with the IRGC. In April 2011, the former deputy representative of the Supreme Leader in the IRGC is reported to have said that by using the cyber army, Iran had successfully hacked a number of "enemy sites."

Basij Paramilitary Force

The Basij Paramilitary Force was reorganized in 2007. The armed units of the Basij became members of the ground forces of the IRGC, while the nonmilitary units became responsible for "soft war" and for cyber warfare. The Basij Paramilitary Force is largely made up of inexperienced individuals who engage in the less complex hacking or infiltration operations on sites and e-mails, while the more sophisticated operations are undertaken by Iran's cyber army. There is a Basij Cyber Council, which is responsible for the tasking of hackers under the supervision of IRGC specialists. One report stated that 1500 "cyber war commandoes" had been trained.

In a December 2014 from Cylance,[2] the types of offensive activities that Iran has been involved in were described:

> Since at least 2012, Iranian actors have directly attacked, established persistence in, and extracted highly sensitive materials from the networks of government agencies and major critical infrastructure companies in

the following countries: Canada, China, England, France, Germany, India, Israel, Kuwait, Mexico, Pakistan, Qatar, Saudi Arabia, South Korea, Turkey, United Arab Emirates, and the United States.

The report goes on to detail a wide range of targets for the attacks, which included airlines and their contractors in Pakistan, the United Arab Emirates, and South Korea; and, in the United States, computers belonging to the navy's unclassified computer system, defense contractors, chemical and energy companies, universities, and transportation providers. The activity, which has been given the nickname of Operation Cleaver, is believed to have been carried out by at least 20 hackers.

Research and Development

Universities

A number of Iranian universities are engaged in information warfare research and education:

Amirkabir University

Amirkabir University has two security-related laboratories. The first is the data security laboratory, which gives its role as research and innovation in computers and communications information security fields; and training researchers and engineers in the related ground of information security. This includes designing and analyzing encryption algorithms, software and hardware development for secure data communications, visual communications, processing, and the design and implementation of computerized secure systems, such as secure operating systems. The second laboratory is the secure computerized systems laboratory, which has the role of designing, making, and evaluating secure and reliable systems, distributed secure systems, information security management systems, and network security.

Isfahan University

Isfahan University has a Cryptography and System Security Research Laboratory (CSSRL), which is an interdisciplinary laboratory. The laboratory conducts research into information security, which includes analyzing cryptographic algorithms, security protocols, and systems; developing and providing technical training materials and courses; and providing academic and instructional support for both undergraduate and postgraduate security courses.

Sharif University

Sharif University runs a postgraduate program in information security and has a Data and Network Security Laboratory, which was established in 1999. The laboratory carries out research into data and network security. The main research areas are

- Network security
- Botnets, honeypots, malwares, traffic analysis, network prediction
- Formal evaluation of security of computer systems
- Foundations of information security
- Secure data outsourcing
- Computational trust
- Access control

Tarbiat Modares University

This university runs a Cryptography and Network Security program and has carried out research on topics such as verification of firewalls configuration versus security policies using description logics; a new quantitative approach for information security risk assessment; and identification of the required security practices during e-government maturity.

University of Tehran

The University of Tehran held the 2014 International ISC (Iranian Society of Cryptology) Conference on Information Security and Cryptology (ISCISC), which has been the flagship conference in information security and cryptology. The university runs a postgraduate information assurance program.

Exercises

A report in the *Iran Daily* in December 2012 stated that Iran had staged a cyberwarfare drill at the same time as a naval exercise in the straits of Hormuz. The report stated that the Iranian navy had carried out a cyber attack against the computer network of its defense forces in order to simulate a hack or a virus infiltration by a foreign aggressor.

In February 2013, the IRGC carried out a three-day ground and air military exercise called the Great Prophet 8 war games. The exercise included intelligence-gathering drones, as well tests of the IRGC's cyber-defense systems.

Israel

Policy and Strategy

In 2010, the Israeli Prime Minister announced a National Cyber Initiative, designed to carry out a review of Israel's national cyber policy. The findings of the review highlighted seven main areas of concern: the need to

1. Improve education, from basic best practice to advanced interdisciplinary research and development (R&D)
2. Develop knowledge and an R&D infrastructure
3. Create a statewide "protective shield" based on the products of domestic R&D, while addressing privacy concerns
4. Develop national operational capabilities in cyber space for routine and emergency situations, while confronting moral, legal, and financial challenges
5. Upgrade the defense by combining technical and nontechnical legislative measures
6. Deploy unique technologies, developed cooperatively by domestic scientific and industrial sectors, with the government encouraging local procurement
7. Establish a national agency for comprehensive cyber policy in Israel, as none existed

In August 2011, government resolution 3611, Advancing National Cyberspace Capabilities, adopted the recommendations of the National Cyber Initiative to work toward advancing national cyber-space capabilities and to improve the management of both current and future challenges in cyber space. The resolution stated that it aimed to improve the defense of the essential elements of the national infrastructures and to strengthen those infrastructures against cyber attack. This is to be achieved by advancing Israel's status as a center for the development of information technologies and encouraging cooperation between academia, industry, and the private sector; government ministries; and "special bodies."

In the resolution, it was decided:

1. To establish a National Cyber Bureau in the Prime Minister's Office. The mission of the Bureau was stated to be

   > as an advising body for the Prime Minister, the government and its committees, which recommends national policy in the cyber field and promotes its implementation, in accordance with all law and Government Resolutions.

2. To regulate responsibility for dealing with the cyber field
3. To advance defensive cyber capabilities in Israel and advance research and development in cyber space and supercomputing

The budget for establishing and operating the bureau was in the region of US $130 million each year for the first five years.

In Israel, there are four main organizations that are responsible for Israeli cyber defenses:

Israel Defense Forces (IDF) Unit 8200. Unit 8200 focuses on three areas of cyber war: intelligence gathering, defensive operations, and offensive operations. It is the largest unit in the Israel Defense Forces and is reported to be staffed by several thousand soldiers. It is the equivalent of the US NSA. Unit 8200 is the Israeli army's signals intelligence unit.

National Cybernetic Taskforce. In May 2011, a National Cybernetic Taskforce was created with the role of securing the country against attacks on the critical networks as well as protecting private industry from espionage. It is reported to have a staff of around 80. The task force will also support efforts to improve university research on cyber security and increase the number of students.

Israeli Security Agency (Shin Bet). Shin Bet is responsible for defending government systems, national infrastructure, and financial data. A number of reports in 2014 identified S-74 as the Shin Bet unit that protects Israeli cyber space.

The C4I Corps is responsible for communication and organizing the IDF cyberdefense capabilities for the information systems of the IDF and other government bodies.

Defensive

National Cyber Defense Authority

In July 2014, the Israeli prime minister announced the creation of a National Cyber Defense Authority. Reports indicate that the role of the Authority is to be a link between the civilian and military authorities in the area of cyber security.

National Information Security Authority

The National Information Security Authority in Israel (NISA) is a subdivision in the Prime Minister's Office that focuses on IT and cyber security, including audits of IT and cyber systems and industrial control systems (ICS/SCADA), gap analysis, instruction, guidance, technical aspects, and standards of IT and cyber-security systems and devices, as well as policy management and risk assessment.

In September 2014, the Israeli prime minister announced the establishment of the new National Cyber Defense Authority to protect civilian cyber space. The new organization is to operate alongside the existing Israel National Cyber Bureau; it was decided that in light of the number of attacks that were being experienced in Israel, there was a need for a

> designated body to link the civilian and security spheres, to coordinate between leading experts in the field and lead Israel's overall defensive activity while taking a long-term view of the increasing and developing cyber threats.

Computer Services Directorate's (Lotem) (Telecommunications and Information Technology Unit)

The Computer Services Directorate, which was created in 2003, is the IDF organization that is responsible for the communication, wireless transmission, computerization, command and control over, and defense of information in the IDF. When it was created, it took over some of the functions previously carried out by the C4I Corps.

The Telecommunications and Information Technology Unit (Lotem) has the following subunits:

- Mamram: Center of Computers and Information Systems, responsible for managing military software and computer infrastructure
- Hoshen: responsible for operating the army's communication systems
- Matzov: Center of Encryption and Information Safety, responsible for the protection of digital military data. Matzov is responsible for encryption within the IDF, Shin Bet, and Mossad networks. It also has responsibility for providing intelligence on technological progress among Israel's enemies in the area of computer hacking.
- Ma'of: Systems and Projects, responsible for planning and engineering telecommunication systems
- Shoham: responsible for operational programming and computer services
- Leshem: responsible for human resources and logistics-related software

Offensive

According to an article on the Israel Defence Forces website,[3]

> The IDF has been engaged in cyber activity consistently and relentlessly, gathering intelligence and defending its own cyber space. Additionally if necessary the cyber space will be used to execute attacks and intelligence operations.

According to unverified reports, Israel recently established a cyber task force for cyber warfare against Islam and Pakistan, besides harming the Palestinian cause. A budget of $15 million is reported to have been allocated to this force to carry out various digital-espionage and information-gathering operations against Islam and Pakistan.

Israel Defense Forces (IDF) Unit 8200

During operation Protective Edge (Israel–Gaza conflict), which took place in 2014, members of Unit 8200, the signals unit, sat in a control room and provided real-time instructions to field commanders, telling them where to turn and which buildings housed targets.

Research and Development

Israeli Cyber Experimentation Center

The Inter-University Computation Center (IUCC) established a national Internet security test bed, an experimental infrastructure where next-generation cyber-security technologies can be tested and evaluated on live network traffic. The system, which was set up in 1984, supports all eight of Israel's universities. The IUCC test bed is the foundation of the Israeli Cyber Experimentation (ICE) Center, a partnership with the Israeli National Cyber Bureau (INCB).

Institute for National Security Studies (INSS)

The INSS carries out security research and provides policy analysis and recommendations. The INSS looks at a wide range of security issues, which include cyber security.

Ben Gurion University (BGU) was the first Israeli university to offer a graduate track in cyber security and also to have a cyber-security training center for the Israel Defense Forces (IDF). The university has a cyber-security laboratory, which carries out research into a wide range of security topics.

Tel Aviv University's cyber-research center. In 2014, Tel Aviv University announced the creation, in collaboration with the National Cyber Bureau, of a new Center for Cyber Interdisciplinary Research. The topics to be researched by the center include security software, attacks on hardware and software, cryptography, network protocols, and the security of operating systems and networks, as well as interdisciplinary research on topics such as the impact on national security, society, regulation, and the business sector. One report gave the number of staff at the center as around 40.

A news report in September 2014 stated that Israel had invited India to be part of the Israeli Prime Minister's project, the National Cyber Defense Authority. A news report in October 2014 stated that Britain's Office of Cyber Security and Information Assurance and Israel's National Cyber Bureau had signed a pact to finance joint cyber-defense research.

Exercise Lights Out

In January 2012, the National Cyber Command (NCC) and the Counter Terror Bureau (CTB) ran Israel's first official cyber-terror drill in order to improve response effectiveness in the event of a virtual assault. The exercise simulated a cyber-terror attack from multiple sources.

References

1. Fassihi, F. (2012). Iran's censors tighten grip. *Wall Street Journal*, March 16. http://online.wsj.com/news/articles/SB10001424052702303717304577279381130395906.
2. Cylance. (2014). Operation Cleaver, http://www.cylance.com/assets/Cleaver/Cylance_Operation_Cleaver_Report.pdf.
3. Pesso, R. (2012). IDF defines its activity in cyber space as a platform to improve operational effectiveness and defense. IDF has been relentlessly operating in the field. Israel Defence Forces website, June 3, 2012. http://www.idf.il/1283-16122-en/Dover.aspx.

Chapter 8

Nation-State Defensive and Offensive Information Warfare Capabilities: Asia Pacific Region

The Asia Pacific region includes a large number of countries and is, from an information warfare (IW) perspective, one of the most diverse. The region includes some very Western, first-world countries such as Australia, as well as one of the most isolated and anti-Western countries, North Korea.

Australia

Policy and Strategy

Australia published its National Cyber Security Strategy in 2009. The aim of the strategy is to enable a secure operating environment for both government and private networks in order to ensure security and to take advantage of the economic benefits of information technology.

The strategy identified seven strategic priorities:

- Developing threat awareness and response
- Changing civilian security culture

- Promoting public–private partnerships
- Securing government systems
- Pursing international engagement
- Creating an effective legal framework and building a skilled cyber workforce

The cyber-security policy was initially coordinated by the Cyber Security Policy and Coordination Branch of the Attorney General's Department. In 2011, cyber-policy responsibility was transferred to the National Security Division of the Department of the Prime Minister and Cabinet, together with the policy staff from the Attorney General's Department. Cyber policy is currently being reviewed in a process being led by a Senior Executive Service (SES)-level officer in the offices of the prime minister and the cabinet.

The Attorney General's Department also published a document in 2010 titled "Protective Security Policy Framework: Securing Government Business," which gave details on how the strategy was to be implemented.

The Australian Defence Force (ADF) published the Australian Defence Doctrine publication "Operation Series: Information Activities," Edition 3[1] (ADDP 3.13) in 2013. The aim of this document "is to provide guidance for the planning and conduct of Information Activities in the joint and multinational environments." The document defines information activities as

> Information Activities is the integration, synchronisation and coordination of two or more information-related capabilities (IRC) that generate and sustain a targeted information advantage. An information advantage is a favourable information situation relative to a group, organisation or adversary.

It goes on to define information operations (IO), which is considered a subset of information activities, as

> the operational level planning for and execution of coordinated, synchronised and integrated lethal and non-lethal actions against the capability, will and understanding of target systems and/or target audiences.

The paper explains that information operations are focused on affecting the decision-making of the target audience, while at the same time protecting and enhancing their own. It also makes the point that IO is an integral part of operational plans and supports the commander's decision-making.

In January 2013, the Australian prime minister announced the establishment of a new Australian Cyber Security Centre to enhance Australia's ability to protect networks against cyber attacks. The center combines existing cyber-security capabilities from across the Defence Signals Directorate (now renamed the Australian Signals Directorate), the Defence Intelligence Organisation, the Defence Imagery and Geospatial Organisation (now renamed the Australian Geospatial-Intelligence Organisation), the Australian Security Intelligence Organisation, the Attorney General's Department's Computer Emergency Response Team Australia, the Australian Federal Police, and the Australian Crime Commission. The announcement stated that defense would take the principal role in the operation of the center.

Defensive

Australian Security Intelligence Organisation

The Australian Security Intelligence Organisation (ASIO) is the Australian equivalent of the British MI5. The organization is responsible for the collection, analysis, and provision of advice on matters relating to espionage, foreign interference, politically motivated violence, communal violence, sabotage, attacks on Australia's defense system, and serious threats to Australia's territorial and border integrity. ASIO established a cyber-investigations unit in March 2011, which has a focus on state-sponsored cyber attacks.

The Defence Intelligence and Security Group (DISG) is one of the principal functional areas of the Department of Defence (DoD). The head of the group is a senior civilian official who coordinates intelligence and security policies, capabilities, and operations across the department. DISG comprises four organizations:

- Australian Geospatial-Intelligence Organisation (AGO)
- Australian Signals Directorate (ASD)
- Defence Intelligence Organisation (DIO)
- Defence Security Authority (DSA)

The ASD is responsible for the collection, analysis, and distribution of signals intelligence and is the national authority on communications, information, and cyber and computer security. The ASD includes the Cyber Security Operations Centre, which coordinates and assists with the response to cyber events and provides the government with a consolidated understanding of the cyber threat through a range of capabilities, including intrusion detection, analysis, and threat assessment.

Cyber Security Operations Centre

The Cyber Security Operations Centre (CSOC) was established in 2009 in the Australian Signals Directorate (ASD) to mitigate the cyber threat to Australia's national security, and it will complement ASD's other information security activities. It has a staff of around 130. The two main roles of the CSOC are

- To provide government with a better understanding of sophisticated cyber threats against Australian interests

■ To coordinate and assist operational responses to cyber events of national importance across government and systems of national importance

Australian Cyber Security Centre (ACSC)

The ACSC became operational in late 2014 and has the role of raising awareness of cyber security, reporting on the nature and extent of cyber threats, encouraging the reporting of cyber-security incidents, analysing and investigating cyber threats, coordinating national cyber-security operations and capability, and leading the government's operational response to cyber incidents. The ACSC will have a staff of around 300 by 2017. The ACSC differs from the CSOC in that it is the next generation of the Australian government's cyber-security capability. The CSOC is a defense capability that hosts liaison staff from other government agencies. The ACSC will result in the colocation of the cyber-security capabilities of all contributing agencies in one location. This will include the existing CSOC, the ASD's cyber-security mission; the attorney general's CERT (computer emergency response team) Australia; representatives of the Australian Federal Police and Australian Crime Commission, which focus on cyber crime; and cyber-investigations and telecommunication security specialists from ASIO.

Between 2012 and 2017, the Australian DoD will conduct Phase 2B.2 of a Computer Network Defence (CND) project to develop a survivable Defence Network Operation Centre capability, to enable defense to manage, monitor, and secure its major communications networks and information systems.

A 2008 article by Donald Deakin-Bell[2] in a journal of the Australian Naval Institute gives a perspective of the view of IO at that time in the Royal Australian Navy (RAN). The article states that it is

> the integrated employment of the core capabilities of electronic warfare, computer network operations, psychological operations, military deception and operations security, at to influence, disrupt, corrupt or usurp adversarial human and automated decision making while protecting our own.

The paper explains that IO is an integral part of effects based operations (EBO), and as a result is a major departure from the platform-based mindset predominant in the RAN. It goes on to describe the various levels at which IO must be considered, from the strategic level to the operational and tactical levels, and describes how this is communicated. It then discusses some of the concerns that result from the fact that the RAN will be involved in the implementation of IO while at the same time having little input into the development of the plans. In the paper, the authors also highlight the fact that while the RAN has capabilities in a number of IO areas, including electronic warfare (EW), computer network operations (CNO), information assurance (IA), military deception, operational security (OPSEC), and protective security, it does not coordinate these capabilities when it conducts operations, and each capability operates as a separate activity.

Offensive

Royal Australian Air Force (RAAF) Aerospace Operational Support Group

The Royal Australian Air Force's Aerospace Operational Support Group forms part of the ADF combat capability by providing comprehensive, timely, and integrated operational support to missions. The group has three elements:

- The Information Warfare Wing
- The Air System Development and Test Wing
- The Woomera Test Facility

The Information Warfare Wing is responsible for the supervision, activity coordination, and tasking of

- The Joint Electronic Warfare Operational Support Unit (JEWOSU), which provides EW support to the RAN, the army, and the RAAF. The unit also provides subject-matter advice to the Defence Intelligence Group.
- The RAAF Aeronautical Information Service (RAAF AIS), which provides the ADF with tailored, accurate, and current aeronautical information in both printed and electronic formats to support air operations.
- No 87 Squadron, which produces timely and precise air force intelligence and combat targeting products and expertise to the operational and tactical levels of the RAAF.
- No 462 Squadron, which has the role of exploiting and protecting against the exploitation of the information domain and supports operational commanders in providing a secure information environment to support air operations.
- No 460 Squadron, which is the RAAF's target intelligence squadron. Its task is to produce accurate and timely geospatial intelligence and precision target intelligence for defense and national interests.

Research and Development

Defence Science and Technology Organisation

The Defence Science and Technology Organisation (DSTO) is the Australian defense research organization and describes its core roles as being centered around providing expert and impartial advice and support for the conduct of operations for the current force and for acquisition of future defense capabilities. It has a produced a document that outlines how the DSTO will address the emerging relationship between cyber and electronic warfare, signals intelligence, and communications. The vision highlights the way in which the DSTO will engage with the national community to foster a cohesive, integrated national cyber science and technology capability. It also published a paper in May 2014 titled "Future Cyber Security Landscape: A Perspective on the Future." This is a companion paper to the DSTO "Cyber 2020 Vision: DSTO Cyber Science and Technology Plan"; it looks at the increasing national dependency, threat, and vulnerability and provides a view of the possible future of cyber security.

DSTO Cyber and Electronic Warfare Division

The DSTO Cyber and Electronic Warfare Division undertakes research and development focused on identifying, analysing, and countering threats to Australia's defense and national security through electronic means.

Exercises

No reference could be found to IW, IO, or cyber warfare in any of the Australian military exercises. However, Australia has been seen as an observer on NATO and US-based exercises.

China

Doctrine and Strategy

China has never published a formal information warfare strategy document or a CNO strategy, but a number of high-level, long-term directives, known as the military strategic guidelines, have been published, which give the direction for defense policy and set out a long-term course of action for the modernization of the military. The Chinese have adopted the concept of "information confrontation," which is aimed at integrating all elements of IW, both electronic and nonelectronic, offensive and defensive, under a single command authority.

IW is not specifically addressed in any one issue area. The last time that the Central Military Commission (CMC) updated the military strategic guidelines was in 1993. This update stated that the Peoples Liberation Army (PLA) should prepare to "fight local wars under high-tech conditions." This was then updated again in 2002, when Jiang Zemin, the then-president of the People's Republic of China, stated that the PLA must be able to fight and win "local wars under informationized conditions." This was a minor change in terminology from "local wars under high-technology conditions" but revealed a change in the PLA's strategic focus to *informationization*. This is the ability to link all services and units through a shared information infrastructure so as to enable joint operations. The Chinese strategy incorporates concepts such as that successful warfighting is predicated on the ability to exert control over an adversary's information and information systems, and that this may be achieved preemptively.

China has adopted an approach whereby offensive and defensive IW missions are closely coordinated to ensure that these activities are mutually supporting and are closely integrated with their campaign objectives.

The operational control for the military use of CNO lies within the PLA's Third and Fourth Departments of the General Staff. The Third Department is China's primary signals intelligence organization and is probably responsible for computer network defense and possibly exploitation. The Fourth Department, which is the EW arm of the PLA, is probably responsible for network attack. In 2013, in a document entitled "The Science of Military Strategy," China, for the first time, outlined its approach to Information Operations and identified three different groups. These were

- The PLA's "specialized military network warfare forces," which are military operational units specially employed for carrying out network attack and defense
- "PLA-authorized forces, which are teams of network warfare specialists in civilian organizations such as the Ministry of State Security (MSS), the Ministry of Public Security (MPS), and others that have been authorized by the military to carry out network warfare operations
- "Nongovernmental forces," which are external entities that spontaneously engage in network attack and defense, but can be organized and mobilized for network warfare operations

Defensive

Responsibility for computer network defense and computer network exploitation lies with the Third Department, China's traditional signals intelligence (SIGINT) collector. This department is responsible for the PLA's computer network defense and also has a role in China's national-level information security community, including the management of at least five information security engineering or evaluation centers.

In July 2010, the PLA established an Information Assurance Base, which is believed to be tasked with dealing with cyber threats and safeguarding China's national security. This was followed in June 2011, when the chief of the general staff, Gen Chen Bingde, announced the reorganization of the PLA's Communications Department into the Department of Informationization and indicated that, while the Third and Fourth Departments would retain their normal operational responsibilities, the General Staff Department (GSD) would have a formal mechanism for the coordination of network operations within the PLA. A number of media reports referred to a "Military Information Network Protection Bureau" having been established within the Communications Department as early as 2010, almost a year and a half before the PLA publicly announced the reorganization.

In July 2014, the creation of a Cyberspace Strategic Intelligence Research Center within the General Armaments Department was announced. The role of the new center was reported in the PLA daily as being designed to

> become an authoritative research resource for Internet intelligence, build a highly-efficient cyberspace dynamically-tracking research system, provide high-end services for hot and major issues, and explore approaches of intelligence analysis as well as identification and appraisal with cyberspace characteristics.

According to a 2004 report[3] from the Institute for Security Technology Studies at Dartmouth College, the PLA has cyber-warfare training centers at the Communications Command Academy in Wuhan, the Information Engineering University in Zhengzhou, the Science and Engineering University, and the National Defense Science and Technology University in Changsha.

All of these centers train PLA soldiers, and the PLA officer course curriculum includes

- Basic theory, including computer basics and applications
- Communications network technology
- The information highway
- Units connected by IT
- Electronic countermeasures (ECM)
- Radar technology
- Cyber-warfare rules and regulations
- Cyber-warfare strategy and tactics
- Theater and strategic cyber warfare
- Information systems, including gathering, handling, disseminating and using information and combat command, monitoring, decision-making, and control systems

Research and Development

The Chinese government funds a number of research programs for both offensive and defensive CNO at civilian and military universities and also at commercial IT companies. The main PLA universities are

The Academy of Military Sciences

The Academy of Military Sciences (AMS), located in Beijing, answers directly to the CMC. This is the main Chinese military organization for military science research and strategy and doctrine development. Recent AMS IW research has focused on the operational use of computer network exploitation, US network-centric warfare models, and foreign military information management structures.

National Defense University

The National Defense University (NDU), also located in Beijing, educates and trains China's military commanders and undertakes research into the application of new concepts in military science to the military. NDU researchers collaborate with other researchers in a number of other organizations, including the AMS and the Technical Reconnaissance Bureau. Recent NDU IW research has focused on foreign military informatization and information warfare approaches.

Wuhan Communications Command Academy

The Wuhan Communications Command Academy (CCA), located in Wuhan, is the PLA's communications command institution. The CCA trains Third Department communications-command and automated-management personnel in information warfare and military communications systems. It also carries out work on the development of operational doctrine for information operations. Recent CCA research includes studies into

- Internet routing scalability
- Wireless Internet use in military environments
- Data mining techniques
- Distributed denial-of-service attacks
- US network-centric warfare planning

CCA researchers collaborate with researchers in a number of other organizations, including PLA Unit 61081, the PLA Information Engineering University, the PLA Air Force Dalian Communication Officer School, Tsinghua University, Huazhong University of Science and Technology, Wuhan University of Technology, Xi'an Communications Academy, the China Institute of Electronic System Engineering, and the PLA Air Force Dalian Communication Officer School.

National University of Defense Technology

The National University of Defense Technology (NUDT), located in Changsha, is a technology-based university involved in military research and development. The university answers jointly to the Ministry of National Defense and the Ministry of Education. The research focus of NUDT is electronic and information warfare target recognition, biometrics, nanotechnology, quantum computing, and nonlinear mathematics. NUDT researchers collaborate with other researchers in a number of other organizations, including the PLA Unit 63880, PLA Information Engineering University Beijing University of Technology, Wuhan University, and Shanghai Jiao Tong University.

Information Engineering University

The PLA Information Engineering University (PLAIEU), located in Zhengzhou, has a comprehensive IW and CNO program. The school employs more than 800 professors and senior engineers and 100 part-time professors.[4] Published research papers from members of the university include

- Computer espionage methods
- A Windows rootkit
- Advanced hacking techniques
- An analysis of the security flaws in computer memory and the attack vectors for it
- Password cracking
- Data hiding
- Malware analysis
- Vulnerability analysis and countermeasures for smartgrid
- EW program evaluation methods

PLAIEU has its own journal and researchers, and, together with the organizations that it collaborates with, has published more than 300 articles in the past two years. PLAIEU researchers collaborate with researchers in a number of other organizations, including PLA Unit 61365, the Public Security Marine Police Academy, Zhengzhou University of Light Industry, Luohe Medical College, Xi'an University of Electronic Science and Technology, Hebei University of Science and Technology, Sichuan University, the National Digital Switching Engineering Center, and Nanyang Normal College.

It is worth noting that in February 2013, a number of media reports named Zhang Changhe, an assistant professor at the university, as a hacker who had targeted government agencies in Vietnam, Brunei, and Myanmar; oil companies; a newspaper; a nuclear safety agency; an embassy in mainland China; and personal computers in Taiwan and the Philippines.

Research Funding Programs

There are known to be at least five national funding programs that benefit 50 or more civilian universities for research into IW and the PLA's informationization programs. The main research programs are

The 115 Program, also known as the National Ministry of State Security 115 Program, which appears to be focused on highly sensitive information security research. It appears that most of the projects under the 115 State Security Program are classified as confidential or secret.

The National 219 Information Security Application Demonstration Project, which appears to focus on intrusion detection technology, virtual private networks, and e-security platforms.

The National 242 Information Security program, which is administered by the Ministry of Industry and Information Technology and appears to be focused on government-sensitive information security projects.

The 863 National High Technology Research and Development Program, which covers research into national technological independence through the advancement of advanced science and technology research and includes the areas of information technology and telecommunications and a number of defense-related and dual-use projects.

The 973 National Keystone Basic Research Program, which is managed by the PRC Ministry of Science and Technology (MOST) and whose projects include broadband wireless communication, trusted cloud computing, the Internet of things, integrated networks, and network virtualization.

In addition to these national-level grant programs, other funds for information security research are available from provincial, local, and private grants.

The Chinese government funds are intended to align the research to the strategic priorities of the current Five Year Plan (2011–2016), which are to enhance high-tech capabilities, including informationization within the PLA; and to improve national technical IW capabilities.

The Third Department's central command has the Science and Technology Intelligence Bureau and the Science and Technology Equipment Bureau. The Science and Technology Equipment Bureau oversees three research institutes, which are responsible for computing, sensor technology, and cryptography:

■ The 56th Research Institute. The 56th Research Institute, also known as the Jiangnan Computer Technology Research Institute, is the PLA's oldest and largest computing research and development (R&D) organization. The institute has some of the world's fastest supercomputers and carries out high-performance computing for the creation and breaking of sophisticated codes and passwords. It supports the Third Department and other national-level computer centers. The director of the 56th Research Institute is a member of the 863 Program Expert Working Group on Computing and Software.

■ The 57th Research Institute. The 57th Research Institute, also known as the Southwest Institute of Electronics and Telecommunications Technology, is reported to be responsible for the development of communications intercept and signal processing systems. One of the institute's main focus areas is satellite communications technology, and it is reported that the institute has been working with the China Academy of Space Technology on satellite R&D.

- The 58th Research Institute. The 58th Research Institute is also known as the Southwest Automation Research Institute (SWAI), and its main areas of interest are cryptology and information security technology. The 58th Research Institute is reported to have a cooperative relationship with Nanjing University of Science and Technology.

Offensive

As early as 2000, the PLA had adopted a multilayered approach to offensive IW, which they referred to as the Integrated Network Electronic Warfare (INEW) strategy. INEW is the combined application of CNO and EW, used in an attack on enemy command, control, communications, computers, intelligence, surveillance, and reconnaissance (C4ISR) networks and other key information systems. The objective is to deny an enemy access to information essential for continued combat operations. The rationale for this was to bring together the various components of IW under a single commander.

The Second Department of the PLA GSD is responsible for military intelligence (MI). It may use cyber operations as part of its collection activities.

The Fourth Department of the GSD, formerly the ECM, has the lead for the offensive IW activities in the PLA and oversees ECM regiments, many of which are integrated with group army command structures in most military regions in China.

Known Units

While little is published on the operational units, two have become known as a result of the Mandiant report:

  PLA Unit 61398, based in Shanghai, is believed to part of the 2nd Bureau of the Third Department of the PLA GSD. Unit 61398 is believed to engage in aggressive CNO that include systematic cyber espionage and data theft against government and commercial organizations around the world. According to a Mandiant report, the staff at Unit 61398 are trained in computer security and CNO and must also be proficient in the English language.

  PLA Unit 61486, based in Shanghai, is believed to be part of the 12th Bureau of the Third Department of the PLA GSD. This unit has been alleged to be a source of computer hacking attacks as part of a Chinese campaign to steal trade and military secrets from foreign targets. According to the CrowdStrike report, this unit is also suspected of involvement in "space surveillance" and "intercept of satellite communications" fits, with their observed targeting preferences being Western companies producing technologies in the space and imaging/remote sensing sectors. The size and number of satellite dishes present in the area is also consistent with these activities.

Technical Reconnaissance Bureaus (TRB)

The PLA, probably the Third Department, has a number of units known as technical reconnaissance bureaus, which are thought to be responsible for SIGINT collection missions. Known locations include facilities in the Lanzhou, Jinan, Chengdu, Guangzhou, and Beijing military regions. A number of these units may also undertake CNO activities.

The *Washington Post*[5] reported that a "digital squad" was based in China's southern Guangzhou military region and would have a budget in the tens of millions of yuan. (10 million yuan is equivalent to $1.54 million.) Other reports indicated that the unit would have a strength of approximately 30. Western observers believe that the organization may have been operational for two years or more before the announcement was made.

Information Warfare Militia

The Chinese militia is managed by the PLA to enable it to mobilize support and integrate militia members into provincial military commands, prefectural military commands, people's armed forces departments of counties, and basic-level people's armed forces departments; however, the PLA's command and control structure for IW militias remains unclear.

In recent years, alongside the modernization of the PLA, the modernization of the Chinese militia and reserve forces has mainly focused on the recruitment of new members with skills in essential high-technology areas. This has been undertaken with the aim of forming new units and helping transform existing militia or reserve units by incorporating recruits with advanced education and technical skills in areas that are considered essential. This change in the mobilization and recruitment strategy of the PLA has resulted in an expansion of militia units involved in all aspects of CNO.

Since as early as 2002, the focus has been on creating specialized units and has moved from a reliance on the recruitment of employees from state-owned enterprises to include recruitment from private-sector high-tech industries to meet the need for personnel in units such as communications, reconnaissance, and information technology. One example of the success of this change is reflected in a report by the General Political Department, which states that by the end of 2005, the Chengdu Military Region had created more than 290 separate EW, network warfare, and psychological warfare units as the result of recruiting staff from local information technology companies.

Limited reports of militia IW exercise activities provide an insight into how the PLA intends to integrate militia units with active duty units, in line with the information confrontation principles that the PLA has adopted.

Exercises

In the last decade, an increasing number of PLA exercises have included computer network attack, computer network defense, ECM, and psychological operations together with ground, naval, air, and strategic missile force activities. A number of the main PLA exercises during the period 2009–2011 contained an "information confrontation" focus in an attempt to improve the offensive capabilities of key units or test the defensive abilities of line units against network and electronic warfare attack.

The following are examples of this.

As noted in Chapter 2, the first recorded PLA cyber-warfare exercise took place in October 1997 in the Shenyang Military Region, with cyber detachments conducting both defense and attacks against each other. A group army underwent a computer attack that paralyzed its systems. The group army responded with virus-killing software, and the exercise was termed an "invasion and anti-invasion" event. The reported activities included information reconnaissance, planting information mines, changing network data, disseminating propaganda, information deception, organizing information defense, and establishing network spy stations.

The second exercise took place in October 1998, when the PLA staged an integrated high-technology exercise that united several military regions around the country. The center of gravity of the exercise was the Beijing Military Region, where a joint defense warfare drill used a "military information superhighway" for the first time.

Another exercise took place in October 1999, when the PLA conducted another cyber-warfare simulation. Two army groups of the Beijing Military Region took part in a "confrontation" campaign against computer networks. Reconnaissance and counterreconnaissance, interference and counterinterference, blocking and counterblocking, and air strikes and counter–air strikes were among some of the high-tech tactics practiced during the exercise.

In July 2000, the Chengdu Military Region conducted a confrontational campaign exercise on the Internet.

In 2006, the Xinhua News Agency reported that the PLA had concluded its military exercise Qianwei-206B in Shangdong Province. A land force air unit, EW troop, artillery troop, and special troop participated in the exercise, which lasted for 12 days. The purpose of the exercise was to assess the army's IW capabilities in the Jinan Military District.

According to a report in the PLA daily,[6] one of the areas that were the main focus of the military exercises held in 2010 was to test the confrontation capabilities of the troops under actual-combat conditions and featured the highest degree of informationization and had the most complex electromagnetic environment in naval history. The report stated that

> Today, the information system-based systematic combat capability becomes a basic form of combat effectiveness. The focuses of

informationization construction and military exercises of the PLA are about to shift to improving systematic combat capability.

Joint-2011 (Lianhe-211), a multiservice exercise held in late October 2011 in Shandong Province, included "joint information offensive and defensive operations" as one of the exercise's primary themes.

The *Washington Post*[5] reported that the Chinese military conducted an exercise in 2010 featuring attacks on communications command-and-control systems and another in October 2012 involving "joint information offensive and defensive operations."

According to a report in May 2013 in *Asitimes*,[7] the PLA was going to conduct its first joint combat drills involving cyber warfare, special troops, army aviation, and ECM units in June 2013 to test the integration and coordination of its land and air forces.

Exercise Joint Action-2014A was held in September 2014 in the South China Sea. The exercise focused on a range of subjects, including joint command of maritime operations based on information systems, air-defense and antisubmarine, conventional missile strike and information countermeasures. It tested the joint combat pattern, military tactics, and training methods of various services and arms on a multidimensional battlefield.

India

Policy and Strategy

In 1998, after a review of India's defense posture, the Indian military changed its policy and incorporated EW and IO into its doctrine. This resulted in the modernization of four military areas: information technology, EW, critical infrastructure protection, and army mobility.

In 2005, the Indian Army created the Army Cyber Security Establishment to secure networks at the division level and conduct security audits.

In 2012, the Indian Navy became the first Indian armed force to create a dedicated cadre of officers to provide cyber security to protect its computer-enabled communication networks and to enable the maritime force to carry out a network-center operation. The navy created a new cell in its headquarters under a rear admiral–rank officer as assistant chief of naval staff (communications, space, and network-centric operations).

A report in the *Hindu Times* in June 2013[8] criticized the Indian government for only having 556 cyber-security experts deployed within government agencies, compared to 125,000 experts in China, 91,080 in the United States, and 7300 in Russia. The article went on to state that the government would be recruiting an additional 4446 experts to be deployed in six organizations that would take care of India's cyber-security infrastructure:

- The Department of Electronics and Information Technology (DEITy), which includes the Indian Computer Emergency Response Team (CERT-In) and the National Informatics Centre (NIC)
- The Department of Telecom (DoT)
- The National Technical Research Organisation (NTRO)
- The Ministry of Defence
- The Intelligence Bureau (IB)
- The Defence Research and Development Organisation (DRDO)

The article went on to say that of the 4446 posts, the armed forces were to receive the majority of the experts (1887), followed by NTRO (695), DEITy (590), IB (565), DoT (459), and DRDO (250). The experts are to be responsible for traffic scanning and mitigation, system audit and forensics, assurance and certification, research and development, and coordination.

The National Critical Information Infrastructure Protection Centre (NCIIPC) was established in 2013 under the National Technical Research Organisation to provide cover to take all necessary measures to facilitate protection of critical information infrastructure.

The Indian Ministry of Communications and IT produced a National Cyber Security Policy in July 2013.

In 2014, the National Technical Research Organisation (NTRO) was given authority to protect to several critical sectors. In order to achieve this, it is in the process of establishing a National Cyber Coordination Centre (NCCC), which will be under the authority of the National Information Board and will be responsible for all forms of cyber-intelligence and cyber-security issues. The role of the NCCC is expected to include the screening of all forms of metadata, ensuring better coordination between the various intelligence agencies and streamlining intelligence gathering and sharing. The duties will also include providing alerts to all relevant agencies during a cyber attack. The NCCC will be jointly run by the NTRO and the armed forces.

Defensive

India has a number of units within the Ministry of Defence that are responsible for cyber security. The known units are

- Defence Information Warfare Agency, which coordinates information warfare responses
- Defence Intelligence Agency
- National Technical Intelligence Communication Centre
- Research and analysis wing (RAW) of the prime minister's office
- Defense Research and Development Organization, which built two ranges for testing EW systems

Note: The Defence Intelligence Agency and the National Technical Intelligence Communication Centre have been collaborating to create a joint "cyber squad" that would carry out penetration tests to alert the government to potential cyber vulnerabilities.

The proposed NCCC will coordinate efforts and information exchange between intelligence and cyber-response agencies such as the IB and CERT-In.

Data Security Council of India

The Data Security Council of India (DSCI) is a focal body on data protection in India. It is an independent self-regulatory organization (SRO) that was set up by NASSCOM® to promote data protection and develop security and privacy best practices and standards.

Defence Information Assurance and Research Agency (DIARA)

The Defence Information Assurance and Research Agency (DIARA) is a nodal Ministry of Defence agency mandated to deal with all cyber-security-related issues of the three armed services and the MoD. It coordinates its activities with national agencies including CERT-In and the National Training Research Organisation (NTRO).

Defense Intelligence Agency

The Defense Intelligence Agency (DIA) was formed in 2002 and is responsible for providing and coordinating intelligence for the Indian armed forces. The majority of intelligence work is carried out by the RAW and the IB. One of the roles of the DIA is to act as the liaison between the MoD subunits and other intelligence centers. The DIA coordinates its production activity with other agencies under the supervision of the Intelligence Coordination Group.

Offensive

The National Technical Research Organisation, along with the Defence Intelligence Agency, is responsible for developing offensive cyber capabilities.

Discussions have been underway in India since at least 2013 for the creation of a tri-service Cyber Command. In May 2013, the defense minister said that a cyber command was to be established in the armed forces as part of the efforts to strengthen cyber-security in the country.

The RAW is the primary foreign intelligence agency of India. The primary roles of the RAW are the gathering of foreign intelligence and counterterrorism.

Territorial Army (TA) Battalions for Cyber Warfare

There has been discussion since 2012 of the creation of Cyber Territorial Army battalions, which can provide "surge capability" to bolster India's resources during critical periods or in hostilities. To date, there is no evidence that this has taken place.

Indian Cyber Army

The Indian Cyber Army is a nongovernment organization that was created in 2011 under the Societies Registration Act XXI, 1860, with the mission "to fight Cyber Crime." The stated aim of the Indian Cyber Army is to carry out research, to analyze vulnerabilities and cyber attacks, to implement training, and to develop technology. The organization provides a range of training courses. A group calling itself the Indian Cyber Army has claimed responsibility for a number of hacking attacks, primarily against Pakistan. It is not known if these two groups are one and the same.

Research and Development

Military College of Telecommunications Engineering (MCTE)

The college is a center of excellence that specializes in training in combat communications, EW, communication engineering, computer science, cryptology, cyber warfare, and IT. Within the college, there is a Cyber Security Laboratory, which was created in 2010; in 2014, tenders were published for the establishment of a Cyber Warfare Laboratory.

In January 2013, the University Grants Commission directed technical universities and institutions to add cyber security and information security as subjects for higher studies.

The Prabhu Goel Research Centre for Computer and Internet Security

The Prabhu Goel Research Centre for Computer and Internet Security was established at the Indian Institute of Technology at Kanpur by Dr. Prabhu Goel with a grant of US$1 million. The center has a vision to become the nodal R&D center in the country for all aspects of computer security and to educate various governmental and nongovernmental organizations about security issues. The center undertakes research, training, and consulting activities in the area of computer and Internet security and collaborates with defense and security agencies in the development of security technologies.

Cyber Laboratories Program

The Cyber Labs Program was started by NASSCOM® in 2004 to create a common platform where different stakeholders could come together to deal with the issue of cyber crimes. The mission of this program is to

- Establish cyber labs in major cities where the IT/BPO industry is concentrated
- Develop cyber-forensics capability
- Impart training to police and industry entrepreneurs to effectively deal with cyber crimes
- Standardize the methods of investigation and promote cyber forensics
- Train police and judiciary in the IT Act, 2008
- Organize industry wide surveys to determine trends in cyber crimes
- Suggest measures for prevention of cyber crime

In 2009, the Cyber Labs Program was transferred to DSCI. DSCI has continued the program with a focus on training police officers, prosecutors, military, bank officials, and others on cyber crimes. Through the Cyber Labs Program, NASSCOM® and DSCI claim to have trained more than 10,000 personnel in law-enforcement, prosecution, and judiciary professions; banking and other financial institutions; income tax and customs departments; and the defense services.

The Institute for Defence Studies and Analyses (IDSA) has the role of research and policy-relevant studies on all aspects of defense and security. Its mission is to promote national and international security through the generation and dissemination of knowledge on defense and security-related issues. IDSA has a multidisciplinary research faculty drawn from academia, the defense forces, and the civil services.

The KEONICS Cyber Lab is an initiative of the Department of Information Technology under the IT security promotion campaign that is being implemented by Karnataka State Electronics Development Corporation Limited (KEONICS). The mission of the KEONICS Cyber Lab is to provide training, investigative support, and research and development support to agencies and entities involved in the prevention, investigation, and prosecution of white-collar/cyber crimes.

Exercises

APCERT Annual Drill

The APCERT Annual Drill has been held since 2005. In 2008, the scenario for the drill was of cyber attacks by professional cyber-criminal groups targeting at the Asia Pacific economies. India participated in this exercise together with representatives from 12 other countries.

In March 2009, the Indian Army held an exercise called the Divine Matrix. The exercise was based on a scenario in which China launches a nuclear attack on India in 2017. The purpose of the exercise was to describe how China would launch a cyber attack on India before the launch of the actual nuclear strike.

In 2012, India held a joint exercise with the United States to learn how to develop a robust cyber-security mechanism to safeguard its key and critical infrastructure areas. The Indian CERT-In held a two-day joint exercise based on a scenario in which the CERTs from both countries launch full-scale cyber attacks against each other and try to protect themselves from those attacks.

North Korea

> The basic key to victory in modern warfare is to do well in electronic warfare
>
> **Kim Jong-il[9]**

Policy and Strategy

Information on any type of activity in North Korea is difficult to obtain and verify, and the majority of the information available has come from defectors and Chinese news sources. It is clear that the country has been developing an IW capability for a considerable time. In July 2013, in his opening remarks[10] to the Subcommittee on Asia and the Pacific of the US House of Representatives' Committee on Foreign Affairs, the chairman, Senator Steve Chabot, commented that

> North Korea's growing cyber capabilities present the greatest likelihood of a cyber conflict in Asia. Earlier this year it demonstrated its capabilities in South Korea, where it crippled the operations of banks and news agencies by wiping the hard drives of thousands of computers.

Even today, North Korea has one of the lowest levels of Internet connectivity in the world, with only three Internet service providers, and the average citizen does not have access. According to a report in the *New York Times*,[11] North Korea

> has only 1,024 official Internet protocol addresses, though the actual number may be a little higher. That is fewer than many city blocks in New York have. The United States, by comparison, has billions of addresses.

From as early as the 1970s, the North Korean military has been developing its EW capability as an integral part of an effort to improve its asymmetric capabilities. As with many other countries, this area of capability is thought to have been rapidly expanded following reviews that took place following Operation Desert Storm in the early 1990s.

It is thought that the North Korean assessments of the demonstrated US capabilities came to conclusions similar to those of China. As a result, the North Korean military established an IW capability under the concept of "electronic intelligence warfare" (EIW), which includes the introduction of more modern electronic intelligence gathering equipment, jammers and radars. North Korea's approach to cyber operations seems to have begun toward the end of the 1990s with the creation of *Unit 121* within the Reconnaissance Bureau of the GSD.

In 2012, North Korea is believed to have signed an agreement with Iran to combat "common enemy in cyberspace."

Defensive

Little is known about the defensive capabilities of North Korea; however, in 2002 the country developed its own operating system, known as "Red Star," and version 3.0 of this system was released in the summer of 2013. This, coupled with the low levels of access, gives some level of protection; however, as was observed in December 2014, because of its limited size, the whole infrastructure is liable to denial-of-service attacks.

Offensive

The exact number of personnel who are involved in North Korea's cyber activities is difficult to determine, but there are a number of estimates that put the number at between 3000 and 6000.

The organization of the intelligence and internal security within North Korea is thought to consist of three organizations. These are the cabinet, the Korean Workers' Party (KWP), and the National Defense Commission. Directly subordinate to the cabinet is the Ministry of Public Security. Subordinate to the KWP is the Central Committee Secretary in Charge of South Korean Affairs (CCSKA), which controls four intelligence-related departments:

- The Foreign Liaison Department, also known as the Social-Cultural Department or Liaison Department. The Foreign Liaison Department is reported to be tasked with establishing cells within the Republic of Korea (ROK) and training agents.
- The Unification Front Department, also known as the South-North Dialogue Department. The Unification Front Department is reported to be responsible for "unified front" operations and anti-ROK psychological warfare operations.
- Office 35, also known as the Research Department for External Intelligence or Investigative Department. Office 35 is reported to be tasked with internal and external intelligence collection and infiltration into the ROK.
- The Operations Department, which is reported to be responsible for basic training of anti-ROK agents and infiltration operations.

The National Defense Commission is broken down into the Ministry of People's Armed Forces (MPAF) and the State Security Department.

Ministry of People's Armed Forces

Organizations that are directly subordinate to the MPAF are

- Cadre Bureau
- General Rear Services Bureau
- GSD

- Guard Command
- Representative Mission at Panmunjom
- Military Justice Bureau
- Military Prosecution Bureau
- Security Command

Organizations that are directly subordinate to the GSD are

- KPA ground forces
- Korean People's Air Force (KPAF)
- Korean People's Navy (KPN)
- Workers'-Peasants' Red Guard
- Paramilitary Training Units

There are thought to be around 24 bureaus subordinate to the GSD, which include military academies, universities, and research institutes. Among these bureaus are a number that deal with information and intelligence, including the Classified Information Bureau, the Communications Bureau, the Electronic Warfare Bureau, and the Reconnaissance Bureau.

The Classified Information Bureau is responsible for all aspects of classified information within the KPA. The Communications Bureau is responsible for all communications within the KPA. The Electronic Warfare Bureau is responsible for all SIGINT and EW/EIW assets within the KPA. The Reconnaissance Bureau is responsible for the collection of tactical and strategic MI and strategic special operations throughout the ROK and overseas.

Subordinate to the Reconnaissance Bureau is Unit 121. Unit 121, also known as the Korean People's Army (KPA) Joint Chiefs Cyber Warfare Unit, was originally a specialist unit within the Staff Reconnaissance Bureau, but it was upgraded in 2008 to a department made up of technical reconnaissance teams. Unit 121 has been named in a number of media sources for its role in alleged attacks on South Korea. Its core missions are reported to be to infiltrate computer networks, collect classified information, and place viruses into targeted networks.

According to a paper by Duk-Ki Kim,[12] Unit 121 is made up of approximately 3000 persons, organized into 10 combat teams and 110 research teams.

Also thought to be subordinate to the Reconnaissance Bureau are

- Office 91: responsible for core hacking tasks
- Office 3132: responsible for Electronic Cyber Warfare
- The Document Investigation room: responsible for hacking into social and economic organizations
- Unit 110: Also known as the Technology Reconnaissance Team; carries out cyber attacks on military and other strategic organizations and is thought to have been responsible for the July 2009 Distributed Denial-of-Service attacks against the United States and South Korea

The Central Party Investigative Group, also known as Unit 35, consists of approximately 500 people in 10 technical teams, which are responsible for technical education and training for both offensive and defensive capabilities.

Unit 204 of the Operations Department, the Unification Bureau—also known as the Enemy Secret Department Cyber Psychological Warfare Unit—consists of approximately 100 people and carries out cyber-psychological warfare and organizational espionage.

Also subordinate to the GSD is the Command Automation Department, which, according to one report, encompasses Office 31, which is responsible for developing hacking programs; Office No 32, which is responsible for developing military-related software; and Office 56, which is responsible for developing programs for command and communications.

Research and Development

The Military Training Bureau of the MPAF GSD is responsible for education and training within the KPA, including military schools and academies. It is thought to carry out research and the evaluation of foreign combat operations through a number of research institutes.

A significant part of North Korea's effort to develop its cyber capabilities has been targeted at the educational process and the education and training of its citizens from a young age. A number of defectors have reported that the identification of talented children takes place while they are in primary education, and they are then schooled through the education system.

At least four universities are thought to deliver information security/information warfare courses. These are the Kim Il-sung University, the Kim Chaek University of Technology, the Command Automation University (formerly known as Mirim University), and the Moranbong University for Further Education. Courses at these universities are thought to include lessons in programming, command automation, computerized calculation, technical reconnaissance, and cyber warfare.

Top graduates are then thought to be sent to join units in the Reconnaissance Bureau or the General Staff or are sent abroad for further training to gain increased levels of practical experience.

The Command Automation University, which was established in 1986 by order of Kim Jong-il, is believed to produce more than 100 cyber-warfare experts each year. The university has five departments: electronic engineering, command automation, programming, technical reconnaissance, and computer science. The command automation department is thought to teach defensive and offensive programming and hacking tactics.

Moranbong University, which was established in 1997, is believed to produce around 30 experts in data processing, code breaking, and hacking each year.

Exercises

There are no known IW training exercises; however, a number of activities have been attributed to North Korea.

In 2004, it was reported that Unit 121 had gained access to 33 of the 80 wireless communication networks used by the South Korean military. The attack coincided with joint South Korea and US military exercises.

Operation Troy

Between 2009 and 2013, South Korea suffered a number of high-profile cyber attacks. According to a report by McAfee[13], which named the activity Operation Troy, the activity increased in both frequency and sophistication over the period. While the activity was initially considered to be separate attacks by two groups, the New Romantic Cyber Army Team and the Who is Hacking Team, research by Symantec and McAfee indicated that the attacks were linked. The McAfee report indicates that the activity included Mater Boot Record (MBR) wiping, which resulted in the loss of data, cyber vandalism, and a covert espionage campaign.

Kimsuky Campaign

In September 2013, the Kaspersky Laboratory published its findings[14] from a 6 month investigation into an extensive cyberespionage campaign, which they named "Kimsuky," against 11 South Korean and two Chinese organizations. The findings detailed the discovery of an extensive but unsophisticated attack that was primarily targeted against South Korean military think-tank targets. The attack consisted of a number of malicious programs, which included keystroke logging, directory listing collection, document theft, remote control download, and remote control access.

Pakistan

There is very little open-source information available with regard to the Pakistani national capabilities in the area of IW. This is not too surprising, as the National Cyber Security Council was only established in 2014 and is to set out the strategy for cyber space.

Policy and Strategy

In April 2013, the Chairman of Senate Defence Committee announced a Task Force on Cyber Security Policy, which was to work jointly with the Pakistan Information Security Association, (PISA) under the Senate Defence Committee, to define the nature of the new emerging threats to Pakistan's national security and defense in the digital battlefield and to prepare Cyber Security Policy in consultation and with cooperation of experts and professionals from PISA and government organizations as well.

In April 2014, Pakistan presented its National Cyber Security Council Act as a measure to help build capacity for securing its cyber space. The act called for the establishment of a National Cyber Security Council, to be made up of 21 members of the federal government and members from the private sector and information security professionals. The roles of the council include the development of a National Cyber Security strategy and an International Cyber Security strategy. The tasks that the council was to carry out included

1. To establish an independent National CERT under private public partnership
2. To assist in the establishment of industry and sector specific CERTs
3. Subject to privacy, corporate confidentiality, intellectual property, and national security, to establish a voluntary mechanism, with legislative incentive if necessary, for the sharing of cyber-security-related information and data between the private sector and public sector
4. To establish an accreditation and standardization mechanism for public-sector critical information infrastructure
5. To prepare and issue a national cyber-security strategy and an international cyber-security strategy
6. To facilitate the establishment of a cryptographic product evaluation laboratory

Defensive

Pakistan National Response Center for Cyber Crime

The Pakistan National Response Center for Cyber Crime (NR3C) provides a single point of contact for all local and foreign organizations for all matters related to cyber crimes. It provides training and related security education to persons of government/semi-government and private-sector organizations.

Inter-Services Intelligence Directorate

Inter-Services Intelligence Directorate (ISID) is the main intelligence service of Pakistan, operationally responsible for providing security and intelligence assessment to the government. ISID is the largest of the three intelligence services, the others being the IB and MI.

Offensive

Pakistan Cyber Army

The Pakistan Cyber Army is a group of Pakistani hackers that operate under the name. The group has no formal connections with the government and there is no indication that it is formally endorsed. The group has been responsible for a large number of hacking attacks against India and a number of other countries. There are unconfirmed reports that Pakistani intelligence services and some of these hackers now operate in service under the direction of the ISID.

Research and Development

The Pakistan Army School of Military Intelligence runs courses on both security and intelligence.

References

1. Australian Department of Defence. (2013). *Operation Series: Information Activities* (Edition 3). Australian Defence Doctrine Publication. http://www.defence.gov.au/FOI/Docs/Disclosures/330_1314_Document.pdf.
2. Deakin-Bell, D. (2008). Information operations management in the RAN. *Headmark: Journal of the Australian Naval Institute*. http://navalinstitute.com.au/wp-content/uploads/2014/04/headmark-130.pdf.
3. Billo, C. and Chang, W. (2004). *Cyber Warfare: An Analysis of the Means and Motivations of Selected Nation States*. Hanover, NH: Institute for Security Technology Studies at Dartmouth College.
4. Krekel, B., Adams, P., and Bakos, G. (2012). Occupying the information high ground: Chinese capabilities for computer network operations and cyber espionage, A report prepared for the U.S.-China Economic and Security Review Commission by Northrop Grumman Corporation, March 7. http://www.scribd.com/doc/84582278/USCCReport-Chinese-Capabilities-for-Computer-Network-Operations-and-Cyber-Espionage.
5. Nakashima, E. (2012). China testing cyber-attack capabilities. *Washington Post*, March 8.
6. *PLA Daily*. (2011). Chinese military exercises in 2010 highlight five characteristics. January 21. http://eng.mod.gov.cn/MilitaryExercises/2011-01/21/content_4220801.htm.
7. *Asitimes*. (2013). PLA joint cyberwarfare drill to show new strength and sophistication. May 30. http://asitimes.blogspot.co.uk/2013/05/pla-joint-cyberwarfare-drill-to-show.html.
8. Joshi, S. (2013). An IT superpower, India has just 556 cyber security experts. *Hindu Times*, June 19. http://www.thehindu.com/news/national/an-it-superpower-india-has-just-556-cyber-security-experts/article4827644.ece.
9. Bermudez Jr., J. S. (2005). *SIGINT, EW, and EIW in the Korean People's Army: An Overview of Development and Organization*. Honolulu, HI: Asia Pacific Center for Security Studies. http://www.apcss.org/Publications/Edited%20Volumes/BytesAndBullets/CH13.pdf.
10. Chabot, S. (2013). Chairman of the Committee on Foreign Affairs, Subcommittee on Asia and the Pacific, Asia: The Cyber Security Battleground. Opening statement, http://docs.house.gov/meetings/FA/FA05/20130723/101186/HHRG-113-FA05-20130723-SD001.pdf.
11. Perlroth, N. and Sanger, D. E. (2014). North Korea loses its link to the Internet. *New York Times*, December 22. http://www.nytimes.com/2014/12/23/world/asia/attack-is-suspected-as-north-korean-internet-collapses.html?_r=0.

12. Kim, D.-K. (2011). The Republic of Korea's counter-asymmetric strategy. *Naval War College Review* 65(1). https://www.usnwc.edu/getattachment/8e487165-a3ef-4ebc-83ce-0ddd7898e16a/The-Republic-of-Korea-s-Counter-asymmetric-Strateg.
13. Sherstobitoff, R. and Liba, I. (2013). Dissecting Operation Troy: Cyberespionage in South Korea. McAfee White Paper. http://www.mcafee.com/uk/resources/white-papers/wp-dissecting-operation-troy.pdf.
14. Kaspersky Lab. (2013). Kaspersky Lab analyzes active cyber-espionage campaign primarily targeting South Korean entities, September 11. http://www.kaspersky.com/about/news/virus/2013/kaspersky_lab_analyzes_active_cyber-espionage_campaign_primarily_targeting_south_korean_entities.

Chapter 9

Nation-State Defensive and Offensive Information Warfare Capabilities: Europe

In this chapter, the term Europe is used in the context of the European Union (EU), which consists of 28 countries (Austria, Belgium, Bulgaria, Croatia, Republic of Cyprus, Czech Republic, Denmark, Estonia, Finland, France, Germany, Greece, Hungary, Ireland, Italy, Latvia, Lithuania, Luxembourg, Malta, the Netherlands, Poland, Portugal, Romania, Slovakia, Slovenia, Spain, Sweden, and the United Kingdom), and Switzerland.

The three countries with the best defined information warfare (IW) capabilities and largest standing military establishments (France, Germany, and the United Kingdom) have been reviewed.

France

Policy and Strategy

In June 2008, during the presentation of a white paper on defense entitled "Cyber Warfare Has Become a Reality," which defines the French national security strategy for the coming 15 years, the French president stated that "in terms of defense and security, control and protection of information is now real power factors," and that "cyber warfare has become a reality."

The 2008 French White Paper on defense and national security identified that cyber war was a major concern, and the white paper develops a two-pronged strategy: a new concept of cyber defense, organized in depth and coordinated by a new Security of Information Systems Agency under the purview of the General Secretariat for Defence and National Security (SGDSN); and the establishment of an offensive cyber-war capability, part of which would come under the Joint Staff and the other part to be developed within the special services.

In 2011, France's strategy for information systems defense and security was published. In this document, the strategy is defined by four objectives:

1. Become a world power in cyber defense
2. Safeguard France's ability to make decisions through the protection of information related to its sovereignty
3. Strengthen the cyber security of critical national infrastructures
4. Ensure security in cyber space

The document states that in order to achieve these four strategic objectives, seven areas of action had been identified:

- Anticipate and analyze
- Detect, alert, and respond
- Enhance and perpetuate French scientific, technical, industrial, and human capabilities
- Protect the information systems of the state and the operators of critical infrastructures
- Adapt French legislation
- Develop international collaborations
- Communicate to inform and convince

In the 2013 White Paper on Defense and National Security, 12 key points were identified. Within these 12 key points, cyber warfare is specifically addressed in

- Point 2: Fine-tune the analysis of threats compared with the 2008 White Paper, under "Threats related to power," where cyber attacks instigated by states are identified; and under "Threats and risks intensified by globalization," where cyber attacks are again specifically identified.
- Point 8: Build a new armed forces model, where it states that

   for the first time, the armed forces model includes military cyber defence capabilities, in close liaison with intelligence and defensive and offensive planning, in preparation for or support of military operations.

- Point 9: Cyber defense—a new strategic context specifically addresses the subject and states that the 2013 White Paper "marks a crucial new stage in recognition of cyber threats and development of cyber defence capabilities."

Under this point, they address what is seen as the growing vulnerability of the state and society to what are described as increasingly dangerous attacks. These attacks include attempts to gain access to networks for the purposes of espionage, the remote takeover of systems, the paralysis of networks, and the potential, in the near future, for the destruction of vital elements of infrastructure, weapons systems, or strategic military capabilities.

Under point 9, the white paper is identified as providing the basis of a strategic stance for identifying the origin of attacks, organizing and ensuring the resilience of the national infrastructure, and responding to attacks. Notably, this is seen to include the use of offensive cyber capabilities. The white paper goes on to state that France intends to increase the level of personnel dedicated to cyber defense, and that it intends to enhance the reliability of both state and major industry information systems. It states that France will be developing a unified chain of command for defense and to respond to the increase in the number of threats.

■ Point 10: Giving priority to intelligence. This point deals with the priorities for resource allocation over the coming years, and again, cyber defense is highlighted.

One of the initiatives that came from the 2013 defense white paper was the creation of a specialized master's degree in cyber-crisis management, which will run at the French military academy from 2015. The course is expected to have between 15 and 25 military students in the first intake, although in the future, nonmilitary students might also be accepted.

Defensive

The National Agency for Information Systems Security (Agence nationale de la sécurité des systèmes d'information) (ANSSI), which was established in 2009, has the following missions: detecting and reacting to cyber attack, preventing cyber threats by supporting research and development, and providing information to government and critical infrastructure entities. ANSSI operates under the authority of the French general secretariat for national defense. In 2012, ANSSI was expected to have a staff of around 250 and a budget of €90 million. By 2015, ANSSI will ramp up as it will go from 357 to 500 IT specialists.

In 2011, the French government created the position of Cyber Defense General Officer within the Ministry of Defense. This officer will head a committee that will address the protection of information systems against cyber-security-related risks. The Cyber Defense General Officer is responsible for crisis management and collaborates with the ANSSI.

Within the Ministry of Defense (MoD), there is the Center for the Analysis of Computer Warfare Defense (Centre d'analyse de lutte informatique défense) (Calid), which operates under the authority of the Cyber Defense General Officer and is responsible for contributing to the preparation and conduct of operations on cyber networks and systems of the department of defense. Calid provides centralized network monitoring and support in the case of an incident. Calid currently has a military staff of about 20, but this is expected to increase to 40 by 2015.

The Information System Security Operation Center (Centre opérationnel en sécurité des systèmes d'informations) (COSSI) operates under the authority of the General Secretariat for National Defense and Security (Secrétariat général de la défense et de la sécurité nationale) (SGDN) and has the role of defending government networks and information systems. In addition to its general tasks, it coordinates the actions of French ministries and identifies protection and reaction measures.

In its role, the department of protection and security of defense (DPSD) includes missions against interference and control as well as assistance in the field of cyber security. The Joint Department of Infrastructure Networks and Information Defense Systems is responsible for defense communication and information services (CIS). It was created at the end of 2003, and its role is to provide the most suitable and cost-efficient technical solutions to meet the needs of the department of defense. Among these responsibilities are those of networks (Internet, telephone, transit, roads), security of information systems, frequency management, and support of the nuclear forces networks. In January 2006, the Central Directorate of Telecommunications and Informatics of the Army (DCTEI) merged with DIRISI, which was reinforced by resources from the navy, air force, and the General Secretary for Administration (SGA) and the Armaments Procurement Agency (*Direction Générale de l'Armement* (DGA)). Then, in 2007, the air force, and in 2008, the navy integrated their CIS with those of DIRISI.

The network of cyber citizen reserves was created as a result of the 2012 "Cyber Defence: A Global Issue, a National Priority" report. The cyber citizen reserves aim to make cyber issues a national priority through outreach activities and bring together professionals and students about to graduate or with a close interest in the field of cyber security and cyber defense. It is described as a laboratory for a new form of active patriotic commitment in support of the army and the state.

Offensive

According to an article in *La Tribune* in July 2012, France has developed an offensive cyber-war capability under the authority of the Joint Staff. In addition, both the army and the air force have electronic warfare (EW) units.

In 2008, the French government launched an information weapons program to enable it to better respond to cyber threats. At the international forum on cyber security in Lille in January 2014, Admiral Arnaud Coustillière, the general officer in charge of cyber defense at the MoD, with the role of defending the information systems of the Department of Defense and conducting cyber operations in support of military operations, was quoted as saying

Offensive weapons are clearly present in both the 2008 and 2013 Defence White Papers, which refer to both defensive and offensive capabilities. So the state takes that choice' and 'When we have the right to fire missiles, if we can get the desired effect with a computer weapon it is better.

When asked about the French doctrine with regard to the use of offensive cyber weapons, he stated

There is a prédoctrine in the White Paper of Defence which positions IT offensive weapons as one of the means available to the State to respond to a computer attack.

He went on to explain that the French state doctrine for response to a computer strategic attack is

1. Set up a defensive posture under the auspices of ANSSI.
2. In case of strategic cyber attack, the government reserves the right to respond by all means, including the use of the Department of Defense, without specifying how.

A report in *France-Inter* in July 2014 stated that the Department of Defense employs 1400 cyber combatants and will be recruiting a further 350.

Research and Development

The Armaments Procurement Agency is actually the research and development arm of the Department of Defense. It is in charge of providing equipment to all branches of the armed forces and of developing the future equipment of the armies. The agency manages more than 80 projects and controlled a budget of more than €7.5 billion in 2011.

The French Defense Technical Center for Information Warfare (DGA Information Superiority [DGA-MI]) is responsible for designing and evaluating security components for the DGA and is being expanded; a staff level of 450 is expected by 2019.

The High-Security Computing Laboratory (known as the LHS) was designed to cater for research into the security of networks, Internet exchanges, and associated telecommunications equipment.

Universities

The main research areas of the Center for Scientific Studies of Defense within the University of Marne-la-Vallée are systems and information networks, the spread of weapons, and natural, technological, or cultural vulnerabilities.

The École pour l'Informatique et les Techniques Avancées (EPITA) Graduate School of Computer Science runs a master of computer security program.

The Université de Bordeaux runs an information security program.

The Université Joseph Fourier et INPG runs an information security program.

The Université de Toulon et du Var runs an information security program.

The Université de Limoges runs an information security program.

The Université de Tours runs a telecommunications security program.

The Université Technologie de Troyes runs an information security program.

The École nationale supérieure des telecommunications runs an information security program.

Exercises

France took part in the European project Exercise EUROCYBEX; its main issue was the implementation of a cyber-attack exercise involving a number of EU member states. The aim of the exercise was to test and improve communication procedures between member states. The project started in January 2011 and ended in mid-2012.

Exercise Inter PIRANET 2012 was a national crisis management exercise on the theme of a massive cyber attack. The exercise involved a number of agencies including the ANSSI. This exercise was previously held in 2010.

Exercise DEFNET 2014 took place in September/October 2014. The exercise was used to validate operational procedures for the use of rapid response teams (groupes d'intervention rapide [GIR]). Representatives from the three rapid response teams—land, air, (Joint Department of Infrastructure Networks and Information Defense Systems [DIRISI]) and the navy—used the exercise to develop their ability to respond together in a complex environment to strengthen the intervention capability of the Center for the Analysis of Computer Warfare Defense, when required.

As a member of NATO, France is also a regular participant in multinational exercises including the Cyber Storm and Cyber Coalition series.

Germany

Policy and Strategy

Germany started to develop its IW capability as early as 2005, and its Critical Infrastructure Protection Implementation Plan was created in 2007 based on the 2005 National Plan for Information Infrastructure Protection. In 2011, the German Ministry of the Interior published its Cyber Security Strategy for Germany.[1] In the document, the approach that will be taken by the German government was outlined, together with the organizations that were to be created to enable it. Two of the main organizations identified were the National Cyber Security Council and the National Cyber Defense Center. The strategy focused on protecting the critical information infrastructure, securing and strengthening IT systems, improving law enforcement, promoting international engagement, ensuring reliable and trustworthy information technology, and training the cyber workforce.

The National Cyber Security Council was created within the Federal Government Commissioner for Information Technology and is responsible for the implementation of the government's cyber-security strategy. The council includes representatives from the Federal Chancellery and Federal Foreign Office; several key ministries, including interior, defense, economics and technology, justice, finance, and education and research; and the state governments. The role of the council is to coordinate the development and use of "preventive tools and the interdisciplinary cyber security approaches" of the public and the private sector.

The National Cyber Defense Center (Nationales Cyber-Abwehrzentrum) is under the control of the Federal Office for Information Security and works with the Federal Office for the Protection of the Constitution and the Federal Office of Civil Protection and Disaster Assistance, together with the federal police, intelligence, and customs agencies. The role of the center is to analyze cyber-security incidents and provide recommendations for counterstrategies to the National Cyber Security Council, both on a regular basis and in response to specific incidents. The new center was initially staffed with six members of the German security agency BSI, two from the German Office for the Protection of the Constitution (the domestic intelligence agency) and two from the Federal Office of Civil Protection and Disaster Assistance (BBK). It was subsequently reinforced with staff from the Federal Police, the Federal Office of Criminal Investigation, the Federal Intelligence Service (Bundesnachrichtendienst), the German army (Bundeswehr) and the Customs Criminal Investigation Office (ZKA). The agency was heavily criticized in 2014 as not being "fit-for-purpose."

Defensive

Alliance for Cyber Security

The Alliance for Cyber Security is an initiative of the Federal Office for Information Security (BSI), which was established in cooperation with the German Association for Information Technology, Telecommunications and New Media (BITKOM). The Alliance for Cyber Security is developing an extensive knowledge base and supports the exchange of information and experience between participating organizations. The alliance has more than 973 participating organizations.

In Germany, military preparations were made with the intention of an operational capability being in place by 2010; however, it did not become operational until 2012. The unit, known as the "department of information and computer network operations" is part of the Strategic Reconnaissance Command. The Department of Information and Computer Network Operations is believed to have a staff of around 75.

The Bundeswehr Computer Emergency Response Team (CERTBw) is thought to employ around 40 information technology (IT) specialists and has the role of protecting approximately 140,000 computers in Bundeswehr facilities against attacks from the network.

Offensive

Strategic Reconnaissance Command

The Strategic Reconnaissance Command is the German military intelligence organization. The core mission of the command is to support the tactical information needs of the Bundeswehr and education in the relevant disciplines. The Strategic Reconnaissance Command has the following subordinate units:

- Battalion Electronic Warfare 911
- Battalion Electronic Warfare 912
- Lake Board Intervention Teams for fleet service boats
- Battalion Electronic Warfare 931
- Battalion Electronic Warfare 932
- Airborne component for use in close support, Special Forces EW
- Electronic Warfare Evaluation center
- Bundeswehr School for Strategic Reconnaissance
- Bundeswehr Central investigative body for technical education
- Bundeswehr Center for Geoinformation
- Department of Information and Computer Network Operations

Research and Development

In Germany, the majority of research funding is distributed by the Federal Ministry of Education and Research (BMBF). The BMBF has provided funding of around €66 million for projects in IT security since 2009 and supports research to protect IT systems. The BMBF has supported three IT security centers since 2011 with a view to developing new approaches in this area:

- CISPA: Center for IT Security, Privacy, and Accountability
- EC-SPRIDE: European Center for Security and Privacy by Design
- KASTEL: Competence Center for Applied Security Technology

The competence centers take the resources of the best universities and nonuniversity research establishments in the cyber-security research field.

Exercises

Most of the IW training that has been recorded for the German military has been during NATO exercises, in which they are a regular participant.

Exercise LÜKEX 11

This was a strategic crisis-management exercise based on the theme of a national crisis in the wake of cyber attacks. The aim of the exercise was the training and testing of the actions of the crisis and federal administrative staffs of and the state at the strategic decision level, including private operators of elements of the Critical Infrastructure.

Exercise Cyber Coalition 2013

This exercise took place in Estonia and involved around 400 experts from the field of military and civilian cyber defense from 33 nations.

Exercise Steadfast Jazz 2013

This was a NATO joint exercise in Poland, Latvia, and the Baltic Sea, involving around 6000 troops from all of the NATO countries as well as Sweden, Finland, and Ukraine. In addition to the ground exercise, a simulated cyber attack was carried out.

Exercise Combined Endeavor 2014

This is the 20th anniversary of this series of exercise. This is one of the main interoperability and cyber-defense exercises between NATO and the Partnership for Peace (PfP) nations. In September 2013, more than 1200 people from 40 nations and transnational organizations tested their interoperability and cyber-defense skills in a collaborative environment.

United Kingdom

Policy and Strategy

The United Kingdom's cyber-security strategy was published in 2009. The strategy involves a three-pronged approach that is based on reducing risk, exploiting opportunities, and improving the response to cyber incidents.

The document explains that in order to reduce risks in cyber space, it is essential to reduce the level of vulnerability to attacks and mitigate the impact of cyber incidents. The approach that is outlined in the strategy is of intelligence gathering, government policy promotion, and taking action against adversaries. The document goes on to state that in order to improve the response to an attack, it will be necessary to improve knowledge and awareness, develop doctrine and policy, improve governance and decision-making structures, and enhance both technical and human capabilities.

The 2010 National Security Strategy lists one of the four Tier 1 priority risks as "Hostile attacks upon UK cyber space by other states and large scale cyber crime." Also in 2010, in the Strategic Defence and Security Review,[2] an additional £650 million was allocated over a period of four years (2009–2013) for cybersecurity initiatives. The allocation of the £650 million was broken down as 65% on capabilities, 20% on critical cyber infrastructure, 9% on cyber crime, 1% on education, and 5% on reserves. The budget for the National Cyber Security Program for 2015–2016 was later announced as being £210 million.

The rationale for this additional funding is given in the foreword to the document as being to establish a transformative national program to protect the United Kingdom in cyber space. The strategy document stated that "over the last decade the threat to national security and prosperity from cyber attacks has increased exponentially." It goes on to predict that in the future this trend will be likely to continue to increase in scale and sophistication and that this has huge implications on the nature of future conflicts.

This is expanded on later in the document:

> We will transform our cyber capabilities within Defence by establishing a UK Defence Cyber Operations Group as part of the transformative cross-government approach set out in section 4.C.*

The document predicts that future conflict will see cyber operations conducted in parallel with more conventional actions in all three of the maritime, land, and air environments. The role of the Cyber Operations Group is given as providing a group of experts that will support both UK and allied cyber operations to secure vital national networks and also guide the development of new cyber capabilities. The Cyber Operations Group is intended to bring together existing expertise from across the defense community, which includes the armed forces and the science and technology research community. Part of the role of the Cyber Operations Group is to ensure that the United Kingdom plans, trains, exercises, and operates in a way that integrates its activities in both the cyber and physical space; and to develop, test, and validate the cyber capabilities to ensure that they are compatible with traditional military capabilities. The Cyber Operations Group is to work with other government departments and industry and help in the development of strong international alliances in order to increase resilience and improve joint operational capabilities.

---

* Section 4C of the document is the section on cyber security.

In 2009, the Office of Cyber Security was formed, and in 2010 it became the Office of Cyber Security and Information Assurance (OCSIA). The role of OCSIA is to provide support to the minister for the cabinet office and the National Security Council. The unit provides strategic direction and coordinates the cyber-security program for the government, enhancing cyber security and information assurance in the United Kingdom. The OCSIA collaborates with other government departments and agencies, including the Home Office, MoD, Government Communications Headquarters (GCHQ), the Communications-Electronics Security Department (CESG), the Centre for the Protection of National Infrastructure (CPNI), the Foreign & Commonwealth Office (FCO), and the Department for Business, Innovation & Skills (BIS).

The Cyber Security Operations Centre, which was also established in 2009, is responsible for developing both offensive and defensive cyber capabilities. The center is located within GCHQ. Its primary tasks are given as "to monitor the development and health of government IT systems, analyze trends and improve responses to cyber incidents."

The UK military doctrine[3] states that "Both offensive and defensive exploitation of cyberspace is required, to use the space in support of physical activities and effects and to protect that use" and that commanders should consider a number of broad factors, including

1. The manner and degree to which capabilities are dependent on cyber space and the way in which those capabilities are affected by it
2. The way in which activity in cyber space can be integrated into other activities, or is affected by other activities, in other environments
3. The way in which cyber space may have either positive or negative impacts, and how these can be exploited or mitigated
4. The way in which cyber space affects and connects the military, diplomatic, and economic levers of power
5. The way in which cyber space affects the number and type of adversaries
6. The way in which cyber space can be exploited in a maneuvrist way. This means "to achieve understanding and influence; gain intelligence; seize the initiative; to break or protect cohesion and will; and to support a narrative."

Later in the document, under the section on the maneuvrist approach to operations, special influence methods are defined as "a range of specific or special methods which aim to have direct influence can be grouped together."

The document explains that while the special influence methods are likely to require specialized preparation, it is probable that they will affect most of the operations. The document comments that these special influence methods can have significant consequences in return for relatively low expenditure and risk, but that there will be difficulties with the planning, execution, and assessment of their effect. It goes on to highlight that both agility and rapid communication are essential but are challenging for large organizations. In UK military doctrine, special influence methods are organized into:

1. Information Methods. Information Methods have previously been referred to as *information operations* or *Info Ops*. They are the way in which military staffs coordinate a number of tasks designed to have direct influence. These include
   a. Computer network action. Computer network action (CNA) is also known as computer network operations (CNO). This has attack, defense, and network exploitation applications, all of which can be used in cyber space to support operations.
   b. Psychological methods. Psychological methods, previously known as *psychological operations* or *PsyOps*. These are planned activities directed at selected target audiences to achieve political and military objectives by influencing attitudes and behaviors. They are aimed at weakening the will of the adversary, reinforcing the will of friendly force supporters, and gaining the support of the uncommitted.

It is worth noting at this point that the nomenclature within the United Kingdom has changed and a number of new terms have been used, with information operations (Info Ops) being replaced by information methods, CNO being replaced with CNA, and PsyOps being replaced with psychological methods.

Defense

Centre for the Protection of National Infrastructure (CPNI)

The role of the CPNI is to protect national security by providing advice to the organizations that make up the United Kingdom's national infrastructure. The advice covers all aspects of security, including the physical, personnel, and cyber areas. The CPNI answers to the Security Service and GCHQ.

In 2011, the UK government, together with a number of private firms, jointly established a Cybersecurity Information Sharing Partnership (CISP). This was intended to be a joint government/industry resourced "fusion cell" to provide analysis and support.

Land Information Assurance Group

This is a group of IT specialists who provide high-level management and IS support across the army. The Land Information Assurance Group (LIAG) is a unit that is made up of individuals from a number of corps and regiments, and it currently has members who have served with the Royal Navy, Royal Air Force (RAF), and a range of army units including the Royal Artillery, Military Intelligence, and Infantry Units.

A Territorial Army (reservist), the LIAG was established in 1999 to provide support for all three armed services. The services provided include penetration testing, vulnerability assessment, network traffic analysis, computer forensics, and intrusion detection.

The RAF has an Info Ops Group at the Air Warfare Centre, which provides operational security (OPSEC) training and which has oversight of RAF cyber development and input to the Defence Cyber Security program (DCSP).

The RAF also has the 591 Signals Unit, which provides information assurance for its infrastructure.

The Defence Electronic Warfare Centre (DEWC) of the RAF has the mission of providing accurate and timely Electronic Warfare Operational Support (EWOS) to defense in the form of mission-dependent data (MDD), EW information, doctrine, training, countermeasures advice, and various other products resulting from the fusion of intelligence, information, and doctrine. The DEWC is the United Kingdom's authoritative EW data source, from which all defense EW systems are programmed. This is a joint service unit.

In 2012, in supplementary written evidence from the MoD to the defense select committee, two organizations—the UK DCOG and the Global Operations and Security Control Centre (GOSCC)—were named. The organizations were described thus:

> The UK Defence Cyber Operations Group (DCOG), which is due to be fully operational by March 2015, is a collection of cyber units across defence that will be working closely together to deliver a defence capability. The Group will be responsible for ensuring that cyber security is coordinated and prioritized throughout the MoD and ensuring the coherent integration of cyber activities across the full spectrum of defence operations. This is intended to give the MoD a more highly focused approach to the cyber environment to ensuring the resilience of vital networks and by integrating cyber activities into defence operations, doctrine and training.
>
> The Defence Equipment and Support Organisation through its Information Systems and Services (ISS) Global Operations and Security Control Centre (GOSCC). This is responsible for the delivery and assurance of information and communication services for the UK Armed Forces. It is reported that approximately 200 people (mix of military, MoD civilian and contractor personnel) are employed in the GOSCC. The role of the GOSCC is to deliver, manage and defend the Defence Network and provide worldwide assured communications for the MoD.

The GOSCC has been in existence since at least 2002.

In 2012, it was announced that two joint cyber units were to be established. These were

> The Joint Cyber Unit (Corsham) was established with the role of pro-actively and reactively defending MoD networks against cyber attacks to enable the exploitation of MoD information capabilities across all areas of operations.
>
> The Joint Cyber Unit (Cheltenham), which is hosted by GCHQ and was due to achieve full operational capability by 2015. The role of this unit will be to develop new tactics, techniques and plans to deliver military effects, including enhanced security, through operations in cyber space.

The UK government announced the creation of a Joint Cyber Reserve Unit in September 2013, with an initial budget of £500 million. The unit will have full operational capability by April 2015. The aim of the unit is to recruit hundreds of reservists as computer experts to work alongside regular armed forces. The role of the unit will be to defend national security, and it will also launch strikes in cyber space if necessary.

In October 2014, Scotland Yard approved an expansion of the Falcon Unit (Fraud and Linked Crime Online), its specialist electronic crimes unit, to 500 cyber-crime officers. The unit is reported to be the largest anti-cyber-crime unit in Europe and has an initial team of 300 staff.

The Future Reserves 2020 report[4] that was produced by the Independent Commission to Review the United Kingdom's Reserve Forces and was published in July 2011, identified two additional areas of the reserve forces that require development. These were the Royal Navy, which required the generation of further capability in C4ISTAR and cyber; and the RAF, which required the addition of a new Cyber Security Squadron.

Offensive

In a September 2013 report from the *Financial Times*, the UK defense secretary said, ahead of a party political conference, that the United Kingdom was "developing a full-spectrum military cyber capability, including a strike capability." In a separate report in the *Mail on Sunday*, he is quoted as having stated that a "new 'cyber strike force' costing up to £500 million is being secretly built by Britain to wage war with a regiment of computer geeks instead of bombs and bullets" and that "Fighter planes, warships and regiments face being replaced by futuristic cyber assaults using lethal computer worms and viruses to wipe out enemy targets." The article goes on to say that he had "hailed the changes as the biggest military revolution since tanks replaced cavalry brigades in the First World War a century ago" and that "Britain is the first nation in the world to announce publicly that it has a 'cyber strike capability'."

Research and Development

Defence Science and Technology Laboratory (DSTL)

The Defence Science and Technology Laboratory (DSTL) is the Ministry of Defence's research organization. In January 2014, contracts to a value of £10 million were announced for the funding of research to study the growing culture of computer hackers as well as crowd behavior and how social media can impact upon behaviors in crises, with the aim to "deliver new and innovative ways to understand and influence online behaviour."

DSTL Also Runs the Centre for Defence Enterprise (CDE)

The Centre for Defence Enterprise (CDE) operates in the area of novel, high-risk, high-potential-benefit research, and it works with science and technology providers, including academia and small companies, to develop cost-effective capability advantage for the UK armed forces and national security.

Cranfield Defence and Security (CDS) is a School of Cranfield University that is based at the UK Defence Academy. It is the academic provider to the UK MoD for all postgraduate education at the Defence Academy College of Management and Technology and also provides training in engineering, science, acquisition, management, and leadership. The school also carries out research into a number of areas of Info Ops.

The UK GCHQ, the Department for BIS, and the Engineering and Physical Sciences Research Council (EPSRC) have established a scheme to recognize Academic Centres of Excellence in Cyber Security Research (ACEs-CSR). The scheme recognized the first eight UK universities that are carrying out research in the field of cyber security in 2012, and a further three in 2013.

The universities that were recognized under the scheme are

- University of Bristol for research into the areas of theory, design, implementation, and analysis of protocols and systems that use (or relate to) cryptography
- Imperial College London for research into the areas of operational systems and information assurance and security analysis and system verification
- Lancaster University for research into the areas of resilience, with a key focus on the resilience of networks, cyber-physical systems, and studies of user behavior in order to improve the cyber security of large-scale sociotechnical systems, and the development of cyber-security solutions that benefit society at large, particularly vulnerable user groups

- University College London for research into the areas of secure software and the human and economic aspects of security, privacy, anonymity, and cryptology
- University of Oxford for research into the areas of analysis and verification of software and security protocols, systems security, trustworthiness and usability, and interdisciplinary cyber security, policy, and governance
- Queen's University Belfast for research into the areas of cyber-physical systems security, real-time network analytics and virtualization, and high-performance/resource-constrained cryptography architectures
- Royal Holloway, University of London for research into the areas of theoretical and practical applications of cryptography; the social, technical, and organizational aspects of cyber security; and information assurance and security for radio-frequency identification (RFID) tags, smart cards, and mobile and embedded devices
- University of Southampton for research into the areas of analysis and design of trustworthy software, bio- and cyber metrics, cyber identity, cyber risk analysis, cyber crime, data privacy, international cyber law, provenance and trust, safety and security by design, secure embedded systems, and secure web technologies
- University of Birmingham for research into the areas of design of secure systems, security of embedded systems, cloud computing security, privacy technologies for individuals, network security and malware, and the analysis and verification of systems
- University of Cambridge for research into the areas of systems security, network and operating system security, security and human factors including psychology and usability, security and privacy of mobile systems and social networks, smart-card and banking security, cyber crime, frauds and phishing and anonymity and censorship
- Newcastle University for research into the areas of cyber crime as a sociotechnical issue, security assurance of infrastructures (e.g., identity, cloud computing), and the science of cyber security

A 2012 Cabinet office release stated that

> BIS had announced funding for two Centres for Doctoral Training providing 48 PhDs on multidisciplinary cyber topics, in addition to 30 GCHQ sponsored PhDs also funded through the National Cyber Security Programme.

One of the Centres for Doctoral Training is based at Oxford University, and the other is located at Royal Holloway, University of London.

In addition to the universities that have been recognized under the scheme, there are a number of other universities that also provide cyber-security education and research. These include

- Anglia Ruskin University
- Birmingham City University
- De Montford University
- Glasgow Caledonian University
- Kingston University London
- Liverpool Hope University
- Liverpool John Moore University
- London Metropolitan University
- Loughborough University
- Manchester Metropolitan University
- Middlesex University
- Plymouth University
- Robert Gordon University Aberdeen
- Sheffield Hallam University
- Staffordshire University
- Teeside University
- University of Bradford
- University of Essex
- University of Greenwich
- University of Kent
- University of South Wales
- University of York
- Warwick University

Exercises

As early as 2008, the United Kingdom participated in the Cyber Storm series of exercises, which are run by the US Department of Homeland Security.

In September 2012, a joint US/UK team conducted a series of intensive cyber-defense exercises on the "cyber range" inside the Air Warfare Centre at RAF Station Waddington. The scenario for the exercise was a series of attacks against simulated networks.

In November 2013, the United Kingdom participated in a NATO cyber-defense war game that was held in Estonia. The three-day Cyber Coalition 2013 exercise involved more than 400 cyber experts from 27 NATO alliance and partner countries in a test designed to improve their cyber-defense skills. The scenario for the exercise was a fictitious crisis in which all the participating nations had to ward off simulated cyber attacks.

The United Kingdom takes an active role in NATO exercises.

The United Kingdom has taken part in the Cyber Europe series of exercises, which started in 2010 and are organized by the European Union Agency for Network and Information Security (ENISA).

References

1. Federal Ministry of the Interior. (2011). Cyber security strategy for Germany. https://www.bsi.bund.de/SharedDocs/Downloads/EN/BSI/Publications/CyberSecurity/Cyber_Security_Strategy_for_Germany.pdf?__blob=publicationFile.
2. HM Government. (2010). Securing Britain in an age of uncertainty: The Strategic Defence and Security Review. https://www.gov.uk/government/uploads/system/uploads/attachment_data/file/62482/strategic-defence-security-review.pdf.
3. Chief of the General Staff, Ministry of Defence, Army Doctrine Publication—Operations, November 2010. https://www.gov.uk/government/uploads/system/uploads/attachment_data/file/33695/ADPOperationsDec10.pdf.
4. Ministry of Defence. (2011). The future reserves 2020: The independent commission to review the United Kingdom's reserve forces. https://www.gov.uk/government/uploads/system/uploads/attachment_data/file/28394/futurereserves_2020.pdf.

Chapter 10

Nation-State Defensive and Offensive Information Warfare Capabilities: The Russian Federation

---

The Russian Federation has a large standing military organization and is an old adversary of the West. It has shown a willingness to take action in the countries that surround it, as evidenced by actions in Estonia, Georgia, and Ukraine.

Russian Federation

Policy and Strategy

In February 2010, Russia published its new military doctrine.[1] In the document, the characteristics of modern military conflict are defined as including the integrated use of military force and nonmilitary capabilities, with a greater role for information warfare (IW).

The doctrine states that the

> Early implementation of measures of information warfare to achieve political objectives without the use of military force, and in the future

to generate a favorable reaction of the international community to use
military force

will be one of the characteristics of future conflict. The doctrine also includes one
of the tasks of equipping the armed forces and other troops as "the development
of the forces and means of information warfare," and "the creation of new types of
precision weapons and the development of their information security."

The Russian foreign policy was released in 2013,[2] and the section on
"Strengthening International Security" states that

(the Russian Federation) will take necessary measures to ensure national
and international information security, prevent political, economic and
social threats to the state's security that emerge in information space in
order to combat terrorism and other criminal threats.

Because of the way in which IW is considered in Russia, direct comparison
with Western doctrines is difficult. In a 2014 article,[3] they include in their use of
the term

■ Psychological operations to influence the motivation of enemy soldiers
■ Disinformation—providing false information to the enemy about their capa-
bilities and plans
■ Electronic warfare, the "blinding" of the enemy's electronic intelligence systems
■ Physical destruction of elements of the information systems of the enemy
■ Information attack—the destruction or corruption of information without
visible damage to the carrier systems
■ The protection of their own information

The article goes on to give the Russian view that the aims of IW are

■ To create an atmosphere of immorality and lack of spirituality, in order to
create an atmosphere that is likely to cause conflict within a country and
overthrow the authorities
■ The manipulation of public opinion and the political orientation of social
groups to create a climate of political tension and chaos
■ Destabilization of the political relations to provoke conflict and incite an
atmosphere of distrust and suspicion
■ To aggravate political struggle and to provoke repression against the opposition
■ To cause the outbreak of civil war in society
■ To reduce the level of information support for governing bodies in order to
impede the making of important decisions
■ To spread misinformation within the population about the state authorities
to undermine their authority and discredit the government

- To provoking social, political, ethnic, and religious conflicts
- To cause mass protests, strikes, and riots
- To undermining the international authority of the state
- To cause damage to the vital interests of the state in the political, economic, defense, and other areas.

Defensive

The IW capability in Russia, which covers a wide range of topics including all types of networked and digital activities, electromagnetic warfare, and influencing campaigns, is spread over a number of agencies.

The Federal Protection Service (Federal'naya Sluzhba Okhrani) (FSO), which is thought to have a staff of around 20,000, is responsible for supervising top-level government communications, underground command centers, the special underground train system connecting key government facilities in the Moscow area, and the protection of strategic facilities and resources. Another of its roles is to provide the Kremlin with strategic signals intelligence (SIGINT) from surveillance facilities. The FSO Special Communication and Information Service inherited from FAPSI (its predecessor) responsibility for ensuring the exploitation of special information systems for state agencies. It monitors landline, satellites, and wireless communications as well as the Internet.

The Federal Security Service (Federal'naya Sluzhba Bezopasnosti) (FSB)

The Federal'naya Sluzhba Bezopasnosti (FSB) is the successor to the Federal Counterintelligence Service (Federalnaya Sluzhba Kontrrazvedki) (FSK) and is responsible for counterintelligence, internal security, border security, counterterrorism, and surveillance. On January 15, 2013, Vladimir Putin approved a decree that assigned powers to the FSB to "create a state system for the detection, prevention and liquidation of the effects of computer attacks on the information resources of the Russian Federation."

Information Security Centre of the FSB, Military Unit (VCH) 64829

The Information Security Center is responsible for ensuring the information security of Russia. The center was established in the Office of Computer and Information Security (UKIB), the counterintelligence department of the FSB. The unit investigates crimes in the area of e-commerce and the illicit proliferation of personal data.

Ministry of Foreign Affairs: Department of Information Security

In 2013, it was announced that the Ministry of Foreign Affairs was to create a Department of Information Security. The role of the department was given as promoting the UN conventions "On ensuring international information security" and "Code of Conduct on the Internet," which were developed by Russia and the members of the Shanghai Cooperation Organization to defend Russia's approaches to the regulation of the Internet.

RU-CERT

The RU-CERT (Computer Emergency Response Team) provides a computer incident prevention and response service when the incident in question is related to resources located in the territory of the Russian Federation.

Center for information Technology and Systems of Executive Agencies

This lists its roles as

- The creation and maintenance of national information resources in the field of technical documentation
- The creation of systems for the analysis of information at state and municipal levels, and corporate governance
- The design and construction of corporate telecommunications networks and information technology in education
- The creation and maintenance of databases for the benefit of the UGA (state authorities?) and for monitoring system
- Technology certification of software and automated systems,
- System of training and decision-making in the interests of the Defense Ministry
- Information management systems and automated special purpose
- Protected function-oriented system technology
- The creation of integrated engineering systems safety of informatization,
- Information security system
- Innovative tools for the development of design-solution models
- Information technology semantic analysis
- Effective integration solutions for creating complex control systems
- Simulation technology and automatic programming of complex control systems

Department for Combatting Crimes in the High Technology Sphere (Directorate K)

This unit has the role of fighting computer and telecommunications crime in the sphere of computer information and telecommunications.

Ministry of Internal Affairs: Department for Combating Extremism

The main tasks of the department for combating extremism are

- Organizing the formation of the main directions of the state policy on its activities
- Combating extremism and terrorism
- Cooperating with the Departments of the Ministry of the Federal Executive Bodies and the executive bodies of subjects of the Russian Federation within its competence
- Coordinating with the established order of the territorial Ministry of Internal Affairs of Russia and the subdivisions of the central apparatus of the Ministry of Interior of Russia on the activities of the department
- Providing support and practical assistance to the territorial bodies of the Ministry of Interior of Russia and its structural subdivisions on its activities

Center for Licensing, Certification and Protection of State Secrets (FSB)

The Center for Licensing, Certification and Protection of State Secrets of the FSB is the lead department authorized for the organization and implementation of the licensing activities of enterprises, institutions, and organizations. It is also involved in the regulation of the import and export of cryptographic devices and special technical equipment for secret information.

Offensive

According to an article in *DefenseTech*[4] in 2008, Russia at that time had a cyber capability of around 7300 members of the military with a budget of around US$127 million. The article went on to list the types of weapon that Russia had available:

- Large, advanced BotNet for DDoS and espionage
- Electromagnetic pulse weapons (nonnuclear)
- Compromised counterfeit computer software
- Advanced dynamic exploitation capabilities
- Wireless data communications jammers
- Cyber-logic bombs, computer viruses, and worms,
- Cyber-data collection exploits
- Computer and network reconnaissance tools
- Embedded Trojan time bombs (suspected)

Within the military, where there is a system of collective security, the capability is divided according to the regional principle, with each military district having its own IW resources. These will include signals troops and radio-electronic combat units that deal with electronic warfare on the operational and tactical levels. SIGINT and electronic intelligence (ELINT) capability is provided by land, sea, and airborne units as well as the Strategic Rocket Forces.

The Military Intelligence (Glavnoye Razvedovatel'noye Upravlenie) (GRU) is part of the Defense Ministry and is the main military intelligence organization of the General Staff. The GRU is responsible for Human Intelligence (HUMINT), SIGINT, and imagery reconnaissance and satellite imagery (IMINT).

Although clearly dated information, the Agentura.ru website gives the breakdown of the 6th Directorate of the GRU:

1st Division: Signals Intelligence (SIGINT) department—involved in the interception and decryption of communications channels of foreign countries. Runs the special purpose groups (osnaz). The 1st Division of the 6th Directorate has around 1800 military and civilian personnel.

2nd Division: Electronic Intelligence (ELINT) Department—used the same intercept stations for the same target countries as the 1st. However, the interest of the 2nd Division was in the detection and tracking for military purposes of radio telemetry and other electronic signals emitted by control equipment. To intercept these signals, osnaz were deployed in military districts and groups of forces of the Ministry of Defense.

3rd Division: Technical Section—responsible for interception equipment in the buildings of Soviet embassies, consulates, and trade missions around the world, in addition to separately located intercept stations in Cuba, Vietnam, Burma, and Mongolia.

4th Division: Front Tracking—provided 24-hour tracking of all signals intelligence information. The main task of the department was tracking the military situation around the world and especially the significant changes in the armed forces of the United States.

Foreign Intelligence Service (Sluzhba Vneshney Razvedki)

The Sluzhba Vneshney Razvedki (SVR) currently has 13,000 employees and has the role of providing the government with intelligence on political, economic, defense, scientific-technical, and ecological subjects. This is normally achieved through espionage.

The Special Communications and Information Service of the FSO is the cryptologic intelligence agency responsible for the collection and analysis of foreign communications and foreign signals intelligence.

The center for electronic surveillance of communications (FSB), also known as the 16th Directorate and Military Unit (Vch) 71330, is responsible for the interception, decryption, and processing of electronic communications.

Advanced Persistent Threat No. 28 (APT28)

APT28 is a designation that has been given to a Russia-based group that is involved in collecting intelligence on defense and geopolitical issues that would be of value to the Russian government. The group, which has been active since at least 2007, has regularly updated and developed the malware that it uses and the indications are that this is a stable organization. The malware that has been observed indicates that the group is highly skilled.

A FireEye report[5] states that APT28 have engaged in espionage against political and military targets including the country of Georgia, Eastern European governments and militaries, and European security organizations, including NATO and the Organization for Security and Co-operation in Europe (OSCE), since at least 2007. From the malware that has been observed, it has been noted that they contain Russian language settings that are consistent with the working in the time zone of Russia's major cities, which include Moscow and St. Petersburg.

Russian Business Network

While the Russian Business Network (RBN) was clearly an organized crime endeavor and was not acknowledged by the Russian government, the activities of this organization may well have been condoned. The RBN specialized in activities such as identity theft for resale. It was also well known for hosting illegal businesses, including child pornography, phishing, spam, and malware distribution. The RBN was based in St. Petersburg. The RBN seems to have disappeared during 2007 as a result of increasing pressure from the USA.

Research and Development

Strategic Rocket Forces Academy: Department of Electronic and Information Warfare

The Strategic Rocket Forces Academy in Moscow has a Faculty of Special Weapons and Information-Strike Systems, and the Serpukhov Military Institute of Missile Forces (SVR PB) offers courses that enable students to achieve an electronic warfare qualification.

Voronezh Military Aviation Engineering University's Department for Electronic Warfare offers 5-year courses in "Electronic Warfare" and "Integrated Software Information Security Automated Systems." The content of the Electronic Warfare course includes

- EW observation (exploration) of electronic systems by their radiation
- Penetration of electronic storage media and communication channels of the enemy

- Electronic jamming systems of communication, information sharing, navigation, reconnaissance, control, and so on
- EW destruction of information circulating and stored in the information systems of the enemy
- "Radiodezinformatsiya" (probably translates as *disinformation*) of the information electronic systems of the enemy
- Protection from weapons with avionics guidance
- Protection of electronic systems from electronic intelligence collection and radio interference from weapons

National Research Nuclear University: Moscow Engineering Physics Institute

The Department of Cybernetics and Information Security runs a number of courses on information security.

Federal Protection Service (FSO) Academy

The FSO Academy offers 5-year courses in network technology, communication systems, information technology, and telecommunications information security.

Moscow State Technical University (Bauman): Department of Information and Control Systems

This department runs a number of courses on "information security of automated systems."

Academy of the FSB: Institute of Cryptography, Telecommunications and Computer Science (IKSI)

The academy advertises that it provides the following courses:

- Cryptography
- Information-analytical system security
- Information security telecommunications systems
- Computer security
- Information security of automated systems
- Countering technical intelligence

The Federal Service for Technical and Export Control

This is the State Scientific Research and Testing Institute for the technical protection of information.

Its main activities include

- Developing of a conceptual framework for the protection of information from technical intelligence
- Developing a system of regulatory, legal and methodological documents in the interests of the Federal Service for Technical and Export Control of Russia
- Modeling and forecasting the development of forces and means of technical intelligence, and improving the assessment of their capabilities
- The development of technical means of information and monitoring the effectiveness of information security

Center for Special Development Ministry of Defense of the Russian Federation

This center addresses areas in the field of security and communication and information systems of the Ministry of Defense of the Russian Federation. The main objectives of the center are given as

- Organization and conducting research activities in the field of security problems of information and communication systems
- Organization and conduct of research and development activities in designing and building high-performance, problem-oriented computing systems
- Applied research in the field of microelectronics
- Research and expert analysis of electronic maps of military and civilian personnel of the Russian Defense Ministry for different purposes
- Organization and conduct of examinations and test elements of communication and information systems in support of the Russian Defense Ministry

4th Central Research Institute of the Ministry of Defense

The institute has several research centers and departments involved in research in various areas in the field of missile, space, and aviation systems, and it looks at the problems of military theory and practice of construction, development, training, and combat use of the functional components of strategic deterrence forces and the air force. The main areas of research are

- Strengthening strategic stability in the world at arms reduction, reducing the cost of national defense
- Introducing resource-saving technologies for the creation, operation, and liquidation of arms

■ Developing and implementing dual-use technologies to create new models for weapons
■ Ensuring the safety of information technology and the certification of information security

18th Central Research Institute of the Ministry of Defense

This is the main organization in the development and mass production of special weapons and equipment for the federal executive bodies, to ensure the security of Russia.

27th Central Scientific Research Institute of the Ministry of Defense

The research institute includes several research centers and departments involved in research into control systems, the information infrastructure of the armed forces of the Russian Federation, communication systems, and navigation support. Current research topics are given as

■ Comprehensive research in the field of automation and better management of the armed forces
■ Research and testing in the development and improvement of systems, facilities, and means of military communication systems and ground signals intelligence
■ Improving the navigational support of the armed forces of the Russian Federation.

Federal State Unitary Enterprise Scientific-Technical Center "Orion" of the FSB

The Scientific-Technical Center "Orion" is a state-run business with the objectives of "meeting state and public needs in the area of special hardware and software, as well as making a profit." It has the objective of

■ Creating systems and equipment for special technical means
■ Developing and creating fiber-optic products used for communication and data transfer
■ Designing and creating a complex of special technical equipment used for communication and data transmission over fiber-optic lines,
■ Designing and creating information security.

Nizhny Novgorod State University has a "center for security of information systems and communication." The university teaches information security of telecommunication systems at both the undergraduate and postgraduate levels and carries out research into topics related to information security, including developing methods for using special devices to protect against unauthorized access, specialized software and hardware and software systems for information security, system reliability, fault tolerance, disaster recovery capabilities, and information security technologies.

Russia State Humanities University: Faculty of Information Security

The university offers courses on

- Organization and information security technology
- Integrated protection of objects of information

The Scientific Research Institute of Radio (NIIR), also known as the Radio Research Institute, is a Russian research company that specializes in topics of information and communication technologies, navigation, satellite and terrestrial communications systems (control systems) and ensuring the information security of communication networks of the Russian Federation, including the military-industrial complex and broadcasting.

Operations and Exercises

Starting in 2007, elements that support Russia, which may or may not have been under the control of the Russian government, have carried out a number of operations against other nation-states during times of increased tensions.

Estonia

In April 2007, a large and coordinated set of cyber attacks were mounted against Estonia during a disagreement with Russia about the relocation of the Bronze Soldier of Tallinn memorial. A number of Estonian organizations came under attack, including the Estonian parliament, government ministries, banks, and the media. The majority of the attacks were denial-of-service (DoS) attacks, but there were also web defacements and spamming. The Estonians managed to mobilize sufficient people and resources to withstand the attack, but it was considered to be on a level that had not been seen before. A postincident analysis estimated that more than one million computers were used to mount the DoS attack, and they appeared to be located in in more than 75 countries. The analysts concluded that this attack was carried out by a well-organized group with a good command and control structure. The Nashi Youth movement, which claimed responsibility, and the Russian Business Network were both suspected of involvement in the attacks. The involvement of the Russian government was alluded to in an interview given by State Duma Deputy Sergey Markov,[6] when he claimed that one of his assistants was responsible for instigating the attack.

Georgia

The cyber attacks against Georgia took place in the summer of 2008 in the period running up to the start of the 5-day military conflict between Russia and Georgia. The attacks consisted initially of small-scale DoS attacks against specific targets in June 2008. Then, in July, the number of DoS attacks increased, primarily targeted against the official website of the Georgian president, which was forced to shut down for a period. Then, in August, on the same day that the military offensive started with Russian forces crossing over the borders into Georgia, attacks took place on the websites of the president, the Georgian parliament, a number of ministries, the National Bank of Georgia, and the online media. During the August phase of the cyber attacks, there were DoS attacks and website defacements. Two Russian hacker forums were subsequently identified as the sites where the attacks were organized. The Russian government has consistently rejected any accusation of its involvement in these attacks, and there is no evidence that it initiated or conducted the campaigns. The involvement of the Nashi Youth movement was again suspected.

Ukraine

During the ongoing civil conflict in Ukraine, there has been a relatively low level of cyber activity. Russian and pro-Russian groups have attempted to disable the news media and government websites, and during the early days of the conflict, pro-Russian/separatist groups managed to disable almost all of the Ukrainian government websites. It is also probable that they were able to take control of and monitor Internet and telephone communication lines. During the invasion of Crimea, the communications systems of almost all Ukrainian forces that were based in Crimea were disabled. The mobile communication systems of members of the Ukrainian government were also attacked in order to disrupt communications between government agencies.

The Ukrainian company Ukrtelecom announced that unmarked gunmen had gained access to their infrastructure and that optical fiber and conductor units were disabled, resulting in the collapse of all communications.

In July 2014, the Russian Federation Ministry of Communications carried out a set of exercises to develop measures to disrupt the Internet in Russia. Exercise participants included units from the Defense Ministry, the Federal Security Service, the Interior Ministry, specialists of OJSC "Rostelecom" (one of the largest telecoms providers in Russia), the Coordination Center for the Internet Top Level Domain (TLD) Internet Technical Center and the interaction center Computer Networks "MSK-IX" (Moscow Internet Exchange (MSK-IX)). The exercises were held under the supervision of the minister of communications and mass communications, Nikolai Nikiforovto, in order to assess the state of security and stability of the national infrastructure and the criticality of its connectivity to the global infrastructure and to assess the potential vulnerabilities identified.

On October 25, 2014, Lentra.ru[7] published an article that reported that the State Duma deputy, the head of the legal service of the Communist Party, Vadim Solovyov, had proposed to prohibit the military from posting photos and videos of military units and military exercises with images of specialist equipment and weapons on the Internet. According to the newspaper *Izvestia*, a corresponding bill to make amendments to the federal law "On Military Duty and Military Service" is also being prepared. This shows an increasing awareness of the potential for leakage of information on social media.

References

1. Military Doctrine of the Russian Federation. (2010). Approved by the Decree of the President of the Russian Federation, The Security Council of the Russian Federation http://www.scrf.gov.ru/documents/33.html.
2. The Ministry of Foreign Affairs of the Russian Federation. (2013). Concept of the foreign policy of the Russian Federation. http://www.mid.ru/brp_4.nsf/0/76389FEC 168189ED44257B2E0039B16D.
3. Politikus.ru. (2014). The information war. http://politikus.ru/articles/26176-informa-cionnaya-voyna.html.
4. Carroll, W. (2008). Russia's cyber forces. *DefenseTech*, May 27. http://defensetech.org/2008/05/27/russias-cyber-forces/.
5. FireEye special report. (2014). APT 28: A window into Russia's cyber espionage operations? https://www2.fireeye.com/apt28.html.
6. Asadova, N. (2009). Behind the Estonia cyberattacks. *RIA Novosti*, March 6. http://www.rferl.org/content/Behind_The_Estonia_Cyberattacks/1505613.html.
7. *Lentra.ru*. (2014). In the State Duma a proposal to ban the military upload photos from service. http://lenta.ru/news/2014/09/11/army/.

Chapter 11

International Organizations' Defensive and Offensive Information Warfare Capabilities

There are two international organizations that have to be included in this review—the European Union (EU) and the North Atlantic Treaty Organization (NATO). While some of the countries that have been reviewed belong to one or both of these organizations, the organizations themselves both set policy and, in the case of NATO, have some capability.

European Union

Policy and Strategy

In 2013, the EU published its "Cyber Security Strategy—An Open, Safe and Secure Cyberspace." The strategy takes a comprehensive approach to the subject and addresses, within the remit of the EU's responsibilities, the civil aspects of cyber security in addition to the Cyber Defence for the Common Security and Defence Policy (CSDP). In December 2013, at the EU Council on defense matters, the EU heads of state and government recognized cyber defense as a priority for capability development.

The EU policy states that it

> is solely engaged in cyber self-protection and assured access to cyber space to enable conventional military activity. Offensive cyber capabilities have not been developed, or deployed, under the EU banner.

The EU does not have standing military forces or EU-owned military equipment for EU operations. When the EU launches a military operation, the EU is wholly dependent on force contributions from EU member states or other force contributors. This also applies to cyber defense activities, and the member states are the key to force generation. The EU approach is to encourage the member states to develop and maintain their own cyber capabilities. The policy states that

> in order to be effective, the EU and its member states must develop and deploy a robust inventory of in-depth (layered) cyber defence capability for the military, as part of their national cyber defence strategy and capabilities.

The EU has two organizations that are carrying out work to improve EU cyber defense capabilities: the EU Military Staff (EUMS) and the European Defence Agency (EDA).

Defensive

The EUMS has a staff of around 200 seconded national experts as part of the EU External Action Service (EEAS). The EUMS is responsible for providing the EU with military advice and for providing EU council bodies with military options should the member states decide on a course of military action. The cyber defense role or EUMS is to develop doctrine and policy to ensure that the cyber-protection elements of the different member states in support of an EU military operation, which may be operating independently, will provide a coherent collective protection of the EU force to ensure that no threat or vulnerabilities exist.

Offensive

The EU does not have an independent offensive capability.

Research and Development

European Defence Agency (EDA)

The EDA has a staff of about 130 from different EUMS. The EDA supports member states in a range of areas of military capability development. In 2011, the EDA established a Project Team (PT) cyber defense, which had the task of assessing short-, medium-, and long-term cyber-defense capability requirements and identifying collaborative options in order to improve the cyber-defense resilience of participating member states and CSDP operations.

The European Network and Information Security Agency (ENISA) is an agency of the EU that was created in 2004 and has been fully operational since September 1, 2005. The agency had a budget of €32 million (for the years 2005–2009), and its mandate was extended up to 2012 with an annual budget of €8 million. It has a staff of around 55. The role of ENISA is to assist the European Commission, member states, and the business community in meeting the requirements for network and information security.

Exercises

Cyber Europe Exercise Series

The Cyber Europe Exercise Series was first run in 2010 and has taken place every two years since. In Cyber Europe Exercise 2014, which was organized by ENISA, more than 200 organizations and 400 cyber-security professionals from 29 European countries and the European Free Trade Association took part in the first phase of the cyber-security exercise.

NATO

In 2008, NATO set up a Cooperative Cyber Defence Centre of Excellence in Estonia. The center provides a research and training facility dealing with education, consultation, lessons learned, research, and development in the field of cyber security. The mission of the center is to enhance the capability, cooperation, and information sharing among NATO, NATO nations, and NATO partners in cyber defense by virtue of education, research and development, lessons learned, and consultation. The center has a staff of around 48 personnel from 16 different nations, who have all been sent to work at the center by their respective home organizations.

A 2012 report entitled "NATO 2020"[1] identified the need for the alliance's new "strategic concept" to further incorporate cyber defense. The report highlighted that there was an increasing danger of cyber attacks. The report states that NATO needs to

> accelerate efforts to respond to the danger of cyber attacks by protecting its own communications and command systems, helping Allies to improve their ability to prevent and recover from attacks, and developing an array of cyber defence capabilities aimed at effective detection and deterrence.

NATO Policy on Cyber Defense

NATO has adopted an enhanced cyber-defense policy and an action plan, which was endorsed at the Wales Summit in September 2014. The policy establishes cyber defense as part of the alliance's core task of collective defense, confirms that international law applies in cyber space, and increases NATO's collaboration with industry. The policy identifies that the top priority is the protection of the communications systems owned and operated by the alliance.

The new policy also addresses a streamlined format for cyber-defense governance, procedures for assistance to allied countries, and the integration of cyber defense into operational planning (including civil emergency planning). The policy also defines the ways in which awareness, education, and training and exercise activities are taken forward. Other issues addressed include enhancing information sharing and mutual assistance in preventing, mitigating, and recovering from cyber attacks.

NATO Cyber Range

During the NATO Summit in Wales, the establishment of a Cyber Range Capability was agreed. The range will be provided by Estonia, which will provide NATO with access to the Estonian Defence Forces' national cyber-range facility. NATO has used this facility in the past. In 2013, it was used for the exercise CYBER COALITION 2013. NATO will use the range to carry out cyber-related training, exercises, and education in a secure environment.

NATO Smart Defence Initiative

Cyber defense has also been integrated into NATO's Smart Defence initiative. Smart Defence enables countries to work together to develop and maintain capabilities they could not afford to develop or procure alone. The Smart Defence projects in cyber defense, so far, include the Malware Information Sharing Platform, the Smart Defence Multinational Cyber Defence Capability Development project, and the Multinational Cyber Defence Education and Training project.

NATO Computer Incident Response Capability (NCIRC)

The NATO Computer Incident Response Capability (NCIRC) was established to protect NATO's own networks through centralized and 24/7 cyber-defense support to the various NATO sites. It achieved full operational capability in May 2014, providing enhanced protection to NATO networks and users.

NATO Communications and Information Systems School

The NATO Communications and Information Systems School (NCISS) provides training to personnel from allied (as well as non-NATO) nations relating to the operation and maintenance of some NATO communication and information systems. The NCISS facility is to be relocated to a location in Portugal, where there will be a greater emphasis on cyber-defense training and education.

NATO School in Oberammergau

The NATO School in Oberammergau, Germany, is a NATO training facility for multinational military education. The school conducts cyber-defense-related education and training to support alliance operations, strategy, policy, doctrine, and procedures.

NATO Defence College

The NATO Defence College in Rome undertakes research into strategic thinking on political-military matters, including on cyber-defense issues.

NATO Communications and Information Agency

In July 2012, the NATO Communications and Information Agency (NCIA) was established. The NCIA is a key pillar of the NATO Secretary General's Smart Defence and Connected Forces initiatives. The role of NCIA is to connects forces, NATO, and nations where and when required by providing interoperable communications and information systems and services. It provides NATO-wide IT services and state-of-the-art command, control, communications, computers, intelligence, surveillance, and reconnaissance (C4ISR) capabilities, including cyber and missile defense. The NCIA is in more than 30 locations in Europe, North America, and Southeast Asia in support of its customers and NATO operations.

In April 2014, the North Atlantic Council agreed to rename the Defence Policy and Planning Committee (Cyber Defence) as the Cyber Defence Committee. The Cyber Defence Committee coordinates cyber-defense efforts at the level of defense counselors, who are a part of national delegations to NATO. The committee is also responsible for the development of cyber capabilities through NATO's Defence Planning Process.

NATO Exercises

NATO conducts regular exercises, such as the annual Cyber Coalition Exercise, and aims to integrate cyber-defense elements and considerations into the entire range of alliance exercises. NATO is also enhancing capabilities for cyber education, training, and exercises, including the NATO Cyber Range, which is based on a facility provided by Estonia.

Exercise Baltic Cyber Shield 2010

In this exercise, six teams from the NATO NCIRC, Latvia, Lithuania, and Sweden attempted to defend virtual computer networks against hostile attacks. The aim of the exercise was to increase understanding of the international cyber environment and to enhance international cooperation in handling technical incidents.

One of the main tasks was to defend an initially insecure company network, which contained components of supervisory control and data acquisition (SCADA) systems that were used for monitoring and controlling critical information infrastructure. The exercise was jointly run by the center and the Swedish National Defence College with support from various Swedish institutions and the Estonian Cyber Defence League.

Exercise Locked Shields 2012

Participants in this exercise included teams of experts and specialists from governmental organizations, military units, computer emergency response teams (CERTs), and private-sector companies. The participants came from Switzerland, Germany, Spain, Finland, Italy, NATO NCIRC, Slovakia, Austria, Denmark, Estonia, Latvia, and Norway. As with Exercise Baltic Cyber Shield, teams attempted to defend virtual computer networks against hostile attacks. The main objectives were recorded as being to

- Support the campaign of the Multinational Experiment 7 (MNE 7 is a project regarding the global commons, which are defined as the physical and geographical areas of sea, air, and space domains and the virtual cyber domain that no states have sovereignty over, and that are available to everyone)
- To explore situational awareness technologies in the cyber domain
- To learn from the activities of the team members

Exercise Locked Shields 2013

Taking place in April 2013, exercise Locked Shields was a real-time network defense exercise carried out over a two-day period, in which around 250 participants from 11 nations took part. The theme of the exercise remained the same, with teams attempting to defend virtual computer networks against hostile attacks. Participants came from the NATO NCIRC team and also from countries including Estonia, Finland, Lithuania, Germany, Holland, Italy, Poland, Spain, and Slovakia.

Exercise Locked Shields 2014

Locked Shields was another real-time network defense exercise that was carried out over a two-day period with nearly 300 participants from 17 nations. The theme of the exercise remained the same, with teams attempted to defend virtual computer networks against hostile attacks.

Cyber Coalition Exercises

The Cyber Coalition series of exercises have run for a number of years, and in November 2013, NATO started a three-day cyber-defense exercise named Cyber Coalition 2013. The exercise was to test the alliance's ability to defend its networks from attacks. In excess of 300 cyber-defense experts from 33 nations, including five partner non-NATO nations (Austria, Finland, Ireland, Sweden, and Switzerland) were involved in the exercise, which was the largest exercise of its kind in terms of participating countries. A further 80 experts from the military training facility in Tartu, Estonia, which is the host nation for this year's exercise, also took part in the event. New Zealand and the European Union also attended the exercise with observer status.

International Exercises

Cyber Europe 2010

In November of 2010, Exercise Cyber Europe 2010 took place with the objective of stimulating and testing the cooperation between EU countries in case of attacks on a large scale. About 70 cyber-security experts played out a scenario of defending against a range of attacks on communication between institutions, corporations, and private citizens throughout Europe.

Exercise Cyber Atlantic 2011

In November 2011, the first joint exercise on cyber security between the EU and the United States was held and had the theme of hacking SCADA and advanced persistent threat (APT). The objectives of the exercise were to evaluate the degree of cooperation between the EU member states and the United States in the management of a cyber crisis, to identify the criticalities of cyber-crisis management at an international level, and to exchange good practices on how to tackle a cyber crisis worldwide. The exercise involved 20 EU states, 16 of which had an active role.

Summary

In the last few chapters, we have looked at the cyber-defensive and cyber-offensive capabilities of a number of countries and international organizations. The countries and organizations that have been examined were chosen because it was felt that these were the most relevant to the interests of the United States and the Western world. They do not represent the only countries that have developed or are developing capability.

As you might expect, the level of open-source information that is available for countries varies, and while some of the information can be gathered from official government websites, in some cases it is almost exclusively taken from news reports and research project reports.

One of the ongoing problems is that of the terminology used. Even among the NATO alliance partners, there is a diversity of terms used to describe the same activities. While this book is about information warfare, the term is used (or not used) to describe a range of activities, from computer-based offensive and defensive actions to deception and psychological operations, depending on the country and, in some cases, the part of government that is using the terms.

Reference

1. NATO. 2010. NATO 2020: Assured security; dynamic engagement. http://www. nato.int/cps/en/natohq/topics_85961.htm.

Chapter 12

Nonstate Actors

In this chapter, nonstate global information warfare (GIW) actors will be discussed. Actually, not much has changed since we last discussed these people. More have joined the GIW arena, but under the same headings of individuals and groups.

Individuals and Groups

The individuals remain the same: hackers, fraudsters, or whatever other name one may call them. They are lone individuals who wage global warfare against government agencies, businesses, groups, and other individuals.

Information Warfare Tactics by Miscreants in General

The catch-all of the *miscreant* in general is here for all the other people out there that cannot be classified as either terrorists or activists, but who can still create a significant impact on a country, an organization, or an individual.

The tactics that they will use will depend on the level of skill they possess, the target of their attention, and the effect they are trying to cause.

One small but significant individual can be viewed as an individual or as a group: the anarchist and technoanarchist.

> An-ar-chistan-er-kist, -ar-n 1: *one who rebels against any authority, established order, or ruling order 2: one who believes in, advocates, or promotes anarchism or anarchy; esp. one who uses violent means to overthrow the established order.*[1]

Does their joining together in a common cause mean that they are not true anarchists, or does it mean that the definition is wrong?

Typically, the targets for anarchists have been governments and large multinational companies, but in recent years, there has been a significant shift in targeting toward the meetings of the G8, G20, and other institutions perceived to have an effect on the world economy, such as the World Bank. Recent meetings of the heads of governments have increasingly come under violent attack from anarchists, and this has been mirrored in the activity seen on the Internet. They have also joined and hidden within groups such as those protesting various causes such as killings of minorities in the United States and capitalism—basically, anarchists take any opportunity to hide in plain sight and cause chaos.

The cause of a denial-of-service (DoS) attack from this portion of the population will generally be dependent on the relationship between the attacker and the target. The attack may be the result of a perceived slight of an individual by another individual or an organization, or part of a concerted attack that is part of a wider event.

Some of the easier to remember cases of theft on the Internet are cases that originated in Russia. It is notable that in Russia, according to Anatoly Platonov—a spokesman for the Interior Ministry's "Division R," which handles computer crime—this rise in the number of arrests may reflect increased police effectiveness rather than a growth in crime.

For some in this category, the online collection of intelligence relative to them is an issue. It is now almost irrelevant as to whether you refer to this activity as spying, such as on a web site, social media, etc., as open-source intelligence collection, or as industrial espionage. The net results are very similar, as are the methods used. In the past, if you were planning an action against an adversary, you would carry out a reconnaissance of the target and gain as much information as possible to enable you to identify the specific targets and to learn as much as possible about their habits, practices, and history.

You would visit public offices and libraries and read newspapers to gather background information and you would visit the site to gather more specific information through observation or through methods such as dumpster diving (yes, it did exist before we had computers; it was just that the information that the dumpster diver was looking for was different).

Now, most of the information that exists with regard to a person or an establishment is held in computer text files or databases, so the need for a protagonist to expose themselves to identification by visiting the site or by being seen in local libraries or public offices is greatly reduced. The same applies to those seeking to nullify their effectiveness.

Another form of attack that this category of attacker might use is *identity theft*. It is now trivially easy to gain all the information you need to assume someone else's identity (identity theft) or draw all of the information needed with regard to an organization or a company. Identity theft is still largely confined to the United States and other Western nations; however, the number of recorded incidents has risen dramatically in recent years. If an individual is the victim of an identity theft, the results can be startling, and the restoration of a state that is similar to that which existed before the identity was stolen is extremely difficult and time consuming. It also has terrorist implications, as one can imagine.

Since its early days, the Internet has been exploited for espionage. What better medium could the modern information broker, activist, or spy want? They have been provided with a low-risk means of access to a country and a facility or organization, a means of communication that is both anonymous and untraceable, the potential to use cryptography without raising the slightest suspicion, an updated version of the Cold War *dead letter box*, and a set of obstacles to overcome to gain access to industrial and government information that, in previous times, would have been considered laughable.

The first case of online espionage was allegedly reported when Cliff Stoll documented his actions and discoveries of 1985 in his book *The Cuckoo's Egg*.[2] In this case, the Soviet Committee for State Security (Komitet Gosudarstvennoi Bezopasnosti—KGB) is known to have paid an East German hacker, Markus Hess, to penetrate US defense agency systems. In a present-day case, the heavily reported Moonlight Maze attacks have been occurring for some time, probably since 1997 or before, wherein hackers from Eastern Europe have broken into a large number of systems, including the Pentagon's systems, accessing "sensitive information about essential defense technical research matters." Although the stolen information has not been classified, it is still invaluable to foreign governments, terrorist groups, and private companies because these networks hold information on military logistics, planning, payrolls, purchases, personnel, and routine Pentagon e-mails between departments. The most sophisticated attacks observed to date apparently came from just outside Moscow and were supposedly eventually traced to the laboratory of the Russian Academy of Sciences, the country's leading scientific research body.

The average miscreant in this category will have one of three driving motivators for his/her activity on the Internet: It will either be for curiosity (the "can I do that" factor); for some sort of revenge; or for financial gain.

Another activity carried out by individuals and within groups is the use of the Internet for the purposes of communication. What is being referred to here is the use by individuals and groups, who are engaged in nefarious activities, of technologies that will either allow them to remain anonymous or let them send and receive messages that cannot be intercepted and reduced to a meaningful state by either law enforcement of their opposition. It will always attract them to technology and the Internet.

If the drug cartels and the Mafia have this type of capability at their disposal, and there is no reason to doubt that they do—untraceable money will buy you almost anything—the potential is frightening. There is considerable paranoia regarding the capabilities of various "Big Brother" governments to intercept an individual's e-mail (and just because you are paranoid does not mean that they are not out to get you), but governments are at least voted into office and can be removed. Criminals with the same potential powers have no such constraints placed on them. The use of the Internet for criminal activities has been highlighted by the action that the FBI took in November 2014 against the Silk Road 2, a *dark-web* service that was used to purchase illegal goods, including weapons and drugs, through digital currency (Bitcoin).

Historically, activists were groups of people with a common cause who wanted to bring pressure to bear on the *establishment*. The establishment might be a government, an international organization such as the World Trade Organization, or even an industry sector such as the petrochemical industry or the biotech sector. Another tool in the hands of the activist is the DoS attack. The case below is an illustration of the effect that such an attack can have and the seesaw motion between the capabilities of the hackers and those of the defenders of the systems as they develop countermeasures.

The DoS attacks were/are again a major problem for corporations such as Microsoft, especially after an employee had apparently misconfigured one of the routers on the system. The attackers were able to capitalize on this human error made by one person at Microsoft, and they bombarded the routers with bogus data requests. The defensive measure brought to bear was an intrusion detection system. In this case, Arbor Networks, a relatively new company that has been jointly funded by Intel and Cisco, was about to announce the launch of a managed service that it claims will detect, trace, and block DoS attacks. This type of technology is not unique, and similar services have been produced in the United Kingdom by the Defence Evaluation and Research Agency (DERA) for use by the UK Ministry of Defence and have subsequently been used to provide a service for both government and industry. Other commercial organizations such as IBM and SAIC also offer similar services.

The service relies on sensors that are placed at strategic locations within the network to allow the monitoring agent to detect abnormal behavior on the system. The primary type of activity monitored is system penetration; however, if the sensors are placed in front of the routers, the monitors can collect information about traffic patterns and identify anomalies, such as excessive traffic coming from a given IP address. In some cases, the software is capable of generating a fingerprint that can be used to trace the origins of the attack; however, this type of functionality has proved to have limited success to date. (How do you identify the attacker in a DoS attack that uses thousands of zombies?) Operators at the customer site or Arbor's network operations center can take corrective action, such as blocking excessive traffic.

The defacement of websites or the hijacking of their addresses has been occurring for some time, but it has increased to the point where the website that became famous for its up-to-date reporting of websites that had been defaced stopped trying to keep up with the list of sites that had been damaged.

In the past in Europe, during protests about the cost of fuel and the tax that the governments were levying on fuel, a number of websites came into being that provided not only communications within the local environment but also allowed for the coordination of activity over the wider area. The material that is shown on these pages is from web pages and newsgroups, all of which are semipermanent; but in fact, a great deal of the information that was passed during these and other activities is now passed through services such as the Internet relay chat (IRC) channels, which can be as public or as private as the participants wish, and for which less of a permanent record is created.

Within the United Kingdom, there was an interesting mix of online activists, including concerned citizens who would not normally have been viewed as activists; political parties and groups; the more expected trade group and industry sites; and forums.

The Harsher Side of Activism

Urban terrorists from disparate factions across Europe used the Internet and mobile phones to orchestrate the rioting that marred a European summit. When the International Monetary Fund and the World Bank meet, they are always a target of attacks. Some groups orchestrate thousands of online protesters, employing, for example, DoS tools for people with almost no computer expertise. In addition to the inconvenience resulting from this act, the groups also hoped to cause monetary loss.

Activists are usually cash strapped, preventing them from being able to afford the best technology. This creates a capabilities gap, but that is overcome with creativity. Activists adapt and improvise with what they have to achieve their goals. This has been the case for thousands of years. Today, activists use that creativity and adaptability to bring to bear whatever technologies they can acquire.[3]

As for groups, we have singled out two primary ones: organized criminals and terrorists (whom some consider just another group of organized criminals).

Terrorists

The terrorists practice a fringe form of Islamic extremism that has been rejected by Muslim scholars and the vast majority of Muslim clerics—a fringe movement that perverts the peaceful teachings of Islam. The terrorists' directive commands them to kill Christians and Jews, to kill all Americans, and make no distinction among military and civilians, including women and children. This group and its leader—Al Qaeda and a person named Osama bin Laden—are linked to many other organizations in different countries, including the Egyptian Islamic Jihad and the Islamic Movement of Uzbekistan. There are thousands of these terrorists in more than 60 countries. They are recruited from their own nations and neighborhoods and brought to camps in places like

Afghanistan, where they are trained in the tactics of terror. They are sent back to their homes or sent to hide in countries around the world to plot evil and destruction.

George W. Bush, President of the United States of America

9/11/01: A Date in Infamy

It has been some time since the massacre of September 11, 2001, took place.

The attacks on the World Trade Center and the Pentagon were extreme but conventional terrorist attacks, while some of the retaliatory action that has continued to take place in the following years is occurring in cyber space.

Information Warfare Tactics by Terrorists

The first group examined is terrorists. The motivation of a terrorist is to undermine the effectiveness of a government by whatever means it chooses. It is worth remembering at this point that a terrorist in one country is a freedom fighter in another, and as a result, there is no stereotype. When you take into account the differing cultures around the world and the differing political regimes that exist, it is easy to understand that a whole variety of actions may be terrorist actions when carried out for political means, or the actions of a hooligan, or, in computer terms, the actions of a hacker.

Let us first address a term that is in current and widespread use—cyber terrorism. While it can be accepted that this term can be used to convey a general meaning, it is not possible to accept the current use of the term to be anything more. The following definition of terrorism was adopted by the gateway model in the United Nations in the spring of 1995:

> A TERRORIST is any person who, acting independently of the specific recognition of a country, or as a single person, or as part of a group not recognized as an official part of division of a nation, acts to destroy or to injure civilians or destroy or damage property belonging to civilians or to governments to effect some political goal.
>
> TERRORISM is the act of destroying or injuring civilian lives or the act of destroying or damaging civilian or government property without the expressly chartered permission of a specific government, thus, by individuals or groups acting independently or governments on their own accord and belief, in the attempt to effect some political goal.
>
> All war crimes will be considered acts of terrorism
>
> Attacks on military installations, bases, and personnel will not be considered acts of terrorism, but instead acts by freedom fighters that are to be considered a declaration of war towards the organized government.[4]

A very different definition was offered at the Fifth Islamic Summit, convened some time ago to discuss the subject of international terrorism under the auspices of the UN, which is as follows[5]:

> There is an underlying trend of physical destruction and of the actions being of such a magnitude and type as to cause "terror" to the people. This does not fit well within the "cyber" environment because there is no direct physical destruction (other than "0s and 1s") and, without the effect of the bullet, the blast, or carnage of the bomb, the "terror-ization" of the people is difficult in our current state of technological advancement. It is more likely that as our cultural values change and we become more highly dependent on technology than we currently are, that the cyber-terrorist in the true sense will come into being.

What Do They Want to Achieve?

Let us first look at what a terrorist will want to achieve through the use of the Internet. This may be one or more of a number of things. The purposes for which a terrorist organization may wish to use this medium include but are not limited to

- The transmission of communications between individuals and groups within the organization
- Propaganda
- Recruiting new members
- Inciting terrorist acts
- Threatening nations, groups, and individuals
- Collecting information on targets
- Hacking targets

No attempts are made by the service providers to ascertain that the details provided by a customer are real and actually do relate to the user.

Once the user is online, there are a number of ways that user can further disguise his or her identity. There are anonymous remailers and browsers that can disguise the identity of the user.

There is freely available high-grade encryption that law enforcement cannot yet break and civil liberty groups that want to ensure that this situation remains so. The desire of civil liberty organizations to maintain the privacy of messages on the Internet has actually nothing to do with the terrorist—they have the liberty and privacy of the individual at heart—but the terrorist is just one of the winners of the pressure that they seek to exert.

A well-reported example of the use of the Internet by terrorists in this way is the activity of Osama bin Laden, who is reported to have used steganography (the ability to hide data in other files or on the slack space on a disk) to pass messages over the Internet.[6] Steganography has become a weapon of choice because of the difficulty in detecting it. The technique hides secrets in plain sight and is especially important when there is a concern that encrypted communications are targeted.

It was reported that Bin Laden was "hiding maps and photographs of terrorist targets and posting instructions for terrorist activities on sports chat rooms, pornographic bulletin boards, and other Web sites." According to another report, couriers for Bin Laden who have been intercepted have been found to be carrying encrypted floppy disks.[7] Other references to the use of the Internet by Bin Laden describe the use of a new form of the Cold War *dead letter box*, which was a predetermined place where one agent deposited information to be collected by another agent.

More recently, the group Islamic State of Iraq and Syria (ISIS) (also known as the Islamic State of Iraq and the Levant [ISIL]) has made very effective use of the Internet. Its members have used official communiqués released by their media centre, Al-Hayat, together with "unofficial" messages posted by their members, and they have targeted local, regional, and global audiences with messages in a number of languages. They have used information operations (IO) very effectively in concert with their political and military activities.

Tactics

Having identified some of the types of effects that terrorists might want to use the Internet to achieve, let us now examine the tactics and tools that they would use to realize their aim. In the case of Osama bin Laden, he is apparently communicating via the Internet using steganography and encryption. Dealing with the two issues separately for the purposes of describing the tactics, this is in no way implying that the two (steganography and encryption) do not go together; in fact, quite the reverse. If you are paranoid, and you want to make sure that your messages get through undetected and in a state that is unreadable to anyone that should guess their presence, then the combination of these techniques is a powerful one.

Data Hiding

What is steganography? The word *steganography* literally means "covered writing" and is derived from Greek. It includes a vast array of methods of secret communication that conceal the very existence of the message. In real terms, steganography is the technique of taking one piece of information and hiding it within another. Computer files, whether they are images, sound recordings, text and word processing files, or even the medium of the disk itself, all contain unused areas where data can be stored. Steganography takes advantage of these areas, replacing them with the information that you wish to hide. The files can then be exchanged with no indication of the additional information that is stored within. A selected image, perhaps of a pop star, could itself contain another image or a letter or map. A sound recording of a short dialogue could contain the same information. In a strange twist in the use of steganography, law enforcement, the entertainment industry, and the software industry have all started to experiment with the use of steganography to place hidden identifiers or trademarks in images, music, and software. This technique is referred to as digital watermarking.

How does it work? Well, the concept is simple. You want to hide one set of data inside another but the way that you achieve this will vary, depending on the type of material in which you are trying to hide your data.

You can hide your material in the file by adding to the data that is already there, thus increasing the size of the file.

You can replace some of the data that is already in the file with the information that you want to hide; this will retain the same file length but there will be a slightly reduced quality in the original representation.

This can be explained in more detail: If you are using an image file to hide data, the normal method is to use the least significant bit of each information element as a place to store hidden data. In doing this, the changes to the image are so subtle as to be undetectable to the naked eye. But the changes are significant enough for steganographic software to be able to hide relatively large quantities of information in the image and also for the software to recognize a pattern within the image that it can use to reveal hidden material.

It would not be unrealistic to hide the contents of this chapter in a relatively small image; for example, if you look at the two images that are reproduced in Exhibit 12.1, they are relatively small, and yet it is possible to hide more than 30 pages of text within one of them with no noticeable degradation in the quality of the image.

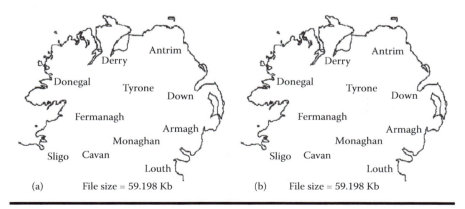

Exhibit 12.1 (a) This picture is the original. (b) This picture has had the entire text of this chapter concealed within the file.

For the most part, the size of the file and the quality of the image are not significant; after all, if you do not have the before and after copies of the file or image on hand, how can you tell that the file has grown or that the image has been degraded? Even when you look at the two images above side by side, it may not be possible to detect any significant difference.

You can even hide messages in music and sound files (MP3) using software that will hide information in these files during the compression process. The data is first compressed and encrypted and is then hidden in the MP3 bit stream. If an opponent discovers your message in an MP3 stream and wishes to remove it, they can uncompress the bit stream and recompress it, which will delete the hidden information. The data hiding takes place at the heart of the encoding process, namely in the inner loop. The inner loop determines the quantity of the input data and increases the process step size until the data can be coded with the available number of bits. Another loop checks that the distortions introduced by the process do not exceed the predefined threshold.

The plethora of choices of software and encoding schema allows the terrorist a wide set of options to suit the chosen method of communication. If the selected method of covering the communications is through a newsgroup that exchanges music, then the use of an MP3 encoder is most sensible. After all, if the other users of the newsgroup have the same taste in music as the sender and recipient of the message, there is no problem; they can download the file, play it, enjoy it, and yet be totally unaware of the hidden content. If the chosen method of communication is one of image sharing, then again, the images can be posted in public, with anyone being able to view the images, but only those who are aware of the additional content are likely to use tools to extract it.

On the plus side of this it is increasingly possible to detect the use of steganography. Software is now becoming available that will identify the use of an increasing range of steganographic packages in use.

While these tools are still limited in the range of data-hiding techniques that they can detect, this will increase rapidly. However, as with viruses and most other forms of malicious code on the Internet, the detection tools will always lag somewhat behind the tools that provide the capability.

Cryptography

It makes sense that if you are a terrorist and you want to communicate using the Internet, you are not going to risk your life or your liberty for the possibility that people will not be able to recognize the use of steganography on its own. Because the steganographic software is not interested in the type of material that it is incorporating into the carrier file, it will hide an encrypted message just as happily as it will hide a clear-text message.

An encryption program scrambles information in a controlled manner through the use of a cryptographic key. In the past, you sent a message encrypted with a particular key to someone, and they had to be in possession of the same key to decrypt the message. This is known as symmetrical cryptography. This, unfortunately, meant that you had to communicate the key to the person to whom you were sending the message.

This was achievable for governments that have the infrastructure to distribute cryptographic keys in a secure manner. However, this type of approach was just not realistic for the general public to consider. In recent years, however, such technology has increasingly been common in the public domain.

Propaganda

Another reason that a terrorist organization might use the Internet is to spread the organization's message and further the cause. For this, the Internet is an outstanding tool. It is the most widely used, uncontrolled medium that has international reach. The number of organizations that have exploited this reach and lack of censorship is huge and has grown with the expansion of social media.

DoS

When a terrorist organization cannot achieve its objective by the means that are normally used—the bullet and the bomb—it has the potential to use the Internet and the connectivity of the systems on which we now rely so heavily to gain the desired impact. There are a number of advantages and disadvantages to this approach, but if the normal techniques cannot be used, it allows another vector of attachment to be utilized that has the advantages of being untraceable to the source and nonlethal.

When compared to the average activity of a hacker, who has limited capability in terms of equipment and sustainability, the terrorist will normally have a greater depth of resources and motivation. A recent example is that of ISIS, who have been selling oil to fund their activities. Someone who takes an action in support of a cause that they believe in will have a much higher motivation to succeed than someone acting on the whim of an idle mind or from simple curiosity.

What Is a DoS Attack?

A DoS attack is characterized by an attempt by an attacker or attackers to prevent legitimate users of a service from using that service. Types of DoS attacks that may be seen include

- Network flooding, resulting in the prevention of legitimate network traffic
- Attempts to disrupt connections between two machines, resulting in the prevention of access to a service
- Attempts to prevent a particular individual from accessing a service
- Attempts to disrupt service to or from a specific system or person

Not all disruptions to service, even those that result from malicious activity, are necessarily DoS attacks. Other types of attack might include DoS as a component, but the DoS itself may be part of a larger attack.

The unauthorized use of resources may also result in DoS. For example, an intruder might make use of your anonymous ftp area as a location where they can store illegal copies of software, using up disk space and CPU time and generating network traffic that consumes bandwidth.

Impact

DoS attacks can disable either the computer or the network, thereby neutralizing the effectiveness of your organization. DoS attacks can be carried out using limited resources against a large, sophisticated, or complex site. This type of attack may be an *asymmetric attack*. An asymmetric attack is one in which a less capable adversary takes on an enemy with superior resources or capabilities. For example, an attacker using an old PC and a slow modem might be able to attack and overcome a much faster and more sophisticated computer or network.

Types of Attack

DoS attacks can manifest themselves in a number of forms and can be targeted at a range of services. There are, primarily, three types of DoS attacks:

Destruction or Alteration of Configuration Information for a System or Network

An incorrectly configured computer may not operate in the intended way, or at all. An intruder may be able to alter or destroy the configuration information and prevent the user from accessing his computer or network. For example, if an intruder can change information in your routers, the network may not work effectively, or at all. If an intruder is able to change the registry settings on a Windows machine, the system may cease to operate, or certain functions may be unavailable.

Consumption of Precious Resources

Computers and networks need certain facilities and resources to operate effectively. This includes network bandwidth, disk space, CPU time, applications, data structures, network connectivity, and environmental resources such as power and air conditioning.

Physical Destruction or Modification of Network Elements

The primary problem with this type of attack is that of physical security. To protect against this type of attack, it is necessary to protect against any unauthorized access to the elements of your system—the computers, routers, network elements, power and air conditioning supplies, or any other components that are critical to the network. Physical security is one of the main defenses used in protecting against a number of different types of attacks in addition to DoS—or any form of the physical destruction of assets.

DoS attacks are normally targeted against network elements. The technique that is normally used in an attack is to prevent the host from communicating across the network. One example of this type of attack is the *synchronize* (SYN) flood attack. In this type of attack, the attacker initiates the process of establishing a connection to the victim's machine. It does this in a way that prevents the completion of the connection sequence. During this process, the machine that is the target of the attack has reserved one of a limited number of data structures required to complete the impending connection. The result is that legitimate connections cannot be achieved while the victim machine is waiting to complete bogus "half-open" connections.

This type of attack does not depend on the attacker being able to consume your network bandwidth. Using this method, the intruder is engaging and keeping busy the kernel data structures involved in establishing a network connection. The effect of this is that an attacker can execute an effective attack against a system on a very fast network with very limited resources.

According to an unclassified document[8] published as far back as November 10, 2001, by the National Infrastructure Protection Center (NIPC), technologies such as Internet relay chat (IRC), Web-based bulletin boards, and free e-mail accounts enable extremist groups to adopt a structure that has become known as "leaderless resistance." Some extremist groups have adopted the leaderless resistance model, in part, to "limit damage from penetration by authorities" that are seeking information about impending attacks. According to the report, which was prepared by NIPC cyber-terrorism experts, "An extremist organization whose members get guidance from emails or by visiting a secure Web site can operate in a coordinated fashion without its members ever having to meet face to face."

In addition to providing a means of secure communications, the range and diversity of Internet technologies also provide extremists with the means to deliver a "steady stream of propaganda" intended to influence public opinion, as well as with a means of recruitment. The increasing technical competency of extremists also enables them to launch more serious attacks on the network infrastructure of a nation-state that go beyond e-mail bombing and Web page defacements, according to the NIPC.

Organized Criminal Groups

The second group examined comprises those involved in organized crime. The motivations of an organized crime group are wide ranging and they will employ whatever means are available to achieve this. For the most part, they make the most of the fact that the Internet is global, whereas laws and law enforcement are primarily nation based. Criminals have done what they always have: followed the money. When the money was in banks, they robbed banks. Now there are much richer pickings on the Internet and the risk of being caught is much lower. Now, the criminal never needs to go to the scene of the crime. In the modern world of CCTV and tracking technologies, this is a huge advantage. Interestingly, at the end of 2013, the British Bankers Association revealed that "traditional" bank robberies (carried out with a mask and a gun), had dropped by 90% in the previous decade. This trend had also been observed in the United States, where the FBI recorded 3,870 robberies in 2012, the lowest figure for several decades.

The criminal can also play the numbers game. If you look at phishing attacks, which are aimed at getting hold of your personal details, they only need a very low proportion to be successful. It costs them nothing other than a little time and effort to send out millions of e-mails purporting to be from your bank asking you to enter your details to reset your account, and they only need a few people to respond to them to generate a good return.

Perhaps the best known organized crime group that has been identified to date was the Russian Business Network (RBN), which operated out of Saint Petersburg in Russia. After a period of criminal activity, the group finally (allegedly) disappeared in 2007. The RBN was a multifaceted Internet-based business that specialized in personal identity theft, but it also managed Internet services for a whole range of other criminal enterprises including child pornography, spam, botnets, and malware distribution.

Since the RBN disappeared, the modus operandi of online criminal gangs has changed, and they now more commonly adopt a *swarm* approach in order to make detection more difficult. A swarm is a group of criminals with a common cause but no obvious leadership, where criminals, often from a number of countries, collaborate online to take part in a joint endeavor.

Other organized crime groups that have been identified include Dreamboard and DrinkOrDie. Dreamboard was a members-only group for a trade in illicit images of children under the age of twelve. It was eventually taken down by a multinational police investigation that started in 2009. When the group was taken down, a total of 72 people in 14 countries across five continents were arrested. The servers for the group were located in the United States, and the group's top-level administrators were located in France and Canada. The group was highly organized, and their network security was very professional. Prospective members were vetted and had to post material on a regular basis to maintain their membership.

The DrinkOrDie group, which appears to have started in Moscow in 1993, specialized in the pirating of copyrighted material and illegally reproduced and distributed software, games, and movies over the Internet. The group had around 65 members in 12 countries including Britain, Australia, Finland, Norway, Sweden, and the United States. DrinkOrDie is most commonly remembered for the illegal distribution of the Windows 95 operating system two weeks before its official release by Microsoft. The group was taken down in 2001, and a total of 20 of its members were arrested.

Organized criminal groups that operate on the Internet have not given up their real world operations—in some cases, they have used the Internet to enhance their operations and in other cases they have created new crimes to make use of the new environment and the opportunities that it has provided.

How big a problem is it? A 2014 report by Security Intelligence[9] states that

> In 2009, the United Nations Office on Drugs and Crime estimated that transnational organized crime (TOC) activities were valued at $870 billion, or approximately 1.5 percent of global GDP. Today, TOC value is well above $1 trillion per year.

The report comments that this amount of money could compromise legitimate national economies and could also have a direct political impact on elections through corruption and bribery. The report goes on to state that a January 2010 US government review of international organized crime (IOC) found that it had grown significantly. As a result of the review has led the government to now view IOC as a serious national security threat. The government has also created a new term to describe the international nature of the organized crime and the potential impact that it has from the converging threats of drugs, human and weapons trafficking, and terrorist groups. It is now referred to as transnational organized crime (TOC).

In reality, it affects every one of us, whether we are affected directly by identity theft or some other crime or indirectly by the increased cost of goods and insurance.

Information Warfare Tactics by Activists

What does an activist seek to achieve by using IW techniques? It is likely that the types of activity that an activist will undertake will be very similar to those of a terrorist group, with the main difference being the scale and the type of target. One of the main aims of an activist is to achieve their goals by exerting pressure through a route other than the government or a corporate process, although they may also use this route. If they can exert this pressure on the targeted organization through DoS or through propaganda, they will do so, but they will also use the Internet to communicate with their colleagues and fellow activists and to gain information or intelligence on their target to identify its weak points.

Activists were, historically, groups of people with a common cause who wanted to bring pressure to bear on the establishment. The establishment might be a government, an international organization such as the World Trade Organization, or even an industry sector such as the petrochemical industry or the biotech sector.

Summary

There are many threat agents to our computers, networks and information. They can be categorized as individual hackers, organized crime groups, activists, terrorists, anarchists, and the like. They all use basically the same tactics to try to achieve their goals. Such things as DoS attacks are common, as are penetrations of our systems in order to take over other computers as weapons to attack other systems, steal information of proprietary or personal nature.

References

1. Merrian Webster Dictionary. http://www.merriam-webster.com/dictionary/anarchist.
2. Stoll, C. (1989). *The Cuckoo's Egg*. New York: Doubleday.
3. FBI. (n.d.). Cyber's most wanted individuals. http://www.fbi.gov/wanted/cyber.
4. Definition of terrorism adopted by gateway model, United Nations, Spring 1995.
5. Ayatullah Muhammad 'Ali Tashkiri. (1987). Towards a definition of terrorism. *Al-Tawhid (A Quarterly Journal of Islamic Thought & Culture)*. Vol. 5, No. 1.
6. McCullagh, D. (2001). Bin Laden: Steganography master? Wired News, February 7. http://archive.wired.com/politics/law/news/2001/02/41658?currentPage=all.
7. Windrem, R., msnbc.com. (2007). http://www.nbcnews.com/id/3907198/ns/us_news-security/t/faq-osama-bin-laden/#.VXV1kdJVhBc.
8. Linda, G. and Martin, G. (eds). (2001). Extremist groups: New organizational models empowered by networked information systems, National Infrastructure Protection Center Highlights, Issue 10-01, November 10. https://www.hsdl.org/?abstract&did=235104.
9. D'Alfonso, S. (2014). Why organized crime and terror groups are converging, security intelligence. *Security Intelligence*. September 4. http://securityintelligence.com/why-organized-crime-and-terror-groups-are-converging/#.VIGgeNKsV8Es.

Chapter 13

The History of Technology

In this chapter, the history of technology will be discussed as one can argue there would not be any global information warfare (IW) if it were not for microprocessor technology.

> What hath God wrought?

Samuel F. B. Morse
The first telegraph message ever sent, 1844

The revolution in technology, especially in high technology, has caused nation-states, corporations, and individuals to become more technology driven, technology supported, and technology dependent. This chapter provides an overview of the history and revolution in technology that has changed the world and discusses how high technology has driven the changes in the ways we live, work, and prosecute wars.

It is not the intent of the authors to provide a detailed history of technology, especially high technology. The intent is to provide a brief, not all-inclusive historic overview. Readers interested in a detailed account of technology history can find numerous websites and books that can provide that detail. However, this overview is provided because it is important for those interested in IW to get some idea as to how we got to our current state of IW through technology, and learning from the past helps us look at where IW will be heading in the future.

What Is Technology?

When we speak of technology, what exactly does that mean? After all, if it was not for technology—high technology—IW would still be relegated to the world of propaganda and written and verbal communication attacks. So, technology is obviously a significant piece of IW. In fact, one cannot discuss modern IW without discussing high technology. It is important to first define what is meant by technology before proceeding any further in the discussion of how the revolution in technology/high technology has impacted how we conduct warfare, especially IW. (Note: Throughout this book, the terms *technology* and *high technology* will be used interchangeably.)

One would expect that by now there would be a common definition for both technology and high technology. However, as with most things related to technology today, there is no easy answer to what appears to be a simple question: What is technology?

According to one dictionary,[1] technology is defined as follows:

> tech·nol·o·gy [tek näl′ Ɛ̩ə jē] (plural tech·nol·o·gies) noun
>
> 1. Application of tools and methods: the study, development, and application of devices, machines, and techniques for manufacturing and productive processes recent developments in seismographic technology
> 2. Method of applying technical knowledge: a method or methodology that applies technical knowledge or tools a new technology for accelerating incubation "…Maryland-based firm uses database and Internet technology to track a company's consumption of printed goods…." Forbes Global Business and Finance, November 1998.
> [Early 17th century. From Greek tekhnologia, literally "systematic treatment," literally "science of craft," from tekhne "art, craft."]

Well, that is fairly general, as should be expected from a general dictionary, but how do those who are involved in technology define it? Well the answer to that is that they cannot—it is too general a term for them and so they prefix it to give it the context that they require to make it useful to them, for instance "green" technology or "high" technology or "automotive" technology.

Also noted on this website were others' definitions of technology:

> Technology is information embodied in a device, the production, use or sale of which may be restricted by law.
>
> **Jonathan Putnam**

Technology is the practical application of knowledge gained through theoretical research to a specific production problem.

Michael J. Patrick
Filament, Renton, WA

Technology is born of a re-search process; institutionalized, glamorized and isolated in its nuclear R&D sheath.

Desmond R. Jimenez
Senior Staff Researcher
AgraQuest Inc.

Technology = knowledge to do something

Alan S. Paau, Ph.D.
Director, Technology Transfer
University of California, San Diego

What it seems to come down to is that the definition of technology is based on one's own perspective, which is biased toward one's own profession. Thus, there are multiple definitions, and all can be applied in discussions of IW.

From Cave Warrior to Information Warrior

The world is rapidly changing. We humans are in the midst of, or have gone through, a hunter-gatherer period, an agricultural period, an industrial period, and now the modern nation-state and its society is in an information-based and information-dependent period. Our global society can no longer function without the aid of automated information and high technology—computers and networks. With computers and global networks such as the Internet come opportunities to make life better for all of us. However, they also make each of us more vulnerable and increase the risk to the high technology we depend on, as well as creating an increased risk of IW and threats to our personal freedoms and our privacy.

Throughout human history, technology has played a role in the development of our species, and it has played a major role in how we prosecute wars. Even the making of fire was probably seen as a technological wonder in the early history of the human race—and it was also used as a weapon of war, such as by setting fire to the enemy's fortifications, houses, and crops. It was also used to help forge tools as weapons of war.

A short look back at that history is appropriate for, as some historian once said, "If you don't know where you've been, you don't know where you are going"—and one might add, "you don't even know where you are." And if you do not know where you are, your survivability in an information-warfare environment is not good. Appendix A provides a short history of technology and its relationship to warfare over the years. The remainder of this chapter is devoted to a discussion of high technology as a basis for IW tactics and weapons.

> Technology drives change.
>
> **Andrew Grove**
> *CEO, Intel Corporation*

From the Twentieth Century to Today: Technology and the Advent of High Technology

The use of technology during the agricultural and industrial time periods saw great numbers of new inventions and improvements in old technologies. This was also the time of the building of the great cities of the world, as well as their total destruction in global wars. Thus, the use of technology for warfare had truly come of age. With the advent of the atomic and subsequent bombs, the entire world could now literally be destroyed. The period also saw great improvements in technology inventions and new inventions such as the telegraph, telephone, air transportation, and computers. This period saw increases in education, mass transportation, and exponential growth in communications—the sharing of information.

During this period, the sharing of information became easier due to the improvement of communications systems, the invention of new communications systems, and the increased consolidation of people into large cities. This also made it easier to educate the people, giving them the skills needed for working in the more modern factories and offices of the period and the skills needed to develop, improve, and implement technologies.

The transition period from the industrial age to the information age in world history varies with each nation-state. In the United States, the well-known authors, the Tofflers, estimated the transition to have taken place in about 1955, when white-collar workers began to outnumber blue-collar workers. Some nation-states are still in various phases of transition from the agricultural period to the industrial period to the information period.

However, no matter when a nation experiences this technology-driven transition, it will see, as the United States and other modern nation-states have seen, that the most rapid changes in all aspects of human existence since humans first walked on this Earth include how wars are prosecuted.

The twentieth century (1900–1999) saw the rapid expansion and use of technology and high technology, to a greater extent than all past centuries combined. It was also the beginning of the concentrated development of technology to specifically develop new and improved weapons of war on a massive scale. This ushered in the era of modern warfare, an era that was sponsored primarily by governments that had the will and the means for such development, and these governments were able to use these new technologically developed weapons to cause death and destruction on a massive scale.

Thus, the twentieth century was the true beginning of technology-based warfare. Due to the technological improvement of older inventions (e.g., submarine, machine gun) and new inventions such as nuclear weapons, never before could so many be killed by so few. Tanks, hand grenades, poison gases, and land mines gave way to chemical/biological/nuclear weapons, carpet bombings, smart bombs, and the beginning of true IW.

> In 1962…the CIA quietly contracted the Xerox Company to design a miniature camera, to be planted inside the photocopier at the Soviet Union's embassy in Washington. A team of four Xerox engineers… modified a home movie camera equipped with a special photocell that triggered the device whenever a copy was made. In 1963, the tiny Cold War weapon was installed by a Xerox technician during a regular maintenance visit to the Soviet embassy.[2]

This period included many significant technology-driven inventions too numerous to mention here in their entirety. In the medical field alone, we have seen the rapid invention of literally thousands of new drugs, procedures, and devices, many of which saved possibly millions of war fighters' lives over the years. Some other significant technologically driven inventions during this century that contributed to changes in war fighting include

Zeppelin
Radio receiver
Polygraph machine
Airplane
Gyrocompass
Jet engine
Synthetic rubber
Solar cell
Short-wave radio
Wirephoto

The twentieth century also saw the development and improvement of more modern warfighting offensive and defensive devices, equipment, and weapons, such as

Kevlar
Hovercraft
Atomic, hydrogen, and other sophisticated bombs
Helicopter

Liquid-fueled rocket
Nuclear submarine
Jeep
Tommy gun
Tank
Gas mask
Vast array of weapons too numerous to list

This period also saw the beginning of the development of our modern era's amazing electronic inventions, leading to the computer and its peripherals:

Electronic amplifying tube (triode)
Radio tuner
Robot
Digital computer
UNIVAC I
Sputnik
Explorer I satellite
Laser
OS/360 IBM operating system
Minicomputer

Photocopier
Computer
Integrated circuit
BASIC language
FORTRAN
Compact disk
Computer mouse
Computer with integrated circuits
RAM, ROM, EEPROM
ARPANET

Optical fiber
Cray supercomputer
Space shuttle
IBM PC
Videotape recorder
Graphic user interface (GUI)
Cathode ray tube
Television
FM radio
Voice recognition machine

Daisy wheel printer
Floppy disk
Dot-matrix printer
Liquid-crystal display (LCD)
Computer hard disk
Modem
Mobile phones
Transistor
World Wide Web
Browsers

Other Significant Twentieth-Century Technological Developments and Events

Some of the other significant technological events and inventions that took place in the twentieth century, and which have led to our rapidly changing information-based societies, information dependencies, and assisted in the development of new methods of prosecuting warfare, include[3]

1930: Shannon's doctorate thesis explains the use of electrical switching circuits in modern Boolean logic.

1934: Computing-Tabulating-Recording becomes IBM.

1936: Burack builds the first electric logic machine.

1940: Atanasoff and Berry design a computer with vacuum tubes as switching units.

1943–1946: Mauchley, Eckert, and Von Neumann build the ENIAC, the first all-electronic digital computer.

1947: The transistor is perfected.

1955: Shockley Semiconductor founded in Palo Alto, California; Bardeen, Shockley, and Brattain share the Nobel Prize for the transistor.

1957: Fairchild Semiconductor founded.

1962: Tandy Corporation buys chain of Radio Shack electronic stores.

1964: Kemeny and Kurtz, Dartmouth College, develop the BASIC computer language.

1968: Intel founded.

1969: Intel produces integrated circuits for Japanese calculators; Data General releases Nova.

What Is High Technology?

We could not come up with a nice, clean definition of technology, but what about *high technology*? Someone once said it was "technology before it became high." That is not bad, but unfortunately it does not help in this instance. One of the better discussions on the topic came from a government website[4] and is quoted below.

High-Tech: A Product, a Process, or Both?

There is no universally accepted definition of *high-tech*, nor is there a standard list of industries considered to be high-tech. Today, nearly every industry contains some element of technology, and even the most technologically intensive industry will include low-tech elements.

Nevertheless, several groups have developed lists of industries they consider high-tech using US Standard Industrial Classifications (SIC).

The breadth of these lists depends on two factors: (1) the goals of the organization and its customers and (2) whether the organization ascribes to the argument that only industries that produce technology can be considered high-tech or to the argument that industries that use advanced technology processes can also be categorized as high-tech.

Any industry-based definitions of high-tech will be imperfect, but none of the definitions discussed here should be considered incorrect. The important factor to consider is the perspective from which any list is derived.

Most high-tech industry classifications have common elements, yet may vary significantly in scope. Let us consider four classifications of high-tech industries developed by the following respected and often quoted organizations: the American Electronics Association (AEA), RFA (formerly Regional Financial Associates), One Source Information Services Inc. (formerly Corp Tech), and the US Bureau of Labor Statistics (BLS).

The different missions of these four organizations influence how they define high-tech. AEA is a trade association made up of mostly electronics and information technology companies. Its members generally produce technology and ascribe to the limited definition of high-tech based only on the nature of an industry's product rather than its process. RFA is a national consulting firm. Its clients include builders and contractors, banks, insurance companies, financial services firms, and government. The industries with the greatest growth potential and those reflective of their clients' interests are included in RFA's list of high-tech industries. While both AEA and RFA have narrowly defined high-tech, One Source and BLS use broader definitions that include industries with both high-tech products and processes.

One Source gathers and sells corporate information on technology firms for use in sales and marketing. As it has built its database of firms, One Source has expanded its list of what should be considered a high-tech industry. BLS is a federal agency responsible for collecting and analyzing data on the national labor force. It has defined those industries with the highest concentration of technology-based occupations, such as scientists and engineers, as high-tech industries.

The Trade Association: AEA

AEA recently released Cyberstates 4.0, its annual report on technology employment, based on AEA's limited definition of high-tech industries, which fall into three categories: (1) computer, communication, and electrical equipment; (2) communication services; and (3) computer-related services. AEA's list is the most restrictive of the four classifications. Absent from the list are areas such as drug manufacturing, robotics, and research and testing operations.

The Consulting Group: RFA

RFA's high-tech sectors are similar to those selected by AEA. However, RFA does not include household audio and video equipment or telephone communications, but it adds drugs and research and testing services.

Information Provider: One Source

Unlike the short lists compiled by AEA and RFA, the One Source list classifies 48 sectors as high-tech. Major additions include a number of manufacturing industries, such as metal products and transportation equipment, and several service industries.

The Research Group: BLS

BLS has further refined its high-tech industry definition by separating sectors into two groups. Those industries with a high concentration of research-oriented occupations are labeled intensive, while those with a lower concentration are considered nonintensive. The differences shown here illustrate why knowing how data are defined is essential to understanding what the data mean. Once again, those wishing for a simple answer will be frustrated. It is not the data that have failed them, but the reality of a complex system (the economy) and the human factor that must determine how to best reflect that system using data.

As we have found, trying to get a handle on this thing called technology—any kind of technology—is like grabbing air. Even low technology was once considered high technology in its day. For example, when the first plow was invented, it was probably considered a technological wonder. Then, after hooking it up to a horse or water buffalo, it increased the productivity of the farmers and it certainly drastically changed farming methods. When the wooden plow was integrated with a steel blade, certainly that was considered high technology in its day. One must remember that high technology today will undoubtedly be considered low technology 25–50 years from now. So, high technology is also based on a reference point, and that reference point is time—perception and time are also key factors in IW.

As we have seen, it is not easy to come to grips with this phenomenon called high technology. For our purposes, a narrowly focused definition is better. In today's world, the microprocessor drives the technological products that drive the information age and IW. So, we will define high technology based on the microprocessor.

High technology is defined as technology that includes a microprocessor.

The Microprocessor

In 1971, Intel introduced the Intel 4004 microprocessor. This was the first microprocessor on a single chip and included the central processing unit (CPU), input and output controls, and memory. This made it possible to program "intelligence into inanimate objects," and was the true beginning of the technology revolution that has caused so many changes in the world and ushered in the beginnings of the age of IW.

The microprocessor was developed through a long line of amazing inventions and improvements on inventions. Without these dramatic and often what appear to be new, miraculous breakthroughs in microprocessor technology, today's IW phenomenon would still exist only in the dreams of science-fiction writers, the likes of Jules Verne and George Orwell. However, because of the amazing developments in the microprocessor, IW is beginning to come to the forefront in modern-day warfare.

Today, because of the microprocessor, its availability, miniaturization, power, and low cost, the world is rapidly developing new high-technology devices, procedures, processes, and networks, and of course IW and conventional warfare weapons. The global information infrastructure (GII) is just one example of what microprocessors are making possible. GII is the massive international connections of world computers that carry business and personal communication as well as that of the social and government sectors of nations. Some say that GII will connect entire cultures, erase international borders, support "cyber economies," establish new markets, and change our entire concept of international relations.

The GII is based on the Internet, and much of the growth of the Internet is in developing nations such as Argentina, Iran, Peru, Egypt, Philippines, Russia, Malaysia, and Indonesia. The GII is not a formal project but it is the result of thousands of individuals', corporations', and governments' need to communicate and conduct business by the most efficient and effective means possible. The GII is also a battlefield in the IW arena.

Moore's Law

No discussion of high technology and IW weapons would ever be complete without a short discussion of Moore's Law. In 1965, Gordon E. Moore, Director of the Research and Development Laboratories at Fairchild Semiconductor, was asked by *Electronics* magazine to predict the future of semiconductors and its industry during the next 10 years. In what became known as Moore's Law, he stated that the capacity or circuit density of semiconductors doubles every 18 months or quadruples every 3 years.[5]

The interesting thing about Moore's comments is that they became sort of a high-technology driver for the semiconductor industry and, even after all these years, Moore's Law has been pretty much on track as to how semiconductors have improved over the years. Its power, of course, depends on how many transistors can be placed in how small a space. The mathematical version of Moore's Law is Bits per square inch = 2 (time−1962).[6]

Some of the high-technology "inventions" of the twentieth century that depended on the microprocessor include

Ethernet (1973)
Laser printer (1975)
Ink-jet printer (1976)
Magnetic resonance image (1977)
VisiCalc (1978)
Cellular phones (1979)
Cray supercomputer (1979)

MS-DOS (1981)
IBM PC (1981)
Scanning tunneling microscope (1981)
Apple Lisa (1983)
CD-ROM (1984)
Apple Macintosh (1984)
Windows operating systems (1985)
High-temperature superconductor (1986)
Digital cellular phones (1988)
Doppler radar (1988)
World Wide Web/Internet protocol (HTTP); HTML (1990)
Pentium processor (1993)
Java computer language (1995)
Digital versatile disc or digital video disc (DVD) (1995)
Web TV (1996)
Apple Ipod (2001)

The Pioneer 10 spacecraft used the 4004 microprocessor. It was launched on March 2, 1972, and was the first space flight and microprocessor to enter the asteroid belt.

Other Significant Twentieth-Century High-Technology Developments and Events

Some of the significant high-technology computer events and inventions that took place in the twentieth century and led to our rapidly changing methods of prosecuting a war include[3]

1971: Intel develops the 8008; Wozniak and Fernandez build the "Cream Soda Computer."

1972: Kildall writes PL/1, the first programming language for the Intel 4004 microprocessor; Gates and Allen form "Traf-O-Data"; Wozniak and Jobs begin selling Blue Boxes.

1973: Wozniak joins HP; Kildall and Cooper build "astrology forecasting machine."

1974: Intel invents the 8080; Xerox releases the Alto; Torode and Kildall begin selling microcomputers and disk operating systems.

1975: Microsoft (previously known as "Traf-O-Data") writes BASIC for the Altair; Heiser opens the first computer store in Los Angeles.

1976: Kildall funds Digital Research; work on the first Radio Shack microcomputer started by Leininger and French; first sale of the CPM operating system takes place.

1977: Apple introduces the Apple II. TRS-80 developed.

1978: Apple ships disk drives for the Apple II and begins development of the Lisa computer.

1980: HP releases the HP-85; Apple III is announced; Microsoft and IBM sign an agreement for IBM's PC operating system.

1981: Osborne I developed; Xerox comes out with the 8010 Star and the 820 computers; IBM presents the PC.

1982: Apple Lisa is introduced; DEC develops a line of personal computers (e.g., DEC Rainbow 100).

1983: IBM develops the IBM PC Jr.; Osborne files for Chapter 11 as the microcomputer market heats up.

1984: Apple announces the Macintosh microcomputer.

1986: Intel develops the 8086 chip.

1987: Intel develops the 8088 chip.

1990s: Intel, already the leader in microprocessors, announces the 286, 386, and 486 chips, followed rapidly by the Pentium chips, which now reach speeds of 1.7 GHz as we enter the twenty-first century.

Moore's Law is still holding true, although some believe we will soon hit the silicon wall, based on the laws of physics. Some of these doomsayers have been saying such things for years. Others are more optimistic and believe that other material will be found to replace silicon, or that silicon will be somehow enhanced to "defy" the laws of physics. If the past is any clue to the future, the future of high technology will not be impaired by such minor impediments as the laws of physics.

According to the US General Accounting Office in a report to Congress,[8] the rapid developments of the telecommunications infrastructure in the United States have resulted in the creation of three separate and frequently incompatible communications networks:

Wire-based voice and data telephone networks
Cable-based video networks
Wireless voice, data, and video networks

In the future, this problem will become a nonissue as integration and commonality, forced by business and government needs for total information compatibility, will take place. It is already happening in many areas (e.g., cellular phones and notebook computers, television, and Internet access).

The Internet

The real issue is control. The Internet is too widespread to be easily dominated by any single government. By creating a seamless global-economic zone, anti-sovereign and unregulatable, the Internet calls into question the very idea of the nation-state.[8]

John Perry Barlow

It is in the context of this phenomenal growth in high technology and human knowledge that the Internet arises as one of the mechanisms to facilitate sharing of information and as a medium that encourages global communications. The Internet has already become one of the twenty-first century's information-warfare battlefields.

The global collection of networks that evolved in the late twentieth century to become the Internet represent what could be described as a "global nervous system" transmitting facts, opinions, and opportunity from anywhere to anywhere. However, when most people think of the Internet, it seems to be something either vaguely sinister or of such complexity that it is difficult to understand. Popular culture, as manifested by Hollywood and network television programs, does little to dispel this impression of danger and out-of-control complexity.

The Internet arose out of projects sponsored by the Advanced Research Project Agency (ARPA) in the United States in the 1960s. It is perhaps one of the most exciting legacy developments of that era. Originally an effort to facilitate the sharing of expensive computer resources and to enhance military communications, it has over the last 26 years, from about 1988 until 2014, rapidly evolved from its scientific and military roots into one of the premier commercial communications media. The Internet, which is described as a global metanetwork, or network of networks (p. 11),[8] provides the foundation on which the global information superhighway has been built.

However, it was not until the early 1990s that Internet communication technologies became easily accessible to the average person. Prior to that time, Internet access required mastery of many arcane and difficult-to-remember programming language codes. However, the combination of declining microcomputer prices and enhanced microcomputer performance, and the advent of easy-to-use browser* software, were key enabling technologies that created the foundation for mass Internet activity. When these variables aligned with the developing global telecommunications infrastructure, they allowed a rare convergence of capability.

> *E-mail.* Although e-mail was invented in 1972, it was not until the advent of the "modern Internet system" that it really began to be used on a global scale. In 1987, there were approximately 10,000 Internet computer hosts and 1000 news messages a day in 300 newsgroups. In 1992, there were more than 1,000,000 hosts and 10,000 news messages a day in 1000 newsgroups. By 1995, the number of Internet hosts had risen to more than 10 million, with

---

* Software that simplifies the search and display of World Wide Web–supplied information.

250,000 news messages a day in over 10,000 newsgroups.[10] By 2014, the majority of e-mail traffic originated from the business world, which accounted for more than 108.7 billion e-mails that were sent and received every day.[11]

Internet protocols. In the 1970s, Internet protocols were developed to be used to transfer information.

Usenet newsgroup and electronic mail. Newsgroups and electronic mail were developed in the 1980s.

Gopher. In 1991, personnel at the University of Minnesota created the Gopher as a user-friendly interface that was a menu system for accessing files.

World Wide Web. In 1991, Tim Berners-Lee and others at the Conseil Européene pour la Recherche Nucléaire (CERN) developed the Web. In 1993, the Web had approximately 130 sites, and in 1994, it had about 3000 sites; in April 1998, this had grown to more than 2.2 million sites, and in January 2015 it had reached 1,169,228,000.[12]

The most commonly accessed application on the Internet is the World Wide Web (Web, WWW). Originally developed in Switzerland, the Web was envisioned by its inventor as a way to help share information. The ability to find information concerning virtually any topic via search engines, such as Google, Bing, Alta Vista, HotBot, Lycos, InfoSeek, and others, from among the rapidly growing array of Web servers is an amazing example of how the Internet increases the information available to nearly everyone. One gains some sense of how fast and pervasive the Internet has become as more television, radio, and print advertisements direct prospective customers to visit their business or government agency websites. Such sites are typically named www.companyname.com, where the business is named "company," or www.governmentagency.gov for government agencies.

From the past century until now, the Internet has rapidly grown from an experimental research project and tool of the US government and universities to the tool of everyone in the world with a computer. It is the premier global communications medium. With the subsequent development of search engines and, of course, the Web, the sharing of information has never been easier. Sites such as Google.com state that in 2013, they searched through 30 trillion Web pages!

It has now become a simple matter for average people—even those who had trouble programming their VCRs—to obtain access to the global Internet, and with this access to search the huge volume of information it contains. Millions of people around the world are logging in, creating a vast environment often referred to as cyber space and the global information infrastructure (GII), which has been described as the virtual, online, computer-enabled environment, one distinct from the physical reality of "real life."

By the end of the twentieth century, worldwide revenues via Internet commerce had reached perhaps hundreds of billions of dollars, an unparalleled growth rate for a technology that has only been really effective since the early 1990s! The "electronic commerce" of the early twenty-first century already includes everything from online information concerning products, purchases, and services to the development of entirely new business activities (e.g., Internet-enabled banking and gambling).

An important fact for everyone to understand, and one of supreme importance to those interested in IW, is that the Web is truly global in scope. Physical borders as well as geographical distance are almost meaningless in cyber space; the distant target is as easily attacked as the local one.

The annihilation of time and space makes the Internet an almost perfect environment for IW. When finding a desired adversary's* server located on the other side of the planet is as easy and convenient as calling directory assistance to find a local telephone number, information warriors have the potential to act in ways that one can only begin to imagine. Undeterred by distance, borders, time, or season, the potential bonanza awaiting the information warrior is a chilling prospect for those who are responsible for safeguarding and defending the assets of a business or government agency.

Because of religious beliefs in many faiths, Internet access to material considered pornographic is generally not acceptable. One of society's struggles will be how to provide access to the world's information without causing some moral decay of society. This will be a struggle for many countries, and it is believed that information warriors will have a major impact on the society of such developing countries.

The Internet is the latest in a series of technological advances that are being used not only by honest people to further their communication, but also by miscreants, juvenile delinquents, and others for illegal purposes. As with any technological invention, they can be used for good or for illegal purposes. They are really no different than other inventions such as the handgun. The handgun can be used to defend and protect lives or to destroy them. It all depends on the human being that is using the technology.

The High-Technology-Driven Phenomenon

Internet Service Providers

Using an Internet search engine and searching for "Internet service providers (ISPs)," 96,900,000 "hits" were identified in a search that took, according to Google, 0.60 seconds! The CIA World Factbook[13] gives a figure of more than 7000 ISPs in the United States—nearly 10 times as many as any other country. Canada has the second highest number with 760, but China, for example, has only three, and North Korea has only one.

---

* The term "adversary" is used more often these days to describe an enemy than the word "enemy" because it seems it is not as harsh a term, although the intent is still to disable or kill them.

In other words, there are thousands of ISPs operating and connected all across the globe. We all know by now (hopefully) that our e-mails do not go point-to-point, but hop around the Internet. They are susceptible to being gleaned by all those with the resources to read other people's mail or steal information to commit crimes (e.g., identity theft, competitive intelligence information collections, and, of course, useful information for information warriors).

So, what is the point? The point is that there are ISPs all over the world with few regulations and absolutely no protection and defensive standards. Some ISPs may do an admirable job of protecting our information passing through their systems, while others may do nothing. Furthermore, as we learn more and more about netspionage (computer-enabled business and government spying), we learn more and more about how our privacy and our information is open to others to read, capture, change, and otherwise misuse. In addition, with such programs as SORM in Russia, Internet monitoring in China and elsewhere, global Echelon, and the US FBI's Carnivore (still Carnivore no matter how often they change the name to make it more politically correct), we might as well take our most personal information, tattoo it on our bodies and run naked in the streets for all to see. Well, that may be a slight exaggeration; the point is that we have no concept of how well ISPs are protecting government, business or individuals information. Through your ISP, how susceptible are you to the threats of IW? Do you know if your ISP is protecting or monitoring you? If it is monitoring you, for whom?

Faster and More Massive High-Technology-Driven Communications

We are quickly expanding into the world of instant messages (IMs) through ISPs. After all, the more rapidly our world changes, the more rapidly we want to react and we want everything—now! A 2014 report by Juniper networks stated that Instant messaging apps will account for 75% of mobile messaging traffic, or 63 trillion messages, by 2018. Furthermore, it can be used to transfer files and send graphics, and unlike the telephone and normal e-mails, with IM one knows whether or not the person being contacted is there. Interesting ramifications—check to see if a person is online; if not (after already setting up a masquerade or spoof), take over that person's identity and contact someone posing as the other—instantly. Of course there are perhaps hundreds, if not thousands, of examples of ISPs being penetrated or misused. As far back as approximately November 1995, for example, the *Wall Street Journal* ran a story entitled "America Online to warn users about bad e-mail." We all know about the basic issues of viruses and other malicious codes being sent via ISPs. So, the problem has existed for quite some time.

Solar Storms Could Affect Telecommunications. Intense storms raging on the sun…could briefly disrupt telecommunications.… The eruptions triggered a powerful, but brief, blackout Friday on some high-frequency radio channels and low-frequency navigational signals…forecast at least a 30 percent chance of continuing disruptions…. In addition to radio disruptions, the charged particles can bombard satellites and orbiting spacecraft and, in rare cases, damage industrial equipment on the ground, including power generators and pipelines.[14]

High technology is vulnerable to nature and the universe in general. What a great time to launch an IW attack on an adversary. Is it sunspots or an adversary causing these outages? By the time the adversary finds out that it is you and not three days of sunspots, the war could be over.

The Beneficial Effect of Hacker Tools and Other Malicious Software on Network Security with Dual Roles as IW Tools

The following malicious software was selected as a representative sample of those that are available. They have been selected for their range of functionality and additionally for their range through time from 1991 to present, and they can be and are being adapted and adopted for use in IW.*

Hacker Tools

Of the hacker tools that were reviewed, while the intentions of the originators of the tools were mixed, with some being malicious and some well intentioned, they can all be used to strengthen the security of a network or to monitor the system for illicit activity. This can be achieved if the system owner uses hacker tools to identify the weaknesses that exist in the security of the system and to identify appropriate remedial action before a person with malicious intent attempts to exploit the weaknesses. A number of the tools can also be used to monitor the system for illicit activity even before software patches are available, so that the system owner can make informed decisions on appropriate action to prevent or minimize damage to their system. As an information warrior, how will you use such tools to attack an adversary?

Viruses

Viruses have no direct beneficial effect on the security of a system except to provide a visible indication that there has been a breakdown in procedures for the transfer

---

* A number of other tools were reviewed, but these contain no obvious property or functionality that was considered to be both beneficial and a potential IW weapon; that is, they modified the system to exploit vulnerabilities or they were purely malicious and caused a denial-of-service. These are tools that are "pure" IW tools.

of software or data between systems. The negative effect of viruses is the cost in terms of time and the antivirus software to check data and software being imported or exported to and from the system, as well as the cost of rectifying a problem when an infection has occurred, which can be considerable. In an abstract way, the advent of the virus has actually been beneficial to the computer security manager because the impact of a virus on the user is a visible and constant reminder of the need to observe good computer security practices. In the majority of cases, the virus is detected before it can activate its payload, so the damage is normally limited to the inconvenience and cost of cleaning up the system to remove the virus. As an IW weapon, it is a valuable and cheap weapon that can cause devastating results when used against the unprepared information systems of an adversary.

Worms

The release onto the Internet on November 2, 1988, of the Internet worm written by Robert T. Morris, Jr., quickly caused widespread disruption and the failure of a large proportion of the network that existed at that time. The problem was compounded by the fact that some of the servers that had not been affected were taken offline to prevent them from becoming infected, thus placing a higher load on already affected sections of the system and denying those elements of the network that had gone offline access to the patches that would protect them, as the normal distribution method for patches was over the Internet itself. To date, there have been no security benefits derived from worms, other than, in the case of the Robert T. Morris worm, to highlight the urgent need for effective and early communication of information on incidents. The potential for the use of this type of program in a way that would aid the security of systems has been postulated in the form of autonomous intelligent agents that would travel through the system and report back predefined information, such as the system assets, the condition and identity of system elements, and the presence or absence of specific types of activity. As a weapon for prosecuting IW, worms have excellent potential and may even be considered a "weapon of mass destruction" because of the damage they can cause a high-technology, information systems–dependent adversary. Of course, we now have many "colored" worms being written and traveling around the GII, NIIs, and other networks.

Easter Eggs

Easter eggs have no beneficial effect other than to highlight that even proprietary software can include large sections of code that are redundant to the functionality for which they were intended, and also that the quality control procedures for the production of software by well-known organizations is poor if the Easter eggs were not detected during production. Can you think of any way to use these eggs in an IW battle?

Trojan Horses

The Trojan horse, by definition, carries out actions that are normally hidden from the user while disguising their presence as a benign item of software. They are difficult to detect because they appear to be a legitimate element of the operating system or an application that would normally be found on the system. Given that the purpose of a Trojan horse is to hide itself and its functionality from legitimate users, there have been no beneficial effects derived from them—unless you are an information warrior.

Logic Bombs

Logic bombs, like Trojan horses, carry out actions that are unexpected and undesirable. Some may cause relatively minor damage, such as writing a message to a screen, while others are considerably more destructive. They are normally inserted by disaffected staff or by people with a grudge against the organization. Again, they are difficult to detect before they have been activated and, as a result, can be expensive to rectify. Logic bombs are correctly named as they can have the same effect against the system of an adversary as a physical bomb might have against a building—Boom! It is gone!

The clear implication of the issues discussed above is that some hacker tools can have a beneficial effect on the security of computer systems if they are used by the system staff before they are used by personnel either within the organization or outside it to identify shortcomings or flaws in the operating system or applications software, the configuration of the system, or the procedures used to secure it. Viruses, while providing no direct benefit, do provide a detectable indication that there has been a breach in the security of the system, either by an exploitation of a flaw in the security procedures or by a shortcoming in the system software (it allowed a virus through any barriers that had been created to prevent access to the system). Worms currently have no beneficial effect on system security management. However, the concept that was used to disseminate the Robert T. Morris worm may have an application in the mapping of large networks if applied to autonomous agents. The Trojan horse and the logic bomb, which, by their very nature, are covertly inserted into the system without the owner's knowledge, have no beneficial effect and have only malicious applications. However, as noted above, for purposes of prosecuting IW, these have some excellent potential and are, in fact, being refined and improved on for the IW arsenals of individuals, corporations, and nation-states.

Other High-Technology Tools in IW

IW through high technology is being fought on many fronts—on the personal privacy, corporate netspionage,[14] and nation-state battlefields of the world. Even such innocent-sounding words as "cookies" take on new meaning in the IW arena.

These cookies—the computer kind, not the ones you eat—are beneficial, except when they are used to profile customer habits and gather an individual's private information, which is then sold. High-technology cookies are files that a website can load onto a user's system. They are used to send back to the website a user's activity on that website, as well as what web sites the user has previously visited. They are also a potential tool of the information warrior.

Intel's Pentium III included a unique processor serial number (PSN) in every one of its new Pentium III chips. Intel claimed that the PSN could identify an individual's surfing through electronic commerce and other Internet-based applications. It was noted that by providing a unique PSN that can be read by websites and other application programs, an excellent IW tool could be created. Although the PSN is designed to be used to link user activities on the Internet for marketing and other purposes, one can easily imagine other uses, from an IW perspective, that can be made of this high-technology application. And as for Microsoft's new operating system, XP, imagine the IW possibilities.

Steganography is another use of high technology that can be used in IW[14]:

> Hiding information by embedding a file inside another, seemingly innocent file is a technique known as "steganography." It is most often used with graphics, sound, text, HTML, and PDF files. Steganography with digital files works by replacing the unused bytes of data in a computer file with bytes that contain concealed information.

Steganography (which translated from Greek means covered writing) has been in use since about 580 B.C. One technique was to carve secret messages into wooden objects and then cover the etched words with colored wax to make them undetectable to an uninitiated observer. Another method was to tattoo a message onto the shaved messenger's head. Once the hair grew back, the messenger was sent on his mission. Upon arrival, the head was shaved, thus revealing the message—obviously not time dependent. The microdot, which reduced a page of text to the size of a typewriter's period so that it could be glued onto a postcard or letter and sent through the mail, is another example.[17]

Two types of files are typically used when embedding data into an image. The innocent image that holds the hidden information is a *container*. A *message* is the information to be hidden. A message may be plaintext, ciphertext, other images, or anything that can be embedded in the least significant bits (LSB) of an image.[16]

Steganographic software has some unique advantages as a tool for netspionage agents. First, if the agents use regular cryptographic software on their computer systems, the files may not be accessible to investigators but will be visible, and it will be obvious that the agents are hiding something. Steganographic software allows agents to "hide in plain sight" any valuable digital assets they may have obtained until they can transmit or transfer the files to a safe location or to their customer. As a second advantage, steganography can be used to conceal and transfer an encrypted document containing the acquired information to a digital dead drop. The agents could then provide the handler or customer with the password to unload the dead drop, but the steganographic extraction phrase will not be divulged until payment is received or the agents are safely outside the target corporation. As a final note, even when a file is known or suspected to contain information protected with steganographic software, it has been almost impossible to extract the information unless the passphrase has been obtained.

Welcome to Twenty-First-Century Technology

As we left the twentieth century and began the twenty-first century, our dependence on technology continued to increase, as did our interconnectivity on a global basis: our integration of devices—or platforms—and use of wireless, mobile technology. This has increased our vulnerabilities to successful attacks on a global scale. It has also made protection of our systems, information, and so on much more difficult—maybe even impossible.

As we progress into the twenty-first century, we continue to fall behind in our defenses and ability to react quickly and successfully to attacks from around the world. As the sophistication of attacks continues to increase, so do vulnerabilities to our vital information infrastructures.

> Top cybersecurity experts echoed a dire warning from a top intelligence chief on the vulnerability of the U.S. power grid, with one telling FoxNews.com that state-sponsored hackers could send America's nerve centers on an "uncontrollable, downward spiral."[17]

That has also has been made more difficult by advances in technology and also in social networks, where users continue to not only provide information very useful to IW warriors but have also made individuals, groups, corporations, and governments more open to attacks due in part to information that users innocently provide the world on social networks of all kinds.

Let us look at some of the major technology advances thus far in the twenty-first century:

The power of cell and Wi-Fi phones as they have come to be used not only as telephones but also as more all-in-one communication devices, with, for example, voice, text, e-mail, storage, and video and digital camera capabilities. Not far behind are tablets, which offer the same mobility as cell phones but have bigger screens and often more power, storage, memory capacity, and speed.

Twitter, Facebook, You Tube, blogs and other facilities offer social connectivity as never before, wherein individuals, businesses, and governments on a global, mobile scale share information. This activity includes accidentally or purposefully posting sensitive or maybe even classified information as users go unchecked. It is also a great platform for blackmail, marketing, and spreading false information and propaganda, and of course collecting information useful in GIW and conventional wars and battles.

More sophisticated game machines and games can be used to help train info-warriors and in fact are being used to do so.

Driverless vehicles including trams, trains, and cars are turning into computers on wheels. They are loaded with technology. Imagine once they are taken over and controlled by an info-warrior, they can easily be turned into weapons, given new status as car bombs where the drivers do not have to sacrifice their lives.

Electric vehicles will become more prevalent over time. Since we are unable to store electricity as well as we can gas, what would happen to our ability to use electric vehicles, especially for emergencies, once our power grids go down and they cannot be recharged? As we race to be "eco-friendly," are we considering what to do to mitigate this up-and-coming vulnerability? No, of course not.

We are also approaching the time when we will truly be able to use artificial intelligence and possibly become dependent on it. What happens it is then taken over and changed by info-warriors and made into weapons support?

The use of nanotechnology will continue to be enhanced, and as it does, it can be embedded in our infrastructures to destroy them, injected into our bodies. Also, as we depend more on robotics, from manufacturing to medical devices and even for surgeries, what happens when they are taken over by info-warriors?

Looking back at what has been accomplished just in our short lifetimes, imagine twenty-first century technologies and their GIW implications coming in the future.

Summary

If you are involved in any activity in which technology is used as a tool to help you accomplish your work, you are aware of the tremendous and very rapid advances that are being made in that arena. It is something to behold. We are in the middle of the most rapid technological advances in human history, but this is just the beginning. We are not even close to reaching the potential that technology has to offer, nor to realizing its impact on all of us—both good and bad.

It is said that there have been more discoveries in the past 50 years than in the entire history of mankind before that time. We have just to read the newspapers and the trade journals to look at every profession and see what technology is bringing to our world: new discoveries in medicine, the advent of online and worldwide information systems, the ability to hold teleconferences across the country and around the globe, and hundreds of other examples that we can all think of.

High technology is the mainstay of both our businesses and government agencies. We can no longer function in business or government without them. Pagers, cellular phones, e-mail, credit cards, teleconferences, smart cards, tablet and notebook computers, networks, and private branch exchanges (PBXs) are all computer based and all are now common tools for individuals, businesses, and public and government agencies. Information warriors are also relying more and more on computers. As computers become more sophisticated, so do the information warriors. As international networks increase, so does the number of international information warriors.

Networking and embedded systems, those integrated into other devices (e.g., automobiles, microwave ovens, medical equipment), are increasing and drastically changing how we live, work, and ply. According to a study financed by the US ARPA and published in the book *Computers at Risk*:

> Computers have become so integrated into the business environments that computer-related risks cannot be separated from normal business risks, or those of government and other public agencies.
>
> Increased trust in computers for safety-critical applications (e.g., medical) leads to the increased likelihood that attacks or accidents can cause deaths (Note: It has already happened).
>
> Use and abuse of computers is widespread with increased threats of viruses, credit card, PBX, cellular phones, and other frauds.
>
> Unstable international political environment raises concerns about government or terrorist attacks on information and high technology-dependent nations' computer and telecommunications systems.
>
> Individual privacy is at risk due to large, vulnerable databases containing personal information, thus facilitating increases in identity theft and other frauds.
>
> If I want to wreak havoc on a society that, in some cases, has become complacent, I am going to attack your quality of life.
>
> **Curt Weldon, R-PA**
> *US House, Armed Services Committee*[18]

Personal computers have changed our lives dramatically, and there is no end in sight. High technology in general has improved the quality of life for societies, made life a little easier, and yet it puts an information-dependent way of life more at risk than ever before. The use of modems has been commonplace with all newly purchased microcomputer systems,* which come with an internal modem already installed and ready for global access through the Internet or other networks. Wireless networks are being increasingly used and there are now millions of Wi-Fi

---

* Microcomputers had been a term used to differentiate them from minicomputers and main-frame computers. The computers' power and what the manufacturer decided to call them differentiated these systems. However, with the power of today's microcomputer equaling that of larger systems, the issue is unclear and basically no longer very relevant. What these systems are called, coupled with notebooks, PDAs, workstations, desktops, etc., are not that important because they all basically operate the same way.

"hotspots" to which a person can connect their phone, laptop, or tablet wherever they are. Therefore, these devices and the networks that they are using potentially represent some of the most serious and complex crime scenes of the information age. This will surely increase as we begin the twenty-first century.

> it is computerized information, not manpower or mass production that…will win wars in a world wired for 500 TV channels. The computerized information exists in cyberspace—the new dimension created by endless reproduction of computer networks, satellites, modems, databases, and the public Internet.[19]

Neil Munro

High-technology development continues to play a dual role in information-based nation-states. High-technology devices have been turned into tools that have been used to determine the adequacy of information systems' security and defenses, and these have been adopted and adapted by global hackers and other miscreants. They now have been using those tools for probing and attacking systems, especially through the Internet interfaces of corporations and nation-states as well as the GII and NIIs of nation-states. These same hacker techniques have been readily adopted and enhanced by the information warriors of nation-states and others.

References

1. Soukhanov, A. H. (1999). *Encarta World English Dictionary*. New York: Bloomsbury. (Microsoft Corporation. All rights reserved. Developed for Microsoft by Bloomsbury Publishing Plc.)
2. Stover, D. (1996). The CIA's Xerox spy-cam. *Popular Science,* January 1996 Issue.
3. Freiberger, P., and Swaine, M. (1999). *Fire in the Valley: The Making of the Personal Computer.* McGraw-Hill; 2nd Revised edition (1 Dec. 1999).
4. Incontext. (2000). June 2000, Vol. 1, No. 5. http://www.incontext.indiana.edu/2000/june00/spotlight.asp.
5. Schaller, B. (1996). The origin, nature, and implications of "Moore's law"—The benchmark of progress in semiconductor electronics. September 26. http://research.microsoft.com/en-us/um/people/gray/moore_law.html.
6. Phillips, W. (2000). Chapter 2—Computers and intelligence. In *The Extraordinary Future* (learning module). The MindProject. http://www.mind.ilstu.edu/curriculum/extraordinary_future/PhillipsCh2.php?modGUI=247&compGUI=1944&itemGUI=3397.
7. US Government Accountability Office. (1995). Information superhighway—An overview of technology challenges, GAO-AIMD 9523, p. 12. Jan 23, 1995.
8. Barlow, J. P. (1996). Thinking locally, acting globally. *Time,* January, p. 57; as quoted in Davidson, J. D. and Rees-Mogg, L. W. (1999). *The Sovereign Individual.* New York: Touchstone, p. 197.

9. *Microsoft Personal Computing.* Internet guide. http://www.microsoftt.com/magazine/guides/internet/history.htm.
10. Radicati, S. (2014). Email statistics report, 2014–2018. Palo Alto, CA: The Radicati Group. http://www.radicati.com/wp/wp-content/uploads/2014/01/Email-Statistics-Report-2014-2018-Executive-Summary.pdf.
11. *Internet Live Stats.* (2014). Total number of websites. http://www.internetlivestats.com/total-number-of-websites/. Accessed Jan 21, 2015.
12. *Encyclopedia of the Nations.* CIA World Factbook. http://www.nationsencyclopedia.com/WorldStats/CIA-Internet-Service-Providers-ISPs.html
13. Solar flare goes off the charts. (2010). http://www.tldm.org/News3/Solar_flare.htm.
14. Boni, W. C., and Kovacich, G. L. (2000). *Netspionage: The Global Threat to Information.* Woburn, MA: Butterworth-Heinemann.
15. Beal, V., Steganography (n.d.). http://www.webopedia.com/TERM/S/steganography.html.
16. Neil, F. J. Steganography. (n.d.). http://www.jjtc.com/Steganography/.
17. Zimmerman, M. (2014) Intel boss' warning on cyber attacks no joke, say experts. Fox News, November 23. http://www.foxnews.com/world/2014/11/23/intel-boss-warning-on-cyber-attacks-no-joke-say-experts/.
18. Curt Weldon, Armed Services Committee, Speaking at an InfoWar conference in Washington, DC, in September 1999, http://www.zdnet.com/article/info-war-or-electronic-saber-rattling-5000103202/.
19. Neil, M. (1995). The Pentagon's new nightmare—An electronic Pearl Harbor. *Washington Post*, July 16, p. C3.

Chapter 14

Corporate and National Resilience

In this chapter, the ability to defend and bounce back from global information warfare (GIW) attacks is discussed. The potential impact of GIW on both nation-states and corporations will be reviewed in the context of the changed environment.

In the period since the first edition of this book was produced, we have seen and experienced a huge change in information technologies and the applications to which they are put. The Internet has continued to grow at a massive rate, with the number of users growing from about 361,000,000 in 2000 to about 2,800,000,000 in 2014, a growth of nearly 680%. At the same time, the technologies have allowed us to use the networks and the information that they transport, store, and process in ever more ways. We have and are continuing to become ever more dependent on the Internet, and it is increasingly integrated into all aspects of our lives. Governments, businesses, and individuals are now much more dependent on the Internet to communicate and carry out their functions, and as a result, the risks of cyber attacks are continuing to increase.

Several questions must be asked: Can we afford to continue to put more and more reliance on an infrastructure that is so vulnerable to attack? How do we make sure that we can continue to operate when it is attacked?

We are now living in the start of the age of the *Internet of things*, where an increasing range of devices that we interact with on a daily basis are connected to the Internet. The Internet of things is the connection of a whole range of embedded computing devices to the Internet. The range of applications that are already connected include devices and systems for transport systems, environmental monitoring systems, infrastructure management systems, industrial applications such as industrial control systems that are used in manufacturing, energy management systems such as smart grids, medical systems, and building and home automation systems. According to a report by Gartner, there will be nearly 26 billion devices on the Internet of things by 2020. Other reports indicate that while at the moment most communications over the Internet are initiated by humans, in the future the majority of communications will be from machine to machine.

There are already a number of large-scale deployments of the Internet of things in cities such as Abu Dhabi, which has plans to be a "smart city" by 2030; and Songdo in South Korea, which will be the first fully equipped and wired smart city.

Another example is the use of the Internet by the New York Waterways in New York City to connect all their vessels. The network provides coverage on the Hudson River, East River, and Upper New York Bay. In the United Kingdom, a number of cities are also currently planning integrated transport systems.

The problem with the Internet of things is that, with increasingly the complex systems that are being developed, providing adequate security and protection to the systems and ensuring that they are resilient also becomes increasingly complex.

There is also a growing concern that because of the Internet's power, influence, and importance, some governments are trying to move past just censoring its content to actually controlling it, with some wanting to place it under United Nations (UN) management. When something like that happens, its freedom will be sorely limited and censored.

Imagine the Internet being controlled in a similar fashion as the UN Security Council, or having China and Russia as its permanent members and dictatorships and terrorist nations on its rotating council.

Big Data

Big data is a term that is now being used for any collection of data sets that is so large and complex that it has become difficult to process using traditional data processing applications. The whole area of big data and the associated big data analytics and data mining is developing rapidly to meet the needs of large and complex systems. Big data is characterized by the three Vs: velocity, which describes the speed with which data moves in and out of the system; volume, which describes the ever-increasing quantity of data; and variety, which describes the range of data sources and types. Big data requires a whole range of processes, tools, and techniques that are used to collect and process large amounts of data to extract new information. The problem with this is that the ever-larger data sets and the complexity of the systems makes them increasingly difficult to secure and, as a result, provides the potential for attacks.

Most organizations have naturally focused on the potential advantage of big data systems, and it is estimated that the United States currently has a shortage of 140,000 to 190,000 people with analytical expertise and 1.5 million managers and analysts with the skills to understand and make decisions based on the analysis of big data. While resilience is an issue that receives some discussion, security is rarely mentioned in literature on the subject. A draft paper entitled "Big Data and Data Protection," issued by the Information Commissioners Office in the United Kingdom (Information Commissions Office 2014), is currently in circulation. This paper examines the issues of the requirements for the protection of personal information in big data systems. Some of the issues that this paper is addressing are highlighted in paragraphs 10 and 11 of the executive summary, which state:

10. One key data protection requirement is to ensure that processing of personal data is fair, and this is particularly important where big data is being used to make decisions affecting individuals. Fairness is partly about how personal data is obtained. Organisations need to be transparent when they collect data, and explaining how it will be used is an important element in complying with data protection principles. The complexity of big data analytics is not an excuse for failing to obtain consent where it is required.

11. Big data analytics can involve repurposing personal data. If an organisation has collected personal data for one purpose and then decides to start analysing it for completely different purposes (or to make it available for others to do so) then it needs to make its users aware of this. This is particularly important if the organisation is planning to use the data for a purpose that is not apparent to the individual because it is not obviously connected with their use of a service.

This draft paper deals specifically with personal information that is held in big data systems, but of equal importance to the organization will be the issue of the protection of the businesses' critical data. From this it is clear that in the United Kingdom, the government is starting to address the problems of the security of big data systems, but no evidence could be found in publications from other nations that the same level of progress has been achieved.

The use of big data creates its own set of unique security problems and, as has been seen with the introduction of many other technologies, this is an inevitable part of the development and optimization of the resource. However, as with many of the technologies that have been adopted in the past, the security and resilience of the systems are not the main drivers for adoption, and there will be an inevitable gap in our abilities to protect these systems.

Big data systems, by their nature, normally rely on distributed architectures, and in addition, much of the data that is used in big data systems will be unstructured. Security is neither inherent in these systems nor easy to achieve. In the past, the vendors did not design security measures such as firewalls and intruder detection systems (IDS) for distributed computing architectures. As a result, both the organizations that use big data and the vendors that develop the systems are having to retrofit security into the systems. One of the ongoing issues that is exacerbated by big data systems is that of the classification of data. Organizations are, historically, very bad at understanding the value of their data and classifying it correctly. As the systems get larger and more complex, this becomes increasingly important, because without the ability to identify and classify the data, it will be impossible to provide the appropriate level of protection for it or to understand which elements of the data are essential in ensuring that the systems are resilient and can continue to operate. Another major problem with the classification of the data will be that, particularly in big data systems, the ownership of the data may change when the data is processed and aggregated, and unless the ownership at each stage can be identified, it will not be possible to correctly classify the data.

Cloud Computing

Cloud computing is not new but is an evolved technology that has changed the methods by which data is stored and processed. The computing paradigm has shifted from desktop and laptop computers and mobile devices to cloud computing. Cloud computing is increasingly popular; the low entry cost and the saving on capital expenditure, together with its flexibility, have made cloud computing an attractive option for many organizations.

Talking about putting your eggs all in one basket! If you outsource your information to a third-party vendor, do you verify their security? Do you maintain separate, internal backups or rely on the vendor to do so? In the future, do not be surprised to hear of more and more attacks focused on clouds, such as the one that allegedly took place against "iCloud" not long ago.

Cloud computing has a number of definitions. The National Institute of Standards and Technology (NIST) defines cloud computing as

> a model for enabling convenient, on-demand network access to a shared pool of configurable computing resources (e.g., networks, servers, storage, applications, and services) that can be rapidly provisioned and released with minimal management effort or service provider interaction.

NIST identifies five characteristics for cloud computing:

■ On demand self-service
■ Ubiquitous network access
■ Resource pooling
■ Rapid elasticity
■ Pay-per-use business model

There are a number of service and deployment models that are commonly accepted, and these are categorized by the type of computing resources that are provided to the end users. The commonly accepted models are

- Software as a Service (SaaS): Applications are delivered as a service over the Internet; for example, by Google Mail.
- Platform as a Service (PaaS): The development platform is provided as a service; for example, Microsoft Azure.
- Infrastructure as a Service (IaaS): The server(s), storage, and hardware are delivered as a service; for example, Amazon Simple Storage Service (S3).

The problem is that when data is stored and processed in a shared, multitenant, and elastic pool of resources, both security and resilience are proving to be difficult to achieve. Examples of the types of problems that are already being encountered include that which was encountered by Mat Honan, a reporter for *Wired* magazine, when an Apple employee reset his iCloud password at the request of a hacker posing as Honan and used it to remotely wipe all of his devices. In another incident at Dropbox, hackers gained access to a list of customer e-mail addresses from a Dropbox employee's Dropbox account. More recent occurrences have included the now infamous iCloud incident, in which celebrity naked photos were hacked and Snapchat images stolen.

The issue of government access to data stored in the cloud was highlighted by the release of files that were stolen by Edward Snowden, a former National Security Agency subcontractor; these files identified a program called Prism, a surveillance system that was launched in 2007 by the US National Security Agency (NSA). A leaked presentation, dated April 2013, stated that it allows the organization to gain access to e-mails, video clips, photos, voice and video calls, social networking details, login details, and other data held by a number of US Internet companies. The list of companies included Apple, Microsoft (including Skype), Google (including YouTube), Yahoo, Facebook, and AOL. Also detailed in the presentation was the cost of the program, which was given as $20 million a year.

As a result of the leaks, James R. Clapper, the director of National Intelligence, put out a press release on June 6, 2013, which confirmed the existence of the program and justified its activities under Section 702 of the Foreign Intelligence Surveillance Act. The press release went on to state that

> Section 702 is a provision of FISA that is designed to facilitate the acquisition of foreign intelligence information concerning non-U.S. persons located outside the United States. It cannot be used to intentionally target any U.S. citizen, any other U.S. person, or anyone located within the United States.

Another example of government access to data was revealed when details of a July 2013 court order were leaked that directed Verizon Business Network Services to hand over to the NSA "on an ongoing daily basis" the "following tangible things":

> All call detail records or "telephony metadata" created by Verizon for communications (i) between the United States and abroad; or (ii) wholly within the United States, including local telephone calls.

One outcome of these breaches has been that the trust that is essential for organizations to use cloud computing is being eroded. According to a report in *Computing*, Dr. Kevin Curran, a senior member of the Institute of Electrical and Electronics Engineers (IEEE), stated that

> Transparency will be listed on the front page of many cloud services due to the appalling manner in which the NSA has treated the US-based large cloud providers. Trust has gone for now in US cloud providers. It will be some time before it will return.

In the current world, where the Internet does not recognize national boundaries and where data is often stored overseas, the effect of these hacks and government snooping has severely damaged any trust that existed and has elicited strong reactions from other governments.

When there is a data breach in the cloud, the issues of responsibility and liability increasingly come to the fore. A June 2014 report by the Ponemon Institute[1] examined this issue and highlighted a number of problems.

The Ponemon report introduced the concept of the "cloud multiplier effect" for data security problems and produced estimations of the costs of data breaches. The report determined

- That there was a cost of $201.18 dollars per compromised record
- That the average likelihood of a data breach involving 100,000 or more questions was approximately 11.8% over a two-year period
- That, based on these figures, if an organization had a data breach involving 100,000 customer records lost or stolen in the cloud, the cost would be $2.37 million

The report goes on to say that

> Cloud computing is not necessarily less secure, but that is the perception among many of the study's respondents who view on-premises data breach as easier to control and less costly as a result.

The report highlights that if a company does not have the ability to view what is happening with their data, it is hard for them to check that the service provider is taking the proper steps to protect the data.

Another issue that is affecting trust in cloud computing is that of "outages," when service to the end user is lost. There are already a number of examples of significant outages, including

> In August 2009, PayPal suffered an outage[2] that left millions of merchants around the world with no way to sell their goods or services. The service suffered a complete outage for around an hour and provided intermittent service

for several more hours. A hardware failure was blamed for the outage. In January 2013, PayPal suffered more outages that lasted for around 3 hours.

Also in 2009, a Microsoft owned subsidiary, Sidekick, suffered a nearly week-long service outage[3] that left users without access to e-mail, the calendar, and other personal data. The problem was exacerbated when it was revealed that Microsoft had lost the cloud-stored bits and could not restore them. The postevent analysis and lessons learned from this included that, for crucial data, an organization should never assume that someone else will be taking the steps required to protect that organization, and steps need to be taken to ensure that the data will be saved and stored appropriately. Organizations were also advised to ensure that they understand the cloud provider's disaster recovery setup and, if necessary, to make their own arrangements.

In March 2010, Terremark's vCloud Express service went off line[4] for about 7 hours, and users were unable to access data stored in the center for the entire period.

In 2010, Microsoft's Hotmail service experienced database errors[5] that resulted in tens of thousands of empty inboxes. According to Microsoft, the problem was caused by a script that was intended to delete dummy accounts that were created for automated testing. Unfortunately, the script also erroneously deleted 17,000 real accounts. The problem took Microsoft 3 days to sort out and to restore service for most of those users. A small number of users had to wait an additional 3 days before their data was restored.

In June 2010, Intuit, which runs a number of cloud services including TurboTax, Quicken, and QuickBooks, had two outages[6] within a few weeks. The first outage, which was attributed to a power failure, resulted in the systems being off line for a period of 36 hours. The second outage, a few weeks later, was also attributed to a power failure.

In 2012, Amazon's Northern Virginia data center suffered an outage[7] after a network upgrade, when a misrouted traffic shift sent a cluster of Amazon EBS (Elastic Block Store) volumes into what was referred to as a remirroring storm. That set off a series of events that ultimately took down much of the company's US East Region services for nearly 4 days. But while many businesses struggled, others such as Netflix took the outage in its stride. The reason that they continued to operate was given in a "Lessons Netflix learned from the AWS outage" blog post, which stated that "Our architecture avoids using EBS as our main data storage service, and the SimpleDB, S3, and Cassandra services that we do depend upon were not affected by the outage."

The key to survival is designing your systems with these types of failures in mind.

In August 2013, a hardware failure at Amazon's US-East data center led to problems at a number of popular online services,[8] including Instagram, Vine, AirBnB, and the mobile magazine app Flipboard. The outage, which was referred to as a "grey partial failure," was blamed on a single networking device and resulted in data loss. This incident lasted 49 minutes.

Most of the cloud providers advise that their customers should try to operate the concept of geographical redundancy and that customers should spread out their services among multiple data centers so that, in the event of one failing, another can be used to continue operations. The issue here is that, having entrusted their data to the cloud service provider, it does not seem reasonable, or in many cases realistic, to expect the end user to undertake this. Surely it is the service provider who should be taking care of this? The problem then is the cost of achieving it.

James Hamilton, an Amazon engineer, wrote on his personal blog that "inside a single facility, there are simply too many ways to shoot one's own foot," and that "with incredible redundancy, comes incredible cost."

The reality is that organizations have used cloud to achieve greater flexibility and to reduce costs, but if they move to employing backup data centers, it will result in increased expenses and will also exacerbate the latency in the system (the lag time a user experiences when using the organization's websites or applications). It is also difficult for an organization to use multiple providers, as the majority of the main cloud providers are not enthusiastic about supporting this kind of interoperability. To date, it appears that OpenStack, which is an open-source project that can plug into the services of Amazon, Google, and others, is the only one that has been created with the aim of making this easier.

How Do Organizations Reduce the Risks?

Some of the things that organizations can do to mitigate or reduce the risk of a breach are to vet their cloud provider's security policies and practices and to carry out audits of their data that is stored in the cloud. It is amazing how many of the organizations that are relying on cloud services are not doing this, particularly when they had regularly checked their security practices and procedures when the services were carried out in house.

Service Level Agreements (SLAs)

Organizations need to ensure that they have appropriate service level agreements (SLAs) in place (and understand them) with the service providers. In the SLAs, there needs to be statements on the security and resilience measures that the service provider is implementing and also provision for the user organization to audit these measures. Also, liability and insurance matters should be addressed—who is liable under what circumstances?

Data Encryption

It may seem an obvious suggestion, but if the data that is stored in the cloud is encrypted, you have added a whole level of complexity for the people that have gained access to it. These days it is not difficult to achieve, but there are still very few organizations that have done it. Organizations are required by law to take "reasonable measures" to protect some information, and it would seem that this is a very achievable measure to take.

Sensitive Data

Consideration should be given as to whether sensitive data is uploaded to the cloud at all or instead retained within the infrastructure of the organization. At least then, when it is compromised, you will know where it was leaked from.

Business Continuity

It may seem an obvious thing to say, but if an organization is relying on the cloud for its computing services, it is essential that it is confident that the service provider has effective and robust business continuity plans in place. This is in addition to the organization's own business continuity plans. The question then is, while the organization can test its own business continuity plan (and we all know how difficult that is), how can they ensure that the service providers are also testing theirs?

Layered Security

Protecting business-critical and sensitive information is essential, but not all of the information that is collected, processed, and stored by an organization requires the same level of protection. By identifying and classifying the information that does need the greatest protection, effort and resources can be channeled appropriately.

Data Destruction

This is an issue that, to date, has not been well researched or addressed. When data has reached the end of its life cycle, it should be destroyed, but how, in a multitenant cloud environment, can an organization be confident that all traces of it have been effectively destroyed? Moreover, when it has been destroyed, how does the organization audit the fact? They need to ensure that the agreements that they have in place with the service provider allow for this.

Data Breaches in the Cloud: Who Is Responsible?

For most business and government organizations, it is essential that they achieve a comprehensive security and compliance posture across the whole of the system that they are using. Some of the infrastructure will almost certainly be in house, and some of it will be in the cloud. When deciding who is to be responsible for the security and resilience controls, they need to take into account the service delivery and deployment model that has been selected. The responsibility for delivering these controls will need to be contractually assigned during the procurement process, and service level agreements alone will not be sufficient. The balance of who is responsible for what will vary depending on the model that has been adopted for the cloud computing service. In the software-as-a-service (SaaS) and platform-as-a-service (PaaS) models, much of the responsibility for data security and control is typically borne by the service provider, as there is not much opportunity for the user organization to deploy data security or governance solutions in these environments. In the infrastructure-as-a-service (IaaS) model, there is normally more of a shared responsibility. The IaaS provider will typically provide a baseline level of security (firewalls and load balancing) to mitigate distributed denial-of-service (DDoS) attacks, but responsibility for securing the data will normally belong to the organization.

Ultimately, the responsibility lies with the organization that owns the data. An example of this can be seen in the European Union (EU), where a business that stores personal data about its customers is considered to be the "controller" of that data under the EU Data Protection Directive (DPD), even when the data is stored in the cloud.

What Do You Do in the Event of a Breach?

When a security breach is first identified, there are a range of actions that need to be taken, such as

- Notifying the appropriate people, both internally and externally
- Getting together a response team, including forensic specialists and legal counsel
- Putting in place your incident response and business continuity plans,
- Taking memory dumps and saving network logs
- Remediating the vulnerabilities
- Keeping records of all actions taken and storing relevant logs, etc.
- Determining the business impact
- Identifying the latest backup of data that is unaffected and is viable
- Restoring the backup once the systems are clean

Once the breach has been dealt with, a number of actions will have to be taken. These will include

- Reviewing the incident to identify areas where security can be improved
- Using the incident to improve awareness among staff
- Reviewing, and if necessary revising, security measures
- Testing the revised security measures
- Documenting the lessons learned
- Preserving the evidence collected
- Reviewing the status of security provided with third-party services such as cloud
- Informing anyone affected and regulatory bodies as required

Internet of Things (Also Known as the Internet of Everything)

The *Internet of things* is a relatively new term that is used to describe the interconnection of uniquely identifiable embedded computing devices to the Internet, and it is normally used to refer to the connection of devices, systems, and services. Many of these connections will be machine-to-machine communications, with no human input.

Typically, we currently think of the types of objects that will be connected as the smart meter for the electricity, the home security system, the fridge, or the washing machine, but in reality there are already a huge number of applications in use. The interconnection of these embedded devices will enable increasing automation in a greater number of areas, including applications such as Smart Grids. It is the development of the Internet of things that is enabling the wider use of cyber physical systems (CPS).

The problem is that the more things we connect to the Internet, the more potential there is for them to be abused and for the data that they are generating to be stolen. While much of the data has little value on its own, the potential for abuse has already been recognized.

Cyber Physical Systems (CPS)

The term cyber physical system (CPS) is used to describe a collection of collaborating digital systems that are controlling physical entities or monitoring physical processes. There are already a number of CPS in use in areas as diverse as manufacturing, the civil infrastructure, aviation, and road and rail transport, as well as in domestic appliances. Current systems normally consist of embedded devices, communications links, and the computers that are used to coordinate the activities of the individual devices. Some implementations of CPS include the driverless trucks and trains that Rio Tinto is testing in Australia[9] and the pod system at Terminal 5 at Heathrow airport in the United Kingdom.[10] The development of CPS is a recognized area of importance within the EU.[11]

Around the world, many cities, including Milton Keynes in the United Kingdom, Abu Dhabi and Dubai in the United Arab Emirates, Singapore, and Hong Kong have developed or are developing intelligent transport systems in order to address the ever-increasing issues of growing urban populations and congestion in existing road transport systems. The types of systems and networks that are being introduced are public transport systems, including high-speed, driverless rail and rapid transit systems such as trains, trams, buses, and individual-use vehicles; as well as improved infrastructures to encourage walking and cycling.

The problem is that these are integrated, highly complex systems that are increasingly being deployed around the world. While they are designed to be "fail safe," the impact of a failure or the manipulation of the system by someone with malicious intent can be huge. One of the most (in)famous examples of a cyber attack on a CPS, in this case the (isolated) uranium-enrichment facility in Natanz, Iran, was the Stuxnet worm, which was reported to have been designed to affect computerized industrial control systems and to alter the operations of the system to subvert its operation and cause centrifuges to destroy themselves. Events such as this have created an interest in the security of CPS.[12]

In another case, during a strike by city engineers in 2006, two Los Angeles traffic engineers hacked into the city's signal system and programmed the signals so that red lights would be extremely long on the most congested approaches to inter-sections, causing gridlock. As a result, traffic backed up at Los Angeles International Airport, at a key intersection in Studio City, at access onto the Glendale Freeway, and in the streets of Little Tokyo and the Los Angeles Civic Center areas. The problem lasted for several days.

As we increasingly move toward the introduction of these systems, the potential for massive disruption increases.

Smart Grids

Smart grid is the modern electrical grid that uses either analogue or digital information, together with communications technology, to collect and act on information to improve the efficiency, reliability, and sustainability of the production and distribution of electricity. The problem with smart grid systems is that we have failed to learn the lessons of the past from systems such as Supervisory Control and Data Acquisition (SCADA), a system that was developed for the management and control of program-mable logic controller (PLC) systems for use on private networks.

When the private networks were connected to the Internet, the potential harm that could be caused by hackers gaining access to the systems and changing settings was not understood, and the result was the increased exposure of these SCADA systems to attacks. One example was the November 2011 hacking attack at a US water plant, where the attacker managed to access a SCADA controller and take over systems. The hacker used the system to turn a pump off and on several times, which resulted in it failing, although in this case, no serious damage was caused by the attack.

Another example was reported in 2014, when the Havex Remote Access Trojan (RAT) was said to have been used in a number of known information warfare (IW) attacks against organizations in the energy sector. Havex is reported to be programmed to infect the industrial control system (ICS) software of SCADA and ICS systems, which are used in hydroelectric dams, nuclear power plants, oil and gas production and refining, and power grids, as well as in many other areas. Havex is reported to have been used to carry out industrial espionage attacks against a number of companies in Europe that use or develop industrial applications and machines.

The lessons that have not been learned in the development of smart grids are that, in many cases, security has not been built into the systems, and in many implementations, we seem doomed to repeat the past.

Advanced Persistent Threat (APT)

Over the past few years, a new term has been coined—the advanced persistent threat (APT). The term was first used to describe the ongoing range of attacks that were thought to be orchestrated from China, but it is now used in a more general way to describe any ongoing and persistent attack.

An APT is normally seen as a set of stealthy and ongoing cyber attacks targeting a specific organization or industry. The advanced aspect is that they often use sophisticated techniques such as malware to exploit vulnerabilities in the systems. The persistent aspect is that they normally use an external command and control system to continuously monitor and extract data from the target. The threat aspect is that posed by the individual or organization that is orchestrating the attack. The term APT is normally used to refer to a group or government with both the resources to mount the attack and the intent to carry out the attack.

Because of the persistent aspect, the term has most often been used to refer to IW espionage attacks that use a variety of intelligence gathering techniques to access a whole range of information. The normal methods of attack include socially engineered e-mails that contain Trojan horses and infected media.

The first targeted, normally socially engineered attacks were identified in 2005, although the term APT is believed to have originated from the US Air Force in 2006.

The 2013 FireEye Advanced Threat Report (ATR)[13] reported that the main objectives of the APTs that they had examined were to

- Steal intellectual property
- Eavesdrop on sensitive government communications
- Undermine the overall security of national security–related sites

The report went on to state that

> [it] offers strong evidence that malware infections occur within enterprises at an alarming rate. It also shows that advanced attackers can penetrate legacy defenses such as firewalls and anti-virus (AV) defenses with ease.

The report goes on to give statistics for APTs, identifying that in 2013 there were 4,192 attacks by APT actors (more than 11 per day on average). The report also identifies the top ten countries that are the targets of these attacks:

1. United States
2. South Korea
3. Canada
4. Japan
5. United Kingdom
6. Germany
7. Switzerland
8. Taiwan
9. Saudi Arabia
10. Israel

Is it strange that China, Russia, and North Korea are not on this "top ten" list?

How Do You Make Your Organization More Resilient?

The reality is that the environment in which we operate and on which we increasingly rely for everyday activities is both hostile and difficult to protect. The infrastructure of the Internet was never designed to be secure, and the software that we use is inherently flawed and provides endless potential for the discovery of new vulnerabilities.

Both at the national and the organizational levels, the networks are incredibly complex and rely on rapidly changing technology, all of which makes protection difficult. In the past, governments attempted to achieve "absolute security" but eventually realized that it was not achievable. This was the time when we moved from the concept of risk avoidance to that of risk management. What many failed to grasp is that when you move to a risk management approach, you are accepting that an incident will occur; all you are doing is trying to put it off for as long as possible.

There is a recognition by many governments, particularly in the West, that we do not have enough skilled people to enable us to provide the level of protection that we increasingly need to secure our infrastructure. The problem is that in an environment that is changing so rapidly, how do you train, recruit, and retain the necessary skill sets?

In the software development arena, many of the companies that are providing the operating systems and applications that we are using have not grasped that it is impossible to secure a piece of software that is inherently flawed due to poor design and quality control.

If the software is not of a high quality and has not been well tested, it is inevitable that any weaknesses will be found once it is in widespread use. Effort needs to be put into schemes that promote the production of high-quality code, and it may be that regulations need to be changed to punish software manufacturers who produce flawed products. The current situation, wherein software is supplied with known weaknesses that are then "patched" throughout their life cycle, does not help in providing protection to the user.

Organizations need to consider not only their own infrastructures but also those of their service providers when they are looking at the resilience of their environment to make sure that they have the measures in place to survive an attack.

At the national level, in many countries there is already infrastructure and resources in place to provide intelligence on new attacks and to support investigations into existing attacks. The problem here is that there will never be enough of these resources available, as they are in short supply and are expensive.

Defense in Depth

It is commonly held that the best security is achieved through defense in depth. Defense in depth covers all aspects of security—physical, personnel, procedural, and electronic. This covers topics such as staff and contractor vetting, access control, firewalls, data compartmentalization, and monitoring. While none of these is sufficient on its own, when they are put in place and operate together in an effective and integrated manner, they provide the best possible protection.

As we have increasingly adopted new technologies, including the cloud and smart devices, it has become more and more important to ensure that protection is provided for the endpoint with things such as secure browsing applications and hardware and transaction signing devices. There is also an increasing need for session monitoring to compare behavior and with normal patterns. We must move away from the concept of the "fortress" or perimeter defenses, where we put a wall around the organization, toward one where protection is provided for each device.

Another way in which protection can be enhanced and targeted against new threats is through the collection and sharing of intelligence both within the organization and the wider community.

Improved Detection

In addition to the traditional log reviews, there is a need to monitor for out-of-profile activity or unusual traffic. Particular attention should be given to high-risk areas of the organization. This should include the idea of "forensic preparedness," where thought is given to what monitoring and log collection will be required in the event of an incident. Remember that knowing of an attack still occurs after it has occurred or while it is occurring. Prevention of course is always best choice, but, for reasons discussed throughout this book, this is not often achievable these days.

Employee Security Awareness

The first line of defense is the people in the organization. It is the person who is likely to be the one who makes an error, such as opening a spear-phishing e-mail, but it is also the person who may notice that there is something unusual happening. If they are trained correctly and have the right level of awareness, they not only make fewer mistakes but also act as a huge sensor network for the organization.

Organized Crime

Organized crime has been one of the major issues for a number of years. This is because "crime follows the money," and the money has gone online. The Internet has provided an almost perfect environment for the criminal. They no longer have to go to a bank with a gun to rob it; they can attack an organization in one country from another, and the likelihood of being caught (and successfully convicted) is low. We have seen criminal organizations such as the Russian Business Network (RBN), which was a multifaceted cyber-crime organization that began specializing in identity theft as early as 2006. In addition to identity theft, the RBN was also known to have carried out DoS attacks and hosted spamming, phishing, and malware services and Internet access to criminals, and it is reported to have earned around US$150 million in one year.

According to the 2014 INTERPOL report[14] "The Internet Organized Crime Threat Assessment (iOCTA)":

> Traditional organised crime groups (OCGs), including those with a mafia-style structure are beginning to use the service-based nature of the cybercrime market to carry out more sophisticated crimes, buying access to the technical skills they require.

The report also states that

> Over the past few decades the digital underground has evolved and matured from a few small groups hacking and phreaking for fun and prestige, to a thriving criminal industry that costs global economies an estimated USD 300+ billion per year.

One of the tools used by criminals is darknets. These offer a high level of anonymity and are used to host hidden marketplaces and provide services for the more traditional types of crime, such as the drug trade, selling stolen goods, selling stolen or fake IDs, and human trafficking. One of the best known examples of a darknet is the Silk Road, which first became known in 2011 and was taken down by a multinational law-enforcement effort at the end of 2013. The services that were offered by the Silk Road have since been offered on a new site that quickly replaced the original.

Terrorism

The use of the Internet by terrorists is nothing new. They have long used it for communication and fundraising and to promulgate their messages. However, with the rise of Islamic terrorist groups such as Al Qaeda and the Islamic State of Iraq and Syria (ISIS), also known as the Islamic State of Iraq and the Levant (ISIL), there has been a significant increase in the usage. Much of this is probably due to the fact that these terrorists represent the first generation that has grown up with the Internet. ISIS has shown considerable understanding of and skill in using the power of social media, and it has used it to great effect; it has used Twitter to post tweets on a regular basis. An example of one of the ways in which ISIS has used the Internet is given in an article from the *Telegraph* newspaper,[15] which reported that a 14-year-old boy had been arrested on suspicion of planning a series of bombings in Vienna. He had been recruited over the Internet and was promised a "special position" and US$25,000 by ISIS to carry out the attacks.

> The Internet is a prime example of how terrorists can behave in a truly transnational way; in response, States need to think and function in an equally transnational manner.
>
> **Ban Ki-moon**
> *Secretary-General of the United Nations*

A UN Office on Drugs and Crime report[16] identifies the ways in which terrorists have used the Internet and highlights a number of areas where they have been effective. These include

- Propaganda
- Recruitment
- Incitement
- Radicalization
- Financing
- Training
- Planning

Their use of the Internet can be expected to continue and to increase.

Impact on Nation-States

The impact that an IW attack will have on a nation-state will vary depending on that nation's size and its level of reliance on the electronic infrastructure. Perhaps the most graphic example that has been seen to date was the attacks on Estonia in 2007. Estonia is a relatively small country with a population of only around 1.325 million people, but it is technologically advanced and relies on networked services for many of its business and governmental functions. The attacks were mounted against a number of elements of the critical infrastructure, but Estonia managed to survive the onslaught.

For a country such as the United States, it could be said that it is under constant attack from APTs. In the current environment, while an attacker may cause disruption and inconvenience to geographic regions or to business sectors, it is unlikely that they could cause a long-term problem. While the cost of responding to such attacks might be high, there are, in most cases, resources in terms of equipment and people that can be used to tackle the attack.

If an attack was made against a number of elements of the critical infrastructure at the same time, this would be more difficult to respond to, but it would also require significant resources on behalf of the attacker that would probably be traceable. Ultimately, a nation might decide to reduce or totally cut its level of interaction with international networks until it could contain the problem.

Impact on Corporations

The impact on a corporation could be significantly different. There are many examples of the impact of both accidental outages and security breaches as well as hostile attacks that show that the effects can be devastating.

The range of effects of a cyber attack may include

- The loss of intellectual property and sensitive data
- The cost of remediation, countermeasures, and insurance
- The loss of business
- Brand and reputation damage
- Disruption of services
- Potential job losses
- Fines, penalties, and compensation payments to customers

Some examples of the impact of a cyber attack can be seen in reports of the attack on the Target Corporation, in which 110 million customer accounts were compromised. Target reported a 46% drop in its profits during the following quarter. Another example is the 2011 attack on Sony, when the PlayStation network was breached. Now look at the current escalation of attacks on Sony, which have caused serious repercussions and threats between the United States and North Korea, the alleged attacker. In this case, 77 million users were potentially affected by the breach, and it is estimated that Sony spent US$171 million on the costs of repair, enhancing its security, identity theft protection for customers, and offering customers free digital content as an apology. Another example of the devastating effect of a cyber attack on a corporation can be seen in the August 2012 malware attack on the computer networks of Saudi Aramco, the world's largest oil producer. The corporation was attacked by a self-replicating virus called Shamoon, which infected around 30,000 of its computers. It took nearly two weeks to recover from the damage, and experts were called in from the United States, Europe, and Asia to assist in the operation. It has been estimated that the final cost of the attack could run into billions of dollars.

Summary

When all is said and done, the methods used to protect networks, clouds, and the globally changing computer-based communications environment are basically the same as they have always been. However, the threats and attack methods are more sophisticated than ever as the networks and protection methods have become more sophisticated. As always, security lags far behind.

References

1. Keralapura, R. (2014). Data breach: The cloud multiplier effect. Ponemon Institute, June. http://go.netskope.com/rs/netskope/images/Ponemon-DataBreach-CloudMultiplierEffect-June2014.pdf.
2. Fowler, G. A. (2009). PayPal users hit by global service outage. *Wall Street Journal.* http://www.wsj.com/articles/SB124933612758802715.
3. Fried, I. (2009). Sidekick users share their horror stories. Cnet, October 12. http://www.cnet.com/uk/news/sidekick-users-share-their-horror-stories/.
4. *Business Wire.* (2010). Terremark's vCloud express services experience outage at Miami Data Center. March 18. http://www.businesswire.com/news/home/20100318006471/en/Terremark%E2%80%99s-vCloud-Express-Services-Experience-Outage-Miami#.VK6kRNKsV8E.
5. Leonhard, W. (2011). Hotmail fail: Microsoft lays an egg in the cloud. *Infoworld Tech Watch,* January 5. http://www.infoworld.com/article/2624887/saas/hotmail-fail--microsoft-lays-an-egg-in-the-cloud.html.
6. Whiting, R. (2011). Intuit service outages leave frustrated customers in their wake. *CRN,* March 28. http://www.crn.com/news/applications-os/229400407/intuit-service-outages-leave-frustrated-customers-in-their-wake.htm.
7. Malik, O. (2012). Severe storms cause Amazon Web Services outage. *GIGAOM,* June 29. https://gigaom.com/2012/06/29/some-of-amazon-web-services-are-down-again/.
8. Stone, B. (2013). Another Amazon outage exposes the cloud's dark lining. *Bloomberg Business Week,* August 26. http://www.businessweek.com/articles/2013-08-26/another-amazon-outage-exposes-the-clouds-dark-lining.

9. McGagh, J. (2014). Internet of things world forum. *Rio Tinto Mine of the Future*, Chicago, October. http://www.riotinto.com/documents/141014_Presentation_Internet_of_ Things_World_Forum_John_McGagh.pdf.

10. Heathrow T5, Ultra Global PRT. (2014). http://www.ultraglobalprt.com/wheres-it-used/ heathrow-t5/.

11. European Commission. (2014). Directorate General, Communications Networks, Content and Technology, Cyber Physical Systems, http://ec.europa.eu/dgs/connect/ en/content/cyber-physical-systems-european-ri-strategy.

12. Peisert, S., Davis, M., Jonathan, N., David, M., Khurana, H., Sawall, C. (2014). Designed-in security for cyber-physical systems. *Security & Privacy, IEEE* 12(5): 9–12.

13. FireEye Advanced Threat Report. (2013). Security reimagined. http://www2.fireeye. com/rs/fireye/images/fireeye-advanced-threat-report-2013.pdf.

14. INTERPOL. (2014). The Internet Organised Crime Threat Assessment (iOCTA), 2014. https://www.europol.europa.eu/sites/default/files/publications/europol_iocta_ web.pdf.

15. Huggler, J. (2014). ISIL jihadists 'offered teenager $25,000 to carry out bombings in Vienna'. *Daily Telegraph*, October 30. http://www.telegraph.co.uk/news/worldnews/ islamic-state/11199628/Boy-14-who-planned-Vienna-bombings-was-recruited-on-internet-by-Isil.html.

16. UNODC. (2012). The use of the Internet for terrorist purposes. http://www.unodc. org/documents/frontpage/Use_of_Internet_for_Terrorist_Purposes.pdf.

Chapter 15

Awareness

In this chapter, there is a general discussion of aspects of *awareness* of Global Information Warfare (GIW) threats, vulnerabilities, and risks, and of related topics that will be explored on a nation-state, business, group, and personal level. *Collateral damage*, for example, private citizens, also requires that awareness be at all levels.

Definitions to Consider

There is sometimes confusion as to what training versus briefings, awareness, indoctrination, and even propaganda has been done under the guise of one or more of the others, as they tend to overlap. So it is best to start a discussion on awareness with some basic definitions. That way, if you are responsible for providing information warfare (IW) awareness as a separate program or integrated into an overall assets protection awareness program, you can be quite confident that is what you really had in mind, and if not, maybe one of the other definitions* can be the basis for meeting your IW objective in that regard.

Awareness is defined as "having knowledge or perception of a situation or fact"

Training is defined as "the action of teaching a person…a particular skill or type of behavior"

Briefing is defined as "a meeting for giving information or instructions…the information or instructions given"

Indoctrination is defined as "teach a person or group to accept a set of beliefs uncritically"

---

* All definitions quoted from the New Oxford American Dictionary.[1]

Propaganda is defined as "chiefly derogatory information, esp. of a biased or misleading nature, used to promote or publicize particular political cause or point of view"

Education is defined as "the process of giving or receiving systematic instruction"

Establishing and Managing a GIW Awareness Program

The first thing that should be decided is whether or not a GIW awareness program should even be established. The answer is basically that it all depends.

Let us look at whether or not such a separate program should be established by looking at the entity that is considering such a program.

On a Nation-State Level

First, let us look at it from the perspective of a national government. Many governments do not have a GIW concern because they have limited technology or they do not have the funds for such a national program.

If we look at it from the perspective of a modern, technology-dependent nation-state, it would probably not be cost-effective as it can easily be folded into the awareness program related to computer security, information systems security, assets protection, or whatever that nation-state calls it.

In these cases, such an awareness program is primarily directed at all those systems/networks users that are employed by the nation-states' agencies and their government contractors. It does not make sense to have a separate program because the GIW defenses are generally the same as the normal digital security needs. It would not be cost-effective, and, even with today's attacks, the amount of funding available for defense is limited. Therefore, the funds spent on an awareness program as part of the overall digital defense program is very limited.

The exception may be those agencies chartered to perform some specific GIW functions. In that case, maybe the general digital defensive security measures may be couched more in terms of GIW defenses and thus the awareness programs would also be looked at from that perspective.

Generally speaking, government agencies have not developed any formal awareness programs targeting their citizens, although they have them for their government employees separated by individual agencies. They leave it up to businesses, groups, and individuals to do their own.

That makes sense as each business, group, and individual has their own culture, cost-benefits decisions to make, and so on. It would be cost prohibitive. Furthermore, who wants some additional "Big Brother" to tell private businesses, groups, and individuals what they should do. We have seen that the slowest and least efficient way to do anything is to get some government agency involved.

On a Business Level

In general, businesses have been involved in some sort of digital security/defenses for decades—although their track record of doing it well has been generally abysmal.

In the private business environment, even using the term GIW, or even warfare, to management would be counterproductive. It is already difficult enough to get their support for basic digital defenses. Management would probably look at you as some right-wing nut case and say in no uncertain terms, arguing that warfare is for the government and military to take care of and not their business.

On a Group or Association Level

When it comes to some associations—nonprofit groups or charitable organizations, for example—there is little thinking or effort that goes into digital defenses other than a user name and password, if that, and definitely no consideration of such things from a GIW perspective.

However, the larger the association—for example, a national one—the better the chance that some attention is given to general information and systems defenses. However, these are often relegated to its members having user identification and passwords.

Although such groups or associations may be targeted by hackers, terrorists, and the like, they seem to be less of a target than nation-states, businesses, and even prominent individuals.

Furthermore, they are probably even more limited in terms of funds, and anything past explaining passwords is therefore cost prohibitive, let alone having the in-house expertise or funds for outsourcing such things.

On a Personal Level

On a personal level, one learns about risks, vulnerabilities, and such when one watches the news or when one has to log in to some government agency, business, or association website. It is these entities that, almost by accident, provide awareness to the individual by forcing them to follow certain guidelines when creating user identification and establishing passwords.

It would take little effort for such an entity to provide an expanded online document that must be read and acknowledged by the user before they are allowed system access. However, most would just click "agree" and get on with their access as many do when downloading vendor files, for example. At least with such an awareness document, any user whose personal information—for example, credit card details—was compromised may have a difficult time taking legal action if it could be shown that the user did not follow the proper procedures when establishing online access.

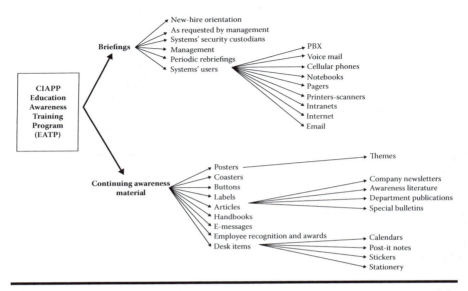

Exhibit 15.1 CIAPP Education Awareness Training Program. (From Kovacich, G. L. *Information Systems Security Officer's Guide*. Burlington, MA: Elsevier, 1998. With permission.)

An Awareness Program Incorporating GIW Aspects

Basically, we pretty much will agree that, with very few exceptions, a separate GIW awareness program would not be well received by any entity; however, aspects of additional GIW defenses can easily be incorporated into an overall digital defensive awareness program (DDAP), assets protection awareness program (APAP), corporate information assets protection program (CIAPP), or whatever name you want to call it.

Such a program can be elaborate, as shown in Exhibit 15.1, or as simple as the user reading and signing a one-page document when they are hired.

Profile of an Awareness Program

Such a program should be developed based on the laws, rules, regulations, policies and procedures, and culture of the entity developing, implementing, and managing such a program.

It should target newly hired people before they are allowed access to any digital information and systems. They should also be periodically provided with refresher courses, and a process should be in place to expeditiously provide new information relative to changes in defensive policies, procedures, and the like.

A more sophisticated program will incorporate training, briefings, education, and indoctrinations; and yes, some cultures may even use propaganda to meet their defensive requirements.

Such a program will also target the users by their positions within the entity, as some may have more access to proprietary information than others and maybe defensive measures are more sophisticated and require more stringent protection processes; for example, need to know.

To be cost-effective, the use of technology should be used where shown to enhance awareness at a lower cost; for example, in establishing online briefings and training. Such a process will also provide more expeditious awareness to users of changes. For example, just before a person logs on, a bulletin shows on the screen explaining changes, requiring acknowledgment before logging on. Yes, the old adage does apply: "You can lead a horse to water but you can't make them drink." However, such a system allows the entity to at least show such information was provided in the event that disciplinary action takes place because the processes were not followed.

As this program incorporates GIW defensive measures, its nature should depend on how vulnerable the entity believes it is to GIW attacks. Obviously, the more vulnerable the entity, the more sophisticated the GIW defensive strategies and tactics in place should be, and therefore it is more important to have an equally sophisticated awareness program in place.

Measuring the Cost and Effectiveness of an Awareness Program

Example of a Security Education and Awareness Training*

The Security Education and Awareness Training (SEATP) mission is to ensure all employees and support personnel (e.g., in-house contractors, suppliers, and part-ners) are aware of their responsibilities to protect assets. One objective of the SEATP is to teach them how to protect those assets. Through periodic security briefings, reinforced by the development and distribution of security awareness materials, the chief security officer (CSO) must continue to work to raise the level of security consciousness within the organization.

In addition, the CSO will have charged the security staff supporting the SEATP to manage this function as efficiently and effectively as possible. This includes ensuring the security staff is well prepared to develop and deliver security train-ing materials specific to the needs of the entity. However, for our purposes in this chapter, we will concentrate on the two functions: security awareness and how to protect assets.

---

* For more details, see *Information Systems Security Officer's Guide, Second Edition*[3] and *The Manager's Handbook for Corporate Security*,[4] both published by Elsevier and cited here with permission.

Once all the administrative security tasks—for example, policies, procedures, plans, and processes are in place—those that are expected to comply with them must know about them. After all, they would be useless if employees and other personnel did not know that these policies, procedures, plans, and processes even existed or what the employees and others need to do to comply with them.

The entire corporate assets protection program (CAPP) consists of security or assets protection *layers*. One of the foundation layers is employee vigilance and understanding as to how to protect corporate assets. That understanding, and hopefully the motivation to protect corporate assets, are learned and developed through the use of SEATP tools (briefings, videos, pamphlets, and other security training and awareness material).

What is *education*? Basically, we are talking about acquiring information and knowledge through some form of teaching and learning experience. In the case of SEATP, it is used to make the employees aware of explicit assets protection policies and procedures and how to comply with them. The objective of the program is for everyone at the entity to protect corporate assets, supported by the employees having a clear awareness as to why and how to properly protect the assets.

The SEATP is based on effective communications, with constant feedback supported by measurement to determine if the SEATP is meeting its established goal of lowering assets' threats, vulnerabilities, risks, and losses through informed and supportive organization employees and a robust CAPP.

SEATP Drivers and Flowcharts

US court decisions have shown that if a corporation does not adequately protect its assets, and the employees do not know and understand their responsibilities relative to the protection of those assets, it is highly unlikely that a corporation will have a successful lawsuit against an employee for such things as theft of corporate property or proprietary information. If a complaint is accepted and the employee is prosecuted, the judge is likely to find that, if the employee was unaware of the rules, the employee could not have been expected to follow them. In addition, judges in the United States have ruled that if a corporation does not do a proper job of protecting its assets, it should not rely on the court to do it for them.

After gathering a fair amount of information, one first has to look at security drivers: specifically, the drivers for any company to protect assets. In other words, why is an SEATP needed in the first place? The security drivers identified are:

- Need to comply with federal, state, and local laws and government regulation
- Need to comply with the laws of the nation-states where the entity does business
- Need to comply with internal policies, procedures, and directives

- Need to comply with contractual requirements related to assets used by others and the use of others' assets by a business, for example
- Loss of valuable assets would adversely impact the ability to successfully compete in the global marketplace.

SEATP Metrics*

How does a CSO really know the impact of an SEATP on the company? Is the SEATP effective? To learn this, it will be necessary to measure the program in some way.

There must be measures put in place to track the costs, benefits, causes, and effects of an SEATP on the protection of the organizations' assets, as well as the time spent (potential productivity loss) by employees because they spend time attending training sessions that take them away from doing the hands-on job they were hired to do.

Every hour lost by workers (time not spent producing the goods or services of the corporation) has an adverse impact on total productivity. If the SEATP adversely affects the productivity of workers, it must be able to demonstrate how it contributes to the protection of company assets, offsetting that loss of productivity; in essence, it must be able to justify itself. Security metrics management program (SMMP) techniques can assist in doing that.

One of the SEATP goals is to provide all briefings and training required to all applicable employees. The goal is, at the end of the year, to have reached 100% of the employee and support persons population. The effectiveness of training is measured by the correlation analysis of hours of training/employee at each site to all applicable assets-protection policies and procedures at each location. The goal is a positive downward trend of the loss (theft, damage, destruction, etc.) of company assets. A reduction of security violations throughout the company is another potential indicator of success.

Each of the subfunctions and their products' development processes should be analyzed to determine their costs in terms of labor and materials. A useful tool to accomplish this is to flowchart the process. In that way, each step in that process can be understood in the necessary detail to help determine its value. This will assist the CSO in developing an understanding of the real costs involved in the development of security products and to assess the cost-benefits of each part of the SEATP. For example:

- What is the cost and benefit to developing and distributing awareness material such as posters displayed throughout the company containing a security message?

---

* See *Security Metrics Management*[5] published by BH/Elsevier and excerpts published here with permission.

- Do the use of these and other SEATP products cause the employees to better protect the organizations' assets?
- If not, what other purpose do they serve?
- Are they just a "nice-to-have" item with no visible return on investments?

A SMMP will help the CSO make this determination. In times of corporate frugality, such products may be seen as too expensive, and the CSO, when placing much reliance on them, may be looked upon as not understanding the business world of costs and profits. After all, a good business person must be able to demonstrate a return on investment. Using the tested measurement process, the CSO can demonstrate the value of the program. If the program has little value, the CSO must change or eliminate it. If the program demonstrated more of a benefit than it costs, the CSO should continue the program but also continue to strive to make it more effective and efficient.

Other considerations for the CSO include the effectiveness of the employee awareness briefings: Are they being accomplished cost-effectively? Are the security specialists conducting the briefings doing them for large audiences and thereby operating more cost-effectively by providing fewer briefings? By providing fewer briefings for more attendees per session, the security specialist frees up some of his or her time. That is time that can be used to perform other duties contributing to the security program in others way or making up for a shortage of security resources in other areas.

Data Collection and Metrics Management

Some of the questions that may be asked by a CSO or a CSO's staff responsible for the SEATP are:

Who should track the functional metrics input data? As with all security functions, the tracking of the data should be done by the person at the lowest level who is responsible for the day-to-day SEATP activity.

What to track? To begin with, all major tasks should be tracked and gradually, data can be collected in more detail as one moves through the work breakdown structure of the SEATP. To start, the tracking and data collection should be basic, recording the number of briefings, the number of attendees at those briefings, and the associated costs (which will provide a baseline of information to work with); the type, number, and costs of all awareness material; and the costs of meeting all requirements (remember the security drivers) mandated action (e.g., laws and regulations).

Why track it? First and foremost, it is difficult at best to manage what you do not know. Therefore tracking data and measuring performance is essential if one is to know the basics about a process and what it does. Any process of high cost or frequency must be tracked as it is likely to get much attention. Once these factors can be quantified and qualified, then the process of analysis can begin to determine more cost-effective ways of providing the SEATP service and support to the CAPP and thus the organization.

How to track it? It is actually a simple process. To begin with, the tracking of costs and lost productivity of workers can be accomplished by maintaining a record of attendees (having a sign-in log for those attending the briefings) and the amount of time each spends at the presentation. This can then be entered into a spreadsheet, and the total time spent at the briefing can be calculated, as well as the average time spent by each employee. This time can then be added to the average time it takes for an employee to get to the briefing and return to their place of work. Multiply that time by the average employee pay rate plus benefits and you will have the total cost of time of lost productivity due to attending SEATP briefings.

Of course, the next thing to do would be to quantify the value of the briefings. This is a more difficult task. As the organizations' CSO, how would you go about doing that? (See the case study toward the end of this chapter.)

When to track it? The tracking of various data from the processes making up the SEATP can be done at different intervals (weekly, monthly, bi-monthly, etc.) and should be done in a way consistent with your organizational needs. Again, the criteria that should be used are how often the data is needed for analysis along with special actions and follow-up for CSO assignments and projects. To keep the process as simple as possible, data collection should occur as often as briefings are conducted and as often as awareness materials are distributed.

For distributed awareness material, the cost in time and other resources should be collected as awareness materials are developed. Added to that would be the publication and distribution cost, including material, labor, and other resources. So, for awareness material, the data would be collected at the end of each project. The total costs of all projects relative to the development of awareness materials would be summed on a monthly basis, again on a quarterly basis, and also on an annual basis; or whatever your specific need happens to be.

The use of awareness material such as security calendars, pamphlets and brochures, and other related items is a common approach to enhancing security education efforts often used by corporations and government agencies. However, if they can't be qualified or quantified in terms of their value and benefits to the SEATP and ultimately to employee security consciousness and the protection of assets, then you may consider eliminating them. Using a tool for which the benefit cannot be derived is a luxury that can't be afforded in these times of global competition.

Where to track it in the functional process? Each briefing's data would be collected at the end of each briefing and entered into the spreadsheet or database. Each awareness material development, production, and distribution would be collected at the end of the project for each awareness material project.

In analyzing these SEATP charts, the CSO can see if the ratio of attendees to briefings is cost-effective. Changes can be implemented on a trial basis to see if it has a positive impact resulting in a more cost-effective briefing program. If so, excellent! If not, make another adjustment. The beauty of measurement is that it helps the CSO or security professional manage change, track results, and continue to make positive adjustments in the process, working toward the most effective and efficient process possible.

Another measure the CSO can use is the cost of lost productivity due to the fact that each employee must attend an annual briefing in person, and thus they are not spending that time being productive (in terms of their normal assignment and responsibilities). Assume an average wage of $50 an hour per employee, which includes benefits. Then assume that it takes about 30 minutes for each employee to shut down their work and go to the briefing location and another 30 minutes to get back to the office and return to their primary duties. That means if you multiply the number of attendees by $50, you can estimated the cost factor of the employee's "travel" time alone. Now factor in another hour each at $50 an hour for the time taken to listen to the one-hour briefing. So, you see, learning can be expensive. The most critical point is what you get for that learning.

Suppose that you, as the CSO, learn employee security awareness must be achieved to a minimum standard in order to ensure all employees understand their responsibility to protect corporation assets. Essentially, your security awareness briefings are now required by federal law. What does this mean to you?

The law requires that the employees be made aware of their duties and responsibilities for the organizations' assets protection. This may be interpreted (here you want to get a representative of the legal staff to provide you, the CSO, guidance) to mean that a briefing can be through the simple distribution of a security awareness pamphlet or an online briefing where employees can acknowledge their responsibilities as they go through charts and take a simple test to demonstrate they have learned the basic information. Which to choose? Keep in mind, your goal should be to determine which is most efficient and effective.

By placing the briefing online, there are advantages. It can be rapidly updated and tied to security software—used to collect data—so the relevant data can be collected in a centralized database for later metrics analyses. Furthermore, the travel time is eliminated, and thus $50 per employee per briefing can be claimed as a saving, in addition to an increase in the employees' productivity.*

---

* We use the word "potential" here, recognizing that realistically, one can usually not count on a 100% productivity increase as one never knows what the employee will do before or after the briefing. However, it would be realistic to assume that time savings represent cost savings and a gain in employees' productivity; that is, they are available for working at their primary duties instead of traveling to and from a briefing.

There is of course the unknown factor: If employees attend the briefings in any format, does that make them more aware of their assets protection responsibilities and are they then more apt to comply with the organizations' CAPP and properly protect the organizations' assets? If so, how do you know? If not, why not?

Case Study

The organization's CSO met with the security department's investigations manager, who stated that there was an ongoing security problem in the organization. That problem was the theft of the information technology assets used by employees; for example, the theft of notebook computers out of the vehicles of the employees when the employees were out on business trips. It became particularly problematic when it was discovered that many of these stolen notebooks contained sensitive information about the organization. In many cases, this information was considered to be competition-sensitive, that is to say, if the organizations' competitors were to obtain that information, the organization could see their competitive advantage negatively affected.

As the CSO, what would be your plan of action to eliminate the thefts and losses of these valuable organization assets and the information they contained?

Of course, you should know by now that this calls for action, which should be managed through a project plan. In this case, the project plan consisted of the following tasks*:

- Collect and analyze all investigative report data on the losses to include the usual who, how, where, when, why, and what.
- Coordinate the results with the SEATP security specialist.
- Develop an organization-wide communication (it may be as simple as a corporate-wide e-mail notice) advising all employees of the problem and how to eliminate it.
- Update the new-hire and annual employees' APP briefings to emphasize the problem and solution.
- Update the CAPP policy to include a statement that all losses of notebooks and other valuable assets due to the employee being negligent in their duty to protect company assets would require them to pay for the loss (or at least the equipment, as its value is easily quantified) out of their salary. This will be an unpopular "pill to swallow" but it may get employees' attention (of course this must be coordinated with and approved by the legal and HR staffs). No employee would be authorized to use a notebook computer or other assets (e.g., PDA, cell phone) unless they signed a statement acknowledging their

---

* Of course a more detailed list of tasks can and should be developed. This case study just shows an example of what would be included.

obligations to protect and had an understanding of the consequences. Failure to agree to such a practice will result in a restriction imposed on them to not remove any asset from the facility.

■ Develop and implement a useful metric as a means of graphically depicting the future loss trends. Keep in mind that the goal is to drive down the number of losses and eliminate that asset protection problem.

Always ensure that you have detailed charts and related documents to back up your overview charts and triple check them for accuracy, as any errors would detract from your reporting. Be sure you never present charts with inaccurate or inconsistent data. The integrity and quality of your charts are a reflection on you, the CSO. Bad charts equal a bad presentation with your message possibly being lost, or worse yet, not believed—at least in the minds of those subjected to this poor performance.

Summary

The SEATP is an important subfunction under the administrative security function. It is primarily responsible for awareness briefings, the development and distribution of awareness material, and administratively managing the security departments' security professionals' training program.

The SEATP costs in terms of lost productivity and the loss of other resources can and should be measured using a security metrics management approach. In addition, it can be used to help eliminate a trend of asset losses by emphasizing the problem and solution through awareness materials and briefings monitored through metrics trend charts.

The basis for an SEATP supported by an SMMP are the following: metrics charts such as the ratio of briefings to employees attending, lost productivity caused by attending briefings, costs and benefits of awareness materials, and cost saving in terms of identifying assets protection loss trends; and mitigating those losses through enhanced awareness materials and briefings.

References

1. *New Oxford American Dictionary*. (2010). Oxford University Press (Third Edition).
2. Kovacich, G. L. (1998). *Information Systems Security Officer's Guide*. Burlington, MA: Elsevier.
3. Kovacich, G. L. (2003). *The Manager's Handbook for Corporate Security*. Boston: Butterworth-Heinemann.
4. Kovacich, G. L. and Halibozek, E. P. (2005). *Security Metrics Management*. Burlington, MA: Elsevier.

Chapter 16

The Tallinn Manual

The *Tallinn Manual on the International Law Applicable to Cyber Warfare* was written by an independent "international group of experts" at the invitation of the North Atlantic Treaty Organization (NATO) Cooperative Cyber Defence Centre of Excellence (CDCE). The manual was the product of a three-year project to examine how existing international law applies to this "new" form of warfare.

The Tallinn manual, in particular, examines the international law that governs the resort to force by states as an instrument of national policy and the international law regulating the conduct of armed conflict (this is also known as the law of war, the law of armed conflict, or international humanitarian law). Other related international laws, such as the law of state responsibility and the law of the sea, were also addressed.

Since the concepts of information warfare/information operations/cyber warfare were first discussed, one of the issues that has challenged governments, the military, and academics has been the status of both offensive and defensive operations in law. Conventional kinetic acts are covered in the Geneva Conventions and have been developed over a long period—globally, there has been a lot of experience.

Information warfare/cyber warfare is relatively very new. The NATO Cooperative CDCE, based in Tallinn, Estonia, commissioned the aforementioned experts to produce the *Tallinn Manual on the International Law Applicable to Cyber Warfare* to examine how existing international laws apply to this "new" form of warfare. The NATO Cooperative CDCE was created when several countries came together to foster cooperation, capabilities, and information sharing between NATO countries on issues related to cyber security. This was as a result of the 2007 Estonian cyber attack, which hit the government, national ministries, banks, the media, the police, and emergency services. The NATO center also conducts research and training on several areas of cyber warfare.

The Tallinn manual group was led by Professor Michael N. Schmidt, the chairman of the International Law Department at the US Naval War College. The document, produced in 2013, is the first in-depth examination of the issues related to the legal status of acts and the responsibilities of the actors in cyber attacks.

This comprehensive document covers a range of topics, many of which have not been considered by the practitioners and academics, and the results are expressed as a set of 95 "rules." For anyone involved in the planning or prosecution of either offensive or defensive cyber actions, this should be an essential read.

In this chapter, we will take a look at the range of topics that are covered in the manual and also highlight some of the major issues that relate to both offensive and defensive information operations.

The manual is divided into two parts. Part 1 concerns international cybersecurity law and is broken down into sections on

- The state and cyber space
- The use of force

Part 2 is broken down into sections on

- The law of armed conflict generally
- Conduct of hostilities
- Certain persons, objects, and activities
- Occupation
- Neutrality

In Part 1, the section on the state and cyber space examines issues of

- Sovereignty
- Jurisdiction and control and the responsibility of the state

The section on the use of force addresses the topics of

- Prohibition of the use of force
- Self-defense
- Actions of international governmental organizations

In Part 2, the section on the law of armed conflict generally examines the issues of

- The applicability of the law of armed conflict
- Geographic limitations
- Characterization of international armed conflict,
- Characterization of noninternational armed conflict
- Criminal responsibility of commandeers and superiors

The section on the conduct of hostilities addresses

- Participation in armed conflict
- Attacks generally
- Attacks against persons
- Attacks against objects
- Means and methods of warfare
- Conduct of attacks, precautions
- Perfidy, improper use, and espionage
- Blockade and zones

The section on certain persons, objects, and activities examines the issues related to

- Medical and religious personnel and medical units, transports, and matériel
- United Nations (UN) personnel, installations, matériel, units, and vehicles
- Detailed persons, children, journalists
- Installations containing dangerous forces
- Objects indispensable to the survival of the civilian population
- Cultural property, the natural environment
- Diplomatic archives and communications
- Collective punishment
- Humanitarian assistance

The section on occupation covers

- Respect for protected persons in occupied territory
- Public order and safety in occupied territory
- Security of the occupying power
- Confiscation and requisition of property

The last section in Part 2 is on neutrality and examines issues including

- The protection of neutral cyber infrastructure
- Cyber operations in neutral territory
- Neutral obligations
- Response by parties to the conflict to violations
- Neutrality and security council actions

As you can see from this very condensed list, the manual covers a very wide range of relevant topics. One of the first issues addressed in the manual is that of the sovereignty of cyber space. The manual argues that, while no nation may claim sovereignty over cyber space *per se*, each nation has sovereignty over the cyber infrastructure located within its territories as well as the activities associated with that cyber infrastructure. The manual points out that this sovereignty has two consequences—the first is that the cyber infrastructure is subject to legal and regulatory control by the state, and the second is that, whether the infrastructure belongs to the government or to commercial or private organizations, it is protected by the state's sovereignty.

What does this mean? That no nation "owns" cyber space (and this includes the Internet—although, as noted in an earlier chapter, some governments or other entities are trying to do so), but each nation has control over the part of it that falls within its jurisdiction and has the right/obligation to protect it. This is taken to mean that a cyber operation by a state against the cyber infrastructure in another state may violate that state's sovereignty, particularly if it causes damage to that infrastructure. What the group of experts could not agree on was whether malware, which causes no physical damage, falls into this category.

From this rationale, it would seem to be fairly clear that malware such as Stuxnet, which did cause physical damage, would be a violation of the sovereignty of Iran. However, the responsibility for the Stuxnet malware, which is believed to have been active since around 2006 but was only discovered in 2010, has never been claimed or attributed beyond any reasonable doubt, and as a result, to date, there is no case to answer for any nation. It is interesting to note that in August 2014, the *UK Mail Online*[1] reported that Retired Marine Gen. James "Hoss" Cartwright, a former vice chairman of the Joint Chiefs of Staff, was under investigation for allegedly leaking classified information about a covert Stuxnet cyber attack on Iran's nuclear facilities.

According to David E. Sanger, chief Washington correspondent for the *New York Times*, President Obama inherited from the Bush administration an operation known as Operation Olympic Games. This was allegedly a covert and unacknowledged campaign to disrupt the workings of Iranian nuclear facilities with a computer virus. The operation was supposedly started by the Bush administration in 2006. He reported in the *New York Times*[2] that

> It appears to be the first time the United States has repeatedly used cyber-weapons to cripple another country's infrastructure, achieving, with computer code, what until then could be accomplished only by bombing a country or sending in agents to plant explosives.

Operation Olympic Games was reported to be a collaborative effort between the National Security Agency (NSA), the Central Intelligence Agency (CIA), and Israel. The CIA, under then-director Michael V. Hayden, lent its covert operation authority to the program.

Other malware that has apparently targeted Iran includes

> DuQu, which was discovered in 2011 and which has a striking similarity to Stuxnet in terms of design philosophy, internal structure and mechanisms, implementation details, and the estimated amount of effort needed to create it.

Flame, which was discovered in 2012 by the MAHER Center of the Iranian national Computer Emergency Response Team (CERT) and was a highly sophisticated piece of malware that was found to be infecting systems in Iran and elsewhere and was believed to be part of a well-coordinated, ongoing, state-run cyberespionage operation.

Wiper, which was a virus that was first reported by the Iranian Maher Computer Emergency Response Team Coordination Center in January 2013 as a virus capable of wiping the data on infected PCs. The virus had been active for at least two months. The malware, also known as Batchwiper, continuously erased data from drive partitions starting with the letters D through I on the Windows operating system, in addition to files stored on the user's desktop.

In August 2012, the Saudi Aramco Company was hit by the Shamoon virus and was forced to shut its internal network for more than a week, although the website came back online within a couple of days. Shamoon infected 30,000 of Aramco's computers, wiping their hard drives. It did not, however, affect oil production, which is controlled from separate networks. It has been speculated that this may have been an attack sponsored by Iran.

The Tallinn manual continues on the subject of sovereignty by stating that if the cyber operation against another state is intended to coerce the government, it may constitute a prohibited "intervention" according to the UN Charter, Article 2(1) or a prohibited "use of force." The result of this is that a cyber attack that qualifies as an "armed attack" would trigger the right of individual or collective self-defense. Actions that did not constitute an "armed attack" but that were in violation of international law could enable the target country to resort to countermeasures; however, actions that are authorized by the UN Security Council would not constitute a violation of the target nation's sovereignty.

One effect of sovereignty is that a state is allowed to restrict or prevent access to the Internet without prejudice to applicable international law, such as human rights or international telecommunications law. The Tallinn manual addresses the increasingly important issue of attacks on the cyber infrastructure of a state by non-state actors, although it does not offer any "rules" to address this. This is not surprising for two reasons. The first is that the concept is still very new, and the second is that nonstate actors have historically not conformed to the Geneva Conventions!

The next issue addressed by the Tallinn manual is that of jurisdiction. Having established the issue of sovereignty, the manual addresses jurisdiction over individuals or groups involved in cyber activity on a state's territory and of the cyber infrastructure located on its territory and also extraterritorially in accordance with international law.

While this may seem to be straightforward, the problems of mobility, cloud, and grid computing, wherein systems may span national borders and where it is possible to dynamically reallocate both processing power and storage, mean that it may be difficult to determine which state has jurisdiction over specific data at any one point in time. Another problem that affects jurisdiction is that of mobile devices, where a process or a query may be initiated in one location.

The view on this from the European Court of Justice is that there are two views on jurisdiction—subjective and objective. The subjective view is that the state has jurisdiction on actions that were initiated in their jurisdiction but which were completed elsewhere, even if the actions had no effect on the state concerned. The objective view is that the state has jurisdiction on actions that were initiated elsewhere but were completed within its jurisdiction. An example of this is the events in Estonia in 2007, when the attacks were initiated, at least in part, from abroad. As the acts violated Estonian laws, Estonia had jurisdiction over the individuals who perpetrated the acts, wherever they were located. The result of this subjective and objective jurisdiction is that two or more states may have jurisdiction over the same individuals or objects as the result of the same event.

Another issue that is raised is that no state should knowingly allow the cyber infrastructure located within its jurisdiction to be used for acts that adversely or unlawfully affect other states, and the obligation is placed on a state to respect the territorial sovereignty of other states. This is easier said than done as, given the nature of cyber space, a state may be unaware of the preparation for and the execution of an attack from its territories. The issue is further complicated if the state in question is neither the state in which the actions were initiated or the target but is merely the conduit through which the activity is routed. All of this is further complicated by the significant problem of being able to attribute actions that have been taken in cyber space to their source.

What the Tallinn manual is clear on is that a state has a legal responsibility for cyber operations that are attributed to it that constitute a breach of its international obligation. In cyber space, this may be a breach of the UN Charter, for example, a use of force carried out through cyber means or a violation of the obligations of the law of armed conflict. Interestingly, espionage is not covered by international law unless it violates a specific legal prohibition such as diplomatic communications.

As a result, an advanced persistent threat that has been attributed by a number of sources[3–5] to China does not appear to be covered by international law. However, if a state takes action or contracts with private organizations to undertake cyber operations on their behalf or calls on the services of cyber volunteers, the state is still responsible for the effect of these actions. This responsibility does not extend to private individuals who act as "hacktivists" or "patriotic hackers" who are acting on their own initiative. Put simply, if the state sponsors a cyber operation, then they carry responsibility for it, but they cannot be held responsible for the actions of individuals acting on their own initiative. The unfortunate reality is that it is currently almost impossible to attribute, with certainty, state involvement in a cyber attack.

Rule 7 of the Tallinn manual deals with cyber operations that are launched from a governmental cyber infrastructure. This highlights the fact that even though a cyber attack is launched from a governmental cyber infrastructure, this does not represent sufficient evidence that the state is responsible but is an indication that the state is associated with the operation. In addition, this only applies to the governmental cyber infrastructure and does not apply to other infrastructures, even though they are located within the states territories. Now call me a cynic, but if I was in charge and wanted to avoid responsibility for an action, might I not use a system that fitted the description of a "nongovernmental cyber infrastructure"?

Rule 8 deals with attacks that are routed through a state's infrastructure and points out that this does not make the state responsible. The activity that became known as Solar Sunrise[6] represents a good example of this, where some of the attacks were routed through China and the United Arab Emirates but were eventually attributed to two kids in Cloverdale, California.

Rule 9 of the Tallinn manual looks at the countermeasures that a state that has been attacked may take, which are derived from Articles 22, 49, and 53 of the International Law Commission's Articles on State Responsibility. The rule describes countermeasures as "necessary and proportionate actions" that the "victim state" takes in response to a violation of international law by an "offending state" and says that any such measures must be intended to "induce compliance by the offending state with international law." Interestingly, according to the manual, countermeasures can only be taken to persuade the offending state to desist in their activities, and once they have stopped, so must the countermeasures.

Countermeasures can only be used to persuade the offender to operate within international law and cannot be used for punishment or retribution. The panel agreed that "cyber countermeasures" could not escalate to the level of an "armed attack." However, the panel of experts accepted that states often do not comply with this and that the whole area was "far from settled."

A related area that is addressed in the manual relates to those actions taken as a result of a "plea of necessity." This is described as protective (cyber) measures that are taken by a state that violate the interests of another state, such as shutting down part of the cyber infrastructure, if this is the only way of protecting themselves against a "grave and imminent peril," even if doing so affects the cyber infrastructure of another state or states in general. It also allows for the possibility of "counter hacking" if a state was faced with significant cyber operations against its critical infrastructure.

The next part of the manual deals with the use of force. A cyber operation that was conducted by a state's armed forces or intelligence agencies or by a private contractor working on behalf of the state would be considered to be a "use of force." Unfortunately, Article 2(4) of the UN Charter does not apply to nonstate actors such as terrorist groups. A cyber operation is defined as the use of force when "its scale and effects are comparable to non-cyber operations rising to a level of the use of force." However, there is currently no definition of what constitutes a "use of force."

The manual does give the example that a nondestructive cyber-psychological operation intended solely to undermine confidence in a government or economy does not qualify as the use of force. A current example of this type of operation would be the activity being undertaken by Russia against Ukraine. According to *Defense Update*,[7] the largest military cyber attack was the attack implemented by the Russian Military Intelligence (GRU) on the armed forces of Ukraine, as reported by the BBC.[8] According to the law-enforcement agencies of Ukraine, Russian cyber attacks collapsed the communication systems of almost all the Ukrainian forces that were based in Crimea that could pose a danger to the invading Russian troops. Attacks of a lesser scale were directed at government websites and news and social networks.

Another report in the *Smolensk Crash News Digest*[9] highlighted another form of attack when it reported that

> The Russian Federation is actively using the religious factor to promote its conditions for stabilizing the situation and to spread false statements about a peaceful settlement of the war. There are many eye-witness accounts of sermons by priests of the Ukrainian Orthodox Church of the Moscow Patriarchate about "militant heroes," "holy war," and the "Kyiv junta," not only in the Donbas but also in the Sumy and Chernihiv oblasts. Another direction that is actively pursued is the spreading of rumors. The instruments of distribution are not only specific individuals and Russian TV, but also informational messages delivered through the printed press, leaflets, and local cable broadcasts.

The manual also deals with the "threat of force," which it defines as "a cyber operation or a threatened cyber operation, constitutes an unlawful threat of force when the threatened action, if carried out, would be an unlawful use of force." While this may seem in itself to be self-explanatory, it can be used to describe two different scenarios. These are described in the manual:

> The first is a cyber operation that is used to communicate a threat to use force (whether kinetic or cyber). The second is a threat conveyed by any means (e.g. public pronouncements) to carry out cyber operations qualifying as a use of force.

This part of the manual deals with what a state can do in self-defense against an armed attack, and this includes attacks that are entirely carried out in the cyber domain and do not include a kinetic element.

The consensus of the international panel that wrote the manual was that any use of force that injured or killed people or damaged or destroyed property would satisfy the "scale and effects" criteria for an armed attack. They also agreed that cyber-intelligence gathering, cyber theft, and cyber operations that only caused brief or periodic interruptions to nonessential cyber services would not satisfy those criteria. Also addressed is the issue of whether a number of minor attacks from the same source can be aggregated to meet the criteria of scale.

The international experts took the view that in the period up to 2012, no cyber incidents had been publicly and unambiguously characterized as having reached the threshold of an armed attack. They highlighted two specific cases as examples. The first was the fact that the 2007 incidents in Estonia were not characterized by either the Estonians or the international community as an armed attack. They then looked at the 2010 Stuxnet incident, which did cause physical damage to the centrifuges at the Iranian Natanz nuclear facility, and they felt that this would reach the threshold of an "armed attack" (unless it could be justified on the basis of "anticipatory self-defence") if it could be attributed to an "originator."

The manual then deals with the issue of the use of force, including cyber operations, by a nation in an act of self-defense being both proportionate and necessary. An act of force that is undertaken by a state must be "needed" to successfully prevent an imminent armed attack or to defeat one that is taking place. The issue of proportionality is that of how much force is permissible once the use of force is deemed to be appropriate, and this encompasses the scale, scope, duration, and the intensity of the response. It also deals with the issues of imminence and immediacy. Article 51 of the UN Charter refers to the situation in which an armed attack occurs but does not actually address the situation of defensive action in anticipation of an armed attack.

It gives an example in which a state gains incontrovertible evidence that another state is preparing to launch a cyber attack against its primary oil pipeline, one that would cause the microcontrollers along it to increase the pressure in the pipeline so as to cause a series of explosions within the subsequent two weeks. The intelligence does not include the vulnerability that is to be exploited but does indicate that the perpetrators will be at a specific location at a specific time. The expert group concluded that the necessity of self-defense was imminent and that strikes against the perpetrators would be lawful. The issue of immediacy distinguishes an act of self-defense from one of retaliation and considers the period following an armed attack when a state may reasonably respond in self-defense.

It may be that the authors of the manual were looking for relevant examples from the past on which to base their scenarios, as the choice of an example of the destruction of an oil pipeline bears a strong similarity to reports in the media in 2004[10] of a 1982 CIA operation to sabotage Soviet industry through the use of booby-trapped software to trigger a huge explosion in a Siberian gas pipeline. The explosion was, according to a report in the *Washington Post*, "the most monumental nonnuclear explosion and fire ever seen from space." According to the report, "The software was programmed to reset pump speeds and valve settings to produce pressures far beyond those acceptable to pipeline joints and welds."

The next section of the manual deals with the law of cyber armed conflict and, as a first step, looks at the law of armed conflict generally and its applicability. The manual states that the law of armed conflict applies to cyber operations in the same way that it would to any other operations undertaken in the context of an armed operation. To illustrate the point being made, the manual looks at the activities in

Estonia in 2007 and in Georgia in 2008. For most people who are not lawyers, the nuances of the difference between the incidents do not appear to be significant, but the findings reveal two very different situations.

As stated earlier, Estonia was the target of persistent cyber operations, but the situation did not rise to the level of armed conflict. On the other hand, in Georgia, because the cyber operations took place in furtherance of a kinetic armed conflict, the relevant law of international or noninternational armed conflict applies. This means that the law of armed conflict does not apply to cyber operations if they are conducted on their own and do not reach the level of an armed conflict. However, if they are conducted in conjunction with other kinetic operations that do reach that level, then the law does apply to them. The manual does highlight the fact that it is often difficult to determine that a cyber operation is taking place, and even if this can be determined, its origin, purpose, and effects may be very difficult to identify.

The manual looks at the subject of the support of a state for an armed nonstate group in another state, such as was seen in Ukraine in 2014. The example that is used in the manual is of one state shutting down the communications capabilities of another state to support the rebels in that state. It is interesting that the manual was published before the situation in Ukraine occurred, but the example quoted is very similar to what actually took place. *Defense Update*[7] reported that

> Russia has managed to hit almost all Ukraine government websites and it was able to take control and to put on surveillance and monitoring all the Internet and telephone communications lines, before the invasion and occupation of Crimea by its military. Russian Special Forces managed to derail all important communications systems through direct physical impact on them by combined field and high-tech operation.

Using the arguments of the case put forward in the manual, as Ukraine relied on the communications systems for its military communications, this attack may be enough to "internationalize the conflict."

Rule 24 of the Tallinn manual deals with the issue of the criminal responsibility of commanders and superiors. This rule starts by stating that (a) commanders and other superiors are criminally responsible for ordering cyber operations that constitute war crimes, and (b) that commanders are also criminally responsible if they knew or, owing to the circumstances at the time, should have known their subordinates were committing, were about to commit, or had committed war crimes and if the commanders failed to take all reasonable and available measures to prevent their commission or to punish those responsible.

The rule emphasizes that commanders and other superiors (including civilians) do not escape responsibility even though they did not personally commit the act. The example given of what would constitute a war crime is cyber attacks against civilians who are not directly participating in hostilities.

This makes the use of a cyber attack extremely difficult, given the cyber infrastructure—how would you ensure that the attack only affected the intended target? If we look at Stuxnet, the intended target was the centrifuges of the Iranian uranium-enrichment program. Unfortunately, as with most malware, it spread from the initial target and subsequently affected computers in Russia, the United States, China, Germany, India, Pakistan, Azerbaijan, Kazakhstan, and Indonesia. All of these would probably be considered to be "civilians who are not directly participating in hostilities."

This section of the manual also deals with the issue of "participants" in an armed conflict and the rules and consequences that apply to them. It highlights three in particular: combatant immunity, prisoner of war status, and targetability. While the first two are well understood by the members of the armed forces of most countries, the third—targetability—is one that bears further consideration.

Rule 35 highlights that a civilian participant in a conflict will lose certain protections that they would normally enjoy during the time that they participate. The good news is that if you are working for the government, but not in the armed forces, you are covered by combatant immunity as you would be considered to be a "state organ" and, as a result, meet the requirements. However, if a person is engaged in cyber operations during an armed conflict and is a member of an organized armed group not belonging to a party of the conflict, they would not be covered; they would be considered an "unprivileged belligerent" and would not enjoy combatant immunity or prisoner of war status.

Combatant status requires that individuals can be identified through the wearing of a "fixed distinctive sign," normally achieved by the wearing of a uniform. This is somewhat difficult to achieve in the cyber domain.

The manual explains that the participation of a civilian in cyber attacks related to an armed conflict qualifies as direct participation. So also do acts in preparation for such an attack, such as identifying vulnerabilities in the target system or developing malware that will be used for intelligence gathering or conducting a DoS attack. Such an act of direct participation would render the person liable to targeting for the period in which they are engaged in the act of direct participation. This would include the time when the person might be traveling to a location to use the computer that was to be used for the cyber attack.

The manual also addresses the problem of mercenaries who engage in cyber operations and states that they do not enjoy combatant immunity or prisoner of war status.

The manual also addresses the issue of status of an object, such as civilian Internet services, civilian social networks, civilian residences, commercial businesses, factories, libraries, and educational facilities, that may be a potential target of a cyber attack. If the object is normally used for civilian purposes but is being used to make an effective contribution to military action, the manual determines that a careful assessment must be undertaken to ensure that there is no doubt. If there is any doubt, then it should not be attacked. The manual also points out that civilian objects that have become military objectives through use will revert to their civilian status as soon as the military use stops, unless they are likely to be used again in the future for military objectives.

The problem here is that with the Internet, determining which specific element is being used for military objectives is extremely resource intensive and almost impossible to prove. The ubiquity of the Internet also means that it is possible to rapidly move the use of one set of resources to another. For example, if a particular laboratory was being used to mount a cyber attack, the resources could be very quickly recreated in another laboratory in another location. Consider the time and level of resources it took during operation Solar Sunrise to identify the source of the attack and also look at the level of success that has been achieved in identifying the protagonists who operate under the banner of "Anonymous." Achieving a level of confidence that a particular civilian object has been converted to military use, unless it is in operation for a considerable period, will be problematic.

The identification of "protected" objects such as those dedicated to religion, art, science, or charitable purposes; historic monuments; hospitals; and places where the sick and wounded are collected must be aided by the defenders by the use of distinctive markings or must be notified to the attacker beforehand, as defined in Article 27 of the Hague regulations. Again, this is going to be problematic for both attackers and defenders. While the use of the red cross or red crescent has historically been used to denote physical hospitals and medical facilities, how do you do this in cyber space? To date very little work has been undertaken in how to identify systems that support the same functions in cyber space.

Rule 41 of the Tallinn manual gives definitions on the means and methods of warfare; it defines the "means of cyber warfare" as cyber weapons and their associated cyber systems and "methods of cyber warfare" as the cyber tactics, techniques, and procedures by which hostilities are conducted. A distinction is drawn between a computer system, which qualifies as a means of warfare, and the cyber infrastructure (e.g., the Internet) that connects the computer to the target. The cyber infrastructure is not a means of warfare as it is not under the control of the attacking party.

The manual gives an example of a botnet that is being used to carry out a DDoS attack against a target. The botnet is the means of cyber warfare and the DDoS attack is the method of cyber warfare.

It goes on to address the issue of "indiscriminate" means and methods, which they define as methods that cannot be directed at a specific military objective or are limited in their effects as required by the laws of armed conflict and as a result will strike both military and civilian objects without distinction. These are unlawful, but this essentially means those cyber weapons that by their nature generate effects that cannot be controlled and therefore can spread into civilian and other protected computers and networks and cause harm. The manual uses the specific example of the release of Stuxnet-like malware and concludes that, while it did spread beyond the initial target, it would not be unlawful as it only caused damage to specific "military" targets.

Rule 44 of the Tallinn manual states that it is forbidden to employ cyber "booby traps" associated with certain objects specified in the laws of armed conflict. The rule is derived from the Mines Protocol and the Amended Mines Protocol (UN Convention on Prohibitions or Restrictions on the Use of Certain Conventional Weapons which may be deemed to be Excessively Injurious or to have Indiscriminate Effects), which define a "booby trap" as "any device or material which is designed, constructed or adapted to kill or injure, and which functions unexpectedly when a person disturbs or approaches an apparently harmless object or performs an apparently safe act." It may be difficult to envisage a scenario where a cyber "booby trap" could kill or injure someone, but the manual gives an example of an individual who works in a water treatment plant who receives an e-mail, purporting to come from his physician, which contains a "kill switch."

When he opens the e-mail, the embedded malware causes the water purification process to be suspended, resulting in untreated water being released into the system that serves both the civilian and military populations and causes illness. This booby trap is unlawful because the worker believes that opening an e-mail from his physician is safe to himself and others and because it relates to medical activities (one of the "protected" objects). Another rule (45) in the manual that relates to this example is that it is also unlawful to use starvation as a means of cyber warfare, and this includes the deprivation of water.

The manual next looks at the issue of cyber attacks on clearly separated and distinct military objectives. It states that a cyber attack that treats as a single target a number of clearly discrete cyber-military objectives in a cyber infrastructure primarily used for civilian purposes is prohibited if to do so would harm protected persons or objects. What this means is that if, for example, military computers were connected to a civilian network but they could be individually identified (say by their Internet protocol [IP] address) and attacked, it would be unlawful to use a method of cyber attack that would also damage the civilian computers.

However, the manual does go on to deal with the issue of "proportionality" and acknowledges that potential "collateral damage" does not necessarily render an attack unlawful as long as the target of the attack was a military objective. In simple terms, as with a kinetic attack on a military target, there is always the potential for civilians to be affected. The manual states that "if [this] expected harm is excessive in relation to the anticipated military advantage of the operation, the operation would be forbidden."

The manual also deals with the precautions that should be taken during hostilities that include cyber operations. These include "constant care," verification of targets, the choice of means and methods, proportionality, choice of targets, cancellation of attacks, and warnings.

During hostilities involving cyber operations, "constant care" must be taken to spare the civilian population, individual civilians, and civilian objects from harm. The law of armed conflict does not define the term "constant care," but it does state that particularly during cyber operations, which have a high probability of affecting civilian systems, commanders must maintain situational awareness of the effects of these operations. The defenders, on their part, also have a duty to respect the civilian population; as a result, it is unlawful to use the presence of civilians to shield a lawful target from cyber attack, and it is specifically forbidden to use medical facilities for the purpose of shielding.

The planners of cyber operations are required to do everything feasible to verify that the objectives to be attacked are not civilians or civilian objects and that they are not subject to special protection.

When choosing the means and methods that are to be employed during a cyber attack, the planners must take all reasonable precautions to avoid or minimize the incidental injury to civilians, the loss of civilian life, and damage to or destruction of civilian objects. This will include the consideration of both cyber and kinetic weapons to minimize collateral damage.

As with all military operations, the planners must consider proportionality and refrain from launching any cyber attack that may cause excessive incidental loss of civilian life, injury to civilians, or damage to civilian objects in relation to the concrete and direct military advantages gained. This would also apply during the conduct of an operation if it became apparent that it was unexpectedly resulting in excessive collateral damage. In this situation, the operation should be terminated.

Where there are a number of military targets that could be attacked in order to achieve military advantage, then the one(s) that will cause the least collateral damage should be selected for cyber attacks.

If during the course of an attack it becomes apparent that the objective is not a military target or is subject to special protection, or the collateral damage would be excessive, then the cyber attack should be terminated or suspended.

Warnings of cyber attacks that will affect the civilian population should be given unless the circumstances do not permit this. One example of this may be in a situation where a dual-use system is to be attacked; the attackers may decide to inform the enemy of the impending attack so as to allow them to warn the civilian population to take precautions to minimize the collateral damage. Another option may be to warn the civilian population directly. However, the act of informing the enemy or the civilian population may prejudice the outcome of an attack, and circumstances may not permit a warning to be given.

The manual goes on to address the issue of precautions against the effects of cyber attacks and highlights that all parties involved in an armed conflict must, to the maximum extent feasible, take the precautions necessary to protect the civilian population, individual civilians, and civilian objects under their control from the dangers that result from cyber attacks. This may include actions such as the segregation of military and civilian cyber infrastructures, the segregation of civilian systems on which the critical civilian infrastructure depends, the backing up of important civilian data, preparations for the timely repair of important computers, the digital recording of important cultural or spiritual objects to aid reconstruction in the event of their damage or destruction, and the use of antivirus software to protect civilian systems. One issue that does not appear to be addressed in the manual is the physical "marking" of "cyber" assets to protect them from kinetic attacks.

The measures that can be taken to protect the civilian cyber infrastructure and the examples given are all sensible and rational, but they do raise the question of why any state would wait to put these measures in place until there was the threat of a cyber attack. The reality is that the entire cyber infrastructure is under constant threat of attack from a host of both state and nonstate actors, and many of these measures should already be in place. Issues such as the separation of the military and civilian cyber infrastructure are always desirable, but even in the United States, the connectivity of military systems and the critical civilian cyber infrastructure to the Internet is widespread and in many cases essential.

The next section of the manual deals with the issues of perfidy, improper use, and espionage. Perfidy, which is also known as treachery, is defined in Article 37(1) of Additional Protocol I of the Geneva Conventions as

> [a]cts inviting the confidence of an adversary to lead him to believe that he is entitled to, or is obliged to accord, protection under the rules of international law applicable in armed conflict, with the intent to betray that confidence.

An example is given in the manual of sending a perfidious e-mail to the enemy inviting them to a meeting with the International Committee of the Red Cross, with the intention of leading them into an ambush. Another example would be that, while it is not required for military systems to be marked as such, it would be perfidious to make a military website appear to have civilian status with the intention of deceiving the enemy in order to kill or injure.

Perfidy is distinguished from espionage and ruses, both of which are permissible under the laws of armed conflict. Cyber espionage is the process of gathering information directed at an adversary during an armed conflict. Ruses are acts that are intended to mislead the enemy or to induce the enemy forces to act recklessly. The range of acts that might be classed as cyber ruses include creating "dummy" computer systems to simulate nonexistent forces, transmitting false information, creating honeypots and honeynets, feigning cyber attacks, the issuing of false orders purporting to have been sent by the enemy, carrying out psychological warfare activities, and the use of enemy codes, signals, and passwords. Other related issues include the prohibition on the improper use of protective emblems, signs, or signals such as the red cross, red crescent, or red crystal; the UN emblem or those of neutral states; and the improper use of enemy indicators such as flags, military emblems, insignia, or uniforms while visible to an enemy during an attack.

In some ways, this prohibition does not fit well for cyber operations, as it would be allowable to feign enemy authorship of a cyber communication. Another example that the manual cites to highlight the issues in the cyber realm is that of gaining electronic control of an enemy's surface-to-air missile system, which would be marked with enemy emblems; as the attacking force would not be physically present at the site, it would not be possible to remove the emblems before the resources were used. This would be considered to be lawful.

In the physical world, one tactic that may be employed is that of blockade, normally of port facilities, airports, or territories. It is possible that cyber operations could be used in support of the physical operations, and the view of the group of experts was that this would be lawful. The manual then goes on to look at the issue of the use of a cyber blockade to prevent cyber communications to and from territory controlled by the enemy. The group of experts concluded that it would also be lawful to apply the law of blockade to such a cyber operation.

The manual addresses the issue of protected objects. The law of armed conflict makes specific provision for the protection of certain persons, objects, and activities. These include medical personnel, hospitals and medical convoys, religious personnel, cultural sites, objects indispensable for the survival of the civilian population and works, installations containing dangerous forces (dams, dykes, nuclear power plants) and UN personnel, installations, matériel, units, and vehicles. One aspect that is specifically addressed is that of medical computers, networks, and data.

The manual is clear that there is a responsibility for both protagonists in a conflict to ensure that the resources are protected and not attacked. The responsibility of the defending state is to take measures to protect the resources by both physical and electronic means and to ensure that the resources are clearly marked with a distinctive emblem. The responsibility of the attacking force is to ensure that such resources are not targeted. The difficulty that exists here is that there is currently no agreed protocol or convention on how data and communications can be effectively marked in the cyber environment.

The data relating to detailed personnel such as prisoners of war and interned protected persons also needs to be protected, and the manual gives an example of this being achieved by storing this data separately from data or objects that constitute a military objective. An interesting point here is that this also applies to the correspondence of detailed persons. While this has historically been in the form of letters, it should also apply to electronic communications.

The next section of the manual deals with specific groups of people such as children and journalists. There is a prohibition on children (under the age of 15) being conscripted or enlisted to take part in hostilities, and this includes cyber operations. With regard to journalists, who do not enjoy protected status but who must be "respected" because of the dangers of the profession, particular emphasis is placed on them because of their reliance on computers and networks in the conduct of their jobs.

The next section of the manual deals with the issue of installations that contain "Dangerous Forces." Dangerous forces are defined as dams, dykes, and nuclear electric generating installations, but they currently do not include chemical and fuel production or processing plants. Article 56 of Additional Protocol I and Article 15 of Additional protocol II to the Geneva Conventions provide that, subject to certain exceptions, these works and installations cannot be attacked, even when they are military objectives, if such an attack may cause the release of dangerous forces and result in severe losses among the civilian population.

An example is given of a malware attack on a nuclear power station, which is intended to reduce the enemy's capability to produce electricity by taking it off line. If sufficient safeguards are built into the malware to prevent a core meltdown by ensuring that the integrity of the cooling system was built in, this would not be unlawful.

The next part of the manual deals with those protected objects that are considered to be indispensable to the survival of the civilian population. The manual states that attacking, destroying, removing, or rendering useless objects indispensable to the civilian population by means of cyber operations is prohibited. Additional Protocols I and II of the Geneva Conventions give examples of the objects covered by this protection: foodstuffs, agricultural areas for the production of foodstuffs, crops, livestock, drinking water installations and supplies, and irrigation works.

Food and medical supplies are also generally accepted as being protected. The manual points out that the Internet and communications systems themselves are not considered to be covered; however, the cyber infrastructure that is used for the functioning of electricity generation, irrigation, the supply of drinking water, and the production of food may, depending on the circumstances, be covered.

The next group covered under the protected objects section is that of cultural property. The manual states that the parties (on both sides) of an armed conflict must respect and protect cultural property that may be affected by cyber operations or that are located in cyber space. In particular, they are prohibited from using digital cultural property for military purposes. The actual definition of "digital cultural property" was not agreed on by all the experts on the panel, but the consensus was that it would apply to a digital copy of a physical object, such as a painting, where the original object has been destroyed. However, once multiple copies of the digital version of the object had been created, then it would no longer be protected.

The manual goes on to state that any alteration, damage, deletion, or destruction of the data, as well as its use for military purposes, are prohibited. Again, the problem of marking the protected object with an emblem in cyber space is an ongoing issue that has not yet been resolved. Some possible solutions that are offered in the manual include file-naming conventions, the use of tagging data with machine-interpretable encoding schemes, publishing lists of IP addresses for digital cultural property, or using generic high-level domain names.

The natural environment also enjoys protected status, and the manual states that State Party to Addition Protocol I (of the Geneva Conventions) are prohibited from employing cyber methods or means of warfare which are intended, or may be expected, to cause widespread, long-term, and severe damage to the natural environment. The manual gives an example of such an unlawful act as the purposeful release of oil into a waterway to cause environmental damage.

Diplomatic archives and communications also have protected status and are protected from cyber operations at all times. This protection applies to their confidentiality, integrity, and availability.

The manual next addresses the issues of collective punishment and interfering with humanitarian assistance. The manual states that collective punishment by cyber means is prohibited. The example that is given is that of confiscating all of the personal computers in a village in retaliation for cyber attacks carried out by a small cell of insurgents; this would be a violation of the prohibition. The topic of humanitarian assistance is addressed by the statement that cyber operations shall not be designed or conducted to interfere unduly with impartial efforts to provide humanitarian assistance. In the cyber environment, this would probably be most applicable to the communications and other cyber activities of nongovernment organizations offering humanitarian assistance.

The final two sections of the manual deal with the rules relating to occupation and neutrality. The manual states that there is no legal notion of occupation of cyber space. However, cyber activity can be used both in support of the occupying force or to disrupt or degrade the computer systems of the occupying power. The manual goes on to state that protected persons in occupied territory must be protected from the harmful effects of cyber operations, and that the occupying power must make all efforts to ensure the continuance of computer operations that are essential to the survival of the civilian population in the occupied territory.

An occupying power can lawfully take control of the cyber infrastructure and systems of the occupied territory. The issue of neutrality is addressed because of the global nature of the cyber infrastructure and the ease with which neutral states can be affected by cyber operations. The cyber infrastructure of a neutral state is protected by that state's territorial sovereignty, and belligerent acts against it are prohibited. This includes any elements of the cyber infrastructure that are located in high-seas areas, international airspace, or outer space. Neutral states also have obligations and may not knowingly allow the exercise of belligerents rights by the parties to the conflict from cyber infrastructure located in its territory or under its exclusive control. If they fail to do so, the aggrieved party may take steps, including cyber operations, to counter the activity.

The Tallinn manual, which was sponsored by the NATO Cooperative CDCE and developed by an international panel of experts, is the first informed and comprehensive attempt to address the issues of the laws of war in cyber space. In this chapter, we have tried to capture the main points that are addressed in the manual and to give relevant examples. The laws of war are comprehensive and complex and have to be viewed in the context of each potential scenario; however, a failure to take account of them when planning and conducting cyber operations could have serious repercussions.

While the rules of war and the Geneva Conventions are well understood by members of the military, other agencies, businesses, individuals, and nongovernment organizations will probably not have the same level of knowledge and understanding of the requirements and may expose themselves to legal action.

Summary

The *Tallinn Manual on the International Law Applicable to Cyber Warfare* was discussed in detail as it applies to dealing with today's IW tactics, strategies, and such from a global and legal perspective. It was written at the request of the NATO Cooperative CDCE in order to examine how extant international law norms apply to this "new" form of warfare.

Putting yourself in the position of an international judge and using this document, and assuming North Korea had attacked Sony as it was alleged beginning in 2014 and was aided by China with a counterattack coming from the United States, how would you apply the laws applicable to global information warfare (GIW) to all parties concerned?

If in fact North Korea did perpetrate this attack, aided by its ally, China, and legally the United States did counterattack in its defense, how would you judge the parties involved: guilty or not guilty, or that the cited laws did not apply? Furthermore, if one or more of the parties were guilty, what punishment would you determine and consider fair?

References

1. *Mail Online.* (2013). U.S. general under investigation for leaking details of covert Stuxnet cyber attack on Iran's nuclear program. June 28. http://www.dailymail. co.uk/news/article-2350654/Stuxnet-US-general-investigation-leaking-details-covert-cyber-attack-Irans-nuclear-program.html.
2. Sanger, D. E. (2012). Obama order sped up wave of cyberattacks against Iran. *New York Times*, June 1. http://www.nytimes.com/2012/06/01/world/middleeast/obama-ordered-wave-of-cyberattacks-against-iran.html.
3. Leyden, J. (2013). Advanced persistent threats get more advanced, persistent and threatening. *The Register*, April 4, 2013. http://www.theregister.co.uk/2013/04/04/apt_trends_fireeye/.
4. Gold, D. (2013). Unit 61398: Chinese cyber-espionage and the advanced persistent threat. Infosec Institute, March 26. http://resources.infosecinstitute.com/unit-61398-chinese-cyber-espionage-and-the-advanced-persistent-threat/.
5. Mandiant. (2013). APT1: Exposing one of China's cyber espionage units. http://intel-report.mandiant.com/Mandiant_APT1_Report.pdf.
6. Minihan, K. A. (1998). Director, National Security Agency. (1998). U.S. must combat weak computer security in government information systems. http://www.defense.gov/speeches/speech.aspx?speechid=704.

7. Tsipi, S. (2014). The Ukrainian crisis: A cyber warfare battlefield. Defense Update, April 5. http://defense-update.com/20140405_ukrainian-crisis-cyber-warfare-battlefield.html#.VAhpycVdV8E.
8. Lee, D. (2014). Russia and Ukraine in cyber "stand-off". BBC News Technology, March 5. http://www.bbc.co.uk/news/technology-26447200.
9. Smolensk Crash News Digest. (2014). Parubiy: Russia's war against Ukraine and the world. August 6. http://www.smolenskcrashnews.com/Russian-propaganda-war-against-Ukraine-and-the-world.html.
10. Russell, A. (2004). CIA plot led to huge blast in Siberian gas pipeline. *The Daily Telegraph*, February 28. http://www.telegraph.co.uk/news/worldnews/northamerica/usa/1455559/CIA-plot-led-to-huge-blast-in-Siberian-gas-pipeline.html.

Chapter 17

A Look at the Future: The Crystal Ball

If you consciously try to thwart opponents, you are already late.

Miyamoto Musashi
Japanese philosopher and samurai, 1645

In this final chapter, we will look to the future and some of its possibilities as they relate to our global, more-interconnected-than-ever society; governments', businesses', groups', and individuals' actions and reactions; technology; and the impact all that these topics have on information warfare.

When the first edition of *Global Information Warfare* (GIW) was published in 2002, we discussed the future based on the impact of the topics identified above. Much of what is required for defensive information warfare (IW) operations and systems is based on proven computer security techniques that have been around for decades.

Although you will find much of the following has become redundant since the book's first edition, it has not been repeated because we are too lazy to start anew. It has been done because the issues and the basic methods to solve them have not changed any more than the threats that the future holds. So, let us take out our crystal ball and see what the future continues to hold for all of us.

Unfortunately, even the basic computer security standards that have been around for decades have often not been meet. In fact, even US Federal Government computer security standards, those required to be followed by government agencies, are often not followed.

> U.S. Secret Service refused to provide data on its computer security systems to the Department of Homeland Security…preventing it from being able to verify if it was complying with security policies.…The service, "…refused to comply with mandated computer security policies," according to the report by the DHS inspector general.[1]

Will this change in the future? Maybe, but probably not if history is any indication; and if it does, it will probably not be to the extent needed.

In the business world, the same applies under the guise that it is not cost-effective. However, now and into the future, as a lack of security impacts the bottom line, hopefully that will change.

One of the problems is that we base our security requirements on the basis of "risk," and business is fundamentally based on risk taking. When you base your security requirements on the concept of managing risk, you are accepting that you are only buying time and that, at some point, an incident will happen. However, as constant successful attacks show, it costs more to patch systems; pay out money in lawsuits and for the adverse public relations issues that follow; and compensate for losses in stock values as they plummet, rather than to "do it right the first time" and continuously update and improve over time. Corporate management just does not get it and maybe never will. Governments, groups, and individuals have declared war. Will that increase or decrease in the future? All indications point to an increase.

Although not officially confirmed, at least one major business was successfully attacked because the default passwords that came with the software were never changed. That was identified as an issue at least as far back as the 1980s if not before. That first hacker attack based on that vulnerability can be traced to at least the first 300-baud external modem, based on a hacker software program using the BASIC program language. For those of you who do not know what we are talking about because you were not even born at that time, it proves our point.

Why will these leaders in businesses, industries, and governments not change? Some of the blame rests in democratic nations where people enjoy at least some semblance of freedom, and being told what to do and how to do it is something that they do not like and try to avoid. Security and law-enforcement personnel are always telling people what to do and not do. In the future, a way must be found to make them willing to do it or make security totally invisible to them where not even a password or biometric access control will be needed, unless error-free, and the user does not have to take any action. An "avatar" that is secure, maybe? Not an easy task.

Surviving into the Future

Senior corporate and government leadership support continues to be missing and is necessary to develop the appropriate planning, guidance, strategy, skilled workforce, plant, and equipment. Corporations and nation-states need to boldly accept the new reality lest they wish to lose—and not be able to reattain—the competitive edge. Bureaucracy has no place in an IW environment where nanosecond attack weapons require nanosecond responses. As the past and present have shown, corporations and nation-states have not changed, and personally we do not hold out much hope for that to change in the future.

Senior leadership is essential for security to be meaningful to the bottom line or the national security of nation-states. Corporate espionage will continue to be as big a threat as government espionage—maybe more so. Netspionage* has become a valuable tactic in support of a corporation or government agency's overall espionage strategy.

IW attacks against global corporations have dramatically increased since we discussed that topic in the first edition of this book. They have grown in sophistication and are expected to do so, their targets ranging from governments to individuals around the world. Sadly, IW has also never been easier. Financial losses due to IW attacks have been caused by successful security breaches, ranging from financial fraud and theft of proprietary information to identity theft, sabotage, and blackmail. A new term has come into use over the past few years: advanced persistent threat (APT), which is used to describe an ongoing set of stealthy computer hacking attacks, often targeting a specific business sector, organization, or system.

The motivation for an APT can be business or political gain. As the name implies, APT consists of three elements: the attack is of an advanced type, it is persistent, and it poses a threat. The term was first used to describe an ongoing series of attacks that originated in China, but it is now more widely used. It is clear that we can expect these types of attack to not only continue but to increase. Why would they not? We are not very good at detecting and responding to them, and as long as the benefits outweigh the cost, it is worthwhile for the nation-state or group that is carrying them out.

There is no silver bullet, no one-time expenditure of money to "fix the problem," and no means of putting the genie back in the bottle. Enlightened and dedicated leadership that is willing to stay the course is necessary to guide governments and businesses into the future.

---

* For a basic overview on that topic, see the classic *Netspionage*.[2]

New-Old Approach to Security: Defensive IW

The approach that responsible governments, businesses, and other entities must take in the future to ensure that we have the correct environment to endure is to at least get the basic security processes in place!

This will require a significant change in the attitude and approach that is taken at all levels of governance and management. We have been saying this since the 1980s, and we say it here once again in 2015. We must get on a war footing. Good grief!

What will be required in order for the structures that we understand to survive is a large-scale adjustment in the attitudes taken to the whole subject. In the past, we have said that "the threats are real; and the adversaries are serious about IW," and this must be realized. To a certain extent, that realization takes place generally only after a massive, successful attack. However, after it is over and everyone has calmed down and begun to forget it, management goes back to business as usual and so do government agencies. We do not seem to be able to learn from either our own past or that of other organizations and seem to be doomed to continue to repeat it.

There has been fear (and still is) that a "pearlharbor.com," as Winn Schwartau puts it, is coming. We have already seen it in the physical world. Can the virtual world's Pearl Harbor be far behind? Mini ones are taking place globally and daily. However, as those of us in the profession have said that for so long, it is like the boy crying wolf, or like the year 2000 "the world will end as we know it" crisis due to the millennium bug crash that never happened; we must in the future choose our words more carefully and present the probable risks in a more objective way.

The Changing Environment

To the present day, we have a history of understanding the issues that are related to IW, which are imposed by physical, procedural, or personnel means. We also now understand the IW offensive and defensive worlds better than ever before, and we hopefully will get better at understanding the issues into the future, but understanding the issues and doing something about them are two different things.

The Need for Enlightened and Dedicated Leadership

If an environment in which organizations can feel safe to operate in, free from successful IW attacks, is to be achieved, there needs to be significant changes in the attitudes of both government and management at all levels of organizations.

An infrastructure, at an international level, for collaboration between governments and law-enforcement agencies already exists, but until *all* countries sign up to this and allocate sufficient resources to make it effective, there will continue to be issues. There are currently countries that provide "safe harbor" to both organized criminals and terrorists that are using the Internet to carry out IW attacks. Allegedly, China is doing this for North Korea's IW warriors, who are operating in facilities on China's mainland. There are also other countries that are, themselves, conducting IW operations. While this continues, our defensive IW needs to be improved to meet every possibility.

Perhaps one measure that can be put in place will be the establishment of forums in which incidents can be reported in a suitable manner by individuals, companies, and governments, and where best advice can be gained without worrying about political and power-play games. While these exist in some countries and communities, they must be ubiquitous and easy to access. If attacks are taking place at Internet speeds over structures that do not recognize national borders, then any impediment that the current structures and organizations impose will encourage the perpetrator.

In the governments of most democratic nations, an individual who will champion the cause of creating the correct environment for the protection of information systems is a conundrum. It would require a political nominee that is willing to put the cause that they were supporting not only above their own ambitions (information systems security is not an area that has a track record of producing new party or national leaders) but also above party loyalty. They would need to have seniority within their own party, cross party support, and tenure in the post for a period of more than one term of office if they were to have any significant effect.

Will that happen? We doubt it. When something happens, they will hold public hearings, look for scapegoats, get their faces on the news, and pontificate from on high, but afterwards they will go back to their old ways. If they want to find those partially responsible, they have but to look in the mirror.

Global Trends[3]

It is imperative that when looking at GIW, one should begin by understanding the global trends, because that is the environment that will dictate much of the GIW offensive and defensive environments and tactics; this will also help one to understand the reason for such attacks as well as defensive IW needs and solutions.

As you can see from the reference above, every four years the US National Intelligence Council (NIC) publishes an update of its *Global Trends* series, which identifies key drivers and developments likely to shape world events a couple of decades into the future.

In the "Report of the National Intelligence Council's 2020 Project," the NIC included an Executive Summary, some of which is quoted below:

> At no time since the formation of the Western Alliance system in 1949 have the shape and nature of the international alignments been in such

a state of flux....The role of the United States will be an important variable in how the world is shaped, influencing the path that states and nonstate actors choose to choose...

New Global Players: The likely emergence of China and India as well as others, as new major global players—similar to the advent of a united Germany in the 19th Century and a powerful United States in the early 20th Century—will transform the geopolitical landscape, with impacts potentially as dramatic as those in the previous two centuries...how we mentally map the world in 2020.

New global players are not really that new; however, their power and impact on the world stage has increased. Such shifts and changes are causing the status quo to fade away. Thus, there will be more nation fighting, and with that, the use of GIW tactics in order to assist nations in gaining dominance.

Impact of Globalization

Globalization as an overreaching "mega-trend," a force so ubiquitous that it will substantially shape all other major trends in the world of 2020...the world economy is likely to continue to growing impressively: by 2020, it is projected to be about 80% larger than it was in 2000, and average per capita income will be roughly 50% higher.... Yet the benefits of globalization won't be global....The greatest benefits of globalization will accrue to countries and groups that can access and adopt new technologies....China and India are well positioned to become technology leaders, and even the poorest countries will be able to leverage prolific, cheap technologies to fuel—although at a slower rate—their own development....

...More firms will become global, and those operating in a global arena will be more diverse, both in size and origin, more Asian and less Western in orientation. Such corporations, encompassing the current, large multinationals, will be increasingly outside the control of any one state and will be key agents of change in dispersing technology widely, further integrating the world economy, and promoting economic progress in the developing world....Thus sharper demand driven competition for resources, perhaps accompanied by a major disruption of oil supplies, is among the key uncertainties.

Today's economic wars have included IW offensive operations, and these are expected to increase in volume and sophistication as the demand for economic power is supported and made more vulnerable by the world's dependency on technology.

New Challenges to Governance

The nation-state will continue to be the dominant unit of the global order, but economic globalization and the dispersion of technologies, especially information technologies, will place enormous new strains on governments...political Islam will have a significant global impact leading to 2020, rallying disparate ethnic and national groups and perhaps even creating an authority that transcends national boundaries....The so-called "third wave" of democratization may be partially reversed by 2020—particularly among the states of the former Soviet Union and in Southeast Asia, some of which never really embraced democracy...

...With the international system itself undoing profound flux, some of the institutions charged with managing global problems maybe overwhelmed by them.

Technology can free us or help enslave us. We are ever so much closer to the predictions made by George Orwell in his book *1984*. It all depends who has dominant power over technology in each nation, business, or group, including religious groups.

Since the first edition of this book was written and we discussed terrorists' offensive use of IW tactics and techniques, their use of IW weapons has drastically increased, and it is expected to continue to do so into the future. Terrorists still prefer the propaganda effect of barbaric acts such as bombing, kidnappings, beheadings, and the like; however, they are ever increasingly relying on IW to exploit the vulnerabilities of their enemies.

In the past, they have had to rely on the news media of the nations involved to propagate their messages, whereas now they have the means to get their messages to anyone that is willing to listen. Blogs and social media are great propaganda tools for spewing their hatred, and they are also a great recruiting tool as we have seen with *lone wolf* attacks. While these are indeed physical attacks, those who carry them out have been recruited online.

Pervasive Insecurity

Even as most of the world gets richer, globalization will profoundly shake up the status quo—generating enormous economic, cultural, and consequently political convulsions....The transition will not be painless and will hit the middle classes of the developed world in particular....Weak governments, lagging economy and extremism, and youth bulges will align to create a perfect storm for internal conflict in certain regions...

...The likelihood of great power conflict escalating into total war in the next 15 years is lower than at any time in the past century, unlike during previous centuries when local conflicts sparked world wars.... Countries without nuclear weapons—especially in the Middle East and Northeast Asia—might decide to seek them as it becomes clear that their neighbors and regional rivals are doing so.

We must also remember the power that individuals now have to exploit those that they feel are against them, whether it be governments, businesses, groups, or other individuals—for example, even school bullying causes some to commit suicide—and on a global warfront. The worse the economy gets, the more hostile and dissatisfied a nation's citizens become. So, we may not have a global World War III, but we are certainly having thousands of global IW skirmishes 24/7, and this too is certain to increase into the future.

Transmuting International Terrorism

The key factors that spawned international terrorism that has no signs of abating over the next 15 years....We expect that by 2020 al-Qa'ida will be superseded by similarly inspired Islamic extremist groups....Our greatest concern is that terrorists might acquire biological agents or, less likely, a nuclear device, either of which could cause mass casualties

This has already taken place with the advent of the Islamic State of Iraq and Syria (ISIS), and surely more groups will follow and even look at other terrorist groups as their enemies as they all continue vying for global domination. Surely their use of IW attacks will not be limited to only nonterrorist groups.

Policy Implications

Although the challenges ahead will be daunting, the United States will retain enormous advantage, playing a pivotal role across the broad range of issues—economic, technological, political and military—that no other state will match by 2020....While no single country looks within striking distance of rivaling US military power by 2020, more countries will be in a position to make the United States pay a heavy price for any military action they oppose. The possession of chemical, biological, and/or nuclear weapons...also increase the potential cost of any military action by the US...

...A counterterrorism strategy that approaches the problem on multiple fronts offers the greatest chance of containing—and ultimately reducing—the terrorist threat....Over the next 15 years the increasing centrality of ethical issues, old and new, have the potential to divide worldwide publics and challenge US leadership.

While governments around the world continue to think in terms of twentieth-century weapons in this twenty-first-century world, we must remember how vulnerable our technology-dependent governments and businesses are to successful IW attacks. The more "advanced" a nation is and the greater its dependency on technology, the greater the exposure to IW attacks.

It is a sad commentary, but the chances are that the use of IW offensive operations will continue to increase and the lack of viable defensive IW operations will allow more and more attacks to be successful, causing greater scales of damage as these IW weapons continue to increase in sophistication while defensive IW continues to lag behind.

Table 17.1 is a summary of "The 2020 Global Landscape," which was part of the report cited here.

Offensive-Defensive GIW Attacks

When will we get to the point where a person, group, business, or government is going to say "I'm mad as hell and I'm not going to take it anymore!" We are fast approaching that time, if not already past it.

If an entity is attacked, it is about time that the victims, in self-defense, go after those attacking them rather than relying on someone else to protect them. Obviously, agencies such as the FBI and local police investigators come in after the attacks, run their investigations, and may even identify the adversary. Then what? No jurisdiction, so no prosecution. So, basically, maybe it is time for a little "Wild West" independent action?

What we need in the future is a covert *mirror-image* software program that will not only deflect the attack but have that program turn on itself and bounce back to attack the attacker.

Yes, some government agencies we have alluded to in this book are beginning to take covert, offensive-defensive actions. However, more is needed at all levels of victimization. The "reap what ye have sown," "eye for an eye," old style ideas of philosophy and justice maybe need to come back into vogue?

Some will criticize vigilante justice, warning that we cannot be like them or chaos will reign. The ones saying that are primarily those in law enforcement, who fear dependency on them will wane; politicians who fear losing power; and those who have "no skin in the game," among others.

The Future of the Internet

Because of the power and influence of the Internet, some nations want to control it, while others want to have the United Nations be responsible for its management. Governments do not like something they cannot control to their benefit. The day

Table 17.1   The 2020 Global Landscape

Relative Certainties	Key Uncertainties
Globalization largely irreversible, likely to become less Westernized.	Whether globalization will pull in lagging economies; degree to which Asian countries set new "rules of the game."
World economy substantially larger.	Extent of gaps between "haves" and "have-nots"; backsliding by fragile democracies; managing or containing financial crises.
Increasing number of global firms facilitate spread of new technologies.	Extent to which connectivity challenges governments.
Rise of Asia and advent of possible new economic middle-weights.	Whether rise of China/India occurs smoothly.
Aging populations in established powers.	Ability of EU and Japan to adapt work forces, welfare systems, and integrate migrant populations; whether EU becomes a superpower.
Energy supplies "in the ground" sufficient to meet global demand.	Political instability in producer countries; supply disruptions.
Growing power of nonstate actors.	Willingness and ability of states and international institutions to accommodate these actors.
Political Islam remains a potent force.	Impact of religiosity on unity of states and potential for conflict; growth of jihadist ideology.
Improved WMD capabilities of some states.	More or fewer nuclear powers; ability of terrorists to acquire biological, chemical, radiological, or nuclear weapons.
Arc of instability spanning Middle East, Asia, Africa.	Precipitating events leading to overthrow of regimes.
Great power conflict escalating into total war unlikely.	Ability to manage flashpoints and competition for resources.
Environmental and ethical issues even more to the fore.	Extent to which new technologies create or resolve ethical dilemmas.

Table 17.1 (Continued) The 2020 Global Landscape

Relative Certainties	Key Uncertainties
US will remain single most powerful actor economically, technologically, militarily.	Whether other countries will more openly challenge Washington; whether US loses S&T edge.

Source: U.S. Department of the Air Force. The 2020 global landscape. http://www. au.af.mil/au/awc/awcgate/cia/nic2020/map_global_future_es.pdf

the Internet falls into political hands, it is doomed and a GIW battle lost, its users the casualties of the GIW.

That being said, some are optimistic that new technology will allow global users to reconnect on a global scale using another form of technology as it supersedes the "old-fashioned" Internet. In fact, global users may even be able to establish their own mini-Internets and connect to other mini-Internets through advanced communications, even using embedded microprocessor technology as a form of cyber telepathy. They become their own Internet Service Providers (ISPs).

> There will be so many IP addresses…so many devices, sensors, things that you are wearing, things that you are interacting with that you won't even sense it. It will be part of your presence all the time…
>
> Eric Schmidt, Google exec chairman, speaking about the technology future (Varney and Company, Fox Business News Channel, January 23, 2015)

Summary

The saying "the more things change, the more they stay the same" certainly seems to be holding true. Although we have and will continue to have advances in technology allowing for more sophisticated offensive GIW attacks and defenses, we are fighting more GIW battles and losing more of them than ever before.

In the future, we must reconsider our defensive approaches, fund them as a high priority in every entity, and go on the offensive as a defensive approach.

> The future is disorder. A door like this has cracked open five or six times since we got up on our hind legs. It is the best possible time to be alive, when almost everything you thought you knew is wrong.
>
> **Tom Stoppard**
> *Arcadia*

References

1. Chiacu, C. (2014). Secret Service needs to beef up IT security: Report. Reuters, December 22. http://news.yahoo.com/secret-needs-beef-security-report-193616952. html.
2. Boni, W. C. and Kovacich, G. L. (2000). *Netspionage: The Global Threat to Information.* Woburn, MA: Butterworth-Heinemann.
3. Office of the Director of National Intelligence. (n.d.). National Intelligence Council: Global trends. http://www.dni.gov/index.php/about/organization/national-intelligence-council-global-trends (accessed Dec. 14, 2014).

Appendix: A Short History of Technology and Its Relationship to Warfare

Technology from the Chinese

Some of the earliest known traces of humans, if not the earliest, are found in China. The "Yuan Mou Man" is said to date back to 1.6 million years B.C.[1] This was followed by Lan Tian Man and Peking Man in about 700,000–500,000 B.C., when, as indication show, humans used stone tools and fire. Other technological wonders, some believe, started in China and were later reinvented or were part of a technology transfer to Europe and the rest of the world. Many can be related, directly or indirectly, to prosecuting wars.

There may be some who say that several inventions attributed to the Chinese were in fact invented in Europe. However, those inventions (e.g., the flame-thrower) were "invented" in Europe hundreds of years later. Therefore, it is more likely that technology transfer had taken place between the Chinese and European merchants, or the European inventors did not know that the technology had already been invented when they "invented" it.

Abacus

From the Greek word *abax*, meaning "calculating board" or "calculating table," the abacus was invented by the Chinese. The first record of the abacus (see Exhibit A.1) was from a sketch in a book from the Yuan Dynasty (fourteenth century). Its Mandarin name is *Suan Pan*, which means "calculating plate." Its inventor is unknown, but the abacus is often referred to as the "first computer" because it was used as a mathematical model for early electronic computers.[2] Some believe that it may have been invented as far back as 3000 B.C.

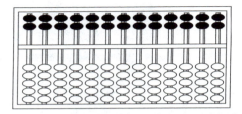

Exhibit A.1   An abacus.

One can argue that many inventions have been modified to directly support warfare. Some technologies have also indirectly supported warfare, such as through logistics, because many noncombatant technologies had a dual use, similar to the way in which the computerized weapons of today have a dual use (e.g., commercial off-the-shelf software [COTS]) (see Table A.1).

Some of the technological devices invented by the Chinese that could be used indirectly to support the offensive, defensive, and exploitative aspects of warfare include the following:

- Medical needles and medical observations (2205–1766 B.C.)
- Piston bellows; gas and petroleum as fuel; compass* (722–481 B.C.)
- Manned kites (403–206 B.C.)
- Steel from cast iron (206–220 B.C.)
- Sliding calipers; belt drive (206–9 B.C.)
- Water, chain pumps; rudder; seismograph (5–220 A.D.)
- Multiple masts; battened sails; watertight ship compartments (220–280 A.D.)
- Use of algebra in geometry (265–316 A.D.)
- Enhanced steel making process (317–420 A.D.)
- Block printing; mechanical clock (589–618 A.D.)
- First use of the symbol for "zero" (in India, 876 A.D.)
- Chain drives (907–960 A.D.)
- Mercator map projection; flares (960–1279 A.D.)

Western Technology†

Having noted the early inventions of the Chinese, one can easily understand how they have impacted societies and their ability to wage wars on each other. If the technological

---

* Some historians believe that the type of compass with a magnetic pointer was developed around 1190. Others believe that in China, Shen Kua, in his *Meng Chi Pi Than* (*Dream Pool Essays*), written around 1080, provided an accurate description of a compass (http://inventors. about.com/science/inventors).

† See the books by Alvin and Heidi Toffler for more information on the transitions of human societies (appendix).[3–5]

Table A.1 Chinese Technological Devices Used For or Could Be Adapted to Warfare

Approximate Dates	Chinese Technology
403–206 B.C.	Chemical warfare, crossbow
206–220 B.C.	Parachute
317–589 A.D.	Propeller
618–907 A.D.	Gunpowder[a]
960–1279 A.D.	Flame-thrower
960–1279 A.D.	Bomb
960–1279 A.D.	Rocket
960–1279 A.D.	Grenade

[a] Some say gunpowder was invented around the third century B.C., but the true gunpowder formula was first published around 1040 by Tseng Kung-Liang (http://inventors.about.com/science/inventors).

inventions of the Chinese impacted how wars were prosecuted, the Europeans brought it to the stage of a fine art. Then, during the last half of the twentieth century and into the twenty-first century, the United States took the lead in technological development for warfare, and especially for information warfare, purposes.

Sixteenth-Century Technology

Using the Gregorian calendar to mark time, it was noted that the sixteenth century (1500–1599) showed little in the way of major technological inventions. It also showed little new in terms of how wars were prosecuted. The main technological invention directly related to warfare during this period was the "hand gonne," actually more of a handheld cannon. It was not very reliable, as is usually the case with the first few attempts at new warfare technology. Later, "miniaturization" took place, and improvements led to the matchlock design that included a cover plate and flash pan. This weapon, known as the "matchlock," was the weapon used by early explorers of empires and nation-states when they set out to colonize the New World, as well as to continue the subjugation of the Old World.

Seventeenth-Century Technology

In approximately 1642 A.D., Pascal designed a mechanical calculator. Thus, from the abacus in 3000 B.C., to the use of the symbol for "zero" in 876 A.D., to Pascal's calculator in 1642 A.D., we see increasing thought about the use of mathematics for developing technology. There also seemed to be more of an inclination to use technology to assist the human race, as well as to control some of us. That was about to significantly increase due to the technological developments of the seventeenth century and beyond.

During the seventeenth century (1600–1699), there were some significant technological inventions. Although some may have had indirect uses in warfare, the majority of them were used to enhance society, including the following:

- Telescope
- Reflecting telescope
- Human-powered submarine
- Steam turbine
- Blood transfusion
- Calculating machine
- Adding machine
- Micrometer
- Barometer
- Air pump
- Pocket watch
- Steam pump

Some of the other technological inventions of this period could be used in warfare but probably were used more by the noncombatants of the period. The major technological weapon created during this time appeared to be the flintlock rifles and pistols that led to experiments with different weapon designs such as rotating cylinders. This was a key warfare discovery and just the beginning of the revolution of rifles and handguns. The human-powered submarine was just a primitive invention and was of no real value as a warship during this period.

Eighteenth-Century Technology

The eighteenth century (1700–1799) saw little change in most of the inventions vis-à-vis warfare technology. However, as in past centuries, the eighteenth century did witness technological inventions that assisted in making life a little better for people (excluding the guillotine, but that of course depended on what end of the blade you were on). The inventions of the period included

- Steam engine
- Fire extinguisher
- Electric telegraph
- Steamship
- Submarine (non human powered)

- First demonstration of the European parachute
- Hot-air balloon
- Guillotine
- Bicycle
- Ambulance
- Smallpox vaccination
- Battery

Although invented in the 1700s, the non-human-powered submarine did not truly come into its own as a great technological weapon until the twentieth century. Such things as the electric telegraph and hot-air balloon could be considered indirect weapons of war because they could be used for military communication and surveillance, respectively. While the parachute was interesting, no reliable type of airplane had yet been invented.

Nineteenth-Century Technology

The nineteenth century (1800–1899) began the period in which the technological inventions of the era that contributed to warfare really began to take off. Although starting slowly, the inventions developed in sophistication and increased in number at an ever-growing rate—a rate that still has not shown any signs of slowing down; in fact, it is speeding up.

However, this century, as with the previous one, also saw continued refinements and "better-invented" technological devices and improvements on previously invented devices. This period also saw an increase in the ability to communicate and conduct surveillance. And as we know, communication is vital to battlefield coordination. Also, surveillance—knowing where the enemy is located, their troop strength, and other battle issues—is a key ingredient to the successful prosecution of warfare.

Even in today's information warfare environment, communication, miscommunication, communication interception, and impeding the adversary's communications are key to defeating that adversary. Surveillance of the adversary remains a key ingredient in warfare today. Some of the major technological inventions of the 1800s are noted in Table A.2.

The following is a short summary of the history of communication and the technology used to store, process, and transmit information.*

- *Telegraph.* Samuel Morse developed the Morse code and the first really successful electric telegraph in 1837. He is credited with digitizing the alphabet.
- *Pony Express.* In 1860, the Pony Express mail service began but only lasted about 18 months due to the development of telegraph lines through to

---

* Based on a communications history (from the *Orange County Register* newspaper[6]).

Table A.2   Major Technologically Driven Inventions of the Nineteenth Century

Printing press	Blueprint
Amphibious vehicle	Facsimile
Armored warship	Anesthesia for tooth removal
Revolver	Sewing machine with a motor
Ether anesthesia	Demonstration of the principles of fiber optics
Telegraph	Barbed wire
Repeating rifle	Toilet paper
Tin can	Metal detector
Barbed wire	Roll film for cameras
Telephone	Radar
Machine gun	Matchbook
Typewriter	Internal combustion engine
Paper-strip Photographic film	Incandescent light bulb
Photography	Improved submarine
Improved propeller	Steam locomotive
Telegraph	Portland cement
Morse code	Dynamite
Bicycle	

California. The Pony Express' objective was the fast delivery of communications through the form of mail. It was one, if not the first, system that was to be eliminated due to a new technology—the telegraph system.

■ *Trans-Atlantic cable.* The cable was installed in approximately 1866, and by 1900, there were 15 cables across the Atlantic Ocean. The first successful trans-Atlantic cable brought fast communication across the ocean. Thus, communication that had previously taken weeks and sometimes months by ship was now accomplished in seconds.

■ *Typewriter.* In 1867, the keyboard layout of the first practical typewriter—the same basic layout as the one used today—was created. This provided a faster means to write the communications that were to be transmitted by telegraph, and later formed the basis for keyboards for inputting to computers.

■ *Telephone.* Alexander Graham Bell is credited with inventing the telephone in 1876, and we all know the results of that invention. However, no one could have dreamed of the power of today's telephone when coupled with the computer. Although the basic telephone was a great technological breakthrough, when coupled with the computer, it exponentially changed the way we share information.

This period saw the evolution and revolution in firearms from rifles and pistols, including such weapons as the Enfield rifle and Colt breech-loading revolver. However, the weapon that truly had a devastating effect on prosecuting wars, especially beginning in the twentieth century with World War I in Europe, was the machine gun.

Also during the nineteenth century, we begin to see the first serious signs of the human use of machines to do their calculations for them. It is true that earlier scholars and inventors had used mathematics for centuries and did invent some primitive ways of looking at the use of mathematics to help them better understand their universe. However, when in 1823 Babbage began work on "algebraic solutions mechanisms," we see the first baseline and model of things to come. This was followed in 1888 by Marquand's designing what was called an "electronic logic machine," followed in 1890 by Hollerith's designs for a "tabulating machine." Now, looking back at those three designs, we begin to see signs of the true beginning of modern-day technology, which led to high technology.

References

1. Smith, R.L. History of Chinese invention and discovery: The West's debt to China. http://www.computersmiths.com/chineseinvention/.
2. http://qi-journal.com/action.lasso?-Token.SearchID=Abacus&-Response=culture.asp.
3. Toffler, A. (1999). *Future Shock*. Turtleback Books. October.
4. Toffler, A. (1980). *The Third Wave*. William Morrow. February.
5. Toffler, A. and Toffler, H. (1994). *War & Anti-War in 21st Century: Survival at the Dawn of the 21st Century*. Little, Brown.
6. *Orange County Register*, September 21, 1997.

Index

A

Abacus, 331–332

Abu Dhabi, 268, 278

Academic Centres of Excellence in Cyber Security Research (ACEs-CSR), United Kingdom, 199

Academy of Military Sciences (AMS), China, 164–165

ACEs-CSR, *see* Academic Centres of Excellence in Cyber Security Research (ACEs-CSR), United Kingdom

ACSC, *see* Australian Cyber Security Centre (ACSC)

Acupuncture warfare, 39

ADF, *see* Australian Defence Force (ADF)

Advanced persistent threat (APT), 45, 223, 279–280, 304, 321

Advanced Persistent Threat No. 28 (APT28), Russia, 209

Advanced Research Project Agency (ARPA), 253, 263

Advancing National Cyberspace Capabilities, Israel, 152

AEA, *see* American Electronics Association (AEA)

AFIWC, *see* Air Force Information Warfare Center (AFIWC)

AFRL/RI, *see* Air Force Research Laboratory Information Directorate (AFRL/RI)

AFSPC, *see* Air Force Space Command (AFSPC)

AFTAC, *see* Air Force Technical Applications Center (AFTAC)

Agentura.ru website, 208

Ahmadi, M., 49

Airborne Warning and Control Systems (AWACS), 79

Air Force Cryptologic Support Center Securities Directorate, 113

Air Force Information Warfare Center (AFIWC), 113, 115
mission of, 115–117

Air Force Institute of Technology Center for Cyberspace Research (CCR), 134

Air Force Intelligence, Surveillance and Reconnaissance Agency, 130–132

Air Force Research Laboratory, 133

Air Force Research Laboratory Information Directorate (AFRL/RI), 144

Air Force Space Command (AFSPC), 131

Air Force Technical Applications Center (AFTAC), 131

Air Intelligence Agency, 113

Air University, 76, 78

Air War College study, 80

Alexander, K. B., 125

Al-Hayat, 232

Alliance for Cyber Security, Germany, 191–192

Al Qaeda, 87, 90, 229, 283

AMAN, *see* Israeli Military Intelligence (AMAN)

Amazon, 68, 273

American Electronics Association (AEA), 248

Amirkabir University, Iran, 150

AMS, *see* The Academy of Military Sciences (AMS), China

Anonymous (hacking group), 67

ANSSI, *see* National Agency for Information Systems Security (Agence nationale de la sécurité des systèmes d'information) (ANSSI), France

Anthem Inc., 65

APT, *see* Advanced persistent threat (APT)